*Also by*
*Michael McLaughlin*

◆ ◆ ◆ ◆ ◆ ◆ ◆ ◆ ◆ ◆ ◆

THE SILVER PALATE
COOKBOOK
*by Julee Rosso and Sheila Lukins*
*with Michael McLaughlin*

THE MANHATTAN CHILI CO.
SOUTHWEST-AMERICAN
COOKBOOK

# THE NEW
# AMERICAN
# KITCHEN

## MICHAEL McLAUGHLIN

**SIMON AND SCHUSTER**

*New York   London   Toronto   Sydney
Tokyo   Singapore*

**Simon and Schuster**
Simon & Schuster Building
Rockefeller Center
1230 Avenue of the Americas
New York, New York 10020

Copyright © 1990 by Michael McLaughlin

Designed by Laurie Jewell
Manufactured in the United States of America

1   3   5   7   9   10   8   6   4   2

Library of Congress Cataloging in Publication Data

McLaughlin, Michael.
The new American kitchen / Michael McLaughlin.
p.   cm.
1. Cookery, American.   2. Menus.   I. Title.
TX715.M47436   1990
641.5973—dc20          90-37063
CIP

ISBN 0-671-65826-3

♦ ♦ ♦ ♦ ♦ ♦ ♦

*This one is for me*

♦ ♦ ♦ ♦ ♦ ♦ ♦

# ACKNOWLEDGMENTS

♦ ♦ ♦ ♦ ♦ ♦ ♦ ♦ ♦ ♦ ♦

THIS BOOK HAS BEEN a long time in the making and there are many people without whom it might still be "in progress." Among those who have helped to get it to this final stage are the publishers, editors, and test kitchens of the magazines for which I write, and in which much of this work originally appeared. Many thanks go especially to Barbara Fairchild, William Garry, Jan Weimer, and Zack Hanle at *Bon Appétit*; Mary Goodbody, Susy Davidson, and Judith Hill at *COOK'S*; Susan Wyler, William Rice, and Ila Stanger at *Food & Wine*; Sarah Belk at *House Beautiful*; Joan Steuer at *Chocolatier*; and Nadine Kolowrat at *Phillip Morris Magazine*. Their advice, sympathy, encouragement, and frequent checks have been most welcome.

I came to New York in 1979, a rank greenhorn in the food business. For better or for worse (mostly for better) Julee Rosso, Sheila Lukins, and John Werner knew a likely thing when they saw it and gave me the chance to prove I had something to offer. Later, also for better or for worse (mostly for better), Bruce Sterman and Luba Pincus shared my feelings about food and joined me in putting them to the commercial test at The Manhattan Chili Co. Many of the recipes in this book were first tasted in their kitchen.

The rest were cooked in the wonderful apartment I rented for many years at 563 Tenth Street in Brooklyn. My landlady Helen Laszczewski and her family, especially Jean Szelkowski, provided me with much more than mere shelter for nearly nine years. I miss 563 and I miss them.

At Simon and Schuster, many people shared my enthusiasm, understood my point, and amplified it into a book. My special thanks to Kerri Conan (who took the handoff without a fumble), Lisa Kitei, Eve Metz, Laurie Jewell, Joel Avirom, and Stacy Holston.

Agents and editors make books happen, and mine deserve extra special thanks. Susan Lescher believed in this project almost before I did, and she found me a publisher who cared; Carole Lalli inspired me to write it and then gave me the time and space to finish the job.

A writer needs friends; the best of them are understanding, patient, and willing to go for a year or two with nothing but an occasional cranky phone call to sustain them. Of my many good friends, I especially thank Linda Norris, Perry Woods, Lou Ekus, Phyllis Wrynn, Mitch Friedlin, Nancy Hoffman, John Mijac, Birdie Allen, Steve Lange, Peg O'Byrne, Fraser Ellis, Derek Hodel, Marc Glick, Michael Honstein, Pamela Morgan Maxwell, and Francine Maroukian, who even when she's not there, is there.

Another friend, Victor Fabrizio (forever Warren to me), taught me that making food for a living could be exciting, challenging, occasionally rewarding, and almost always fun, even when people throw things at you.

Among good friends, some are extraordinary. Lisa Ekus is a great pal and also a great publicist who has done as much to help me make this book happen as anyone I know. It sustains me to think we have years of barbecue and chardonnay ahead of us.

And finally, speaking of checks and of patience, extremely special thanks go to my parents, Jim and Shirley, who've waited for years for me to live up to the promise of my high school English medal. I hope this is a suitable beginning.

◆ ◆ ◆ ◆ ◆ ◆ ◆ ◆ ◆ ◆ ◆ ◆ ◆ ◆ ◆ ◆ ◆ ◆ ◆ ◆ ◆ ◆ ◆ ◆ ◆ ◆ ◆ ◆ ◆ ◆ ◆ ◆ ◆ ◆ ◆ ◆ ◆ ◆ ◆ ◆ ◆ ◆ ◆ ◆ ◆ ◆ ◆ ◆

# CONTENTS

# INTRODUCTION

I am more modest now, but I still think that one of the
pleasantest of all emotions is to know that I, I with my
brain and my hands, have nourished my beloved few,
that I have concocted a stew or a story, a rarity or a
plain dish, to sustain them truly against the hungers of
the world.

—M. F. K. FISHER
*The Gastronomical Me*

THESE ARE GOOD TIMES to be cooking, and the American kitchen
right now is a very exciting place to be. The recent past—the late
seventies and the early eighties—was a time of fads, rapid change,
and silly innovation, but we're in calmer culinary waters now and
have entered a new era of solid but imaginative cooking, simpli-
fied entertaining, and confident personal style.

The change came about thanks to a collection of influences:
Writer-teachers (Julia Child, James Beard, Craig Claiborne,
Marcella Hazan, and many others); restaurateurs (Alice Waters,
Jeremiah Tower, Paul Prudhomme, Larry Forgione); merchants
and caterers (Joel Dean and Giorgio DeLuca, Julee Rosso and
Sheila Lukins, Lee Bailey); and the revitalized food press (magazines, newspapers, influential behind-the-scenes cookbook editors). The revolutionary political spirit as well as the health food
concerns of the sixties must be given their due, and I'm even
immodest enough to suggest that an oddly endearing cookbook,
named after a Manhattan carry-out food shop and written by
three novices (*The Silver Palate Cookbook*), also contributed to
this new spirit of adventure.

The grill, the pizza oven, and the pasta maker are among the
technical "innovations" that have helped us to look at old favorites in new ways. Sun-dried tomatoes, wild mushrooms, goat
cheeses (domestic, please), ginger, mustards, pepper (black,
white, green, pink), peppers (red, yellow, orange, Dutch, expensive), chiles, balsamic vinegar, and extra virgin olive oil became
the product icons that symbolized a whole new approach to cooking food in America with staples from around the world.

A crowd of bright, inventive, well-trained young restaurant chefs grew up already impatient with the classics. They discovered or rediscovered or reinvented Southwestern American cooking, Oriental mystery, Italian style, and Cajun-Creole fire and poked into every corner of the United States looking for new thrills. The rare (fiddlehead ferns, singing scallops, lobster mushrooms, Mexican corn fungus) and the familiar (maple syrup, crab cakes, meatloaf, barbecue) were of equal interest, and got stirred together with equal fervor—and occasionally with equal success. These chefs have matured, and calmed down, and restaurant food is better—and more affordable—than it has been in years. Who says nothing good ever comes of a stock market crash?

Home cooks have followed suit, eager to duplicate what they are tasting in restaurants and reading about everywhere. As the recipes have trickled down and the ingredients have begun to appear in specialty shops, catalogs, and even supermarkets, it has become clear that many of the changes in the American kitchen were for the better and are here to stay.

Perhaps this book should be called My *New American Kitchen,* since, like contemporary cooks everywhere, I've assimilated all this lovely new culinary information in a most personal way. On the other hand, while I have my own approach to cooking and eating, and while I write about food and cook for a living, I still go into the kitchen under the same time constraints and economical limitations as you do. I shop at markets not so very different from yours, and my hopes for the finished product are identical—I want unfussy food, straightforward to prepare, easy to appreciate, entertaining to cook and to eat, free from bizarre pretense or frivolous obfuscation.

Despite the "new" in the title, this is an old-fashioned book, and I am an old-fashioned cook. These recipes and menus are not designed for people who hate to cook. They are meant in my old-fashioned way, for people who love to cook well, and to eat well, but who no longer have the time to do so. It's paradoxical that just as cooking has become more adventurous and entertaining, the demands of modern life have drastically reduced the hours most of us have to spend in the kitchen.

Some solutions to this time crunch can be found in this book, but I have concentrated on simple menus, rather than clever shortcuts. Here are meals for many occasions, some small, some grand, but all designed, coordinated, and deliberately down-scaled in order to make producing them the pleasure good cooking ought to be. Some of my basic principles:

• Food should fit comfortably into the social scene and complement, not dominate, the people and the event.

• Food should be seasonal, celebrating the best and the freshest in the market. (I know people who think this ought to be a given nowadays, but it can't be repeated often enough.)

• The best of this food should adapt easily to feed family or company, and it's possible to see the two gradually merging. The family is often no longer nuclear, and while I might be watching too many episodes of "The Golden Girls," I think communal clusters of friends may well become a newly dominant social group. (The real estate industry even has a name for this trend: "mingles.")

• The best food engages the intellect. Well-planned menus and well-prepared meals *are* challenging and stimulating.

• In this book, if a complex dish is featured, the remainder of the menu is kept simple. The endless parade of courses that once characterized a "respectable" home meal, on a daily basis, at least, is passé. The restaurant equivalent, featuring small tastes of many courses, is beyond the manpower of the average home.

• Vice versa. Some "dishes" are simple to the point of not being cooked at all. This is particularly true of appetizers or first courses and desserts. A dish of olives, a few toasted almonds, or a fresh, locally produced goat cheese and good bread are so satisfying no one will accuse the chef of dereliction. Similarly, a ripe, perfect pear, accompanied by perfectly ripe Camembert, is rare and delicious enough to impress the most demanding guest.

• Some dishes can be merged, which simplifies the kitchen timetable considerably. I'm especially fond of starch–vegetable side dishes that do double duty. Many of the main courses are garnished with enough vegetables to balance the meal, and in some menus a simple green salad is more appropriate (and less work) than an involved vegetable side dish.

• Such casual menus, which frequently consist of a one-dish meal, are often best accompanied by a single appropriate wine, rather than an expensive and daunting array. Quality, *on a daily basis*, rather than an expensive quantity expended on a single occasion, is the rule in my kitchen, both in food and in wine.

• Some of the best of this casual cuisine is food that can—or must—be prepared in advance and either reheated without loss of flavor or texture or served at room temperature. Good chili, any wonderfully braised stew, or loaves of homemade bread are impossible if you limit your kitchen time to twenty minutes. Such aerobic cooking may be occasionally necessary for daily survival (particularly with hungry children to accommodate), but it's no end in itself. On the other hand, chili, stew, and bread all keep well in the refrigerator or freezer and can become a major part of your strategy for eating and cooking well every day.

• In general, I've called for the minimum amount of so-called foundation cookery in this book. If you make your own stocks, I admire your industry; using them in these recipes will yield splendid results. However, the truth is that most of these recipes were conceived to create their own stocks as they simmer, and they were all tested using ordinary canned broths. At times, canned pumpkin puree, frozen spinach, or dried herbs have yielded results as good as—if not better than—their fresh counterparts. Puff pastry from scratch, homemade pâtés and sausages, or fresh pasta are occasional technical projects for those so inclined, but for these menus, I have kept them to a minimum. When such lengthy basic preparations are called for, they are featured as stars in a menu, not bit players, and will let the industrious cook (you) take plenty of credit.

• The best of this food is self-garnishing—colorful, appetizing, and eye-pleasing on its own, without unnecessary and time-consuming embellishment.

• Above all, this casual cuisine means taking pleasure in simple things. If kitchen time is precious, and good ingredients costly, the results had better taste good. Think of a rich and garlicky beef stew, a slice of homemade bread (still warm), a tart salad crunchy with real croutons, a glass of lemonade, or a wedge of warm fruit pie served with a scoop of homemade ice cream, and you'll know what I mean.

Though it is possible to love cooking for its own sake—for the plain and simple joy of transforming raw ingredients into finished food—the good cook should never forget that the main reason one cooks is to feed oneself or another. To do that with style and skill and simplicity is a challenge with its own reward.

♦ ♦ ♦ ♦ ♦ ♦ ♦ ♦ ♦ ♦ ♦ ♦ ♦ ♦ ♦ ♦ ♦ ♦ ♦ ♦ ♦ ♦ ♦ ♦ ♦ ♦ ♦ ♦ ♦ ♦ ♦ ♦ ♦ ♦ ♦ ♦ ♦ ♦ ♦ ♦ ♦ ♦ ♦ ♦ ♦ ♦ ♦

# MAKING MENUS

◆◆◆◆◆◆◆◆◆◆

COOKS, EVEN GOOD ONES, I have learned, are sometimes intimidated by planning menus. I have also learned that menu books can often be intimidating: When confronted by a difficult technique or a hard-to-find ingredient in an otherwise appealing menu, some cooks would rather turn the page and skip the whole thing. Is there, then, somewhere, a cookbook of menus featuring easy, delicious, stylish recipes no one has heard of, requiring equipment everyone already owns, using inexpensive ingredients from the neighborhood supermarket? Or, better yet, is there a book that will teach us to make creative, well-balanced, stylish menus on our own? Or, best of all, is there some nice person who will just come to our house and tell us what to cook?

I'm too busy to make house calls, but I do have some advice that might make your life easier. The menus in this book work for me, but they are, above all, suggestions only. If you're insecure, let them guide you; if technical problems crop up, be flexible. Within the index to the book, you will find separate listings of recipes by my own arbitrary but useful categories—Fish and Shellfish, Chocolate, Eggs, etc. Browsing here can let you make creative substitutions to personalize my menus into your own. I also suspect you have another cookbook or two (or two hundred), and there's no reason not to take my general menu ideas and mix and match recipes from favorite cookbooks. I do it all the time.

When I plan a menu from scratch, however, several things guide me. No one aspect of menu planning is more important than another, but at times one stage or another takes precedence. First, consider ability. No menu should take you where you haven't the skill, the free time, or the cash to enjoy yourself and do a good job. A big dinner for the boss is not the time to make your first game pâté. Who are you trying to impress?

Remember the season. Choucroute garnie is much easier to cook and to eat in December than in August. Apples cost less in the winter than in the summer, and they're also tastier. Heavy flavors like Roquefort are better appreciated when there's a chill in the air. Oysters are best—firmer and more flavorful—in cold months. A menu for a dinner in January, using these foods, rather than one featuring grilled basil salmon, beefsteak tomatoes, and raspberry ice-cream cones, will be more successful.

Respect geography. Certain combinations of ingredients or of dishes within a menu have become classic because generations—centuries—of cooks and eaters have proven over and over that they go well together. Menus *are* more fun than ever and there *are* fewer rules, but a menu of ricotta- and pesto-stuffed ravioli, chicken enchiladas *mole poblano*, and kumquat-ginger compote will still be a jumble, no matter how good the dishes taste individually. However, with a few substitutions (chèvre and oregano in the ravioli, grilled lime-marinated chicken instead of enchiladas, and a pineapple-mango compote) the menu, while fresh, now hangs together with a Cal-Mex theme that adds welcome coherence. The best modern menus strive to add flair to basic combinations with which we are already comfortable.

Be aware of—but not a slave to—repeated textures, colors, and ingredients. Generally, avoiding excessively soft and tender meals, more or less one-color meals, or meals with more than one use of the same ingredient makes safe sense; you'll never go wrong following these guidelines. No one wants béchamel sauce, red bell peppers, or cured meats to appear more than once in a menu. On the other hand, you may miss out on some terrific meals if you play things too safe. Who hasn't enjoyed smoked salmon as a first course, followed by a fresh seafood—even a fresh salmon—entrée? What's not to like with tender, brown pot roast, soft mashed potatoes with brown gravy, apple sauce, and moist, brown gingerbread served on a wintry Sunday night?

Like the rules of matching wines to foods or owning all the right plates and forks and serving dishes, the rules of menu planning made sense at sometime to someone. And over the years they've become the dogma that we've adhered to strictly, as if to say there's something wrong with relaxing, cooking, and eating the foods we enjoy. A friend, who has a higher sense of taste and design than almost anyone I know, once called me in a panic to say that her table service was inappropriate for a dinner she was preparing. The food was eclectic but coherent, featuring prime ingredients from some of Brooklyn's best Italian and Middle Eastern purveyors. Her plates, silver, and serving dishes, lovingly collected over the years, were all American, from the twenties, thirties, and forties. The evening was destined to be a unique dining experience for the rather stuffy guests, and yet my friend was worried that her stemware—all nearly antique and all lovely, but from several patterns—didn't divide neatly into those for red wine and those for white wine.

Good taste is innate, and knowing with certainty when and how to break the rules (and when not to) is a talent few possess. On the other hand, being aware of what you are comfortable cooking and serving, knowing food traditions and their histories and respecting them, and learning and adjusting from less-than-successful menus are simple enough habits to acquire. Menus and meals are not isolated events but rather happenings along a continuum of experience, and if you—like me—are serious about food, you'll continue to make mistakes and learn from them and continually think about and improve upon the ways you combine your food into your menus. This book—thick as it is—is only a snapshot of the many meals I've cooked and menus I've planned over the years. These are my menus, my recipes, and with luck some will become yours. Good hunting!

♦ ♦ ♦ ♦ ♦ ♦ ♦ ♦ ♦ ♦ ♦ ♦ ♦ ♦ ♦ ♦ ♦ ♦ ♦ ♦ ♦ ♦ ♦ ♦ ♦ ♦ ♦ ♦ ♦ ♦ ♦ ♦ ♦ ♦ ♦ ♦ ♦ ♦ ♦ ♦ ♦ ♦ ♦ ♦ ♦ ♦ ♦ ♦ ♦

# BRUNCHES, LUNCHES, AND SUPPERS

HESE ARE THE SMALL MEALS, the ones Donna Reed and Jane Wyatt turned out without much apparent fuss or planning, the ones so hastily abandoned in our hectic times. Nowadays we've ceded much of the home turf to the pizza delivery man or to carry-out cuisine. A supper with mate or friends is more often than not an urban safari, with bagging the head of the hottest new chef the evening's primary goal. Lunch, as a shared experience, hardly exists, unless the family joins you for tuna salad at your desk, or you crash the school cafeteria—frequently a row of vending machines—to join the kids for candy and soda. Brunch—once meant to be an extended and mellow mingling of friends and food—has become a boozy excuse for dropping a bundle of cash in the middle of an otherwise uneventful day off.

If you are nostalgic for the small meals the way they used to be, consider making them, if only occasionally, a priority in your life. Break the rules, stop the clock, think small and intimate, and concentrate on entertaining only your closest friends and family. After all, it is the company and not the food that makes the event, and in the new American kitchen, even a sandwich can be a celebration.

The following menus, pared down to solid, simple essentials, and celebrating hearty, often regional American fare, are my solution to the problem of finding time to break bread on a more modest scale. Frequently my brunches and lunches can just as easily be suppers, and with do-ahead steps to simplify preparation (and plenty of hungry guests and willing hands to assist with final assembly) you'll find yourself feeling as cool, calm, and collected as Donna and Jane ever were. Now if you can just locate a frilly apron . . .

# MENU

........................

TABASCO ALMONDS AND CASHEWS

◆

POACHED EGGS AND
CORNMEAL-CRUSTED TOMATOES
IN HAM AND THYME CREAM

◆

RASPBERRY-ORANGE
CUSTARD TARTLETS

EGGY MEALS were frequent economy suppers when I was growing up, but they never seemed like hardship food, and eggs and pancakes or bacon made a nice change from pork chops, meatloaf, or chicken. This menu not only provides a festive, southern-accented brunch (and a good excuse for using up some leftover ham), but it also makes an elegant little supper for four good friends.

## TABASCO ALMONDS AND CASHEWS

♦♦♦♦♦♦♦♦♦

**D**ESPITE THE PRODIGIOUS quantity of Tabasco sauce, these crisp nuts build slowly to a pleasantly spicy but comfortable peak. Other pepper sauces may be much hotter (or milder) than Tabasco; adjust the amount accordingly.

In two large skillets heat the oil over medium heat. Add the nuts and cook, tossing and stirring often, until they are crisp and brown, about 10 minutes. Transfer the nuts to a large, shallow pan (such as a jelly-roll pan). While stirring them, drizzle the Tabasco over the nuts. Still stirring, sprinkle them with the salt. Cool to room temperature and store in an airtight container. *The recipe can be prepared 3 days ahead. Reheat the nuts on a cookie sheet in a 350-degree F oven before serving if desired.*

*Makes 1½ pounds, serving at least 10*

3 tablespoons olive oil
¾ pound jumbo, unsalted, roasted cashews
¾ pound jumbo, unsalted, roasted almonds
2 tablespoons Tabasco sauce
½ tablespoon coarse kosher salt

## POACHED EGGS AND CORNMEAL-CRUSTED TOMATOES IN HAM AND THYME CREAM

♦♦♦♦♦♦♦♦♦

**U**SE EITHER DRY-CURED HAM (see Cook's Sources) or "ordinary" (fully cooked, brine-cured) ham in the creamy, thyme-enhanced sauce. The best, thickest, tastiest English muffins (like those from Wolferman's, see Cook's Sources) will make this dish especially delicious.

···  🥘  ···

½ cup yellow cornmeal

1 teaspoon freshly ground
black pepper

1½ cups whipping cream

4 ounces firm, lean, smoky
ham, trimmed and cut
into ¼-inch dice

1 tablespoon minced fresh
thyme

2 tablespoons fresh lemon
juice, strained

4 tablespoons unsalted
butter

2 large tomatoes, trimmed
and cut into 8 thick
slices

2 teaspoons salt

8 eggs

4 English muffins, split
and toasted

On a plate stir together the cornmeal and ½ teaspoon of the pepper.

In a small, heavy saucepan over medium heat combine the cream, ham, and thyme. Bring to a boil, then lower the heat, and simmer, stirring once or twice, until reduced to 1 cup, about 20 minutes. Remove from the heat and stir in the remaining pepper and the lemon juice. Cover and keep warm.

In a large skillet over medium-high heat melt the butter. Dredge the tomatoes in the prepared cornmeal and fry them in the skillet, turning once, until lightly browned on both sides, 6 to 8 minutes.

Meanwhile, bring a shallow pan with 2 inches of water to a simmer. Stir in the salt. One at a time, break the eggs into a small dish and slide them into the water. Adjust the heat to keep the water from exceeding the simmer and cook the eggs to desired doneness, 2 to 4 minutes.

Arrange 2 muffin halves on each of 4 plates. Top each muffin half with a tomato slice. With a slotted spoon remove the eggs from the water, drain, and set an egg atop each tomato slice. Spoon the cream sauce over and around the eggs and muffins and serve immediately.

━━● *Serves 4*

◆◆◆◆◆◆◆◆◆◆◆◆◆◆◆◆◆◆◆◆◆◆◆◆◆◆◆◆◆◆◆◆◆◆◆◆◆◆◆◆◆◆◆

## RASPBERRY-ORANGE
## CUSTARD TARTLETS

◆◆◆◆◆◆◆◆◆◆

**C**ONCLUDE WITH these tiny tartlets, combining orange custard and fresh berries in a buttery pecan crust. Set them out on a plate, pour plenty of strong black coffee, and let guests nibble as they please.

*For the custard* Whisk the eggs and egg yolks together in a small, heavy, nonreactive saucepan until foamy. Whisk in the sugar, orange juice, orange zest, and lemon juice. Set the pan over low heat and cook, stirring constantly, until the mixture thickens and leaves a track on the back of the spoon when a fingertip is drawn across it. (This happens rather suddenly, after about 8 minutes.) Immediately remove the pan from the heat and whisk in the butter. When the butter is absorbed whisk in the liqueur. Cool completely, cover with plastic wrap, pressing the wrap onto the surface of the custard, and refrigerate overnight. *The custard can be prepared up to 3 days ahead.*

*For the pastry* In a food processor combine the flour, pecans, sugar, and salt. Add the butter and process with short bursts of power until the mixture resembles coarse meal. With the machine running, add enough of the cream to form a soft dough. Process until the dough forms a ball. On a lightly floured surface shape the dough into a flat disc. Wrap in plastic and refrigerate 30 minutes.

Divide the dough into 8 pieces. Flatten, 1 piece at a time, into discs (cover and refrigerate the remainder). Between sheets of wax paper roll the dough out to a round about ¼ inch thick. Peel the round off the paper and fit the dough into a 3½-inch fluted, 1-inch deep tartlet mold. Trim the edges. Repeat with the remaining dough. Refrigerate the formed tartlet shells, wrapped in plastic, for at least 30 minutes. *The pastry can be prepared to this point up to 1 day ahead.*

Position a rack in the center of the oven and preheat to 375 degrees F. Prick the tartlet shells with the tines of a fork. Bake until lightly browned, about 10 minutes. Cool in the molds on a rack for 5 minutes, unmold, and cool completely. *The shells can be baked up to 1 day ahead. Wrap in plastic and store, airtight, at room temperature.*

ORANGE CUSTARD

*2 eggs*
*2 egg yolks*
*¼ cup sugar*
*¼ fresh orange juice, strained*
*2 tablespoons minced orange zest*
*1 tablespoon fresh lemon juice, strained*
*4 tablespoons unsalted butter, chilled and cut into small pieces*
*1½ tablespoons Cointreau liqueur*

PECAN PASTRY I

*1 cup unbleached all-purpose flour*
*½ cup (2 ounces) pecans, finely ground*
*2 tablespoons sugar*
*¼ teaspoon salt*
*6 tablespoons (¾ stick) unsalted butter, chilled and cut into small pieces*
*2 tablespoons (about) heavy cream, well chilled*

GLAZE

*½ cup currant, raspberry, or strawberry jelly*
*1 tablespoon sugar*

*1 pint fresh raspberries, picked over*

*For the glaze* In a small, heavy saucepan over low heat combine the jelly and sugar. Stir to dissolve the sugar. Raise the heat and boil hard for 3 minutes, stirring occasionally. Cool to room temperature. *The glaze can be prepared to this point up to 1 week ahead. Refrigerate, covered, bringing the glaze back to room temperature before using.*

To assemble, fill each tartlet half-full with custard. Arrange the raspberries over the custard, covering it completely. Brush the raspberries with the glaze. *The tartlets can be assembled up to 30 minutes in advance and refrigerated.*

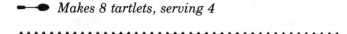 *Makes 8 tartlets, serving 4*

# MENU

◆◆◆◆◆◆◆◆◆◆◆◆◆◆◆◆◆

PAN-FRIED DUCK AND
SWEET YELLOW PEPPER SAUSAGES
WITH RED WINE SAUCE
*page 133*

◆

SCRAMBLED EGGS

◆

SLICED TOMATOES

◆

GRITS WITH BLACK OLIVE BUTTER

◆

BUTTERMILK BISCUITS

SAUSAGE-MAKING is a labor of love, and this brunch is one to serve to your nearest and dearest. I take the duck sausages along whenever I visit my good friends Lou and Lisa Ekus; the menu is just right for a lazy Sunday brunch around the big table in the dining room of their New England farmhouse.

Since the sausages need a day or two of refrigerated rest to develop full flavors, the actual last-minute effort isn't any different from cooking store-bought sausages, and the resulting good eating is hard to beat. For brunch, the rich red wine sauce seems out of place, so you can skip that step. For early morning convenience, the sausages can be pan-fried but, for extra flavor, grill the sausages over some smoky hickory or apple wood chips.

## GRITS WITH
## BLACK OLIVE BUTTER

♦ ♦ ♦ ♦ ♦ ♦ ♦ ♦

**T**HIS PUNGENT olive-salty butter adds unexpected *oomph* to humble grits, and it goes a long way toward converting those who still haven't discovered the virtues of this corn product.

2 tablespoons unsalted
    butter
½ cup finely diced onion
3½ cups canned chicken
    broth or homemade stock
¾ cup regular-cooking
    white hominy grits (not
    instant or
    quick-cooking)
Black Olive Butter (recipe
    follows)

In a medium-size, heavy saucepan over low heat melt the butter. Add the onion and cook, covered, stirring once or twice, until tender, about 10 minutes. Add the chicken broth and raise the heat. When the broth boils, slowly stir in the grits in a steady stream, lower the heat, and cook, covered, stirring once or twice, until thick, 15 to 20 minutes. Remove from the heat and let stand, covered, 5 minutes.

To serve, top each portion with a dollop of Black Olive Butter and pass the pepper mill.

*Serves 4*

## BLACK OLIVE BUTTER

♦ ♦ ♦ ♦ ♦ ♦ ♦ ♦

¾ cup (1½ sticks)
    unsalted butter, softened
12 brine-cured, imported
    black olives, preferably
    Calamata (see Cook's
    Sources), pitted

In a food processor, using brief pulses of power, blend the butter and olives until almost smooth. Transfer to a storage container and cover. *The butter can be prepared up to 3 days ahead and refrigerated or frozen for up to one month.* Return it to room temperature before using.

*Makes about 1½ cups*

## BUTTERMILK BISCUITS

**A** GOOD, BASIC BISCUIT RECIPE THAT, with a little practice, will go together in only a few minutes.

Position a rack in the upper third of the oven and preheat to 450 degrees F.

In a large bowl stir together 3¾ cups of the flour, the baking powder, and salt. Cut in the butter and shortening until the mixture resembles bits the size of peas. Stir in the buttermilk until a rough dough forms. Turn the dough onto a surface heavily floured with the remaining ¼ cup of flour and knead about 20 seconds, or until the dough just coheres. Roll the dough out ½ inch thick. With a 2½-inch cutter, form the biscuits, transferring them to an ungreased baking sheet. Gather the scraps into a ball and roll again. Cut out the remaining biscuits.

Bake the biscuits about 12 minutes, or until they are puffed, crisp, and golden. Serve immediately.

*Makes about 15 large biscuits*

*4 cups unbleached all-purpose flour (to measure, stir the flour with a fork, spoon it into measuring cups, and sweep level)*
*2 tablespoons baking powder*
*1¼ teaspoons salt*
*6 tablespoons unsalted butter, chilled and cut into small pieces*
*⅓ cup solid vegetable shortening, chilled and cut into small pieces*
*1½ cups buttermilk, chilled*

**SERVING STRATEGY** Eggs are a personal matter, and preparing them for more than one can leave you scrambling for a solution to the firm versus creamy dilemma. Your best bet is to take a survey, then remove some eggs from the skillet while creamy and continue cooking the rest until firm. (Eggs will continue to cook after removed from the skillet.) Personally, I eat scrambled eggs barely broken up and still obviously yellow-and-white, but for a group it's best to whisk them thoroughly and season them well with salt and pepper. Be generous with the sweet butter, and consider stirring in several tablespoons of whipping cream or crème fraîche just before serving.

For four it's an easy matter to serve this meal on separate plates, but for a crowd (the menu multiplies easily), mound the eggs on a platter and surround them with the tomatoes and sausages, pass the grits in a large bowl, offer the black olive butter in a crock, and serve the biscuits in a napkin-lined basket.

◆◆◆◆◆◆◆◆◆◆◆◆◆◆◆◆◆◆◆◆◆◆◆◆◆◆◆◆◆◆◆◆◆◆◆◆◆◆◆◆◆◆◆◆◆◆

# MENU

◆ ◆ ◆ ◆ ◆ ◆ ◆ ◆ ◆ ◆ ◆ ◆ ◆ ◆ ◆

CHUNKY GUACAMOLE
*or*
ROMAINE AND RED ONION
SALAD WITH FRESH
OREGANO DRESSING
*page 80*
◆

WEST TEXAS ROAST BEEF HASH
◆

BUTTERMILK BISCUITS
*page 27*
◆

GRITS AND HONEY PUDDING

THE DAYS WHEN FAMILIES regularly had plenty of leftover roast beef following Sunday's big dinner are almost gone, and the pleasure of turning those leftovers into sandwiches, shepherd's pie, or roast beef hash is also a thing mostly of the past. When on the rare occasion it happens in your house, I hope you'll turn to this recipe; when the nostalgia for homemade hash is so great you're driven to impetuous improvisation, you can even substitute roast beef purchased from the deli. Either way, top your hash with eggs, serve it up with suitable panhandle fixin's, and enjoy it for brunch, lunch, or supper.

One practical note: To have enough salad for eight, you'll need to double the recipe on page 80.

## CHUNKY GUACAMOLE

♦ ♦ ♦ ♦ ♦ ♦ ♦ ♦ ♦

¼ cup minced yellow
   onion
¾ cup coarsely chopped
   cilantro leaves
2 tablespoons minced fresh
   marjoram or oregano
   leaves
1 to 1½ fresh jalapeños,
   stemmed
1 teaspoon salt
4 ripe but firm Hass
   avocados
2 large, ripe tomatoes,
   seeded and cut into
   ¾-inch chunks
⅓ cup finely diced red
   onion
Lightly salted corn tortilla
   chips

THE BEST GUACAMOLE is the simplest and freshest, made with buttery avocados (the wrinkled, black-skinned Hass or a near relative), ripe tomatoes, fresh jalapeño or serrano chiles to taste, a bit of onion, and—in my house, at least—a generous dose of cilantro.

That said, though, there *are* variations and no cook need ever get into a rut. One of my favorite twists is marjoram. Since its pungent taste is almost as southwestern to my palate as cilantro, I decided to combine the two, and the resulting guacamole—chunky and assertive indeed—is more an avocado and tomato salad than a mere dip. It's a great appetizer when served with corn chips, but it will also be appreciated when served alongside smoky grilled meats or rolled into tortillas with fajitas. If you don't have fresh marjoram or oregano, don't substitute dried; just increase the cilantro, as you see fit.

In a small food processor or blender combine the yellow onion, cilantro, marjoram, jalapeños, and salt. Process until smooth.

Halve and pit the avocados. Using the dull side of a knife, score the flesh into ¾-inch chunks. Scoop the chunks out of the skins and place in a medium-size bowl.

Add the herb puree, tomatoes, and red onion to the avocado and toss gently until just mixed. *The guacamole can be prepared up to 1 hour before serving. Cover tightly with plastic wrap and let stand at room temperature.* Serve with the tortilla chips.

*Serves 6 to 8*

## WEST TEXAS
## ROAST BEEF HASH

♦ ♦ ♦ ♦ ♦ ♦ ♦ ♦ ♦

**A**LTHOUGH HOMEMADE ROAST BEEF hash often contains a bit of catsup, I think you'll find that using barbecue sauce produces a more interesting result. Select a good-quality, fairly thick sauce, preferably one with a bit of hot spice and smoke to it. Some folks skip the eggs, but in my house, it wouldn't be hash without them.

In a saucepan cover the potatoes with cold water. Stir in 1 tablespoon of salt, set over medium heat, and bring to a boil. Lower the heat and simmer, stirring occasionally, until the potatoes are tender but still hold their shape, about 5 minutes after the water reaches a boil. Drain immediately and reserve.

In a large skillet over medium heat melt the butter. Add the onion and thyme and cook, uncovered, stirring occasionally, until the onion just begins to brown, about 15 minutes. Add the beef, the potatoes, the barbecue sauce, and the beef juices. Bring to a simmer and cook, about 5 minutes, or until the mixture is thick. Season to taste with salt and the pepper. *The hash can be prepared to this point 1 day ahead. Cool, cover, and refrigerate. Bring the hash back to a simmer before proceeding.*

Preheat the broiler. Spoon the hash mixture into 8 individual shallow gratin dishes. Bring a shallow pan with 2 inches of lightly salted water to a simmer. One at a time, break the eggs into a small dish and slide them into the water. Maintain the water temperature at just below an active simmer until the eggs are done to your liking, 2 to 4 minutes.

Meanwhile, set the gratin dishes under the broiler and cook until the beef and potato cubes on top are browned and the hash is sizzling, about 2 minutes.

*2 pounds boiling potatoes, peeled and cut into ½-inch dice*

*Salt*

*4 tablespoons unsalted butter*

*1 medium onion, peeled and chopped*

*½ teaspoon dried thyme, crumbled*

*1½ pounds leftover roast beef or pot roast, trimmed of fat and cut into ½-inch dice (see note)*

*¾ cup hot and smoky, prepared tomato-based barbecue sauce*

*1½ cups beef braising juices or canned or homemade broth*

*Freshly ground black pepper*

*8 eggs*

With the back of a spoon, make a shallow depression in the center of each portion. With a slotted spoon, remove the eggs one at a time from the water, drain, and set them atop the hash in the depressions formed by the spoon. Serve immediately.

NOTE Brisket makes sublime hash. See page 59 for information on and directions for braising beef brisket.

*Serves 8*

♦♦♦♦♦♦♦♦♦♦♦♦♦♦♦♦♦♦♦♦♦♦♦♦♦♦♦♦♦♦♦♦♦♦♦♦♦♦♦♦♦♦♦

## GRITS AND HONEY PUDDING

♦♦♦♦♦♦♦♦♦

4 cups milk
Salt
1 cup regular-cooking
   white hominy grits (not
   instant or
   quick-cooking)
1 cup golden or dark
   raisins, or a combination
   of the two
5 egg yolks
¾ cup honey
3 egg whites
1 tablespoon sugar
Unsweetened whipped
   cream, as optional
   garnish

**A** STURDY, SWEET, AND SIMPLE conclusion to the hearty menu, this pudding has great kid-appeal, and it may convince those dubious about grits to try them in other unsweetened forms. The recipe makes extra servings; enjoy some as a midnight snack.

♦♦♦  ♦♦♦

In a heavy-bottomed, 3-quart saucepan combine the milk and ½ teaspoon of salt. Bring to a boil and slowly add the grits in a steady stream, stirring constantly. Add the raisins, lower the heat, and cook, covered, stirring once or twice, until very thick, about 15 minutes.

In a mixing bowl whisk together the egg yolks and honey. Whisk in 1 cup of the hot grits mixture, then slowly whisk this mixture back into the hot grits. Return the grits to low heat and cook, stirring constantly, until the mixture just reaches a boil, about 5 minutes. It will be very thick. Remove from the heat.

In another mixing bowl, whisk the egg whites and a pinch of salt to soft peaks. Sprinkle with the sugar and continue to whisk until the whites are firm and glossy. Stir one-quarter of the egg whites into the grits mixture, then fold in the remaining whites until just combined. Cool to room temperature and cover with plastic wrap, pressing the wrap onto the surface of the pudding.

Refrigerate at least 6 hours before serving. *The pudding can be prepared up to 3 days before serving.* Top, if desired, with whipped cream.

*Serves 8 to 10*

♦ ♦ ♦ ♦ ♦ ♦ ♦ ♦ ♦ ♦ ♦ ♦ ♦ ♦ ♦ ♦ ♦ ♦ ♦ ♦ ♦ ♦ ♦ ♦ ♦ ♦ ♦ ♦ ♦ ♦ ♦ ♦ ♦ ♦ ♦ ♦ ♦ ♦ ♦ ♦ ♦ ♦ ♦

♦ ♦ ♦ ♦ ♦ ♦ ♦ ♦ ♦ ♦ ♦ ♦ ♦

WARM SALAD OF SOFT-COOKED
EGGS AND SMOKED FISH

♦

TOASTED PUMPERNICKEL
RAISIN BAGELS

♦

BOURBON-BUTTERSCOTCH
BAKED APPLES

THIS IS A LITTLE SUPPER I would like to come home to, perhaps after an evening of theater- or concert-going, but the elements are also very brunchlike, and, with the addition of the Sunday papers, I suspect it would taste very good in the middle of a long and lazy weekend. Because I'm a New Yorker, smoked fish makes me think of bagels, but you may freely substitute any bread you choose.

## WARM SALAD OF SOFT-COOKED EGGS AND SMOKED FISH

♦♦♦♦♦♦♦♦♦

**A**T A GRANDER BRUNCH this salad would make an admirable starter course for, say, eight people. However you serve it, pour beer or champagne. If you're feeling especially flush, you might omit the smoked fish and top the eggs, after the salad has been assembled and dressed, with a generous dollop of caviar.

Remove and discard the spinach stems. Trim away any wilted outer leaves of lettuce. Wash and dry the greens and tear them into bite-size pieces. Store in plastic bags and refrigerate. *The greens can be prepared to this point up to 1 day ahead.*

In a small, nonreactive saucepan whisk together the vinegar, sugar, mustard, and salt. Gradually whisk in the oil and cream, first by drops, then in a slow stream. Set the pan over low heat and bring to just below a simmer. Stir in the dill, remove from the heat, and cover to keep warm.

Arrange the greens on 6 plates, dividing them equally. In a medium-size skillet over low heat melt the butter. Break the eggs into a bowl, whisk them briefly (do not overmix or salt the eggs), and pour them into the skillet. Cook, stirring, until softly set, about 5 minutes. Fold the smoked fish into the eggs and immediately spoon the mixture into the center of each salad. Pour the warm dressing over the eggs and greens. Garnish each salad with the onion and serve immediately.

— ● *Serves 6*

*2 medium bunches (about 1½ pounds) fresh spinach*

*1 head of Boston or Bibb lettuce*

*3 tablespoons white wine vinegar*

*½ tablespoon sugar*

*2 tablespoons Dijon-style mustard*

*Pinch of salt*

*½ cup corn oil*

*¼ cup heavy cream*

*¼ cup minced fresh dill*

*4 tablespoons (½ stick) unsalted butter*

*8 eggs*

*⅓ pound thinly sliced or flaked smoked salmon, whitefish, sturgeon, or trout (see Cook's Sources)*

*1 small red onion, peeled and sliced into very thin rings*

## BOURBON-BUTTERSCOTCH BAKED APPLES

6 large baking apples
(Rome Beauty, Granny
Smith, or Golden
Delicious), cored
½ cup (1 stick) unsalted
butter, cut into small
pieces
¾ cup light brown sugar,
firmly packed
¾ cup bourbon
¾ cup whipping cream
1 tablespoon vanilla
1 tablespoon fresh lemon
juice

♦ ♦ ♦ ♦ ♦ ♦ ♦ ♦ ♦ ♦

THIS DESSERT can't really be made ahead, so plan to bake it while you enjoy the warm salad. Dark rum, cognac, Calvados (applejack), or Scotch can be substituted for the bourbon.

Preheat the oven to 375 degrees F. Remove a ½-inch strip of peel from around the top of each apple, using a vegetable peeler. Set the apples upright in a shallow, flameproof baking pan just large enough to accommodate them. Top the apples with the butter, sprinkle with the brown sugar, and then drizzle the bourbon over all. Bake until the apples are puffed and tender, basting them occasionally with the pan juices, 30 to 50 minutes.

Transfer the apples to a platter and keep warm. Stir the cream into the baking pan and set over high heat. Bring to a boil, then lower the heat to medium-high, and cook, stirring frequently, until the sauce is reduced by half and coats a spoon, 7 to 10 minutes. Remove the sauce from the heat and stir in the vanilla and lemon juice. Spoon the sauce onto dessert plates, set an apple in the center, and serve immediately.

━━● *Serves 6*

# M E N U

◆ ◆ ◆ ◆ ◆ ◆ ◆ ◆ ◆ ◆ ◆ ◆ ◆ ◆ ◆

BACON, LETTUCE, AND
TOMATO CUSTARD

◆

CARROT AND RED PEPPER SLAW

◆

FRESH POTATO CHIPS

◆

NECTARINES POACHED IN
SPICED RED WINE
*page 147*

BRUNCH, LUNCH, AND SUPPER will all be improved by this accommodating menu, featuring a sort of savory bread pudding that incorporates all the elements of the BLT sandwich. It goes together quickly and is good hot or warm. The unfussy accompaniments and a light dessert of poached fruit round out an informal meal.

## BACON, LETTUCE, AND TOMATO CUSTARD

◆◆◆◆◆◆◆◆◆

1 pound of smoked slab
    bacon, trimmed and cut
    into ¼-inch dice
Salt
1 medium head of romaine
    lettuce, trimmed and
    coarsely chopped
10 eggs
⅓ cup mild, deli-style
    mustard
¼ teaspoon cayenne pepper
1 quart whipping cream
4 cups whole wheat bread,
    cut into 1-inch cubes
3 firm, ripe plum tomatoes,
    trimmed and cut into
    thick slices

**E**VERYTHING BUT THE MAYO is included in this savory custard. At lunch or brunch drink freshly squeezed orange juice; later in the day accompany the pudding with a crisp and spicy Gewürztraminer.

◆◆◆  ◆◆◆

In a large skillet over medium heat cook the bacon, stirring occasionally, until it is crisp and brown, about 10 minutes. With a slotted spoon, transfer the bacon to paper towels to drain.

Bring a large saucepan of water to a boil. Stir in 1 tablespoon of salt. Add the lettuce and cook 1 minute. (The water need not return to a boil.) Drain immediately and transfer to a large bowl of ice water. Let stand until cool, drain well, and squeeze dry. Reserve.

Position a rack in the middle of the oven and preheat to 375 degrees F. Butter a 9 × 13-inch rectangular baking dish.

In a large bowl whisk the eggs thoroughly. Whisk in the mustard, 2 teaspoons of salt, and the pepper. Slowly whisk in the cream.

Sprinkle the bacon, the lettuce, and the bread cubes evenly over the bottom of the prepared baking dish. Pour in the egg mixture. Arrange the tomato slices on top.

Bake the custard for 45 to 50 minutes, or until it is puffed, golden brown, and firm in the center. Let it cool on a rack for at least 20 minutes before cutting into squares and serving.

━● *Serves 8*

## CARROT AND
## RED PEPPER SLAW

**♦ ♦ ♦ ♦ ♦ ♦ ♦ ♦ ♦**

**S**WEET, TART, AND CRUNCHY, this carrot slaw is every bit as good as the sort made with cabbage, and it boasts a mustardy balsamic vinegar–based mayonnaise. It keeps well, too, and also tastes great with grilled chicken, burgers, or other simple summer fare.

♦ ♦ ♦  ♦ ♦ ♦

Set aside 2 tablespoons each of the diced peppers and sliced onions, for use as garnish. In a large bowl combine the remaining peppers and onions, and the carrots. Add about two-thirds of the mayonnaise and toss well. *The slaw can be made to this point up to 1 day ahead. Refrigerate, covered. Cover and refrigerate the remaining mayonnaise.*

Line a bowl with the cabbage leaves. Adjust the seasoning of the slaw and add more mayonnaise, if desired. Spoon the slaw into the cabbage-lined bowl and sprinkle with the reserved diced peppers and sliced onions. Pass the remaining mayonnaise at the table.

━● *Serves 8 to 10*

♦ ♦ ♦ ♦ ♦ ♦ ♦ ♦ ♦ ♦ ♦ ♦ ♦ ♦ ♦ ♦ ♦ ♦ ♦ ♦ ♦ ♦ ♦ ♦ ♦ ♦ ♦ ♦ ♦ ♦ ♦ ♦ ♦ ♦ ♦ ♦ ♦ ♦

2 large, sweet red peppers, trimmed and cut into ¼-inch dice
5 green onions, trimmed and sliced thin
2 pounds carrots, peeled and coarsely shredded
Balsamic Mayonnaise (recipe follows)
Leaves of curly green cabbage, as garnish

## BALSAMIC MAYONNAISE

**♦ ♦ ♦ ♦ ♦ ♦ ♦ ♦ ♦**

In a food processor combine the egg yolks, vinegar, mustard, salt, and a generous grind of pepper and process 1 minute. With the machine running slowly add the oils through the feed tube in a slow stream. Adjust the seasoning. Cover and refrigerate. *The mayonnaise can be prepared up to 3 days ahead.*

━● *Makes about 3 cups*

♦ ♦ ♦ ♦ ♦ ♦ ♦ ♦ ♦ ♦ ♦ ♦ ♦ ♦ ♦ ♦ ♦ ♦ ♦ ♦ ♦ ♦ ♦ ♦ ♦ ♦ ♦ ♦ ♦ ♦ ♦ ♦ ♦ ♦ ♦ ♦ ♦ ♦

3 egg yolks
½ cup balsamic vinegar
3 tablespoons prepared Dijon-style mustard
½ teaspoon salt
Freshly ground black pepper
1 cup olive oil
1 cup corn oil

3½ pounds red-skinned
   new potatoes, unpeeled
   and well scrubbed
Vegetable oil, for deep
   frying
Coarse salt

## FRESH POTATO CHIPS

THESE CHIPS ARE a bad habit to get into. The quantity below is enough for eight by any normal standards; on the other hand, this recipe expands easily, and I've never thrown any away. The chips can be made up to twelve hours ahead, stored at room temperature in a paper bag, and rewarmed slightly for serving, but they taste best piping hot, right out of the fryer.

With a knife or in a food processor, slice the potatoes paper-thin. In a large bowl cover the potatoes with cold water and soak 1 hour. Drain and repeat. Drain and pat thoroughly dry.

Fill a deep fryer half-full of oil and heat to 375 degrees F. Add the potatoes to the oil in batches. Stir immediately. The fat will foam when the potato moisture vaporizes. Cook, stirring occasionally, until golden brown, about 6 minutes. Remove the potatoes with a slotted spoon and drain on paper towels. Sprinkle lightly with the coarse salt.

*Serves 8*

# MENU

◆ ◆ ◆ ◆ ◆ ◆ ◆ ◆ ◆ ◆ ◆ ◆ ◆ ◆ ◆

GRILLED SMOKED TURKEY
AND CHEDDAR SANDWICHES WITH
HOT PEPPER JELLY

◆

SIMPLE ORANGE SLAW

◆

FRESH POTATO CHIPS
*page 40*

◆

BITCHIN' BROWNIES
*or*
VANILLA ICE CREAM
WITH BITTERSWEET
DOUBLE CHOCOLATE SAUCE
*page 77*

IF YOU EVER FIND yourself saying, *"Just* a sandwich," when asked, "What's for supper?" something is amiss. A well-made sandwich ought to be a special treat, not something to apologize for, and it deserves to be assembled with care and attention. This menu features an easy (be wary of sandwiches that seem like too much work) favorite of mine that you won't have to apologize for, and teams it with old favorites like chips, slaw, and brownies.

## GRILLED SMOKED TURKEY AND CHEDDAR SANDWICHES WITH HOT PEPPER JELLY

♦ ♦ ♦ ♦ ♦ ♦ ♦ ♦ ♦

*4 thick slices of sourdough or country-style white bread, sliced ½ inch thick from an oval loaf about 7 inches in diameter*

*½ cup hot pepper jelly*

*8 ounces sharp white cheddar cheese, sliced thin*

*1 pound smoked turkey breast, sliced, skin and fat removed*

*4 ounces (1 stick) unsalted butter, melted*

**P**IQUANT SWEET AND HOT pepper jelly is just right on these crusty sandwiches, but a thick and spicy home-made chutney (see page 375), or even cranberry sauce, is delicious too.

♦ ♦ ♦  ♦ ♦ ♦

Spread 1 side of each of the bread slices with 2 table-spoons of the pepper jelly. Lay the sliced cheese over the jelly, dividing it evenly among the 4 slices of bread. Fold each slice of turkey in half and arrange the slices, overlapping slightly, over the cheese on two of the slices of bread. Invert the remaining cheese-covered bread on top of the turkey.

Heat a griddle or large cast-iron skillet over me-dium heat until just warm. Generously brush half of the melted butter over the top surface of the sand-wiches. Flip the sandwiches butter side down onto the heated griddle. Brush the remaining butter over the top of the sandwiches.

Cook, covered, until the bread is crisp and golden brown on the bottom and the cheese is beginning to melt, about 5 minutes. With a wide spatula, turn the sandwiches and brown them on the other side, 4 to 5 minutes.

Transfer the sandwiches to a cutting board and cut them in half using a serrated knife. Serve immedi-ately.

*Makes 2 large sandwiches, serving 4*

## SIMPLE ORANGE SLAW

♦ ♦ ♦ ♦ ♦ ♦ ♦ ♦ ♦

**I**NVENTED DURING a late night search-and-destroy raid on the refrigerator, this coleslaw's easy dressing was improvised from leftover "French Dressing" and a dollop of sour cream. The result is tangy, sweet, and simple. The parslied slaw makes a great side dish, but I like it equally well when made with dill and piled high on a smoked turkey, Gruyère, and pumpernickel sandwich.

♦ ♦ ♦  ♦ ♦ ♦

⅔ cup sour cream
1 recipe French Dressing
 (page 310)
1 medium white cabbage
 (about 2 pounds), cored
 and finely julienned
½ cup finely minced yellow
 onion
⅓ cup finely chopped
 Italian parsley
Freshly ground black
 pepper

In a medium-size bowl whisk the sour cream until smooth. Whisk in the dressing.

In a large bowl toss together the cabbage, onion, and parsley. Add the sour cream and dressing mixture, season generously with pepper, and stir again. *The coleslaw can be prepared and kept, covered and refrigerated, up to 3 days ahead.*

**━● *Serves 6 to 8***

♦ ♦ ♦ ♦ ♦ ♦ ♦ ♦ ♦ ♦ ♦ ♦ ♦ ♦ ♦ ♦ ♦ ♦ ♦ ♦ ♦ ♦ ♦ ♦ ♦ ♦ ♦ ♦ ♦ ♦ ♦ ♦ ♦ ♦ ♦ ♦ ♦ ♦ ♦ ♦

## BITCHIN' BROWNIES

♦ ♦ ♦ ♦ ♦ ♦ ♦ ♦ ♦

**A**CCORDING TO MY DICTIONARY, "quintessence" is the perfect example of a quality. It's also the bad habit of certain cooks who seek to modify and perfect a recipe so devastatingly right that all other recipes for the same food are rendered useless. You know the type—always boasting about their quintessential chili or barbecue sauce or bouillabaisse while forcing you to listen to the tale of its development over yet another perfected portion. Even I succumb to quintessential quisine on oc-

4 ounces unsweetened
  baking chocolate,
  chopped
1½ sticks unsalted butter,
  cut into pieces
1 teaspoon instant coffee or
  espresso
½ teaspoon ground
  cinnamon
3 eggs
1½ cups light brown
  sugar, packed
2 teaspoons vanilla extract
¼ teaspoon salt
1 cup unbleached
  all-purpose flour (to
  measure, stir the flour
  with a fork, spoon it into
  the measuring cup, and
  sweep level)
1 cup chopped walnuts

casion (see page 71 for Perfect Corn Bread). But, although I understand the burning desire to nail a recipe down so utterly, I also recognize that cooking is rather more imprecise than that, and chemistry, hormones, and Mother Necessity play too big a part in producing food to ever let us be certain of our results.

This is to say that while these may not be *the* quintessential brownies, they are real good—moist, dark, fudgy, and not too sweet. Because quintessence was on my mind, the recipe is somewhat detailed, but the results, I think, are worth it. To be firm enough to cut, the brownies must be refrigerated overnight.

Position a rack in the middle of the oven and preheat to 350 degrees F. Butter an 8 × 8-inch metal baking pan.

In the top of a double boiler over hot water melt together the chocolate, butter, coffee, and cinnamon. Stir occasionally. When the mixture is smooth, remove it from the heat and cool to room temperature.

In a large mixing bowl whisk the eggs. Whisk in the brown sugar until the mixture is thick. Whisk in the vanilla and salt. Pour the chocolate around the edge of the mixing bowl. Fold the chocolate into the egg mixture until just combined. Add the flour and fold until just combined. Stir in the nuts. Pour the batter into the prepared pan and bake 25 minutes. The brownies will appear done around the edges, but the center will be unset and slightly liquid. Cool on a rack to room temperature, cover the pan, and refrigerate overnight.

Run a knife around the edge of the brownies and invert the pan on the work surface. Tap the bottom until the brownies drop out. With a long serrated knife, trim away about ¾ inch of crust from each side. Discard the trimmings. Cut the remaining brownies into 18 1 × 2-inch bars and let them come to room temperature, loosely wrapped, before serving.

*Makes 18 brownies*

# MENU

◆◆◆◆◆◆◆◆◆◆◆◆◆◆◆◆◆

TOMATO, WATERCRESS, AND
ENDIVE SALAD
*page 275*

◆

DILLED LAMB SHANKS IN
EGG-LEMON SAUCE

◆

ORZO WITH OLIVES
AND VEGETABLES

◆

SPICE ICE CREAM
WITH BITTERSWEET
DOUBLE CHOCOLATE SAUCE
*page 77*

THE MENU WITH a Greek touch comes alive with vitality and pleasure when one uses simple, earthy, and satisfying foods. For a splashier starter, substitute the Warm Salad with Feta, Tomatoes, and Garlicked Shrimp (page 101); and if you'd like something more than a plain country loaf, add Parslied Garlic Bread (page 67). Pour plenty of uncomplicated red wine.

## DILLED LAMB SHANKS
## IN EGG-LEMON SAUCE

♦♦♦♦♦♦♦♦♦

5 tablespoons olive oil

4 large (about 1 pound
  each) lamb shanks,
  sawed crosswise into
  thirds by the butcher

2 medium onions, peeled
  and chopped

2 carrots, peeled and
  chopped

1 leek, white part only,
  well cleaned and
  chopped

2 garlic cloves, peeled and
  minced

3 bay leaves

3½ cups canned chicken
  broth or homemade stock

1 teaspoon salt

½ teaspoon freshly ground
  black pepper

2 eggs

⅓ cup fresh lemon juice,
  strained

3 tablespoons minced fresh
  dill

**R**ICH LAMB SHANKS, slow-cooked to tender succulence, are finished with the Greek egg-lemon thickener, *avogolemeno*. Minced dill adds a fresh, green note to the silky sauce, and the resulting dish seems brighter and lighter than the usual lamb preparation. You'll find, if you have a good sense of herb cookery in general, and lamb cookery in particular, that the lemony sauce will be equally savory when made with other lamb-compatible fresh herbs—mint, basil, marjoram, or rosemary.

♦♦♦  ♦♦♦

Position a rack in the middle of the oven and preheat to 350 degrees F.

Heat 2 tablespoons of the oil in a 4½- or 5-quart, heavy, flameproof casserole or Dutch oven over medium-high heat. Pat the lamb shanks dry and cook, in batches, browning them on all sides, about 7 minutes. Transfer the shanks to a bowl as they are browned. Discard the fat from the pan.

Set the pan over low heat (do not clean it) and add the remaining oil. Stir in the onions, carrots, leek, garlic, and bay leaves. Cover the pan and cook, stirring once or twice, for 15 minutes, or until the vegetables are tender.

Return the lamb shanks to the pan, along with any juices from the bowl, and stir in the chicken broth, salt, and pepper. Bring to a boil, cover the pan, and bake in the oven 45 minutes. Uncover the pan, stir, and bake another 30 to 40 minutes, or until the lamb is very tender.

Remove the lamb and keep it warm. Strain and degrease the stock, discarding the solids. *The dish can be prepared to this point up to 1 day ahead. Pour the stock over the lamb shanks, cool completely, cover, and*

*refrigerate. Heat the shanks until steaming, then re-*
*move them from the stock before proceeding. To make*
*serving easier, you may remove and discard the shank*
*bones.*

In a bowl whisk together the eggs and lemon juice.
Whisk in the warm stock. Stir in the dill. Return the
lamb to the pan, pour the sauce over the lamb, and set
the pan over low heat. Cook, stirring and basting the
lamb with the sauce, until it thickens slightly, 3 to 5
minutes. Do not let the mixture come to a boil. Adjust
the seasoning, if necessary, with extra salt and pepper.
Serve immediately.

*Serves 4*

◆ ◆ ◆ ◆ ◆ ◆ ◆ ◆ ◆ ◆ ◆ ◆ ◆ ◆ ◆ ◆ ◆ ◆ ◆ ◆ ◆ ◆ ◆ ◆ ◆ ◆ ◆ ◆ ◆ ◆ ◆ ◆ ◆ ◆ ◆ ◆ ◆ ◆ ◆ ◆ ◆ ◆ ◆ ◆ ◆ ◆ ◆

## ORZO WITH OLIVES AND VEGETABLES

◆ ◆ ◆ ◆ ◆ ◆ ◆ ◆ ◆

T HIS IS ONE OF THOSE vegetable-starch side dishes that
can simplify the cook's life. It goes together quickly,
provides color and crunch on the plate, and in a casual
menu that also includes a salad, eliminates the need
for a separate vegetable side dish.

◆ ◆ ◆  ◆ ◆ ◆

In a saucepan bring the chicken broth to a boil. Stir in
the orzo, lower the heat, and simmer briskly, stirring
occasionally, until the orzo is tender, about 9 minutes.
Drain the orzo and stir in 1 tablespoon of the oil. Set
aside. *The recipe can be prepared to this point up to 3*
*hours ahead.*

In a heavy skillet over high heat warm the remaining oil. Add the pepper and zucchini and cook,
stirring and tossing, until lightly browned, 5 to 6 minutes. Season with the salt and remove from the heat.
Cool the pan slightly, then stir in the orzo and the

*4 cups canned chicken*
  *broth*
*1 cup orzo (rice-shaped*
  *pasta)*
*4 tablespoons olive oil*
*1 sweet red pepper,*
  *stemmed, cored, and cut*
  *into ¼-inch dice*
*1 medium zucchini,*
  *scrubbed, trimmed, and*
  *cut into ½-inch dice*
*½ teaspoon salt*
*⅓ cup small black olives,*
  *such as Niçoise or Gaeta*
  *(see Cook's Sources),*
  *rinsed and drained*
*Freshly ground black*
  *pepper*

olives. Set the skillet over low heat and cook, stirring and tossing, until the orzo is just heated through, 3 to 5 minutes. Season with black pepper to taste and serve immediately.

*Serves 4*

◆◆◆◆◆◆◆◆◆◆◆◆◆◆◆◆◆◆◆◆◆◆◆◆◆◆◆◆◆◆◆◆◆◆◆◆◆◆◆

▚▞▚▞▚▞▚▞▚▞▚▞▚▞▚▞▚▞▚▞▚▞▚▞▚▞▚▞▚▞▚▞

## SPICE ICE CREAM WITH BITTERSWEET DOUBLE CHOCOLATE SAUCE

◆◆◆◆◆◆◆◆◆

**4 egg yolks**
**¾ cup sugar**
**½ teaspoon ground cinnamon**
**½ teaspoon ground ginger**
**½ teaspoon freshly grated nutmeg**
**¼ teaspoon ground cloves**
**¼ teaspoon ground allspice**
**3 cups half-and-half**
**1 cup whipping cream**
**2 teaspoons vanilla**
**Bittersweet Double Chocolate Sauce (page 77)**

Cold ice cream with plenty of warm spices makes for an intriguing conclusion to the meal. This ice cream is equally good alongside a big wedge of warm apple pie.

◆◆◆  ◆◆◆

In a large bowl whisk together the egg yolks, sugar, cinnamon, ginger, nutmeg, cloves, and allspice.

In a heavy, 3-quart saucepan bring the half-and-half and whipping cream to a boil. Slowly whisk the hot cream into the egg mixture. Return the mixture to the pan. Set over low heat and cook, stirring constantly, until the mixture thickens and leaves a track on the back of a spoon when a fingertip is drawn across it, about 4 minutes. Strain it into a bowl. Stir in the vanilla. Cool the custard to room temperature, cover, and refrigerate until very cold, preferably overnight.

Transfer the custard to the canister of an ice-cream maker and churn according to manufacturer's directions. Store the ice cream, covered, in the freezer. *The ice cream can be prepared up to 2 days ahead.* Soften the ice cream slightly in the refrigerator and top with the chocolate sauce before serving.

*Makes about 1 quart*

◆◆◆◆◆◆◆◆◆◆◆◆◆◆◆◆◆◆◆◆◆◆◆◆◆◆◆◆◆◆◆◆◆◆◆◆◆◆◆

# MENU

◆◆◆◆◆◆◆◆◆◆◆◆◆◆◆◆

MIXED GREENS WITH
RED WINE VINAIGRETTE
AND CHEESE TOASTS

◆

VEAL CHOPS SMOTHERED
WITH ARTICHOKE, BACON,
AND SHALLOT RAGOUT

◆

ARBORIO RICE CAKE
*page 278*

◆

WARM APPLE CRISP À LA MODE

LUNCH NEEDN'T BE something quick and on the run; supper isn't necessarily a modest family meal between the end of the workday and the beginning of prime-time television. There are occasions when these small meals can mean graceful food served to an intimate few; this menu is a good example.

Veal might not be everyday lunch or supper fare, but when you want to celebrate on a certain scale and know your guests will be pleased by the food and impressed by the casualness of it all, try these chops with their luscious ragout of artichokes, bacon, shallots, and cream. A simple green salad adds color and crunch, the crusty cake of arborio rice is the offbeat starch, and the dessert is a warm, gussied-up version of apple crisp, topped with a scoop of ice cream.

## MIXED GREENS WITH RED WINE VINAIGRETTE AND CHEESE TOASTS

◆◆◆◆◆◆◆◆◆

1 medium bunch of
arugula

1 medium bunch of
watercress

1 small head of Belgian
endive

1 tablespoon red wine
vinegar

2 teaspoons shallot
mustard

Pinch of salt

¼ cup corn oil

¼ cup olive oil

Freshly ground black
pepper

8 thin slices of baguette,
cut on the diagonal and
toasted

6 ounces soft cheese, such
as St. André, St.
Christopher, or
Roquefort, at room
temperature

HERE IS THE MOST BASIC of green salads, composed with an eye toward availability and variety. Use at least three different greens, including one that has an assertive flavor and one that is crisp and crunchy. I keep a jar of shallot Dijon mustard expressly for this salad, and since the dressing is otherwise very simple, I suggest you use only best-quality vinegar and oil.

The toasts are an uncomplicated garnish that elevates the salad into something more than mere roughage; adjust the cheese—triple crème, chèvre, Camembert, blue-veined—to suit market, mood, and menu.

◆◆◆  ◆◆◆

Trim the arugula and watercress. Wash and pat them dry and tear into bite-size pieces. Remove any discolored outer leaves from the endive. Cut the inner leaves into long thin strips. *The greens can be prepared to this point up to 1 day ahead. Store them separately in plastic bags and refrigerate.*

In a bowl whisk together the vinegar, mustard, and salt. Combine the oils and add them to the vinegar mixture in a slow dribble, whisking constantly. Adjust the seasoning, if necessary, and add fresh pepper to taste.

Spread the toasted baguette with the cheese. In a large bowl combine the greens. Add the dressing, toss to mix, and divide the salad among 4 plates. Spoon any dressing remaining in the bowl over the salads. Divide the cheese toasts atop the salads and serve immediately.

━● *Serves 4*

## VEAL CHOPS SMOTHERED WITH ARTICHOKE, BACON, AND SHALLOT RAGOUT

♦♦♦♦♦♦♦♦♦

**M**Y FRIEND FRANCINE the caterer is fond of telling her clients, "You can have veal or you can make the next payment on your summer home, but you can't do both." A properly thick chop of prime veal may well squander a chunk of your savings, so be certain it's money spent on a good cause, like this dish. If time is short, substitute a 9-ounce package of frozen artichoke hearts, thawed and drained, but when made with fresh baby artichokes, the ragout is sublime.

♦ ♦ ♦  ♦ ♦ ♦

Trim the stems and tough outer leaves and halve the artichokes. Bring a pot of lightly salted water to a boil. Add the artichokes, lower the heat, and simmer until just tender, 7 to 10 minutes. Drain and reserve.

In a large, heavy skillet over medium heat fry the bacon, stirring occasionally, until crisp, about 10 minutes. With a slotted spoon, transfer the bacon to paper towels to drain. Pour the drippings off and reserve. Do not clean the skillet. *The recipe can be prepared to this point up to 3 hours ahead.*

In a medium-size saucepan over moderate heat warm all but 2 tablespoons of the bacon drippings. Add the shallots and cook until they are golden brown, stirring occasionally, about 15 minutes. Add the artichokes and cook another 5 minutes. Set aside.

Heat the remaining 2 tablespoons of bacon drippings in the reserved skillet over high heat until very hot. Add the veal chops, lower the heat slightly, and cook until well browned, about 10 minutes. Turn the chops, season them with the pepper, and continue to cook until they are well browned but slightly pink and juicy inside, about 10 minutes. Transfer the chops to a plate and make a foil tent to keep them warm.

*8 baby artichokes*
*Salt*
*½ pound slab bacon, trimmed and cut into ¼-inch dice*
*16 large, whole shallots, peeled*
*4 veal loin or rib chops, 1 to 1½ inches thick (about 3½ pounds), patted dry*
*Freshly ground black pepper*
*1 cup canned chicken broth or homemade stock*
*½ cup whipping cream*

Discard the drippings. Stir in the broth and cream and set the skillet over high heat. Bring to a boil, scraping up any browned bits, and cook hard until reduced to ¾ cup, about 7 minutes. Add the artichoke mixture and the bacon and simmer until heated through, about 2 minutes. Adjust the seasoning. Arrange the veal chops on plates and spoon the artichoke ragout partially over the chops. Serve immediately.

*Serves 4*

♦♦♦♦♦♦♦♦♦♦♦♦♦♦♦♦♦♦♦♦♦♦♦♦♦♦♦♦♦♦♦♦♦♦♦♦♦♦♦♦♦♦♦♦♦♦♦

## WARM APPLE CRISP À LA MODE

♦♦♦♦♦♦♦♦♦

**APPLE PUREE**

*2 pounds (about 4 large)*
*Granny Smith apples,*
*peeled, cored, and*
*coarsely chopped*

*½ cup light brown sugar,*
*firmly packed*

*6 tablespoons (¾ stick)*
*unsalted butter*

*⅓ cup apple juice or cider*

**HAZELNUT CRISP**

*½ cup unbleached*
*all-purpose flour*

*½ cup hazelnuts*

*¼ cup light brown sugar,*
*packed*

*5 tablespoons unsalted*
*butter, chilled and cut*
*into small pieces*

*Ice cream, softened slightly*

THIS DESSERT is inside out and upside down, featuring individual servings of warm apple puree, topped by a scoop of ice cream and a crumble of hazelnut cookie crisp. Make Spice Ice Cream (page 48) or Maple Syrup Ice Cream (page 330), or substitute premium store-bought vanilla ice cream.

♦♦♦  ♦♦♦

*For the puree* In a heavy saucepan combine the apples, brown sugar, butter, and cider and set over medium-low heat. Bring to a simmer and cook, covered, stirring occasionally, until the apples are very tender, about 20 minutes. Cool slightly and force through the medium blade of a food mill or puree until smooth in a food processor. Cool completely, cover, and refrigerate. *The puree can be prepared up to 2 days ahead.*

*For the crisp* In a food processor, combine the flour, hazelnuts, brown sugar, and butter in the order listed. Process just until a moist, crumbly dough is formed. Transfer to a bowl and refrigerate for 45 minutes.

Position a rack in the upper third of the oven and preheat to 375 degrees F. Lightly pat the dough into a 6-inch round in the bottom of a 9-inch metal pan. (The dough will resemble a large, rather sloppy cookie.) Bake until crisp and browned, 15 to 20 minutes. Cool in the pan on a rack. Coarsely crumble the crisp. *The crisp can be prepared up to 1 day ahead. Store in an airtight container at room temperature.*

*To assemble* In a small, heavy saucepan over low heat warm the apple puree, stirring often, until steaming. Spread ½ cup of the puree into a 5-inch round on each of 4 dessert plates. Place a scoop of ice cream in the center of each circle of puree. Sprinkle the crumbled crisp over the puree and serve immediately.

━● *Serves 4*

◆ ◆ ◆ ◆ ◆ ◆ ◆ ◆ ◆ ◆ ◆ ◆ ◆ ◆ ◆ ◆ ◆ ◆ ◆ ◆ ◆ ◆ ◆ ◆ ◆ ◆ ◆ ◆ ◆ ◆ ◆ ◆ ◆ ◆ ◆ ◆ ◆ ◆ ◆ ◆

# MENU

◆ ◆ ◆ ◆ ◆ ◆ ◆ ◆ ◆ ◆ ◆ ◆ ◆ ◆ ◆

**SALAD OF WINTER GREENS WITH
BLUE GOAT CHEESE DRESSING**
*page 225*

◆

**CABBAGE SOUP WITH
LAMB AND RICE MEATBALLS**

◆

**BUCKWHEAT
COUNTRY PUMPERNICKEL BREAD**

◆

**APPLES, CLEMENTINES, AND
BLACK WALNUTS**

SOUP, SALAD, good bread, seasonal fruit—the simplest kind of repast, easy to cook and even easier to enjoy. The buckwheat bread is delicious and unusual, but if you're not a baker, any good, dark bread is easily substituted. White or red wine will complement the hearty, mustard-spiked soup, but a foamy glass of amber or dark beer seems more appropriate.

## CABBAGE SOUP WITH LAMB AND RICE MEATBALLS

◆ ◆ ◆ ◆ ◆ ◆ ◆ ◆ ◆

**P**ASS A VARIETY of prepared mustards, encouraging diners to stir a dollop into their soup before digging in. (This dish is equally good when the meatballs are made of lean ground pork or a combination of pork and veal.)

◆ ◆ ◆  ◆ ◆ ◆

In a small skillet over low heat melt 3 tablespoons of the butter. Add the onion, garlic, and thyme and cook, covered, stirring occasionally, until tender, about 15 minutes. Remove from the heat and cool.

In a saucepan bring a quart of lightly salted water to a boil. Add the rice, lower the heat slightly, and cook, stirring occasionally, until the rice is tender, about 20 minutes. Drain.

In a large bowl combine the sautéed onion mixture, the cooked rice, the ground lamb, the eggs, 1 tablespoon of salt, and the pepper. Refrigerate until very cold, at least 2 hours.

In a large, heavy pot over medium-high heat melt 3 tablespoons of the butter. Working in batches, form the lamb mixture into 1-inch meatballs and add them to the pot. Cook, turning frequently, until lightly and evenly browned, about 7 minutes. Using a slotted spoon, transfer the browned meatballs to a plate. There should be about 48.

Pour off the fat but do not clean the pan. Set it over low heat, add the remaining butter, and stir in the leeks and carrots. Cover and cook, stirring occasionally and scraping up any browned deposits from the pan, until the vegetables are tender, about 15 minutes. Stir in the chicken broth and white wine. Add the meatballs, any juices from the plate, and the bay leaves. Bring the soup to a simmer, lower the heat, partially cover, and cook for 25 minutes. *The soup can be prepared to this point up to 2 days ahead. Remove from the*

9 tablespoons unsalted butter

1 medium onion, peeled and minced

4 garlic cloves, peeled and minced

2 teaspoons dried thyme, crumbled

Salt

½ cup white rice

3 pounds very lean lamb, finely ground

4 eggs, beaten

1 teaspoon freshly ground black pepper

4 leeks, white part only, well cleaned and finely chopped

4 carrots, peeled and diced

8 cups canned chicken broth or homemade stock

⅔ cup dry white wine

2 bay leaves

1 small head green cabbage, trimmed, cored, and finely julienned

*heat, cool completely, and refrigerate. Heat the soup until simmering before proceeding.*

Remove the meatballs and keep them warm. Discard the bay leaves. Add the cabbage to the pot and simmer, uncovered, stirring once or twice, until the cabbage is almost tender, about 12 minutes. Return the meatballs to the soup and simmer until heated through, about 5 minutes. Adjust the seasoning and serve.

*Serves 8*

## BUCKWHEAT COUNTRY PUMPERNICKEL BREAD

2 cups warm water (105 to
115 degrees F)
¼ cup unsulfured
molasses
1 envelope dry yeast
1 tablespoon salt
2½ teaspoons freeze-dried
instant coffee
2½ teaspoons unsweetened
powdered cocoa
2 teaspoons caraway seeds
(optional)
1½ cups buckwheat flour
½ cup whole wheat flour
3 cups unbleached
all-purpose flour
2 tablespoons vegetable oil

BUCKWHEAT—A GRASSY STARCH, not a cereal grain—lends its distinctive color and sweet nutty flavor to this robust pumpernickel bread. The buckwheat is low in gluten, so the dough is soft and sticky, but the results are worth the extra effort. Freeze one loaf for future use—it makes great sandwiches and spectacular French toast.

In a mixing bowl stir together the water, molasses, and yeast and let stand 10 minutes. Stir in the salt, coffee, cocoa, and caraway seeds. Whisk in the buckwheat and whole wheat flours. Stir in 2½ cups of the unbleached flour. Turn the dough out onto a heavily floured surface and knead in as much as necessary of the remaining ½ cup of flour until the dough is smooth, firm, and elastic, about 7 minutes. In a large mixing bowl turn the dough in the vegetable oil to coat it. Cover the bowl with a towel and let the dough stand at room temperature until it is doubled in size, about 2 hours.

Punch the dough down, turn out onto a floured surface, and knead 2 minutes. Return the dough to the bowl, cover it with a towel, and let stand at room temperature until the dough is doubled in size, about 2 hours.

Preheat the oven to 400 degrees F. Butter 2 loaf pans, 9 × 5 × 3 inches.

Turn the dough out onto a floured surface and divide it in half. Shape each half into a loaf. Transfer the loaves to the prepared pans, cover with a towel, and let stand at room temperature for 30 minutes.

Bake the loaves for about 25 minutes, or until they are risen, crisp, and brown and sound hollow when the bottoms of the loaves are tapped. Cool for 5 minutes in the pans, turn the loaves out onto a rack, and cool completely before cutting or wrapping.

●── *Makes 2 loaves*

♦ ♦ ♦ ♦ ♦ ♦ ♦ ♦ ♦ ♦ ♦ ♦ ♦ ♦ ♦ ♦ ♦ ♦ ♦ ♦ ♦ ♦ ♦ ♦ ♦ ♦ ♦ ♦ ♦ ♦ ♦ ♦ ♦ ♦ ♦ ♦ ♦ ♦ ♦ ♦ ♦ ♦ ♦ ♦

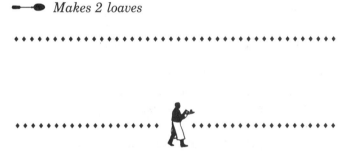

♦ ♦ ♦ ♦ ♦ ♦ ♦ ♦ ♦ ♦ ♦ ♦ ♦ ♦ ♦ ♦ ♦ ♦    ♦ ♦ ♦ ♦ ♦ ♦ ♦ ♦ ♦ ♦ ♦ ♦ ♦ ♦ ♦ ♦ ♦

**SERVING STRATEGY** Clementines, according to Elizabeth Schneider's indispensable *Uncommon Fruits and Vegetables,* are a variety of the common mandarin (some of which we call tangerines). The deepest, most intensely flavored clementines come from Morocco; the season reaches its peak in December and January.

Serve the clementines ice cold, accompanied by black walnuts (see Cook's Sources) and apples. In this informal menu you can even present your guests with baskets of fruits and nuts, a supply of small knives and nutcrackers, and a place to put the peels and shells so that they can nibble as long as they please. Sipping good cognac while eating an icy clementine produces a delicious, instant liqueur-in-the-mouth.

♦ ♦ ♦ ♦ ♦ ♦ ♦ ♦ ♦ ♦ ♦ ♦ ♦ ♦ ♦ ♦ ♦ ♦ ♦ ♦ ♦ ♦ ♦ ♦ ♦ ♦ ♦ ♦ ♦ ♦ ♦ ♦ ♦ ♦ ♦ ♦ ♦ ♦ ♦ ♦ ♦ ♦ ♦ ♦

# M E N U

◆◆◆◆◆◆◆◆◆◆◆◆◆◆◆

**BRAISED BRISKET WITH
HORSERADISH CREAM GRAVY**

◆

**HEAVEN AND EARTH**

◆

**ANADAMA ROLLS
WITH ORANGE BUTTER**
*or*
**BUTTERMILK BISCUITS**
*page 27*

◆

**EGGNOG PIE**

POT ROAST, potatoes, and pie—midwinter buzzwords sure
to excite the simple guy in all of us. I like this menu
just the way it is, with a limited number of dishes and
a muted palate of soft winter colors. You could, however, turn it into something much more than a supper
by beginning with a sprightly and colorful starter of
Shrimp and Celery Salad with Warm Dill Dressing
(page 270) or by following up the entrée with a watercress salad and Hard-Cooked Egg and Mustard Dressing (page 74).

## BRAISED BRISKET WITH HORSERADISH CREAM GRAVY

**B**RISKET IS USUALLY sold as the "flat" (thin) cut or the "point" (thick) cut. Both have their champions. Basically, the flat cut is thin and quite lean, while the point is thick and fatty. Which to use? The choice is yours, and either will work well in the following old-fashioned braise, topped with a creamy brown horseradish gravy.

Position a rack in the lower third of the oven and preheat to 350 degrees F.

In a skillet over medium heat melt the butter. Stir in the onions, thyme, and bay leaf, cover, and cook, stirring occasionally, for 15 minutes, or until tender.

Lay the brisket (fat side up if you are using the point cut) in a heavy casserole. Scrape the onions and herbs over the beef, pour the broth around it, and bake, covered, for about 2½ hours, or until the meat is tender. Regulate the oven temperature to maintain the meat at an even simmer.

Scrape the onions off the meat, transfer the brisket to a pan, and keep it warm. Force the onions and braising liquid through a sieve into a saucepan. Set the pan over high heat and stir in the cream, bringing it to a boil. Lower the heat slightly and simmer briskly, skimming any scum and surface fats, until the gravy is reduced by about one-third, 10 to 12 minutes. Stir the horseradish into the gravy, adjust the seasoning, cover, and keep warm.

Slice the brisket thinly across the grain and on an angle. Arrange the meat on plates, fanning the slices slightly, and drizzle some of the gravy over each portion. Pass the remaining gravy at the table.

*Serves 6*

6 tablespoons unsalted
  butter
2 very large yellow onions,
  peeled and sliced thin
1½ teaspoons dry thyme
1 imported bay leaf
3 pounds beef brisket
3 cups canned beef broth
  or homemade stock
⅔ cup whipping cream
⅓ cup prepared
  horseradish, drained
Salt and freshly ground
  black pepper

▼▲▼▲▼▲▼▲▼▲▼▲▼▲▼▲▼▲▼▲▼▲▼▲▼▲▼▲▼▲

## HEAVEN AND EARTH

♦ ♦ ♦ ♦ ♦ ♦ ♦ ♦ ♦

8 tablespoons unsalted
  butter
2 large, sweet apples, such
  as Golden Delicious,
  cored, peeled, and
  chopped
1 very large onion, peeled
  and sliced thin
Salt
3 medium (about 1½
  pounds) baking potatoes,
  peeled and chopped
3 medium (about 1½
  pounds) turnips, peeled
  and chopped
½ cup canned beef broth
  or homemade stock
Freshly ground black
  pepper
¼ cup minced fresh dill

THE APPLES ARE the "heaven," the potatoes, turnips, and onions the "earth" in this heavenly puree. The dill isn't typical but it makes sense to me; omit it and substitute minced Italian parsley, if you prefer. The rich, subtle flavor of the puree makes it a good accompaniment to duck, goose, or pork.

♦ ♦ ♦  ♦ ♦ ♦

In a skillet over medium heat melt the butter. Add the apples and onions, cover, and cook, stirring occasionally, for 15 minutes. Uncover, raise the heat, and cook, stirring often, until the apples and onions are well browned, about 10 minutes. Transfer the contents of the skillet to a food processor or to a food mill fitted with a medium blade and set over a bowl.

In a saucepan over medium heat cover the turnips and potatoes with cold, lightly salted water. Bring to a boil and cook until the potatoes and turnips are very tender, about 12 minutes after the water boils. Drain, cool slightly, and transfer to the food processor or food mill.

Add the broth and process until the puree is smooth. *The puree can be prepared to this point up to 1 day ahead. Cool, cover, and refrigerate.*

Reheat the puree over low heat until steaming. Adjust the seasoning and add a generous grind of pepper. Stir in the dill, cover, and let stand 1 minute before serving.

—● *Serves 6*

♦ ♦ ♦ ♦ ♦ ♦ ♦ ♦ ♦ ♦ ♦ ♦ ♦ ♦ ♦ ♦ ♦ ♦ ♦ ♦ ♦ ♦ ♦ ♦ ♦ ♦ ♦ ♦ ♦ ♦ ♦ ♦ ♦ ♦ ♦ ♦ ♦ ♦ ♦

## ANADAMA ROLLS
## WITH ORANGE BUTTER

• • • • • • • • • •

**I** ALWAYS GET CRANKY LETTERS when I offer only one of the several possible explanations for the odd name of this delicious Early American bread. Let me just say that 1) Anadama bread should include cornmeal and molasses, 2) the origin of the name is in question, and 3) the rolls, topped with orange butter, taste great with this and many other menus.

• • •  • • •

In a small saucepan slowly whisk the milk into ½ cup of the cornmeal. Set the pan over low heat and bring just to a boil, stirring constantly. Transfer the cornmeal mixture to a medium-size bowl and cool to between 105 and 115 degrees F.

Stir the molasses and yeast into the cornmeal mixture and let stand 5 minutes. Stir in the whole wheat flour and salt. Mix in enough of the all-purpose flour, ½ cup at a time, to form a sticky dough. Knead it on a floured surface until soft, elastic, and only slightly sticky, adding more all-purpose flour if very sticky, about 10 minutes.

Grease a large bowl with the softened butter. Add the dough, turning to coat its entire surface. Cover the bowl with a towel and let the dough rise in a warm, draft-free area until doubled in bulk, about 2 hours.

Punch down the dough, knead it briefly on a floured surface, and return it to the bowl. Cover it with a towel and let it rise until doubled in bulk, about 2 hours.

Sprinkle a baking sheet with the remaining ¼ cup of cornmeal. Punch the dough down. Cut it into 16 pieces and form each piece into a ball. Transfer the balls to the prepared baking sheet, spacing them 1½ inches apart, and cover with a towel. Let the rolls rise until almost doubled in bulk, about 30 minutes.

2 cups milk
¾ cup yellow cornmeal
⅓ cup unsulfured
  molasses
1 package dry yeast
1 cup whole wheat flour
2 teaspoons salt
2½ cups (about)
  unbleached all-purpose
  flour
2 tablespoons (¼ stick)
  unsalted butter, softened
1 egg, beaten
Orange Butter (recipe
  follows)

Position a rack in the center of the oven and pre-heat to 375 degrees F. Brush the tops of the rolls with the beaten egg. Bake until brown and crisp, about 20 minutes. Cool on a rack. *The rolls can be prepared up to 1 day ahead. Wrap and store at room temperature. Reheat in the oven at 325 degrees F about 5 minutes, if desired.*

Serve the rolls warm or at room temperature, accompanied by the Orange Butter.

*Makes 16 rolls*

## ORANGE BUTTER

1 cup (2 sticks) unsalted
  butter, softened
2 tablespoons finely
  minced orange zest

THIS IS A USEFUL ITEM to have on hand in the refrigerator or freezer. The butter is good on cornbread, makes toast a treat, and can dress up an otherwise plain piece of grilled or broiled fish.

Blend the butter and orange zest in a bowl or food processor until well combined. Transfer to a small crock or bowl. *The butter can be prepared up to 3 days ahead and refrigerated or frozen for up to one month. Soften to room temperature before serving.*

*Makes about 1 cup*

## EGGNOG PIE

THIS SWEET LITTLE CUSTARD pie is spiked with dark rum, vanilla, and a generous grating of fresh nutmeg, making it taste unexpectedly grown up.

Refrigerating the pie doesn't do it any good, by the way: the filling gets weepy and the crust, damp. Serve it at room temperature, no more than four or five hours after baking.

*For the crust* In a food processor or a medium-size bowl combine 1¾ cups of the flour and the salt. Cut in the butter and shortening until the mixture is coarse and crumbly. One tablespoon at a time, add enough water to form a soft dough.

Sprinkle the work surface with 2 tablespoons of the flour. Turn the dough out onto the floured surface. Form into a disc, wrap in plastic, and refrigerate 30 minutes.

Sprinkle the work surface with 1 tablespoon of the flour. Place the dough on the floured surface and flatten slightly. Flour the dough with the remaining flour and roll out about ¼ inch thick. Transfer to a 9-inch pan. Trim the overhang, form an edge, and crimp it decoratively. Cover the formed pastry shell and refrigerate at least 30 minutes. *The pie crust can be prepared to this point up to 1 day ahead.*

*For the filling* In a large bowl whisk the eggs until light yellow. Whisk in the sugar. Whisk in the whipping cream, half-and-half, rum, vanilla, nutmeg, and salt. Bring to room temperature.

Set a baking sheet on a rack positioned in the center of the oven. Preheat the oven to 450 degrees F. Line the chilled pastry shell with waxed paper and fill with pastry weights. Set the shell on the heated baking sheet and bake 10 minutes. Immediately remove the weights and waxed paper and fill the shell with the prepared custard. Return the pie to the oven, setting it on the heated baking sheet. Lower the temperature to 325 degrees F. Bake 25 to 30 minutes, or until the filling is puffed and golden. While the custard will not be firm, it will be evenly set from edge to center. Cool the pie completely on a rack before cutting.

*Serves 8*

♦♦♦♦♦♦♦♦♦♦♦♦♦♦♦♦♦♦♦♦♦♦♦♦♦♦♦♦♦♦♦♦♦♦♦♦♦♦♦♦♦

CRUST

*2 cups unbleached all-purpose flour*

*⅛ teaspoon salt*

*5 tablespoons unsalted butter, well chilled and cut into small pieces*

*¼ cup solid vegetable shortening, well chilled and cut into small pieces*

*4 to 5 tablespoons water, chilled*

FILLING

*4 eggs*

*½ cup sugar*

*1 cup whipping cream*

*¾ cup half-and-half*

*¼ cup dark rum*

*1 tablespoon vanilla extract*

*¾ teaspoon freshly ground nutmeg*

*Pinch of salt*

# MENU

◆◆◆◆◆◆◆◆◆◆◆◆◆◆◆◆

GARDEN GREEN BEAN AND
TOMATO SALAD WITH WARM BACON
AND PINE NUT DRESSING

◆

BLUEFISH BAKED WITH CHILE CRUMBS

◆

PARSLIED GARLIC BREAD

◆

BROWN SUGAR ICE CREAM WITH
FRESH STRAWBERRIES

◆

LEMON SUGAR COOKIES

*page 93*

THE FIRST CONVENTION I abandon when I plan a summer lunch or supper is the typical progression of courses and side dishes. That's just too much of a bother in hot weather, and I suspect it's just too much of a bother to eat, as well. If, at the end of the meal, everyone feels properly fed and entertained, I'm happy. This menu is a case in point.

## GARDEN GREEN BEAN AND TOMATO SALAD WITH WARM BACON AND PINE NUT DRESSING

◆ ◆ ◆ ◆ ◆ ◆ ◆ ◆ ◆

**S**TART WITH THIS BIG, gutsy salad, full of flavor and crunch, the smoke of good bacon, and the tang of warm vinegar kicking lazy appetites out of their summer doldrums.

In a saucepan bring 4 quarts of water to a boil. Stir in the beans and 1 tablespoon of salt and cook, stirring once or twice, until just tender, about 5 minutes. Drain immediately and transfer the beans to a bowl of ice water. When cool, drain thoroughly. *The salad can be prepared to this point up to 1 day ahead. Wrap the beans in plastic and refrigerate, allowing them to return to room temperature before proceeding.*

Place the beans in a mound in the center of a serving platter. Arrange the tomato wedges around the beans.

In a small skillet over medium heat cook the bacon, stirring once or twice, until crisp and brown, 10 to 12 minutes. Pour off all but 3 tablespoons of the bacon fat; leave the bacon in the skillet. Add the olive oil to the skillet. Stir in the vinegar, sugar, ½ teaspoon of salt, and a generous grind of black pepper. Bring just to a boil, stirring to dissolve the sugar. Stir in the pine nuts, pour the dressing over the salad, and serve immediately.

NOTE To toast the nuts, spread them in a single layer in a shallow pan and bake in a 400-degree F oven, stirring frequently, 7 to 10 minutes, or until richly browned. Remove from the pan and cool.

━● *Serves 4*

1¼ pounds green beans, trimmed
Salt
2 ripe beefsteak tomatoes (1 red and 1 yellow), washed and cut into wedges
6 ounces lean, smoky slab bacon, rind removed and cut into ½-inch dice
2 tablespoons olive oil
3 tablespoons red wine vinegar
½ teaspoon sugar
Freshly ground black pepper
¼ cup toasted pine nuts (see note)

## BLUEFISH BAKED
## WITH CHILE CRUMBS

✦✦✦✦✦✦✦✦✦✦

1 cup coarse, dry bread
   crumbs
1 tablespoon mild, plain
   chile powder (see Cook's
   Sources)
1½ teaspoons ground
   cumin, from toasted
   seeds (see notes)
1 teaspoon dried oregano,
   crumbled
½ teaspoon salt
½ teaspoon freshly ground
   black pepper
6 tablespoons unsalted
   butter
2 garlic cloves, peeled and
   crushed
2 large bluefish fillets,
   about 2½ pounds total
   (see notes)
Wedges of lime, as garnish

**I**N THIS UTTERLY SIMPLE RECIPE, robustly flavored bluefish is topped with bread crumbs seasoned with chile powder. The crumbs bake into a distinctively crunchy topping—an excellent foil to the rich, dark, and tender fish.

In an unstructured summer menu, I'm content just to serve the fish with the garlic bread. If you want a vegetable or side dish, though, simply put the green bean salad on the same plate with the fish—the time I did, no one complained.

Although I think citrus juices mask the sweet delicacy of fish, most people squeeze lots of fresh lime on this.

✦✦✦  ✦✦✦

Position a rack in the upper third of the oven and preheat to 400 degrees F. In a small bowl stir together the bread crumbs, chile powder, cumin, oregano, salt, and pepper.

In a small skillet over low heat melt the butter. Add the garlic and cook, stirring once or twice, until golden, 5 to 7 minutes. Discard the garlic.

Brush the bottom of a large baking dish with 2 tablespoons of the garlicked butter. Place the fillets, skin side down, in the dish. Sprinkle all the seasoned bread crumbs thickly over the fish, pressing them gently onto the fillets. Drizzle the remaining butter evenly over the crumbs.

Bake the fish 10 to 12 minutes, or until the fillets flake at all but their thickest point and the crumbs are browned. Serve hot or warm, garnished with lime wedges.

NOTES Toasted cumin has a rich, mellow, and nutty flavor that is distinct and delicious. To toast the seeds, spread about ½ cup (prepare a quantity since they keep indefinitely in a covered jar) in a small, heavy, ungreased skillet over low heat. Cook, stirring often, until the seeds are fragrant and brown, 7 to 10 minutes. Remove the seeds from the skillet and cool. Grind in a spice mill or with a mortar and pestle just before using.

Use 2 large rather than 4 small fillets here. The slightly longer baking time required ensures a crumb topping that will be crisp and brown.

━━● *Serves 4*

◆◆◆◆◆◆◆◆◆◆◆◆◆◆◆◆◆◆◆◆◆◆◆◆◆◆◆◆◆◆◆◆◆◆◆◆◆◆◆◆◆

## PARSLIED GARLIC BREAD
◆◆◆◆◆◆◆◆◆

I HAVE FRIENDS who can't make garlic bread, but real butter, fresh garlic, and honest bread are all it takes; here's how it's done.

◆◆◆  ◆◆◆

1 stick unsalted butter, softened
¼ cup minced Italian parsley
2 garlic cloves, peeled and forced through a press
Freshly ground black pepper
1 loaf (14 inches long) crusty bread, split lengthwise

In a small bowl mash together the butter, parsley, garlic, and a generous grind of fresh pepper. *The butter can be prepared up to 3 days in advance and refrigerated, or it can be frozen for up to one month. Soften to room temperature before using.*

Preheat the broiler. Spread the butter mixture down the center of the cut sides of the bread, leaving a ¼-inch border all around. Broil the bread about 5 inches from the heat for 1½ to 2 minutes, or until the edges are crisp and brown and the butter is bubbling. Cut into pieces and serve immediately.

*Variations Gorgonzola Bread:* Blend together ¼ pound young, creamy Gorgonzola cheese; 4 tablespoons unsalted butter; ½ cup finely chopped Italian parsley; 1 garlic clove, peeled and forced through a press; and a generous grind of black pepper. Spread the cheese mixture on a split 14-inch loaf of bread and broil as directed. Serve immediately.

*Pesto Bread:* Spread each half of a split 14-inch loaf with ⅓ cup pesto sauce; broil as directed for Parslied Garlic Bread and season with freshly ground black pepper. Serve immediately.

◆━● *Makes 1 loaf, serving 4 to 6*

## BROWN SUGAR ICE CREAM

◆◆◆◆◆◆◆◆◆

4 egg yolks
1 cup light brown sugar, packed
1 cup whipping cream
3 cups half-and-half or light cream
1½ tablespoons vanilla

SINCE THERE'S no better summer dessert than homemade ice cream, and since a seafood main course always leaves everyone feeling virtuous, indulge in this smooth, old-fashioned sweet. Serve it with sliced strawberries, lightly sugared, and Lemon Sugar Cookies (page 93).

In a large mixing bowl whisk the egg yolks and brown sugar until thick.

In a medium-size, heavy pan over medium heat bring the whipping cream and half-and-half just to a boil. Whisking constantly, dribble the hot cream into the egg mixture. Return to the pan and set over low heat. Cook, stirring constantly with a wooden spoon, until the mixture thickens slightly and leaves a track on the back of the spoon when a fingertip is drawn across it, about 4 minutes. Do not let the custard boil.

Remove from the heat at once and transfer to a bowl. Stir in the vanilla and cool to room temperature. Cover and refrigerate until very cold, preferably overnight.

Strain the custard into the canister of an ice-cream maker and churn according to manufacturer's instructions. Store the ice cream in the freezer. *The ice cream can be prepared up to 2 days ahead.* Let the ice cream soften slightly in the refrigerator before serving.

◆━● *Makes about 1½ quarts*

# MENU

◆ ◆ ◆ ◆ ◆ ◆ ◆ ◆ ◆ ◆ ◆ ◆ ◆ ◆

BAKED BBQ PINTO BEANS
WITH HAM HOCKS

◆

PERFECT CORN BREAD
*or*
BUTTERMILK BISCUITS
*page 27*
*or*
PARSLEY-PEPPER SKILLET BREAD
*page 230*

◆

WHITE RICE

◆

SIMPLE ORANGE SLAW
*page 43*

◆

GRITS AND HONEY PUDDING
*page 32*

IT'S OKAY FOR SUPPERS to be economical, like this practically meatless, Southern-inspired menu. With just a little flair and kitchen time, the results are bound to please both family and company. The hot corn bread, biscuits, or skillet bread will make things particularly congenial, but don't hesitate to serve crusty store-bought bread if time is short.

## BAKED BBQ PINTO BEANS
## WITH HAM HOCKS

**1 pound dried pinto beans, picked over**

**2 tablespoons salt**

**2 cups chopped yellow onion**

**4 garlic cloves, peeled and minced**

**1 cup hot and smoky, prepared tomato-based barbecue sauce**

**1 bottle (12 ounces) dark beer, such as Heineken, Beck's, or Double Dark Prior's**

**⅓ cup dark brown sugar, packed**

**¼ cup unsulfured molasses**

**2 teaspoons Tabasco sauce**

**2 large (about 1 pound each), meaty, smoked ham hocks**

◆◆◆◆◆◆◆◆◆

**F**OR MOST DINERS (and I include myself here), two large, smoked ham hocks will provide enough flavor and meat for this dish to qualify easily as a main course for four, particularly if served with bread and rice. Others may consider it a side dish, and it makes a fine and generous one, served hot or cool with fried chicken, grilled spareribs, or the like.

◆◆◆  ◆◆◆

Soak the beans for 24 hours in cold water to cover them by at least 3 inches. Drain.

In a 4½- or 5-quart, flameproof casserole or Dutch oven combine the beans with cold water to cover them by 3 inches. Set over medium-high heat and bring to a boil. Lower the heat and simmer, partially covered, for 30 minutes. Stir in 1 tablespoon of the salt and continue to cook, stirring once or twice, until the beans are very tender, about 50 minutes. Drain, reserving 1 cup of the cooking liquid.

Preheat the oven to 325 degrees F. In a large bowl stir together the beans, onion, garlic, reserved cooking liquid, barbecue sauce, beer, brown sugar, molasses, Tabasco sauce, and remaining salt. Pour the mixture into a 4-quart baking dish. Bury the ham hocks in the center of the bean mixture. Cover and bake 1½ hours, or until the ham hocks are tender.

Remove the ham hocks and cool. Skin them and remove and dice the meat. Stir the meat back into the beans and bake, uncovered, another 60 to 70 minutes, or until the mixture is reduced and thickened and the beans and meat are very tender.

◆◆ *Serves 4*

▀▄▀▄▀▄▀▄▀▄▀▄▀▄▀▄▀▄▀▄▀▄▀▄▀▄▀▄▀▄▀▄▀▄▀▄

# PERFECT CORN BREAD

♦ ♦ ♦ ♦ ♦ ♦ ♦ ♦ ♦

**C**ORN BREAD IS A PERSONAL MATTER, with regional overtones, and while I'm prepared to acknowledge that you might not think this one is perfect, I do, and I've spent a lot of time getting it this way. The result is sweet, tender, and almost cakelike, a very midwestern corn bread. Southerners might find it rich and on the sweet side, but those who already have the perfect corn bread recipe are urged to substitute accordingly. (The average Southerner will also frequently smother that cornbread with butter and honey, making it at least as rich and sweet as mine.) In any case, the recipe is a generous one, and leftovers—if any—are good reheated the next day, or they can be frozen and used in a future corn bread stuffing.

*1¾ cups stone-ground yellow cornmeal*

*1¼ cups unbleached all-purpose flour*

*½ cup plus 1 tablespoon sugar*

*4 teaspoons baking powder*

*1 teaspoon salt*

*1½ cups buttermilk, at room temperature*

*1 stick unsalted butter, melted*

*2 eggs, beaten*

♦ ♦ ♦ 🥄 ♦ ♦ ♦

Preheat the oven to 400 degrees F. Butter a 9 × 13-inch baking pan.

In a large bowl stir together thoroughly the cornmeal, flour, sugar, baking powder, and salt. In a medium-size bowl whisk together the buttermilk, melted butter, and eggs. Stir the liquid mixture into the dry ingredients until just combined; do not overmix. Pour the batter into the prepared pan, spread it to the edges, and bake until puffed and golden, about 20 minutes. Serve hot or warm.

━● *Serves 8*

♦ ♦ ♦ ♦ ♦ ♦ ♦ ♦ ♦ ♦ ♦ ♦ ♦ ♦ ♦ ♦ ♦ ♦ ♦ ♦ ♦ ♦ ♦ ♦ ♦ ♦ ♦ ♦ ♦ ♦ ♦ ♦ ♦ ♦ ♦ ♦ ♦ ♦ ♦ ♦ ♦ ♦ ♦

**SERVING STRATEGY** Making white rice can addle otherwise competent cooks, and I've never known why. Most boxes of long-grain white rice carry infallible directions (1 part rice added to 2 parts lightly salted boiling water; simmer, covered, without disturbing, for 22 minutes or until all the water is absorbed and steam holes appear in the surface of the rice; remove from heat and let stand, covered, for 5 minutes; fluff with a fork, adding butter or oil to taste, plus a healthy measured of chopped fresh parsley; serve). For me, 22 minutes is also about the time it takes to get a done-ahead entrée heated, the table set, the wine opened, and so on; resorting to converted or precooked rice when the rest of the menu is made from scratch (and fluffy, fresh rice tastes so good) is just silly.

# MENU

••••••••••••••••••

BIBB LETTUCE SALAD
WITH HARD-COOKED EGG
AND MUSTARD DRESSING

•

PORK CHOPS WITH APPLE BUTTER

•

PILAF OF WILD RICE
WITH LEEKS AND MUSHROOMS

•

COFFEE ICE CREAM
WITH BITTERSWEET
DOUBLE CHOCOLATE SAUCE

WHEN I WAS GROWING UP, "supper" frequently meant "pork chops," and now when I think of downscaling my ambitions and getting homey, pork is frequently the meat of choice. This supper menu illustrates several rules of sane menu planning. A separate starter, even a salad, makes a meal seem more important. A starch-vegetable side dish makes the cook's life easier, and this savory pilaf is a good one. If you need a traditional vegetable course consider the Puree of Baked Beets and Baked Garlic (page 136) or the Broccoli with Orange-Shallot Butter (page 277). And for the finale, enjoy premium commercial ice cream topped with your own doubly-chocolaty chocolate sauce.

## BIBB LETTUCE SALAD WITH HARD-COOKED EGG AND MUSTARD DRESSING

♦ ♦ ♦ ♦ ♦ ♦ ♦ ♦ ♦

*2 medium heads of Bibb or*
*Boston lettuce,*
*separated, rinsed, and*
*patted dry*
*Hard-Cooked Egg and*
*Mustard Dressing*
*(recipe follows)*
*½ medium red onion,*
*peeled and sliced into*
*thin rings*

THIS SALAD'S NUBBLY DRESSING is comforting and sooth-ing, but with a slight kick of mustard. It goes particu-larly well with buttery Bibb or Boston lettuce. In another menu, the salad can support the addition of sliced mushrooms, particularly the robust brown cre-mini, sliced, baked beets, or both. (The technique for baking beets is described on page 136.)

Arrange the lettuce leaves on salad plates. Spoon the salad dressing over the lettuce (use all of it, if you wish, or pass some at the table) and garnish the salads with the onion. Serve immediately.

*Serves 4*

## HARD-COOKED EGG AND MUSTARD DRESSING

♦ ♦ ♦ ♦ ♦ ♦ ♦ ♦ ♦

*2 eggs, hard cooked*
*2 tablespoons prepared*
*Dijon-style mustard*
*2 tablespoons white wine*
*vinegar*
*½ teaspoon salt*
*Freshly ground black*
*pepper*
*¾ cup corn or other*
*flavorless vegetable oil*

Shell the eggs and separate the yolks and whites. In a small bowl mash the egg yolks together with the mus-tard. Whisk in the vinegar, salt, and a generous grind of black pepper. Whisking constantly, add the oil in a slow stream. Mince the egg whites. Stir them into the dressing. Adjust the seasoning and serve as soon as possible.

*Makes about 1¼ cups*

## PORK CHOPS WITH
## APPLE BUTTER

◆◆◆◆◆◆◆◆◆

THE MODERN PIG goes to market younger than his recent ancestors did, allowing for pork that is leaner and more healthful. That's good news for people who sell pork, and good news for diners too, I guess, but it makes the cook's job harder. Without that seductive fat it is all too easy to cook pork into something so dry and lifeless that it indeed resembles food that must be good for you.

Chops, particularly the thin ones that most supermarkets sell, are especially susceptible to the drying effects of hot, quick cooking. The solution: Buy thick chops (*very* thick—1 to 1½ inches), and braise them slowly with a bit of moisture in the form of onions, apple butter, and broth. The succulent results can make supper a memorable meal.

2 tablespoons unsalted
  butter
2 tablespoons corn oil
4 thick (about ½ pound
  each) pork loin chops
Salt and freshly ground
  black pepper
3 medium yellow onions,
  peeled and chopped
1½ teaspoons dried thyme,
  crumbled
2 cups canned chicken
  broth or homemade stock
1 cup unsweetened apple
  butter

◆◆◆  ◆◆◆

Preheat the oven to 350 degrees F.

In a 4½- or 5-quart, flameproof casserole over medium heat melt the butter and oil together. Pat the pork chops dry. When the butter is foaming, add two of the pork chops and cook, turning once, until well browned, 7 to 10 minutes. Lightly season the chops with salt and pepper and transfer to a plate. Repeat with the remaining chops.

Set the casserole over medium heat (do not clean it) and add the onions and thyme. Lower the heat, cover, and cook, stirring once or twice, until very tender, 15 minutes. In a bowl stir together the chicken broth and apple butter. Return the chops to the pan. Pour the broth and apple butter mixture over the chops. Raise the heat and bring the liquid to a simmer. Cover the pan and set it in the oven. Bake until the chops have just lost all their pink color but remain juicy, about 30 minutes.

Remove the chops, scraping off any clinging pieces of onion, and keep them warm. Pour the stock mixture through a strainer placed over a bowl. Press hard with the back of a spoon to extract all the juices, discarding the solids. Wipe the pan clean.

Return the braising liquid to the pan. Set over high heat and bring to a boil. Lower the heat slightly and cook, uncovered, skimming any scum and surface fats, until the liquid is reduced by half, about 10 minutes. Adjust the seasoning. Return the chops to the pan, lower the heat, and simmer, basting the chops with the sauce, until they are heated through, about 3 minutes. Serve immediately.

*Serves 4*

♦♦♦♦♦♦♦♦♦♦♦♦♦♦♦♦♦♦♦♦♦♦♦♦♦♦♦♦♦♦♦♦♦♦♦♦♦♦♦♦♦♦♦♦

## PILAF OF WILD RICE WITH LEEKS AND MUSHROOMS

♦♦♦♦♦♦♦♦♦

6 cups canned chicken
  broth or homemade stock
12 ounces wild rice (about
  1⅔ cups), rinsed
Salt
1 bay leaf
1 stick (½ cup) unsalted
  butter
4 cups (about 4 large)
  coarsely chopped leeks,
  the white part only
1½ teaspoons dried thyme,
  crumbled
1½ pounds mushrooms,
  wiped, trimmed, and cut
  into thick slices
Freshly ground black
  pepper
½ cup finely chopped
  Italian parsley

**W**ILD RICE HAS REAL CACHET, making even a simple side dish like this one seem important, and elevating an ordinary supper. The taste of wild rice, pork, and apples together in the mouth is one of the most natural combinations possible. Fresh, "exotic" mushrooms, such as shiitake or porcini, can be used for a truly delicious pilaf. Since I typically serve this as both starch and vegetable, the recipe allows for generous portions; if you are making a separate vegetable, the pilaf will serve six to eight.

♦♦♦  ♦♦♦

In a medium-size saucepan bring the broth to a boil. Stir in the rice, 2 teaspoons of salt, and bay leaf. Lower the heat and simmer, uncovered, until the rice is just tender, about 30 minutes. Do not overcook. Drain and discard the bay leaf.

In a large skillet over medium heat melt the butter. Stir in the leeks and thyme and cook, covered, 10 minutes. Stir in the mushrooms and season lightly with salt. Cook, covered, stirring once or twice, until the mushrooms render their juices, about 10 minutes. *The dish can be prepared to this point up to 3 hours ahead and set aside. Warm over low heat before proceeding.*

Stir the rice into the leeks and mushrooms, and cook, covered, about 10 minutes, or until the rice has absorbed the butter and mushroom juices and is heated through. Adjust the seasoning. Add a generous grind of pepper and stir in the parsley. Serve immediately.

● *Serves 4 to 6*

♦ ♦ ♦ ♦ ♦ ♦ ♦ ♦ ♦ ♦ ♦ ♦ ♦ ♦ ♦ ♦ ♦ ♦ ♦ ♦ ♦ ♦ ♦ ♦ ♦ ♦ ♦ ♦ ♦ ♦ ♦ ♦ ♦ ♦ ♦ ♦ ♦ ♦ ♦ ♦ ♦ ♦ ♦ ♦ ♦

## BITTERSWEET DOUBLE CHOCOLATE SAUCE

♦ ♦ ♦ ♦ ♦ ♦ ♦ ♦

**S**INCE I CAN'T MAKE coffee ice cream as delicious as the ice cream that comes from the folks at Häagen-Dazs, I don't try. I do make the best chocolate sauce in town, however, and this recipe, which produces a generous quantity of astonishingly chocolaty sauce, is always in the refrigerator. It stores well but doesn't last long (if you know what I mean), and it turns even ordinary ice cream into a treat.

♦ ♦ ♦  ♦ ♦ ♦

In a heavy saucepan over low heat melt the butter and chocolate, stirring occasionally, until smooth.

Stir in the sugar. Sift in the cocoa, stirring as you do. Add the instant coffee, cinnamon, and corn syrup. Slowly whisk in the whipping cream. Bring just to a boil, stirring often, then lower the heat. Simmer for 5 minutes, stirring once or twice and scraping down the

*1½ sticks (6 ounces) unsalted butter, cut into pieces*

*6 ounces bittersweet or semisweet chocolate (see Cook's Sources), chopped*

*¾ cup plus 2 tablespoons sugar*

*¾ cup firmly packed unsweetened, Dutch process cocoa powder (see Cook's Sources)*

*1 teaspoon freeze-dried instant coffee*

*¼ teaspoon ground cinnamon*

*½ cup light corn syrup*

*1¼ cups whipping cream*

*1 teaspoon vanilla*

*Coffee ice cream*

sides of the pan with a rubber spatula.

Remove from the heat. Stir in the vanilla and pour immediately into a heatproof container. Cool to room temperature, cover, and refrigerate. *The sauce should rest at least 24 hours to mellow the flavors and texture. It will keep well in the refrigerator for several weeks.*

To serve, remove the desired amount of sauce from the container and reheat in a double boiler or microwave oven, stirring, until hot. Spoon the sauce over coffee—or other—ice cream.

*Makes about 1 quart*

**SERVING STRATEGY** Eating ice cream directly from the carton may be acceptable when you're alone, but witnesses dictate a little more effort. I make and serve ice cream often, and years ago I acquired a set of soda fountain ice cream dishes—the kind whose chunky, naive shape signals the sweet, solid dessert to come. For a more graceful presentation, haul out your best stemware. In either case, owning a good ice-cream scoop is essential for making picture perfect sundaes; an aerated dispenser for genuine whipped cream adds the touch of a real pro. The pairing of coffee ice cream and bittersweet chocolate sauce is particularly colorful and delicious when garnished with fresh raspberries.

# M E N U

· · · · · · · · · · · · · · · · ·

ROMAINE AND RED ONION SALAD
WITH FRESH OREGANO DRESSING

·

FRICASSEE OF CHICKEN
DRUMSTICKS WITH VEGETABLES

·

PARSLIED GARLIC BREAD
*page 67*

·

WHITE RICE OR BUTTERED NOODLES

·

PEARS AND PROVOLONE

I'M CERTAIN I HAVE childhood memories of suppers that consisted of a comfortable, colorful mélange of ingredients, simmered in and served from a single skillet—splendid one-dish meals like this one. I remember such suppers, but my mother doesn't; she swears no meal for three hungry sons ever went together with so little effort. So be it (don't argue with Mom); but if that kind of casual supper sounds good to you, you've come to the right place. *This* is exactly that meal of my memory.

## ROMAINE AND RED ONION SALAD WITH FRESH OREGANO DRESSING

2 heads of Romaine
   lettuce, inner leaves only
Fresh Oregano Dressing
   (recipe follows)
½ medium red onion,
   peeled and sliced into
   thin rings
Freshly ground black
   pepper

**I** LIKE THE SPIKY, pale green and yellow inner leaves of romaine for salads—they're more tender and mild than the coarse outer leaves, which work better in sandwiches or soups.

Rinse and pat the lettuce dry. Arrange the leaves on salad plates. Drizzle the Fresh Oregano Dressing over the lettuce to taste, scatter the onion over the dressing, and season with pepper. Serve immediately.

*Serves 4*

## FRESH OREGANO DRESSING

⅓ cup clean, whole fresh
   oregano leaves
1 egg
3 tablespoons red wine
   vinegar
2 medium garlic cloves
1½ teaspoons salt
½ teaspoon freshly ground
   black pepper
1 cup olive oil

**U** SE FRESH MARJORAM or basil if you have no oregano. The dressing is also good with cooled grilled or seared fish, poached shrimp, or crudités.

In a small food processor combine the oregano, egg, vinegar, garlic, salt, and pepper and process 1 minute. With the machine running add the olive oil in a quick stream. Adjust the seasoning. *The dressing can be prepared up to 2 days ahead. Let it return to room temperature before using.*

*Makes about 1⅓ cups*

# FRICASSEE OF CHICKEN DRUMSTICKS WITH VEGETABLES

♦ ♦ ♦ ♦ ♦ ♦ ♦ ♦ ♦

**W**HETHER MY MEMORY of those colorful one-dish suppers is accurate or not, here is my re-creation. For my mother, who had to feed three teenagers who loved only the drumsticks, the ordinary chicken created a chronic shortage—a situation that this creamy, drumstick-only fricassee remedies.

Frozen artichokes are just right in this casual meal, but for truly superb eating, substitute twelve small, fresh artichokes that have been trimmed, halved, and simmered in lightly salted water until tender.

♦ ♦ ♦  ♦ ♦ ♦

Dredge the chicken in the flour, shaking off any excess. In a large, deep skillet or flameproof casserole over medium heat melt 4 tablespoons of the butter. Add the legs, in batches, and cook, turning, until golden brown, about 10 minutes. Season lightly with salt and pepper and transfer to a dish.

Add 2 tablespoons of the butter to the skillet. Stir in the onion, garlic, thyme, basil, and bay leaf. Lower the heat, cover, and cook, stirring occasionally, until the onions are tender, about 15 minutes.

Return the chicken legs to the skillet, along with any juices from the dish. Add the broth and wine and bring to a boil. Lower the heat, cover, and simmer, turning the legs occasionally, until they are very tender, about 40 minutes. Transfer the chicken to a dish.

Meanwhile, in a medium-size skillet over moderately high heat melt the remaining butter. Add the peppers, a pinch of salt and pepper, and cook, tossing and stirring, until lightly browned, about 5 minutes. Add the artichokes and cook for 2 minutes. Transfer the peppers and artichokes to a dish.

16 chicken drumsticks (3½ to 4 pounds)

1 cup flour

8 tablespoons (1 stick) unsalted butter

Salt and freshly ground black pepper

1 medium yellow onion, peeled and chopped

4 garlic cloves, peeled and minced

1 teaspoon dried thyme, crumbled

1 teaspoon dried basil, crumbled

1 bay leaf

2 cups canned chicken broth or homemade stock

1 cup dry white wine

3 large sweet peppers (1 red, 1 yellow, and 1 orange), stemmed, cored, and quartered

1 package (9 ounces) frozen artichoke hearts, thawed and drained

1 cup whipping cream

Strain the cooking liquid and return it to the medium-size skillet. Set over high heat, stir in the cream, and bring it to a boil. Cook hard until the liquid is reduced by one-third, about 15 minutes. Adjust the seasoning. Return the chicken, peppers, and artichokes, and any juices from their bowls, to the skillet. Simmer gently, basting the chicken with the sauce, until just heated through, about 5 minutes. Serve immediately.

*Serves 4*

✦✦✦✦✦✦✦✦✦✦✦✦✦✦✦✦✦✦✦✦✦✦✦✦✦✦✦✦✦✦✦✦✦✦✦✦✦✦✦✦✦✦✦

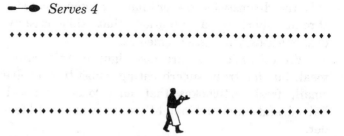

**SERVING STRATEGY** Italians aren't the only "pasta" lovers in the world. A batch of wide, eggy, homemade noodles was frequently my mother's answer to filling the family's constant carbohydrate craving. For the side dish in an easy supper like this one you may not want to make your own noodles, in which case 8 ounces of fresh, store-bought fettuccine (regular, spinach, or a combination of the two), cooked and tossed with sweet butter and parsley to taste, will do very nicely indeed.

A perfect pear takes planing. Red Bartletts are particularly eye-appealing, but, regardless of the specific variety, to enjoy this classic fruit and cheese pairing at its best, several days of room temperature ripening are necessary to ensure a prime, juicy pear. A young provolone, tangy but not fierce, is a pear's best friend, followed closely by an equally youthful Parmesan. Dessert plates and fruit knives are a fine touch if you own them, but the rest of the menu is rustic enough to dispense with that formality. Simply offer the pears in a basket, the cheese on a board, and small plates and simple knives for coring and peeling the fruit.

✦✦✦✦✦✦✦✦✦✦✦✦✦✦✦✦✦✦✦✦✦✦✦✦✦✦✦✦✦✦✦✦✦✦✦✦✦✦✦✦✦✦✦

# PASTA AND A SALAD

SPEAKING OF CASUAL MEALS, pasta, it seems to me, deserves a chapter of its own. Like all revolutions, our revision of pasta's place on the American menu has probably gone too far. Weird combinations, plates swamped with sauce, painfully overcooked (or undercooked) noodles, and ice-cold pastas drenched in acidic vinaigrettes are "innovations" for which we will be apologizing to Italy for years to come.

The general premise, though—that there's more to pasta than red sauce and meatballs—is a sound one, and in the new American kitchen our appreciation of the possibilities pasta has to offer shows that a pasta revolution has been long overdue.

The American cook's bold and unfussy sense of proportion will always overwhelm the Italian sense of balance and restraint, but a reversion to sound principles of pasta cookery is under way and the result—appropriately cooked, combined, and sauced pasta—is an important element of the new American kitchen.

The reasons for the pasta revolution are pretty obvious. We love the speed with which many pastas go together, letting us put a stylish main course on the table in under thirty minutes. We adore the healthy promise of a meal light on meat, long on vegetables, carbohydrates, and flavor. We delight in a plate of lush, cream-sauced pasta that is the only antidote for a bear of a day. And we appreciate the fact that pasta can be a party food, too, where even the most ardent of carnivores will grudgingly allow that occasionally most noodles make a meal. With the addition of one of several possible green and glorious salads, good bread, and decent wine, you've orchestrated a suspiciously easy and immediately appreciated meal for all. *Mangia!*

# M E N U

♦ ♦ ♦ ♦ ♦ ♦ ♦ ♦ ♦ ♦ ♦ ♦ ♦ ♦ ♦

ARUGULA AND ROASTED SWEET
PEPPER SALAD

♦

PENNE WITH VEAL MEATBALLS
IN TOMATO-SHIITAKE SAUCE

♦

BRAIDED OLIVE BREAD

♦

PEARS AND PROVOLONE

THIS MENU IS MEANT to be an easy pasta buffet for twelve, but the spectacular entrée will be just as impressive in the center of a family dining table. It's a simple, straightforward menu, without time-consuming flourishes, but there is room for upscaling things if you would like to. Start with a spread of salami or other Italian meats, or poach some shrimp to dip in Lemon-Basil Dressing (page 130) or in Garlic Mayonnaise (page 295). Add chunks of soft, fresh mozzarella to the salad. Follow the fruit and cheese with a full-fledged dessert or two (or three), and linger over grappa, espresso, and Cornmeal Butter Cookies (page 113).

## ARUGULA AND ROASTED SWEET PEPPER SALAD

♦ ♦ ♦ ♦ ♦ ♦ ♦ ♦ ♦

**T**HIS LITTLE BLACK DRESS of a tossed salad is the kind of basic kitchen know-how that quickly becomes second nature. Of course, like the best of salads, it's only an outline, giving you the bare bones upon which to improvise. The greens will change with what you find in the market, the type and amount of vinegar and oil can be altered to suit your taste, and other garnishing elements—herbs, mushrooms, olives, cheeses—may join or replace the peppers.

♦ ♦ ♦  ♦ ♦ ♦

In the open flame of a gas burner, or under a preheated broiler, roast the peppers, turning them, until the skins are charred. Transfer to a paper bag, or a bowl covered by a plate, and let steam until cool. Rub away the burnt peel, stem and core the peppers, and wipe them with paper towels. Cut the peppers into julienne strips.

In a small bowl combine the pepper strips with 1 tablespoon of the vinegar, 2 tablespoons of the oil, and a pinch of salt and pepper. Let stand at room temperature for 1 hour. *The peppers can be roasted and marinated up to 24 hours ahead. Cover well and refrigerate, allowing them to return to room temperature before proceeding.*

Rub the inside of a large bowl well with the cut sides of the garlic clove. Add the arugula to the bowl. Add the remaining oil and toss to coat the arugula. Add the remaining vinegar, ½ teaspoon of salt, the peppers, and their marinade and toss again. Serve immediately, passing the pepper mill.

━● *Serves 6*

♦ ♦ ♦ ♦ ♦ ♦ ♦ ♦ ♦ ♦ ♦ ♦ ♦ ♦ ♦ ♦ ♦ ♦ ♦ ♦ ♦ ♦ ♦ ♦ ♦ ♦ ♦ ♦ ♦ ♦ ♦ ♦ ♦ ♦ ♦ ♦ ♦ ♦ ♦ ♦ ♦

2 large red, orange, or
   yellow sweet peppers
4 tablespoons balsamic
   vinegar
½ cup olive oil
Salt and freshly ground
   black pepper
1 garlic clove, split
3 bunches of arugula,
   trimmed, rinsed, patted
   dry, and torn into
   bite-size pieces (about
   12 cups)

# PENNE WITH VEAL MEATBALLS IN TOMATO-SHIITAKE SAUCE

◆ ◆ ◆ ◆ ◆ ◆ ◆ ◆ ◆

**TOMATO-SHIITAKE SAUCE**

*⅔ cup olive oil*

*2 medium onions, peeled and chopped*

*6 garlic cloves, peeled and minced*

*4 teaspoons dried marjoram, crumbled*

*3 bay leaves*

*1 large can (35 ounces) and 1 medium can (28 ounces) Italian-style plum tomatoes, with their juices*

*Salt*

*1 pound shiitake mushrooms (see Cook's Sources)*

*1 pound cultivated white mushrooms*

*2 teaspoons freshly ground black pepper*

**Y**ES, THIS *IS* SPAGHETTI and meatballs, and just because it involves homemade tomato sauce, spinach, veal, and exotic mushrooms, doesn't mean it isn't as reassuring and good to eat as the somewhat more prosaic inspiration. Other plusses: The several steps can be gotten out of the way well in advance, in early stages; I've used short pasta quills to make buffet service easier on the guests and rug alike; and the entire dish is so honestly nourishing and tasty that with nothing more than a glass of wine and a chunk of bread a grand meal is at hand.

*For the tomato sauce* In a 5-quart, nonreactive saucepan over low heat warm half of the olive oil. Add the onions, garlic, marjoram, and bay leaves, cover, and cook, stirring once or twice, until the onions are tender, about 15 minutes. Add the tomatoes, breaking them up with the side of a metal spoon, their juices, and 1 tablespoon of salt. Raise the heat and bring the liquid to a boil, then lower the heat, partially cover, and simmer, stirring occasionally, until the sauce is reduced to 7 cups, about 50 minutes. Cool the sauce slightly and puree in a food processor or through the medium blade of a food mill.

Wipe the mushrooms with a dampened towel or soft brush. Discard the shiitake stems. Trim the white mushrooms. Slice all of the mushrooms ¼ inch thick. In a large skillet over medium-high heat warm the remaining oil until hot. Add the mushrooms and cook, stirring and tossing, for 5 minutes, or until softened. Stir in 2 teaspoons of salt and cook another 4 or 5 minutes, or until the mushrooms are tender and have rendered their juices. Stir the mushrooms, their juices, and the pepper into the tomato sauce. Adjust the seasoning. *The sauce can be prepared up to 3 days ahead. Cool completely, cover, and refrigerate.*

*Serves 12*

♦ ♦ ♦ ♦ ♦ ♦ ♦ ♦

*For the meatballs* Position a rack in the upper third of the oven and preheat to 400 degrees F. In a large bowl combine the veal, spinach, eggs, bread crumbs, cheese, parsley, garlic, marjoram, salt, pepper, and nutmeg. Stir well.

Shape the veal mixture in 1-inch balls and lay them in a single layer on an 11 × 17-inch jelly-roll pan. Bake the meatballs, turning them occasionally, until they are cooked through and well browned, 25 to 30 minutes. *The meatballs can be baked up to 1 day ahead. Cool them completely and transfer to a wide, shallow container. Cover and refrigerate. Position a rack in the upper third of the oven and preheat to 325 degrees F. In the oven in a single layer on a jelly-roll pan reheat the meatballs.*

*To assemble* In a heavy saucepan over medium heat bring the tomato-shiitake sauce to a simmer. Bring a very large pot of water to a boil and stir in 4 tablespoons of salt. When the water returns to a boil add the penne. Cook, stirring occasionally, until just tender, about 10 minutes. Drain and return to the pot. Stir in the tomato-shiitake sauce. Add the meatballs and ¾ cup of the parsley and toss gently. Turn the pasta into a large bowl and sprinkle it with the remaining parsley. Serve immediately, offering the remaining cheese on the side.

*Serves 12*

VEAL AND SPINACH MEATBALLS
*3 pounds ground veal*
*2 packages (10 ounces each) frozen spinach, thawed, squeezed dry, and finely chopped*
*3 eggs, slightly beaten*
*½ cup fine, dry bread crumbs*
*½ cup freshly grated Parmesan cheese*
*½ cup minced Italian parsley*
*3 garlic cloves, peeled and forced through a press*
*1 tablespoon dried marjoram, crumbled*
*2 teaspoons salt*
*2 teaspoons freshly ground black pepper*
*1 teaspoon freshly grated nutmeg*

*2 pounds dried penne or other short pasta*
*1 cup minced Italian parsley*
*1 cup freshly grated Parmesan cheese*

## BRAIDED OLIVE BREAD

1 envelope dry yeast

2 cups warm water (105 to
115 degrees F) plus 1
tablespoon, at room
temperature

1 teaspoon salt

5½ cups (about)
unbleached all-purpose
flour

2 tablespoons olive oil

16 Calamata olives (see
Cook's Sources), pitted
and coarsely chopped

12 large green olives,
pitted and coarsely
chopped

3 tablespoons yellow
cornmeal

1 egg yolk

THIS BIG, BRAIDED LOAF, studded with chopped green and black olives, looks good and tastes good. Leftovers are rare, but when you have some, the bread toasts beautifully and makes delicious croutons for a green salad.

In a large bowl stir together the yeast and the 2 cups of warm water. Let stand for 10 minutes. Stir in the salt and enough of the flour—about 4½ cups—to form a manageable dough. Turn the dough onto a floured board and knead about 5 minutes; the dough will remain slightly soft and sticky. Gather the dough into a ball. In a large bowl turn the dough in the olive oil to coat it well. Cover the dough with a towel and let it rise at room temperature until doubled in bulk, about 2 hours.

Punch the dough down and turn it out onto a floured surface. Flatten the dough into a large rectangle and scatter the olives over it. Gather the dough into a ball, enclosing the olives, and knead for about 5 minutes, incorporating an additional ¾ cup or so of flour and distributing the olives throughout the dough. Return the dough to the bowl, cover it, and let it rise until doubled, about 2 hours.

Sprinkle a baking sheet with the cornmeal. Punch the dough down and turn it out onto a floured surface. Cut the dough into thirds and roll each third out into a rope about 18 inches long. Braid the ropes together, tucking in the ends, to form a long, oval loaf. Transfer the loaf to the baking sheet, cover it with a towel, and let it rise at room temperature for 30 minutes.

Preheat the oven to 400 degrees F. In a small bowl beat the egg yolk with the remaining tablespoon of water. Brush the egg mixture over the loaf and bake 30 minutes. Remove the loaf from the baking sheet and brush off any clinging cornmeal. Return the loaf to the oven, setting it directly on the rack. Bake another 7 to 10 minutes, or until the bread is a rich brown and sounds hollow when tapped. Cool completely on a rack before cutting. *The loaf can be baked up to 1 day ahead. Wrap well and store at room temperature.*

➥ *Makes 1 large loaf, serving 12*

✦✦✦✦✦✦✦✦✦✦✦✦✦✦✦✦✦✦✦✦✦✦✦✦✦✦✦✦✦✦✦✦✦✦✦✦✦✦✦

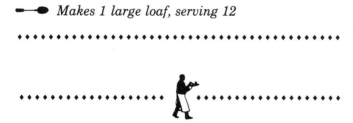

✦✦✦✦✦✦✦✦✦✦✦✦✦✦✦✦✦    ✦✦✦✦✦✦✦✦✦✦✦✦✦✦✦✦✦

**SERVING STRATEGY** I admit to being in a delicious rut when it comes to pears and provolone (see page 82 for the details), and certainly that cheese and fruit combination (or your own favorite) is an easy way to end a meal for twelve. On the other hand, for something much more festive, try pairing the raspberry variation of my Jack Daniel's Chocolate Whiskey Cake (page 200) with a big bowl of either Dark Chocolate–Raspberry Mousse (page 377) or Lemon Curd Mousse (page 302).

✦✦✦✦✦✦✦✦✦✦✦✦✦✦✦✦✦✦✦✦✦✦✦✦✦✦✦✦✦✦✦✦✦✦✦✦✦✦✦✦

# MENU

◆ ◆ ◆ ◆ ◆ ◆ ◆ ◆ ◆ ◆ ◆ ◆ ◆ ◆

WARM CAESAR SALAD

◆

PASTA WITH CREAMY
SAUSAGE-FENNEL SAUCE

◆

NECTARINES POACHED IN
SPICED RED WINE
*page 147*

◆

LEMON SUGAR COOKIES

THIS IS A PASTA MENU with rich, bold flavors, and just a bit of last-minute fussing. As usual with such meals, choose your companions carefully, and invite only those happy to join you in the kitchen to offer welcome kibitz or to lend a hand.

## WARM CAESAR SALAD

◆ ◆ ◆ ◆ ◆ ◆ ◆ ◆ ◆

**A**LL THE PUNGENT ELEMENTS of a classic Caesar salad—anchovy, garlic, Parmesan cheese, and Worcestershire sauce—are even zestier when the salad is served warm. Guests are always delighted with this renovation of an old favorite.

Trim the romaine, discarding any tough or discolored outer leaves. Wash the lettuce, pat it dry, and tear into bite-size pieces. *The lettuce can be prepared up to 1 day ahead. Store in plastic bags and refrigerate.*

In a medium-size skillet over moderately high heat melt together the butter and 2 tablespoons of the oil. Add the bread cubes and toss to coat. Lower the heat slightly and sauté the bread cubes, stirring them often, until they are crisp and golden, 5 to 7 minutes. With a slotted spoon, remove them from the skillet and drain them on paper towels.

Meanwhile, chop the eggs and force them through a sieve into a small bowl. Reserve. Put the lettuce into a large salad bowl and set aside.

In a small, nonreactive saucepan combine the vinegar, anchovy paste, Worcestershire sauce, and garlic. Whisk to blend. Whisk in the remaining olive oil. Set the pan over medium heat and bring the dressing just to a boil.

Immediately pour the hot dressing over the lettuce; toss well. Add the cheese and croutons and toss again.

Divide the salad among 6 plates. Spoon a mound of sieved egg into the center of each salad and season generously with pepper. Serve immediately.

━● *Serves 6*

*2 medium heads of romaine lettuce*

*2 tablespoons unsalted butter*

*¾ cup olive oil*

*1 loaf (8 ounces) sliced Italian bread, crusts trimmed, cut into ¾-inch cubes*

*2 eggs, hard cooked and shelled*

*3 tablespoons white wine vinegar*

*1½ tablespoons anchovy paste*

*1 tablespoon Worcestershire sauce*

*1 garlic clove, forced through a press*

*¼ cup freshly grated Parmesan cheese*

*Freshly ground black pepper*

## PASTA WITH CREAMY
## SAUSAGE-FENNEL SAUCE

*¾ pound sweet
Italian-style sausage
with fennel, casings
removed
¼ cup olive oil
2 garlic cloves, minced
¾ teaspoon crushed red
pepper flakes
1 cup finely diced fresh
fennel (about half a
small, trimmed bulb)
plus ⅓ cup finely
minced fresh fennel
fronds
¾ pound mushrooms, such
as cremini or porcini
(see Cook's Sources),
trimmed and coarsely
chopped
1¾ cup whipping cream
1 cup chicken broth
1 tablespoon salt
12 ounces short dried
pasta, such as fusilli,
rotelle, or penne
1 cup freshly grated
Parmesan cheese*

THOSE WHO BELIEVE that calories consumed along with pasta don't count will be able to enjoy this rich dish without guilt; clearer thinkers will have to decide if the anguish is worth it.

Crumble the sausage into a large skillet and set over medium heat. Cook, stirring often to break up the sausage, until it is lightly browned, about 15 minutes. With a slotted spoon, transfer the sausage to a bowl. Discard the rendered fat. Do not clean skillet.

Add the oil to the skillet and set over low heat. Stir in the garlic and pepper flakes and cook, stirring often, for 2 minutes. Add the diced fennel and cook, stirring occasionally, for 3 minutes. Add the mushrooms, stir to coat them, and raise the heat to medium. Cook, tossing and stirring, until the mushrooms are softened, about 5 minutes. Stir in the cream and chicken broth and bring to a simmer. Cook, stirring once or twice, for 5 minutes, or until slightly thickened.

Meanwhile, bring a large pot of water to a boil and stir in the salt. When the water returns to a boil add the pasta. Cook, stirring occasionally, until the pasta is just tender, 8 to 10 minutes. Drain.

Add the pasta, the sausage, and ½ cup of the cheese to the skillet with the sauce and cook over medium heat, stirring often, until the pasta has absorbed most of the sauce and is hot, 3 to 5 minutes.

Stir in the fennel fronds. Serve immediately, passing the remaining cheese at the table.

*Serves 6*

▼▼▼▼▼▼▼▼▼▼▼▼▼▼▼▼▼▼▼▼▼▼▼▼▼▼▼▼▼▼▼▼▼▼▼▼▼

## LEMON SUGAR COOKIES

♦ ♦ ♦ ♦ ♦ ♦ ♦ ♦ ♦ ♦

**A** CRISP LITTLE LEMON COOKIE is the perfect accompaniment to many fruit desserts, such as Nectarines Poached in Spiced Red Wine (page 147). This is an easy and basic recipe; the dough can be refrigerated for several days or frozen for months.

In a bowl cream together the butter, ½ cup of the sugar, the lemon zest, and salt. Whisk in the egg yolks. Stir in the lemon juice. Add 1¼ cups of the flour and stir until well mixed. Cover the dough and chill it for at least 2 hours. *The dough can be prepared up to 3 days ahead and refrigerated, or it can be frozen for up to 3 months.*

Preheat the oven to 375 degrees F. Butter 2 baking sheets. By rounded tablespoonfuls, measure out the dough and form it into 1- to 1½-inch balls. Place the balls of dough on the prepared baking sheets, spacing them well apart. Use the remaining flour to coat the flat bottom of a drinking glass. Flatten the balls into 2-inch rounds, about ¼ inch thick.

Bake until the cookies are crisp and the edges and bottoms are browned, about 10 minutes, exchanging the positions of the sheets in the oven at the halfway point. With a spatula, transfer the cookies immediately to parchment paper and sprinkle generously with the remaining sugar. *The cookies can be prepared 1 day ahead and stored in an airtight container.*

●━● *Makes 16 to 20 cookies*

♦ ♦ ♦ ♦ ♦ ♦ ♦ ♦ ♦ ♦ ♦ ♦ ♦ ♦ ♦ ♦ ♦ ♦ ♦ ♦ ♦ ♦ ♦ ♦ ♦ ♦ ♦ ♦ ♦ ♦ ♦ ♦ ♦ ♦ ♦ ♦ ♦ ♦

½ cup (1 stick) unsalted
    butter, softened
¾ cup sugar
2 tablespoons minced
    lemon zest
⅛ teaspoon salt
2 egg yolks
3 tablespoons fresh lemon
    juice, strained
1½ (about) cups
    unbleached all-purpose
    flour

# MENU

◆ ◆ ◆ ◆ ◆ ◆ ◆ ◆ ◆ ◆ ◆ ◆ ◆ ◆ ◆ ◆

OYSTERS ON THE HALF-SHELL

◆

CORNMEAL FETTUCCINE
WITH QUAIL AND SHIITAKE

◆

MIXED GREENS WITH RED WINE
VINAIGRETTE AND CHEESE TOASTS
*page 50*

◆

ALMOND-PEAR TORTE
WITH WHISKY CUSTARD SAUCE

MOST PASTA SUPPERS in my house are on the casual and rustic side, but here is a dressier and more stylish pasta menu, perfect for an intimate dinner party for a few friends.

In keeping with the festivities, this menu concludes with what is for me—and for this book—a fairly serious dessert. I'm no baker, and I usually don't tackle such ambitious confections, but this one is special and worth a little effort. Fortunately, although there are several steps, they can all be completed at least a day ahead, leaving just the assembling, serving, and enjoying to be dealt with at the last minute.

## CORNMEAL FETTUCCINE WITH QUAIL AND SHIITAKE

♦ ♦ ♦ ♦ ♦ ♦ ♦ ♦ ♦

THOUGH THE INGREDIENTS are few, they all contribute such rich flavor that the result is a wonderfully complex-tasting dish. The cornmeal pasta is attractive and delicious, but fresh fettuccine from the gourmet shop or supermarket will work almost as well.

♦ ♦ ♦  ♦ ♦ ♦

Cut down each side of the quail backbones from neck to tail. Discard the backbones. Flatten the breastbones with the heel of your hand. Pat the quail dry.

In a large, heavy skillet over medium-high heat melt the butter. Add the quail, breast side down, and cook until lightly browned, about 5 minutes. Turn the quail over, season with salt and pepper to taste, and cook until brown, about 4 minutes. Transfer the quail to a plate.

Add the peppers to the skillet and cook, stirring often, until lightly browned, about 5 minutes. Add the mushrooms and cook, stirring often, for 5 minutes. Season to taste with salt and pepper. Lower the heat and cook until the mushrooms render their juices, stirring occasionally, 5 to 7 minutes.

Raise the heat to high. Add the madeira and boil until it is reduced to a glaze that just coats the vegetables, stirring occasionally, 3 to 5 minutes. Lower the heat. Stir in the broth and cream, scraping up any browned bits, and bring the sauce to a simmer. Add the quail. Partially cover and simmer until the quail are tender and heated through, about 5 minutes.

Meanwhile, bring a large pot of water to a boil and stir in 1 tablespoon of salt. When the water returns to a boil add the fettuccine. Cook until just tender, stirring occasionally, about 4 minutes. Drain.

Transfer the quail to a plate and make a foil tent to keep them warm. Stir 1 cup of the cheese into the

*8 quail (see Cook's Sources)*
*4 tablespoons (½ stick) unsalted butter*
*Salt and freshly ground black pepper*
*2 large, sweet red peppers, stemmed, cored, and cut into ¼-inch strips*
*½ pound fresh shiitake mushrooms (see Cook's Sources), stemmed and cut into ¼-inch slices*
*½ cup medium-dry (Sercial) madeira*
*1½ cups canned chicken broth or homemade stock*
*½ cup whipping cream*
*Cornmeal Fettuccine (recipe follows)*
*1½ cups freshly grated Parmesan cheese*

sauce. Toss the pasta with the sauce and simmer until heated through, 1 or 2 minutes. Divide the pasta among the plates. Arrange 2 quail atop each portion. Spoon any remaining sauce over the quail and serve immediately, passing the remaining cheese at the table.

━━● *Serves 4*

◆◆◆◆◆◆◆◆◆◆◆◆◆◆◆◆◆◆◆◆◆◆◆◆◆◆◆◆◆◆◆◆◆◆◆◆◆◆◆◆◆◆

## CORNMEAL FETTUCCINE
◆◆◆◆◆◆◆◆◆◆

*3 eggs, at room
 temperature*
*¼ teaspoon salt*
*1½ cups (about)
 unbleached all-purpose
 flour*
*½ cup stone-ground yellow
 cornmeal*

In a small bowl whisk together the eggs and salt. In a food processor combine 1¼ cups of the flour and the cornmeal and process briefly to blend. With the machine running, add the egg mixture and blend until the dough just forms a ball. Knead the dough on a lightly floured surface until smooth and elastic, about 5 minutes, incorporating the remaining flour if necessary. Wrap the dough in plastic and let it rest at room temperature for 30 minutes.

Cut the dough in half. Set aside one of the halves and cover with a dry towel. Flatten the remaining piece of dough and fold it in thirds. With a pasta machine on its widest setting, run the dough through the rollers several times until it is smooth and firm, folding it in half before each run and dusting with flour if it becomes sticky.

Narrow the rollers to the next setting and run the dough through the machine without folding it. Repeat, narrowing the rollers after each run until the pasta is ⅟₁₆ to ⅟₃₂ inch thick, dusting with flour as needed. Hang the dough on a drying rack. Repeat with the remaining piece of dough.

When the sheets of dough look leathery, about 20 to 30 minutes, run them through the fettuccine blades of the pasta machine. Arrange the fettuccine in a single layer on towel-lined baking sheets. *The pasta can be prepared up to 1 day ahead, covered loosely with plastic wrap, and stored at room temperature.*

*Variation* To make herbed cornmeal fettuccine, whisk 1 tablespoon minced fresh herbs (thyme, oregano, or rosemary) with the eggs before adding the eggs to the flour.

**➥** *Makes about ¾ pound*

✦ ✦ ✦ ✦ ✦ ✦ ✦ ✦ ✦ ✦ ✦ ✦ ✦ ✦ ✦ ✦ ✦ ✦ ✦ ✦ ✦ ✦ ✦ ✦ ✦ ✦ ✦ ✦ ✦ ✦ ✦ ✦ ✦ ✦ ✦ ✦ ✦ ✦ ✦ ✦ ✦ ✦ ✦ ✦

## ALMOND-PEAR TORTE WITH WHISKY CUSTARD SAUCE

✦ ✦ ✦ ✦ ✦ ✦ ✦ ✦ ✦

**T**HIS DESSERT—fairly plain cake layers filled with warm pears and puddled by a rich, cool custard sauce— is a lovely conclusion to the meal. The smoky presence of a good single malt Scotch whisky is wonderfully at home with both pears and almonds, adding emphasis to the cake, filling, *and* sauce.

If you already have a favorite single malt, by all means use it. But if you're a beginner, you might want to try a personal favorite, the strong and distinctive Laphroig. The remainder of the bottle won't go to waste. You'll learn to enjoy it as the Scots do, sipped with just a splash of cool water. It's also good after dinner, served in a snifter and accompanied by coffee.

*For the custard sauce* In a medium-size bowl whisk together the egg yolks and sugar. In a heavy-bottomed saucepan bring the half-and-half to a boil. Slowly whisk the hot half-and-half into the egg mixture. Re-

WHISKY CUSTARD SAUCE

*4 egg yolks*

*¼ cup sugar*

*1⅓ cups half-and-half*

*¼ cup single malt Scotch whisky*

*¼ teaspoon vanilla*

ALMOND-WHISKY GENOISE

*⅔ cup sugar*

*5 eggs, at room temperature*

*2 tablespoons single malt Scotch whisky*

*⅛ teaspoon almond extract*

*½ cup flour (to measure, sift the flour into a measuring cup and sweep level)*

*½ cup (1 stick) unsalted butter, melted and cooled to lukewarm*

*½ cup finely ground almonds*

*(ingredients continued)*

GLAZED PEAR FILLING

2 tablespoons (¼ stick)
  unsalted butter
2 medium (about 1 pound)
  Bartlett pears, peeled,
  cored, and cut into
  ½-inch chunks
2 tablespoons sugar
1 tablespoon single malt
  Scotch whisky

Powdered sugar

turn the mixture to the saucepan. Set over low heat and cook, stirring constantly with a wooden spoon, until the mixture is thick enough to coat the back of the spoon and leave a track when a fingertip is drawn across it, about 4 minutes.

Transfer to a bowl. Stir in the whisky and vanilla and cool to room temperature. Cover, pressing plastic wrap onto the surface of the custard, and refrigerate. *The custard can be prepared up to 3 days ahead.*

*For the genoise* Position a rack in the center of the oven and preheat to 350 degrees F. Butter two 8 × 1½-inch round cake pans. Cut parchment circles to fit the bottoms and butter the parchment. Flour the pans and tap out the excess.

In a mixer, gradually beat the sugar into the eggs. Continue to beat until the mixture is a pale yellow and a slowly dissolving ribbon forms when the beaters are lifted, 6 to 8 minutes. Beat in the whisky and almond extract. Sift half the flour over the egg mixture and gently fold it in. Fold in 2 tablespoons of butter. Repeat with the remaining flour and butter. Fold in the nuts. Do not overmix.

Divide the batter between the prepared pans. Bake until the edges of the layers are light brown and pulled away from the sides of the pans, 15 to 20 minutes. Cool in the pans on a rack for 10 minutes. Remove the layers from the pans, remove the parchment, and cool completely. *The genoise layers can be prepared up to 1 day ahead. Wrap separately in plastic and refrigerate. Let the layers come to room temperature before assembling the torte.*

*For the filling* In a heavy skillet over medium-high heat melt the butter. Add the pears and cook 2 minutes, stirring often. Raise the heat to high. Add the sugar and whisky and cook, stirring often, until the liquid is reduced to a shiny glaze, about 4 minutes.

*To assemble* Place 1 cake layer on a serving plate. Spread the layer with the warm filling. Cover with the

second layer. Dust the top of the torte with the powdered sugar. Spoon the custard sauce onto plates. Cut
the torte into wedges and set a wedge next to each
puddle of custard.

*Serves 6*

♦ ♦ ♦ ♦ ♦ ♦ ♦ ♦ ♦ ♦ ♦ ♦ ♦ ♦ ♦ ♦ ♦ ♦ ♦ ♦ ♦ ♦ ♦ ♦ ♦ ♦ ♦ ♦ ♦ ♦ ♦ ♦ ♦ ♦ ♦ ♦ ♦ ♦ ♦ ♦ ♦ ♦ ♦ ♦ ♦ ♦ ♦

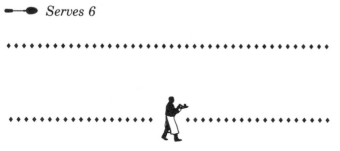

**SERVING STRATEGY** If you don't eat oysters, I'm not
going to change your mind with a few sentences here.
If you do, you'll agree with me that enjoying an icy,
briny few—or more than a few—is a great, light way to
begin this rakish menu. Too often even oyster lovers
partake only in restaurants, in the belief that opening
the delicious bivalves is better left to the pros. In truth,
though, compared to clams, oysters are easy to open.
There are special oyster knives available, though Julia
Child uses a church-key opener. Either gadget, when
slipped between the shells just off the hinge and
twisted, will easily separate the halves. (During this
process the oysters must be held deep side down to
retain the juices.) A knife is then run beneath the oyster to release it from the bottom shell. When opened,
the oysters are transferred on the half-shell to saucers
of cracked ice or salt for serving. More informally (my
choice), gather guests in the kitchen and open and
slurp your oysters more or less to order. This kind of
tasting is a good way to sample and compare several
varieties, and it serves as a great prelude to a plate of
pasta.

♦ ♦ ♦ ♦ ♦ ♦ ♦ ♦ ♦ ♦ ♦ ♦ ♦ ♦ ♦ ♦ ♦ ♦ ♦ ♦ ♦ ♦ ♦ ♦ ♦ ♦ ♦ ♦ ♦ ♦ ♦ ♦ ♦ ♦ ♦ ♦ ♦ ♦ ♦ ♦ ♦ ♦ ♦ ♦ ♦ ♦ ♦

# MENU

◆◆◆◆◆◆◆◆◆◆◆◆◆◆◆

WARM SALAD WITH FETA,
TOMATOES, AND GARLICKED SHRIMP

◆

PASTITSIO

◆

ICE CREAM WITH
MEDITERRANEAN LIQUEURS

◆

CORNMEAL BUTTER COOKIES
*page 113*

A PASTA CASSEROLE is among the most agreeable dishes for serving to a modest-sized crowd. This menu features a Greek specialty, pastitsio, combining pasta and a richly spiced lamb sauce baked under an unctuous, garlicky crust of béchamel. The warm salad requires last-minute work, but the pasta bakes unattended and the dessert is nearly effortless.

# WARM SALAD
# WITH FETA, TOMATOES, AND
# GARLICKED SHRIMP

◆ ◆ ◆ ◆ ◆ ◆ ◆ ◆ ◆ ◆

THIS IS A SPLENDIDLY FRAGRANT, colorful, and satisfying warm starter salad, but it can also be served as a light main course (add a few extra shrimp if you do). I've even used it without the shrimp altogether, alongside plain grilled lamb or chicken, like an elaborate warm vegetable.

◆ ◆ ◆  ◆ ◆ ◆

Trim away the ends and any wilted or tough outer leaves of the arugula, endive, and lettuce. Separate the leaves, wash them well, and dry. Tear the leaves into bite-size pieces. Store the greens in plastic bags and refrigerate. *The salad can be prepared to this point up to 1 day ahead.*

Rinse the feta, pat it dry, and crumble. Let the cheese come to room temperature.

In a large bowl combine the greens and feta and toss. Set aside.

In a large, nonreactive skillet over medium-low heat combine half of the olive oil and the garlic. Cook, stirring frequently, until the garlic begins to sizzle gently, about 2 minutes. Add the shrimp, season with ¼ teaspoon of salt, and cook, stirring, until they are pink, curled, and opaque, about 5 minutes. Do not let the garlic brown. With a slotted spoon, leaving as much garlic as possible behind in the skillet, transfer the shrimp to a bowl and cover to keep warm.

Add the remaining olive oil, the cherry tomatoes, and the oregano to the skillet. Raise the heat to medium and cook, tossing and stirring gently, until the tomatoes are heated through and the oregano is fragrant, about 5 minutes.

*1 large bunch arugula*
*1 head curly endive*
*  (or frisée)*
*1 large head red leaf*
*  lettuce*
*½ pound feta cheese*
*⅔ cup olive oil*
*4 medium garlic cloves,*
*  peeled and forced*
*  through a press*
*1 pound (about 24)*
*  medium shrimp, shelled*
*  and deveined, with tails*
*  left on*
*¼ teaspoon salt*
*1 pint (about 20) ripe, red*
*  cherry tomatoes,*
*  stemmed, rinsed, and*
*  patted dry*
*2½ teaspoons minced fresh*
*  oregano*
*⅓ cup red wine vinegar*

Add the vinegar to the skillet, raise the heat to high, and bring just to a boil. Immediately pour the contents of the skillet over the greens and feta in the bowl and toss well.

Divide the salad among serving plates. Garnish each salad with 3 shrimp. Spoon any dressing remaining in the bowl evenly over the salads and serve, passing a pepper mill.

*Serves 8*

## PASTITSIO

3 tablespoons olive oil

1 large onion, peeled and finely chopped

6 garlic cloves, peeled and minced

1 pound very lean lamb, coarsely ground

2 teaspoons dried oregano, crumbled

1 teaspoon dried thyme, crumbled

1 teaspoon ground cinnamon

1 teaspoon ground cumin, preferably from toasted seeds (see page 66)

½ teaspoon crushed red pepper flakes

½ teaspoon ground ginger

½ teaspoon freshly grated nutmeg

ALTHOUGH MOST OF THE WORLD'S great pasta dishes are Italian, there are exceptions, notably this Greek classic. Pastitsio is most authentic (and, I think, most delicious) when made with ground lamb, but beef or pork can also be used. The long-simmered savory meat sauce, rich and zesty with Middle Eastern spices, can be prepared several days in advance.

In a medium-size saucepan over medium heat warm the olive oil. Add the onion and garlic and cook, stirring occasionally, until the onions are tender, about 15 minutes.

Add the lamb. Cook, stirring, until the meat is evenly cooked and crumbled, about 5 minutes. Stir in the oregano, thyme, cinnamon, cumin, red pepper, ginger, nutmeg, and bay leaf and cook 5 minutes longer, stirring often. Stir in the wine, the tomatoes—breaking them up with a spoon—their juices, and 2 teaspoons of salt. Bring the sauce to a boil, lower the heat, and simmer, covered, for 30 minutes. Uncover and cook, stirring occasionally, until the sauce is thickened and reduced to 4 cups, about 30 minutes. Cool to room temperature, cover, and refrigerate. *The sauce can be prepared up to 3 days ahead. Bring it to room temperature before proceeding.*

Preheat the oven to 350 degrees F.

Bring a large pot of lightly salted water to a boil. Cook the pasta, stirring occasionally, until it is tender, but still firm, about 8 minutes. Drain, rinse well with cold water, and drain again.

In a small, heavy saucepan over low heat warm the Garlic Béchamel. Stir 1 cup of the cheese into the béchamel.

Separate 2 of the eggs. Set aside the egg yolks in a small bowl. Whisk the whites until frothy and stir them into the lamb sauce. In a large bowl toss together the cooked pasta, the lamb sauce, and ½ cup of the cheese. Spoon the mixture into a large, shallow baking dish. Crack the remaining 2 whole eggs into the bowl with the egg yolks. Whisk to blend and stir them into the béchamel mixture. Evenly spread the béchamel over the pasta and sprinkle the remaining cheese evenly over the top. *The pasta can be assembled up to 1 hour before baking. Cover and store at room temperature.*

Bake the pasta until the topping is golden brown, 40 to 45 minutes. Let the pastitsio sit for 15 minutes before cutting.

━━● *Serves 8*

◆ ◆ ◆ ◆ ◆ ◆ ◆ ◆ ◆ ◆ ◆ ◆ ◆ ◆ ◆ ◆ ◆ ◆ ◆ ◆ ◆ ◆ ◆ ◆ ◆ ◆ ◆ ◆ ◆ ◆ ◆ ◆ ◆ ◆ ◆ ◆ ◆ ◆ ◆ ◆

*1 imported bay leaf*

*½ cup dry white wine1 can (14 ounces) Italian-style plum tomatoes, with their juices*

*Salt*

*1 pound short, thick pasta, such as large elbow macaroni, fusilli, or penne*

*1 recipe Garlic Béchamel (recipe follows)*

*1¾ cups freshly grated Parmesan cheese*

*4 eggs*

## GARLIC BÈCHAMEL

3 tablespoons unsalted
  butter
2 medium garlic cloves,
  peeled and minced
3 tablespoons unbleached
  all-purpose flour
2½ cups milk
½ teaspoon salt
Pinch of freshly grated
  nutmeg
Pinch of cayenne pepper

In a small, heavy saucepan over low heat melt the butter. Stir in the garlic and cook, without browning, for 2 minutes. Whisk in the flour and cook, stirring often, for 2 to 3 minutes, without letting the flour brown.

Remove the pan from the heat and add the milk slowly, whisking vigorously to avoid lumping. Return the pan to low heat. Stir in the salt, nutmeg, and pepper, and bring to a simmer. Cook, partially covered, stirring frequently, until the sauce is thick enough to coat a spoon, about 15 minutes. *The sauce can be prepared up to 1 day ahead. Cool, cover, and refrigerate.*

*Makes about 3 cups*

**SERVING STRATEGY** Set up a soda fountain for grownups (no need for a soda jerk, this is all self-service), with an array of intensely flavored Mediterranean liqueurs—Strega, Galliano, Sambuca, Sabra—and let your guests top premium vanilla ice cream with the "syrup" of their choice. Your work consists of shopping for the liqueurs, scooping the ice cream, and encouraging everyone to be spontaneous. This is also a good time to bring out the espresso coffee maker.

# MENU

♦ ♦ ♦ ♦ ♦ ♦ ♦ ♦ ♦ ♦ ♦ ♦ ♦ ♦

ARUGULA AND ROASTED
PEPPER SALAD
*page 85*

♦

SPICY FUSILLI WITH ZUCCHINI,
OLIVES, AND GOAT CHEESE

♦

ORANGE-MINT ICE
*page 126*
*or*
GOLDEN RAISINS, CRISP APPLES,
AND MACADAMIA NUTS

PASTA SUPPERS are frequently meatless, and though cream, cheese, or butter may be involved, they still remain light, healthful, and easy to digest. There is also some medical evidence that carbohydrates eaten with the evening meal promote restful sleep. Sweet dreams!

▼▲▼▲▼▲▼▲▼▲▼▲▼▲▼▲▼▲▼▲▼▲▼▲▼▲▼▲▼▲▼▲▼▲▼▲▼▲▼

# SPICY FUSILLI
# WITH ZUCCHINI, OLIVES,
# AND GOAT CHEESE

♦ ♦ ♦ ♦ ♦ ♦ ♦ ♦ ♦ ♦

1/4 cup olive oil

1 large onion, peeled and
  chopped

1 1/2 teaspoons hot red
  pepper flakes

6 garlic cloves, minced

1 1/2 teaspoons dried basil,
  crumbled

1 teaspoon dried oregano,
  crumbled

1/2 teaspoon dried thyme,
  crumbled

1 bay leaf

1 can (35 ounces)
  Italian-style plum
  tomatoes, crushed, with
  their juices

Salt

5 small zucchini (about
  1 2/3 pounds), scrubbed,
  trimmed, and sliced into
  rounds 1/2 inch thick

Freshly ground pepper

1 pound short corkscrew
  pasta, such as fusilli or
  rotelle

24 wine-cured, imported
  black olives, such as
  Calamata (see Cook's
  Sources)

12 ounces fresh, mild goat
  cheese, rind removed,
  well chilled, and cut into
  1/2-inch chunks

1/2 cup finely chopped
  Italian parsley

**T**HIS CONCOCTION IS COLORFUL, zesty, entirely satisfying, and easy on the cook's schedule. The tomato sauce can be prepared a day or two in advance, helping to make your pasta supper truly casual. The remaining steps go quickly, and the end result—short, curly pasta, coated with a spicy, chunky sauce, topped with slices of browned zucchini, with the surprise of goat cheese melting beneath the surface—is a great mix of flavors and textures.

♦ ♦ ♦ 🍳 ♦ ♦ ♦

In a large saucepan over medium heat warm 2 tablespoons of the olive oil. Add the onion and pepper flakes and cook, uncovered, stirring occasionally, until tender and lightly browned, about 15 minutes.

Add the garlic, basil, oregano, thyme, and bay leaf and cook until the garlic is softened, about 3 minutes. Stir in the tomatoes, their juices, and 1 1/2 teaspoons of salt. Bring to a boil, then lower the heat, cover, and simmer, stirring occasionally, until the sauce is thick and chunky, about 40 minutes. *The sauce can be prepared up to 2 days ahead. Cool completely, cover, and refrigerate.*

In a large, nonstick skillet warm the remaining olive oil over medium-high heat. Add the zucchini, season lightly with salt and black pepper, and cook, turning occasionally, until well browned, 7 to 10 minutes. Set aside, draining them on paper towels and keeping warm.

Meanwhile, bring a large pot of water to a boil. Stir in 1 tablespoon of salt. When the water returns to a boil add the fusilli. Cook, stirring occasionally, until just tender, about 9 minutes. Drain well.

In a large, flameproof casserole or deep skillet over medium heat warm the tomato sauce until simmering. Adjust the seasoning. Add the pasta and cook, stirring, until the pasta absorbs most of the sauce, about 5 minutes. Stir in the olives and cook for 1 minute longer. Remove the casserole from the heat and stir in the goat cheese and parsley. Quickly scatter the zucchini over the pasta, cover the casserole, and let it stand for 1 minute. Serve immediately and pass freshly grated Parmesan cheese at the table.

*Serves 6*

**SERVING STRATEGY** As with other fruit and nut desserts, the combinations and serving suggestions are meant to be flexible to suit your mood and style. Here you might try plump dried apricots or dates in place of the raisins. By all means choose a crisp, firm apple, preferably locally grown, and borrow enough at the bank to stock up on plenty of nuts. The only thing worse than no macadamias is too few macadamias. This would be a good spot to sip a medium-dry madeira, such as Bual.

# MENU

◆ ◆ ◆ ◆ ◆ ◆ ◆ ◆ ◆ ◆ ◆ ◆ ◆ ◆ ◆

ARUGULA AND ROASTED
SWEET PEPPER SALAD
*page 85*

◆

LINGUINE WITH EGGPLANT
AND RICOTTA

◆

PESTO BREAD
*page 68*

◆

ICE CREAM WITH GOLDEN DRIED FRUIT
AND COGNAC SAUCE

◆

LEMON SUGAR COOKIES
*page 93*

HERE IS ANOTHER meatless pasta supper, but there's plenty of kick, thanks to the Jalapeño Tomato Sauce and the eggplant's rich and slightly smoky flavor and satisfying texture. No one will feel shortchanged in the serious eating department when presented with this meal. On the other hand, if you've got a determined carnivore who must be dealt with, consider adding a julienne of good-quality salami or prosciutto to the salad.

## LINGUINE WITH EGGPLANT AND RICOTTA

♦ ♦ ♦ ♦ ♦ ♦ ♦ ♦ ♦

**S**AUCE SHOULDN'T BE SOMETHING spooned over the pasta as a garnish. Instead, it should be integral, cooked into the pasta a bit so that the dish has a unity. Those commercial photos of bright red sauce sitting atop a mound of pale-faced spaghetti would be unrecognizable to an Italian, who knows that pasta needs at least a toss (if not a short simmer) with the sauce before it's served. This linguine is a good case in point, and the spicy tomato-infused pasta, topped with tender sautéed eggplant and a cool dollop of ricotta, is packed with flavor and contrast.

*2 medium (about 1 pound each) eggplants, trimmed and cut into ½-inch cubes*
*2 tablespoons salt*
*1 pound dried linguine or other long, flat pasta*
*1 recipe Jalapeño Tomato Sauce (page 118)*
*⅓ cup olive oil*
*8 ounces ricotta cheese, at room temperature*

In a colander combine the eggplant and 1 tablespoon of the salt. Rest the colander on a plate and let stand, stirring once or twice, for 30 minutes. With paper towels, dry the eggplant cubes as thoroughly as possible.

Bring a large pot of water to a boil and stir in the remaining salt. When the water returns to a boil add the pasta. Cook, stirring occasionally, until the pasta is just tender, about 9 minutes. Drain well.

Meanwhile, in a large saucepan over low heat, bring the Jalapeño Tomato Sauce to a simmer. In a large skillet over high heat warm the olive oil. When it is hot add the eggplant and cook, tossing and stirring occasionally, until the eggplant is browned, 5 to 6 minutes. Add the linguine and eggplant to the tomato sauce and cook, stirring once or twice, until the pasta is just heated through and steaming.

Divide the pasta among 6 plates. Top each serving with a dollop of the ricotta and serve. Offer freshly grated Parmesan cheese at the table.

*Serves 6*

♦ ♦ ♦ ♦ ♦ ♦ ♦ ♦ ♦ ♦ ♦ ♦ ♦ ♦ ♦ ♦ ♦ ♦ ♦ ♦ ♦ ♦ ♦ ♦ ♦ ♦ ♦ ♦ ♦ ♦ ♦ ♦ ♦ ♦

## ICE CREAM WITH GOLDEN DRIED FRUIT AND COGNAC SAUCE

**B**RANDY, ARMAGNAC, or an orange liqueur can be substituted for the cognac.

*4 ounces dried pineapple, cut into large dice*

*8 ounces dried apricots, quartered*

*4 ounces dried cherries (see Cook's Sources)*

*¼ cup cognac*

*¼ cup sugar*

*2 tablespoons fresh lemon juice*

*1½ to 2 pints premium commercial vanilla ice cream, softened slightly*

In a food processor, in batches if necessary, process the pineapple and apricots until finely chopped.

In a medium-size, nonreactive saucepan combine the chopped fruit, cherries, cognac, sugar, lemon juice, and 2 cups water. Set over medium heat and bring to a boil, stirring once or twice. Lower the heat, partially cover, and simmer, stirring occasionally, until the fruit is tender and has absorbed most of the liquid, about 25 minutes.

*The sauce can be transferred to a heatproof storage container and cooled to room temperature before covering and refrigerating. It can be prepared up to 1 week in advance. In a heavy saucepan over low heat reheat the sauce before serving.*

Scoop the ice cream into serving dishes. Top with the fruit sauce and serve immediately.

*Serves 6*

# MENU

◆ ◆ ◆ ◆ ◆ ◆ ◆ ◆ ◆ ◆ ◆ ◆ ◆ ◆

ARUGULA AND ROASTED
SWEET PEPPER SALAD
*page 85*

◆

MACARONI BAKED WITH
TWO CHEESES AND HAM

◆

PESTO BREAD
*page 68*

◆

PINK GRAPEFRUIT WITH STREGA

◆

CORNMEAL BUTTER COOKIES
*or*
AMARETTI DI SARRONNO

THE MAIN COURSE of this comfortable pasta-and-salad supper is a good illustration of the best of the new American cookery. In it, a familiar dish, macaroni and cheese, gets an updating with mild goat cheese substituted for part of the more traditional cheddar. It is a meal at once homey and sophisticated, and I make it often.

The liqueur-marinated grapefruit is easy to prepare and quick to assemble, but if you prefer, offer apples, pears, or grapes.

## MACARONI BAKED WITH TWO CHEESES AND HAM

♦ ♦ ♦ ♦ ♦ ♦ ♦ ♦ ♦

1 recipe Garlic Béchamel
   (page 104)
10 ounces medium-sharp
   cheddar cheese, grated
10 ounces mild, rindless
   goat cheese, crumbled
1 tablespoon salt
1 pound short pasta, such
   as fusilli or rotelle
12 ounces baked, smoked
   ham, trimmed and cut
   into ½-inch cubes (about
   2½ cups)
2 teaspoons freshly ground
   black pepper
2 tablespoons fine, dry
   bread crumbs
2 tablespoons freshly
   grated Parmesan cheese

THERE ARE SEVERAL WAYS to arrive at macaroni and cheese, from simply tossing buttered pasta with Parmesan and giving it a little crisping time in the oven to this more elaborate version. I like the way the béchamel sauce distributes the tangy chèvre-and-cheddar combination throughout the dish, interrupted by the nuggets of good, smoky ham. This macaroni and cheese will not resemble in the slightest your favorite recipe, whether from mom, a box, or a cafeteria, but you'll feel just as good when you've finished it.

♦ ♦ ♦  ♦ ♦ ♦

In a heavy saucepan over low heat warm the béchamel sauce. Whisk in the cheddar and goat cheese until smooth.

Bring a large pot of water to a boil and stir in 1 tablespoon of salt. Add the pasta and cook until just tender, about 7 minutes. Drain immediately, rinse well under cold water, and drain again. *The recipe can be prepared to this point several hours ahead. Cover the béchamel with plastic wrap, pressing it onto the surface of the sauce. Toss the pasta with 2 tablespoons of olive oil and cover.*

Preheat the oven to 400 degrees F. Butter a 3-quart baking dish. In a large bowl combine the warm béchamel mixture and the pasta. Add the ham and pepper and mix thoroughly. Spoon the pasta mixture into the prepared baking dish. In a small bowl combine the bread crumbs and grated cheese. Sprinkle evenly over the pasta. Bake 30 to 40 minutes, or until the top is lightly browned and the pasta is bubbling. Let the dish stand 5 minutes before serving.

━● *Serves 6*

## PINK GRAPEFRUIT WITH STREGA

◆ ◆ ◆ ◆ ◆ ◆ ◆ ◆ ◆

Substitute another italian liqueur—Galliano, Frangelico, or Sambuca—if you prefer.

◆ ◆ ◆  ◆ ◆ ◆

Arrange the grapefruit sections on dessert plates. Drizzle the liqueur over the fruit and chill, covered, for 30 minutes. Garnish with the mint and serve.

—● Serves 4

3 large pink or ruby grapefruits, peeled and sectioned
1/2 cup Strega liqueur
Sprigs of fresh mint, as garnish

◆ ◆ ◆ ◆ ◆ ◆ ◆ ◆ ◆ ◆ ◆ ◆ ◆ ◆ ◆ ◆ ◆ ◆ ◆ ◆ ◆ ◆ ◆ ◆ ◆ ◆ ◆ ◆ ◆ ◆ ◆ ◆ ◆ ◆ ◆ ◆ ◆ ◆ ◆ ◆ ◆

## CORNMEAL BUTTER COOKIES

◆ ◆ ◆ ◆ ◆ ◆ ◆ ◆ ◆

Golden, buttery, and fragile, these simple shortbreadlike cornmeal cookies are the perfect little something alongside such no-work desserts as fresh fruit or store-bought ice cream. Since the dough is soft, the easiest way to handle it is with the usual slice-and-bake refrigerator cookie approach. For a more formal look you may also roll the dough between two sheets of wax paper and cut it into shapes with a cookie cutter.

◆ ◆ ◆  ◆ ◆ ◆

In a medium-size bowl cream the butter and sugar together. Stir in the egg yolk and vanilla. Stir in the cornmeal and salt. Add the flour and stir until the dough is just combined.

Turn the dough out onto a piece of waxed paper. Form the dough into a log 2 inches in diameter, wrap it in the paper, and chill until solid, preferably overnight.

9 tablespoons unsalted butter, softened
1/3 cup sugar
1 egg yolk
1/2 teaspoon vanilla extract
1/4 cup yellow cornmeal
Pinch of salt
1 cup unbleached all-purpose flour

*The dough can be prepared up to 3 days in advance and refrigerated. It can also be frozen for up to 1 month. Soften the dough in the refrigerator for 30 minutes before proceeding.*

Preheat the oven to 375 degrees F. Lightly butter cookie sheets. Slice half the log of chilled dough into ¼-inch rounds; refrigerate remainder. Space the rounds well apart on one sheet and bake about 12 to 15 minutes, or until the cookies are golden and the edges and bottoms are lightly browned. Transfer the cookies to absorbent paper and cool completely. Repeat with remaining dough.

*The cookies can be prepared up to 1 day ahead. Store, airtight, at room temperature.*

━● *Makes about 2 dozen cookies*

◆◆◆◆◆◆◆◆◆◆◆◆◆◆◆◆◆◆◆◆◆◆◆◆◆◆◆◆◆◆◆◆◆◆◆◆◆◆◆◆◆◆◆◆◆

# MENU

♦ ♦ ♦ ♦ ♦ ♦ ♦ ♦ ♦ ♦ ♦ ♦ ♦ ♦ ♦ ♦

WILTED ESCAROLE SALAD
WITH PANCETTA AND GARLIC

♦

PASTA SHELLS STUFFED
WITH SPINACH, GOAT CHEESE,
AND BASIL

♦

LEMON-ESPRESSO ICE

♦

CORNMEAL BUTTER COOKIES
*page 113*

ALTHOUGH THE SALAD and baked pasta both involve some last-minute touches, the major elements of both can be gotten out of the way in advance. Serve this to good friends who won't mind keeping you company in the kitchen.

## WILTED ESCAROLE SALAD WITH PANCETTA AND GARLIC

♦♦♦♦♦♦♦♦♦

2 large heads of escarole

½ pound pancetta (see Cook's Sources), cut into ¼-inch dice (see note)

½ cup olive oil

24 large, whole garlic cloves, peeled

24 brine-cured, imported black olives, such as Calamata (see Cook's Sources)

2 lemons, cut into wedges

**E**SCAROLE IS A WIDE-LEAFED cousin of both the prickly green known as curly endive and the fashionable radicchio. This gutsy salad makes a good first course, but I like it almost as well served alongside a plain grilled or roasted meat entrée, rather like an elaborate hot vegetable. Either way, the contrast between the escarole's coarse ribs, which remain crunchy, and the tender green leaves, which wilt considerably, makes great eating.

♦♦♦  ♦♦♦

Trim away the ends and any wilted outer leaves of the escarole and discard. Separate the leaves and wash and dry them well. Tear the leaves into bite-size pieces, store in plastic bags, and refrigerate. *The escarole can be prepared up to 1 day ahead.*

In a large, deep, nonreactive skillet over low heat cook the pancetta, uncovered, stirring occasionally, until crisp and brown, about 20 minutes. With a slotted spoon transfer the pancetta to a small bowl and reserve. Discard the rendered pancetta fat and wipe the skillet.

In the skillet over medium heat add the olive oil and garlic and cook, uncovered, stirring frequently, until the garlic is lightly colored and tender, about 20 minutes. With slotted spoon, transfer the garlic to the bowl with the pancetta; reserve the oil in the skillet. *The recipe can be prepared to this point up to 3 hours before serving. Rewarm the oil in the skillet over medium heat before proceeding.*

Add the olives to the skillet and warm, stirring, for 1 minute. Add the escarole and the pancetta and garlic cloves, tossing to coat with oil, cover, and cook over medium heat for 1 minute. Toss again, remove the skillet from the heat, and let it stand, covered, another minute.

Divide the salad among 6 serving plates and garnish with the lemon. Serve at once, passing a pepper mill and encouraging diners to squeeze lemon juice onto the salads to taste.

NOTE Pancetta is Italian bacon, salted but not smoked, and is available in some specialty food shops. It can be quite salty, and you may wish to blanch it. Simmer the pancetta in boiling water for 5 minutes, drain well, and pat dry before browning. For a different but equally good salad, substitute smoked slab bacon.

*Serves 6*

◆ ◆ ◆ ◆ ◆ ◆ ◆ ◆ ◆ ◆ ◆ ◆ ◆ ◆ ◆ ◆ ◆ ◆ ◆ ◆ ◆ ◆ ◆ ◆ ◆ ◆ ◆ ◆ ◆ ◆ ◆ ◆ ◆ ◆ ◆ ◆ ◆ ◆ ◆ ◆ ◆ ◆

## PASTA SHELLS STUFFED WITH SPINACH, GOAT CHEESE, AND BASIL

◆ ◆ ◆ ◆ ◆ ◆ ◆ ◆

LIFE MAY, as author Shirley Conran once suggested, be too short to stuff a mushroom, but when it comes to pasta—particularly this savory combination—I always find the time. This pasta is best when eaten as the main course, but I've also served it in smaller portions as a starter, followed by roast chicken and a crunchy sauté of vegetables (see page 371).

In a medium-size bowl mash together the goat cheese and ricotta. Stir in the spinach, cream, egg, basil, and 4 tablespoons of the grated cheese. Season generously with pepper. *The filling can be made up to 24 hours ahead. Cover tightly with plastic wrap and refrigerate. Let the filling return to room temperature before proceeding.*

1 pound fresh, rindless,
  mild goat cheese, at
  room temperature
8 ounces ricotta cheese, at
  room temperature
1 package (10 ounces)
  frozen spinach, thawed,
  squeezed dry, and
  chopped
½ cup whipping cream
1 egg, beaten
1 cup finely chopped fresh
  basil
6 tablespoons freshly
  grated Parmesan cheese
Freshly ground black
  pepper
1 tablespoon salt
8 ounces large pasta shells
Jalapeño-Tomato Sauce
  (recipe follows)
2 tablespoons fine, dry
  bread crumbs

Bring a large pot of water to a boil and stir in 1 tablespoon of salt. Add the pasta and cook, stirring occasionally, until just tender, 10 to 12 minutes. Drain, rinse with cold water, and drain again.

Position a rack in the upper third of the oven and preheat to 400 degrees F. Spoon 1 cup of the tomato sauce over the bottom of a large, shallow baking dish. Stuff each shell with about 1 heaping tablespoon of the filling and place in the baking dish, filling side up. Drizzle the remaining tomato sauce evenly over the stuffed shells.

In a small bowl combine the bread crumbs and remaining grated cheese. Sprinkle the mixture evenly over the shells. Bake until the sauce is bubbling and the top is lightly browned, 30 to 40 minutes. Let the pasta settle about 10 minutes before serving.

━● *Serves 6*

◆ ◆ ◆ ◆ ◆ ◆ ◆ ◆ ◆ ◆ ◆ ◆ ◆ ◆ ◆ ◆ ◆ ◆ ◆ ◆ ◆ ◆ ◆ ◆ ◆ ◆ ◆ ◆ ◆ ◆ ◆ ◆ ◆ ◆ ◆ ◆ ◆ ◆ ◆ ◆ ◆ ◆

## JALAPEÑO-TOMATO SAUCE

◆ ◆ ◆ ◆ ◆ ◆ ◆ ◆

*3 tablespoons olive oil*

*1 large onion, peeled and chopped*

*4 garlic cloves, minced*

*1 fresh jalapeño, including seeds, stemmed and minced*

*1 can (28 ounces) Italian-style plum tomatoes, with their juices*

*1½ teaspoons salt*

THIS ZIPPY BUT OTHERWISE basic tomato sauce is a good one for your files. It accommodates any of the usual additions—sautéed wild mushrooms, broccoli, eggplant, clams, mussels, shrimp, black olives, sausages, heavy cream, and more—and freezes beautifully.

◆ ◆ ◆  ◆ ◆ ◆

In a medium-size, nonreactive saucepan over moderate heat warm the oil. Add the onion, garlic, and jalapeño, cover, and cook, stirring occasionally, until the onion is tender, about 15 minutes.

Add the tomatoes, breaking them up with a spoon, their juices, and the salt. Bring to a boil, lower the heat, and simmer, partially covered, stirring occasion-

ally, for 30 minutes. Uncover and continue to cook until the tomato sauce is reduced by about one-third, 25 to
30 minutes. Cool slightly.

Puree the sauce in a food processor or force through
the medium blade of a food mill. Cool completely, cover,
and refrigerate. *The sauce can be made up to 3 days
ahead and refrigerated, or it can be frozen for up to 1
month.*

━● *Makes about 3 cups*

## LEMON-ESPRESSO ICE

T HIS SHOCKINGLY INTENSE ICE makes a perfect dessert
after the spicy pasta, and it also provides a cool oasis in
the middle of a scorching summer afternoon.

In a medium-size, noncorrosive saucepan combine the
espresso, lemon juice, and sugar. Set over medium heat
and bring just to a boil, stirring to dissolve the sugar.
Remove from the heat, transfer to a heatproof bowl,
and cool to room temperature. Cover and refrigerate
until very cold, preferably overnight.

Churn the chilled mixture in an ice-cream maker
according to the manufacturer's instructions. Cover
and store in the freezer. *The ice can be prepared up to
2 days ahead.* Soften the ice slightly in the refrigerator
if necessary before scooping.

━● *Makes about 1 ½ quarts*

2½ cups brewed strong
  espresso or dark-roast
  coffee
1½ cups strained fresh
  lemon juice (from 8 or 9
  lemons)
2 cups sugar

# PICNICS AND GRILLS

◆◆◆◆◆◆◆◆◆◆◆◆◆◆◆◆◆◆◆◆◆◆◆◆◆◆◆◆◆◆◆◆◆◆◆◆◆◆◆◆◆◆◆◆◆

A
FTER THE PASTA REVOLUTION came the grill revolution, and again the battle was won precisely because the times were ripe and the message was one we wanted to hear. Speedy food, big flavors, and at least the impression of lighter, healthier fare were the foundations upon which the grill people built their takeover; the victory has been overwhelming and complete.

There's something innate about our appreciation of grill cookery, perhaps a primal memory of those first mastodon steaks, that makes it seem the most natural of cooking methods. The desire to get back to the basics, and possibly a rejection of the packaged foods and sanitary fifties suburban kitchens (lacking the sights, sounds, or smells of food preparation), makes the smoke, sizzle, and occasional discomfort of cooking over an open fire an essential part of the eating experience. A spirit of adventure is important too, and while I might not go so far as to say *anything* can be grilled, the memory of a skillet of just-caught trout, sautéed over a smoking hickory-wood fire under a grill cover followed by an apple tart baked over the same fire, leads me close.

This chapter isn't simply about grilling, though, but also about rustic and vibrant summer cooking in general. A picnic is mostly a state of mind, and while you can indeed schlep this food out to some pasture or another and enjoy it hunkered down in a sunny bower, the point really has nothing at all to do with locomotion. In my book picnics are foods of the summer season, simply combined, artfully and zestfully seasoned, served at leisure, warm or cool, and enjoyed for their direct flavors. Much of this food can come from the grill, but big, lush salads, prime vegetables and herbs, pungent fresh cheeses, and perfect fruit all play a part too. There's simply no other time of the year I'd rather be cooking or eating, and it's not by accident that this chapter is one of the longest in this book.

▓▓▓▓▓▓▓▓▓▓▓▓▓▓▓▓▓▓▓▓▓▓▓▓▓▓▓▓▓▓▓▓▓▓▓▓▓▓▓▓

# MENU

◆ ◆ ◆ ◆ ◆ ◆ ◆ ◆ ◆ ◆ ◆ ◆ ◆ ◆

TUNA AND ROASTED
RED PEPPER MOUSSE

◆

GRILLED SEA SCALLOPS WITH
RASPBERRY-THYME BUTTER SAUCE

◆

GRILLED ZUCCHINI
AND SUMMER SQUASH

◆

GRILLED NEW POTATOES

◆

ORANGE-MINT ICE

◆

FRESH MELON

THIS SUMMER SEAFOOD MENU IS centered around the grill, with a do-ahead starter and dessert to make your job easier. Serve something cold, white, and uncomplicated with the mousse and drink a lush Chardonnay with the grilled scallops.

## TUNA AND ROASTED RED PEPPER MOUSSE

♦♦♦♦♦♦♦♦♦

**D**URING THE HOT and sultry height of summer, this rough-textured spread is practically my favorite thing to eat. The ready availability of canned tuna and the abundance of red pepper mean it goes together with minimal fuss, and since the mousse keeps for several days, you can divide the recipe into two batches and get appetizers for more than one meal.

Serve it spread on crusty bread, like an Italian-style semolina, or as a dip, offering sturdy vegetables to scoop with.

♦♦♦  ♦♦♦

2 large, sweet red peppers
2 cans (6½ ounces each)
    oil-packed tuna, drained
6 ounces (1½ sticks)
    unsalted butter, softened
1 tablespoon fresh lemon
    juice
1 tablespoon olive oil
2 teaspoons salt
2 teaspoons freshly ground
    black pepper

In the flame of a gas burner, or under a preheated broiler, roast the peppers, turning them, until the skins are charred. Transfer to a paper bag, or a bowl covered with a plate, and let the peppers steam until cool. Rub away the burnt skin, stem and core the peppers, and blot them with paper towels. Chop the peppers.

In a food processor combine half of the roasted peppers, the tuna, butter, lemon juice, olive oil, salt, and pepper. Process until smooth. Add the remaining roasted pepper and process again with short bursts of power until just finely chopped—discernible bits of pepper should remain.

Pack the mousse into a crock or bowl and refrigerate, covered, for *at least* 24 hours. *The mousse can be prepared up to 3 days ahead. Soften the mousse slightly at room temperature before serving.*

━● *Makes about 3 cups*

♦♦♦♦♦♦♦♦♦♦♦♦♦♦♦♦♦♦♦♦♦♦♦♦♦♦♦♦♦♦♦♦♦♦♦♦♦♦♦

▼▲▼▲▼▲▼▲▼▲▼▲▼▲▼▲▼▲▼▲▼▲▼▲▼▲▼▲▼▲▼

## GRILLED SEA SCALLOPS
## WITH
## RASPBERRY-THYME BUTTER
## SAUCE

♦ ♦ ♦ ♦ ♦ ♦ ♦ ♦ ♦

½ cup fresh raspberries
  plus additional
  raspberries, as garnish
2 tablespoons fresh thyme
  leaves plus additional
  sprigs, as garnish
1 cup medium-dry white
  wine
½ teaspoon sugar
2 cups apple, cherry, or
  peach wood chips
2 tablespoons minced
  shallot
2 pounds large sea
  scallops, of equal size
  and weight
2 sticks (8 ounces)
  unsalted butter, well
  chilled and cut into
  small pieces plus 2
  tablespoons unsalted
  butter, melted
¼ teaspoon salt
⅛ teaspoon freshly ground
  black pepper

THIS DISH is a ravishing combination of effects: The tart, pale pink sauce is light but rich, and it serves as the perfect foil to the sweet and smoky scallops. Garnished with a few tiny raspberries and a sprig of thyme, each plate is also beautiful.

As an alternative to the grilled vegetables, accompany the scallops with wild rice and follow the entrée with a green salad.

♦ ♦ ♦ 🥄 ♦ ♦ ♦

In a small bowl thoroughly crush together the ½ cup of raspberries and 2 tablespoons of thyme. Stir in the wine and sugar, cover, and let stand at room temperature about 1 hour. Soak the wood chips in water for 30 minutes.

Strain the raspberry mixture into a small, heavy, nonreactive saucepan, pressing hard with the back of a spoon. Stir in the shallot and bring the mixture to a boil over moderate heat. Lower the heat and simmer, uncovered, until the liquid is reduced to ⅓ cup, 12 to 15 minutes. Strain the mixture and return it to the saucepan.

Sort through the scallops, reserving any small or odd-shaped pieces for another use. Pull off the small, rectangular muscles from the sides of each scallop (they toughen when cooked). Rinse the scallops, pat them dry, and divide them among 4 long, flat, metal skewers.

Preheat a gas grill, or light a charcoal fire and allow it to burn down until the coals are evenly white. Drain the wood chips.

Warm the raspberry reduction over low heat. Whisk in the 2 sticks of butter, 1 or 2 pieces at a time, whisking well after each addition and adding more butter just before the previous pieces are completely absorbed. Stir in the salt and pepper. Adjust the seasoning, if necessary, and set the sauce aside, covered, in a warm (but not hot) place.

Scatter the wood chips over the fire and heat until smoking. *Begin the grilling with the prepared zucchini and summer squash and new potatoes (recipes follow). After turning once, add the scallops. This will allow you to serve the vegetables and scallops at the same time, hot off the grill.* Brush the scallops with the melted butter and grill, turning them once, until lightly golden and opaque, about 4 minutes on each side.

Divide the sauce among 4 warmed dinner plates. Slide the scallops onto the sauce and garnish each serving with several raspberries and a sprig of thyme. Serve immediately.

*Serves 4*

♦ ♦ ♦ ♦ ♦ ♦ ♦ ♦ ♦ ♦ ♦ ♦ ♦ ♦ ♦ ♦ ♦ ♦ ♦ ♦ ♦ ♦ ♦ ♦ ♦ ♦ ♦ ♦ ♦ ♦ ♦ ♦ ♦ ♦ ♦ ♦ ♦ ♦ ♦ ♦ ♦ ♦ ♦

## GRILLED ZUCCHINI AND SUMMER SQUASH

♦ ♦ ♦ ♦ ♦ ♦ ♦ ♦ ♦

**G**RILLING ADDS A WELCOME smoking crispness to otherwise insipid—but abundant and affordable—zucchini and summer squash.

♦ ♦ ♦  ♦ ♦ ♦

2 medium zucchini, scrubbed, trimmed, and quartered or sliced
2 medium summer squash, scrubbed, trimmed, and quartered or sliced
4 tablespoons olive oil
Salt and freshly ground black pepper

Brush the zucchini and summer squash with the olive oil. Arrange them on a preheated gas or charcoal grill, over wood chips soaked in water for 30 minutes, drained, and spread evenly over the coals, if desired, and cook, turning once, until the vegetables are lightly browned, 3 to 4 minutes. Transfer to a plate, season with salt and pepper to taste, and serve hot, warm, or cool.

*Serves 4*

♦ ♦ ♦ ♦ ♦ ♦ ♦ ♦ ♦ ♦ ♦ ♦ ♦ ♦ ♦ ♦ ♦ ♦ ♦ ♦ ♦ ♦ ♦ ♦ ♦ ♦ ♦ ♦ ♦ ♦ ♦ ♦ ♦ ♦ ♦ ♦ ♦ ♦ ♦ ♦ ♦ ♦ ♦

## GRILLED NEW POTATOES

♦ ♦ ♦ ♦ ♦ ♦ ♦ ♦ ♦

2 pounds small,
  red-skinned new
  potatoes
3 tablespoons olive oil
Softened unsalted butter,
  coarse salt, and freshly
  ground black pepper, as
  accompaniments

**S**ATISFY A PRIMITIVE URGE by pulling these spuds hot and smoky from the grill, slathering them with sweet butter, coarse salt, and fresh pepper, and eating them out of hand.

♦ ♦ ♦  ♦ ♦ ♦

In a medium-size pan over medium heat cover the potatoes with cold, lightly salted water. Bring the water to a boil and cook the potatoes until just tender, about 8 minutes after the water returns to a boil. Drain and cool. *The potatoes can be prepared up 3 hours in advance.*

Thread the potatoes on flat, metal skewers and brush them with the olive oil. Place the skewered potatoes on the grill about 4 inches above a smoky fire. Cook, turning once or twice, until crisp and slightly blackened outside and tender inside, about 6 minutes. Slide the potatoes off the skewers and serve hot or warm, passing the butter, salt, and pepper.

◂━● *Serves 4*

♦ ♦ ♦ ♦ ♦ ♦ ♦ ♦ ♦ ♦ ♦ ♦ ♦ ♦ ♦ ♦ ♦ ♦ ♦ ♦ ♦ ♦ ♦ ♦ ♦ ♦ ♦ ♦ ♦ ♦ ♦ ♦ ♦ ♦ ♦ ♦ ♦ ♦ ♦ ♦ ♦

## ORANGE-MINT ICE

♦ ♦ ♦ ♦ ♦ ♦ ♦ ♦ ♦

4 cups fresh orange juice,
  strained
½ cup fresh lemon juice,
  strained
1⅓ cups sugar
Half a large bunch of mint
  leaves and stems (about
  2 loosely packed cups)

**A**RRANGE THIN WEDGES of chilled cantaloupe, watermelon, and honeydew on dessert plates and garnish them with a scoop of the ice and a sprig of fresh mint. Any leftovers make a sweet, refreshing cooler on a summer afternoon, accompanied by a tall glass of iced coffee. An unexpected but no less delicious effect is achieved by substituting an equal amount of fresh basil for the mint.

In a medium-size nonreactive saucepan over medium heat combine the orange and lemon juices and the sugar. Bring the liquid to a boil, stirring often to dissolve the sugar.

In a medium-size heatproof bowl combine the hot juice mixture and the mint. Cool to room temperature, cover, and refrigerate overnight.

Strain the mixture and discard the mint. Transfer the liquid to the container of an ice-cream maker and churn according to the manufacturer's instructions. Store the ice in the freezer. *The ice can be prepared up to 3 days ahead.* Soften slightly in the refrigerator. Serve immediately.

*Makes about 1½ quarts*

# M E N U

♦ ♦ ♦ ♦ ♦ ♦ ♦ ♦ ♦ ♦ ♦ ♦ ♦ ♦ ♦ ♦

SHRIMP AND CHICKEN SALAD
WITH LEMON-BASIL DRESSING

♦

BULGUR SUMMER SALAD
WITH RICOTTA *SALATA*

♦

HERBED PROSCIUTTO FLATBREAD
*page 162*

♦

SLICES OF RED AND
YELLOW WATERMELON

♦

RED AND GOLDEN RASPBERRIES

TWO PLATTERS of beautiful (and complimentary) salads, crusty bread, and sweet, seasonal fruit form the kind of summer menu that's as undemanding to prepare as it is to eat. Simplify your life further by substituting any good store-bought bread, and don't hesitate to improvise with the best summer fruit your market offers. In this two-salad menu, the salads serve six; if offered singly, each will serve four.

# SHRIMP AND CHICKEN SALAD WITH LEMON-BASIL DRESSING

♦ ♦ ♦ ♦ ♦ ♦ ♦ ♦ ♦

THIS SALAD is long on both eye-appeal and taste. The dressing, by the way, tastes good enough to eat with a spoon, and it can be equally delicious on cool grilled chicken, sliced tomatoes, or when used as the dressing for a perfect summer potato salad.

Although the dressing can be made in advance, the chicken and shrimp will be at their best if cooked shortly before they are served.

♦ ♦ ♦  ♦ ♦ ♦

In a skillet just large enough to hold them in a single layer cover the chicken breasts with cold water. Stir in 2 teaspoons of salt, set the skillet over medium heat, and bring slowly just to a simmer, about 15 minutes, turning the chicken breasts once. Stir in the shrimp and simmer until they are pink, curled, and just cooked through, about 4 minutes. With a slotted spoon remove the shrimp. Let the chicken breasts cool in the poaching liquid to room temperature. Drain them, remove any fat, and cut out the tough central cartilage from each breast.

Line a platter with alternating leaves of radicchio and lettuce. Slice the chicken breasts on the diagonal. Arrange the chicken and shrimp on the leaves and drizzle some of the dressing over them. Garnish with the sprigs of basil. Serve, passing the remaining dressing separately and offering guests a pepper mill.

*Serves 4 to 6*

♦ ♦ ♦ ♦ ♦ ♦ ♦ ♦ ♦ ♦ ♦ ♦ ♦ ♦ ♦ ♦ ♦ ♦ ♦ ♦ ♦ ♦ ♦ ♦ ♦ ♦ ♦ ♦ ♦ ♦ ♦ ♦ ♦ ♦ ♦ ♦ ♦ ♦ ♦ ♦ ♦ ♦ ♦ ♦ ♦ ♦

*4 boneless (about 2½ pounds) chicken breasts*
*2 teaspoons salt*
*12 ounces (about 20) medium shrimp, shelled and deveined*
*1 medium head radicchio, leaves separated, rinsed, and patted dry*
*1 medium head Boston or Bibb lettuce, leaves separated, rinsed, and patted dry*
*Lemon-Basil Dressing (recipe follows)*
*Sprigs of fresh basil, as garnish*

2 cups clean, packed fresh
  basil leaves
1 egg
1 egg yolk
5 tablespoons fresh lemon
  juice, strained
1½ teaspoons salt
½ teaspoon freshly ground
  black pepper
1 cup olive oil
⅓ cup corn or other
  vegetable oil

## LEMON-BASIL DRESSING

♦♦♦♦♦♦♦♦♦

In a food processor fitted with the metal blade combine
the basil, egg, egg yolk, lemon juice, salt, and pepper.
Process 1 minute or until smooth. With the machine
running, pour in the olive and corn oils in a steady
stream. Adjust the seasoning and serve. *The dressing
can be prepared up to 1 day ahead. Refrigerate, allowing it to return to room temperature before using.*

●━● *Makes about 1¾ cups*

## BULGUR SUMMER SALAD
## WITH RICOTTA *SALATA*

♦♦♦♦♦♦♦♦♦

**T**HIS COOL, CRUNCHY, and herb-fragrant grain salad requires almost no cooking. Ricotta *salata,* also called
pressed ricotta, is crumbly, tangy, and salty—a good
contrast to the moist, nutty bulgur. Substitute feta or a
sharp, firm goat cheese if you prefer. The salad also
makes a good main course, served with toasted pita
bread.

2 large sweet peppers (1
  yellow and 1 orange)
1 cup fresh, clean, loosely
  packed cilantro leaves
1 cup fresh, clean, loosely
  packed mint leaves
1 fresh jalapeño, stemmed
5 tablespoons white wine
  vinegar
3 teaspoons salt
¾ cup olive oil
3 cups cold water
2 cups medium-grain
  bulgur (see Cook's
  Sources)
2 large tomatoes, juice and
  seeds removed, cut into
  ½-inch dice

In the flame of a gas burner, or under a preheated
broiler, roast the peppers, turning them, until the skins
are charred. In a paper bag, or in a bowl covered by a
plate, let the peppers steam until cool. Rub away the
burnt peel with paper towels, core and seed the peppers, and cut the flesh into ½-inch squares.

In a food processor combine the cilantro, mint, jalapeño, vinegar, and ½ teaspoon of the salt. Process
until smooth. With the motor running dribble in the
oil. Reserve.

In a small saucepan bring the water to a boil. Stir in the remaining salt. In a medium-size bowl pour the water over the bulgur and let stand, stirring once or twice, for 45 minutes. Transfer the bulgur to a strainer and press with the back of a spoon to extract any water that has not been absorbed.

In a large bowl toss together the peppers, tomatoes, zucchini, onions, and bulgur. Pour the dressing over the mixture and toss to combine. Line a platter with the watercress. Place the bulgur mixture in a mound on the watercress and sprinkle the ricotta over the bulgur. Serve, offering a pepper mill at the table.

*3 medium zucchini,
scrubbed, trimmed, and
cut into ½-inch dice*
*4 green onions, trimmed
and sliced thin*
*1 bunch watercress,
trimmed, rinsed, and
patted dry*
*½ pound ricotta* salata,
*crumbled*

—● *Serves 4 to 6*

♦ ♦ ♦ ♦ ♦ ♦ ♦ ♦ ♦ ♦ ♦ ♦ ♦ ♦ ♦ ♦ ♦ ♦ ♦ ♦ ♦ ♦ ♦ ♦ ♦ ♦ ♦ ♦ ♦ ♦ ♦ ♦ ♦ ♦ ♦ ♦ ♦

♦ ♦ ♦ ♦ ♦ ♦ ♦ ♦ ♦ ♦ ♦ ♦ ♦ ♦ ♦ ♦ ♦      ♦ ♦ ♦ ♦ ♦ ♦ ♦ ♦ ♦ ♦ ♦ ♦ ♦ ♦ ♦ ♦ ♦

**SERVING STRATEGY** When a dessert consists of colorful summer fruits, Mother Nature does most of the work. Red and yellow melons and red and golden raspberries are natural appealing, even when you do no more than arrange thin slices of melon on chilled plates and garnish them with a scattering of multicolored berries (plus an optional sprig of mint by way of greenery). Choose the sweetest raspberries and let the melons' juices provide the rest of the sugaring, and your dessert will be as low in calories as it is high in flavor.

♦ ♦ ♦ ♦ ♦ ♦ ♦ ♦ ♦ ♦ ♦ ♦ ♦ ♦ ♦ ♦ ♦ ♦ ♦ ♦ ♦ ♦ ♦ ♦ ♦ ♦ ♦ ♦ ♦ ♦ ♦ ♦ ♦ ♦ ♦ ♦ ♦

# MENU

◆ ◆ ◆ ◆ ◆ ◆ ◆ ◆ ◆ ◆ ◆ ◆ ◆ ◆ ◆

BISTRO SALAD

◆

GRILLED DUCK AND SWEET
YELLOW PEPPER SAUSAGES WITH
RED WINE SAUCE

◆

PUREE OF BAKED BEETS
AND BAKED GARLIC

◆

LENTILS WITH TUSCAN OLIVE OIL

◆

RASPBERRY-ORANGE
CUSTARD TARTLETS
*page 22*

GRILLING IS TOO FINE and simple a cooking method to be limited to summer, and while this menu is hard to resist at any time, the rich, hearty flavors and deep colors make it most appropriate when the weather turns cooler.

## BISTRO SALAD

♦♦♦♦♦♦♦♦♦

**T**HIS WATERCRESS and endive salad, spangled with Roquefort cheese and dressed with sherry vinegar and walnut oil, is a bistro classic.

In a small bowl whisk together the vinegar, mustard, a pinch of salt, and a generous grind of black pepper. Gradually whisk in the walnut oil in a thin, steady stream. Taste the dressing and adjust the seasoning.

In a large bowl toss together the watercress and endive. Add the dressing and toss well. Divide the greens among 4 salad plates. Sprinkle the salads evenly with the cheese and walnuts and spoon any dressing remaining in the large bowl evenly over the salads. Serve immediately.

━● *Serves 4*

♦♦♦♦♦♦♦♦♦♦♦♦♦♦♦♦♦♦♦♦♦♦♦♦♦♦♦♦♦♦♦♦♦♦♦♦♦♦♦♦♦♦♦

*2 tablespoons sherry wine vinegar*
*1 tablespoon prepared Dijon-style mustard*
*Salt and freshly ground black pepper*
*½ cup walnut oil*
*1 bunch watercress, trimmed, rinsed, and patted dry*
*2 Belgian endives, cored and julienned*
*4 ounces Roquefort cheese, crumbled (about ½ cup), at room temperature*
*½ cup walnuts, toasted (see page 65)*

## GRILLED DUCK AND SWEET YELLOW PEPPER SAUSAGES WITH RED WINE SAUCE

♦♦♦♦♦♦♦♦♦

**D**UCKS ARE FAIRLY TIDY creatures to bone, and this is an efficient recipe, using the carcasses as the base for a glossy and delicious red wine sauce. As much as I like the sausages with the sauce in this menu, I also grill them, skipping the sauce, and serve them with Grilled New Potatoes (page 126) topped with Mustard Bacon Butter (page 152) and a tomato salad, or in the rustic brunch on page 25.

Soak the sausage casing in cold water to cover with the vinegar for 1 hour. Rinse the casing, discarding the

*4 feet (about) pork sausage casings, ordered from the butcher*
*1 tablespoon distilled white vinegar*
*2 ducks (4½ to 5 pounds each), gizzards reserved*
*½ pound fresh pork fat, well chilled and cut into ½-inch pieces*
*2 garlic cloves, peeled and forced through a press*

*(ingredients continued)*

*2 teaspoons salt*

*1½ teaspoons freshly
ground black pepper*

*½ teaspoon dried
marjoram, crumbled*

*½ teaspoon dried thyme,
crumbled*

*¼ teaspoon freshly grated
nutmeg*

*1 large, yellow sweet
pepper, stemmed, cored,
and cut into ⅛-inch dice*

*2 cups of hickory or other
aromatic wood chips*

*Red Wine Sauce (recipe
follows)*

water and vinegar mixture. Slip one end of the casing over the faucet and run cold water through it. Check the casing for holes and cut the casing into 4 sections. Each section should be 1 foot long. In a bowl soak the sections in cold water while preparing the filling.

Skin and bone the ducks, reserving the carcasses and gizzards for use in the sauce. Cut the duck meat, hearts, and livers into ½-inch pieces, discarding any fat or tendons. Cover and refrigerate until well chilled.

In a food processor coarsely chop the pork fat. Add the chilled duck meat, hearts, livers, garlic, salt, pepper, marjoram, thyme, and nutmeg and finely chop using short bursts of power; do not overprocess. Transfer the filling to a bowl and mix in the sweet pepper.

Tie a knot at one end of a section of casing. Insert the end of a pastry bag fitted with a large, plain tip into the open end of the casing, gathering the casing up onto the tip. Fill the pastry bag with one-quarter of the sausage mixture. Force the mixture into the casing, sliding the casing off the pastry tip as it fills. Stop occasionally to shape the sausage. Pierce any air bubbles with a fine needle. Remove the sausage from the pastry tip. Tie a knot in the open end and trim any excess casing. Repeat with the remaining filling and casing. Wrap the sausages well in plastic and refrigerate overnight.

Soak the wood chips in water for 30 minutes. Preheat a gas grill, or light a charcoal fire and let it burn until evenly white. Drain the wood chips, scatter them over the coals, and heat until smoking. Prick each sausage several times with the tip of a knife. Arrange the sausages about 6 inches above the coals. Grill them until lightly browned on all sides, 6 to 8 minutes. The sausage meat should be just light pink and juicy.

Slice the sausages diagonally into 1-inch pieces. Spoon the Red Wine Sauce onto 4 plates and arrange the sausage slices over the sauce.

*Serves 4*

## RED WINE SAUCE

◆◆◆◆◆◆◆◆◆

**B**ECAUSE OF THE INTENSELY reduced nature of the sauce, it is not salted until just before serving. A fresh herb compatible with duck—thyme, marjoram, or basil—can be added, to taste, to the finished sauce.

◆◆◆  ◆◆◆

Chop the carcasses into small pieces. Heat 3 tablespoons of the oil in a large, heavy pot over medium-high heat. Add the carcasses and gizzards and cook, turning occasionally, until very brown, about 20 minutes. With a slotted spoon, transfer the browned pieces to a bowl. Discard the cooking fat but do not clean the pot.

Add the remaining oil to the pot and set over low heat. Stir in the onions, carrots, and leek. Cover and cook, stirring occasionally and scraping the browned bits from the bottom of the pan, for 20 minutes. Add the browned carcasses and gizzards, the wine, and 3 quarts of water and bring to a boil, skimming the surface and stirring occasionally. Add the thyme, marjoram, bay leaves, and peppercorns. Lower the heat, partially cover the pot, and simmer, stirring occasionally, for 2 hours. Strain the stock, discarding the solids. Refrigerate the stock until very cold, preferably overnight.

Remove and discard the hardened surface fats from the chilled stock. In a small saucepan over low heat simmer the stock, skimming and stirring occasionally, until it is reduced to 1 cup, about 50 minutes. Add a pinch of salt and a grind of pepper, adjusting the seasoning, if necessary. Remove from the heat, whisk the butter into the sauce, and serve immediately.

━━● *Makes about 1 cup*

Reserved duck carcasses
  and gizzards, trimmed
  of fat and skin and
  patted dry
6 tablespoons vegetable oil
2 medium onions, peeled
  and chopped
3 medium carrots, peeled
  and chopped
1 large leek, trimmed,
  cleaned, and chopped
1 cup full-bodied red wine,
  such as Petite Sirah
2 teaspoons dried thyme,
  crumbled
1 teaspoon dried
  marjoram, crumbled
2 bay leaves
12 black peppercorns
Salt and freshly ground
  black pepper
2 tablespoons unsalted
  butter

## PUREE OF BAKED BEETS
## AND BAKED GARLIC

♦♦♦♦♦♦♦♦♦

3 tablespoons vegetable oil

12 medium beets, tops
trimmed to ½ inch,
rinsed, and patted dry

12 large garlic cloves,
unpeeled

4 tablespoons unsalted
butter, at room
temperature

3 tablespoons raspberry
vinegar

2 tablespoons sugar

1½ teaspoons salt

½ teaspoon freshly ground
black pepper

**B**AKING (AS OPPOSED TO BOILING) intensifies the natural flavor of the beets, which is further enhanced in this puree by the addition of raspberry vinegar. (When I have my own homemade berry vinegar—see page 374—I use it; when I don't, a good store-bought brand does almost as well.) A dozen cloves of garlic sounds like a lot, unless you remember that baking mellows the taste to a nutty sweetness. The puree is also good with roast duck, goose, pork, or ham.

♦♦♦  ♦♦♦

Preheat the over to 400 degrees F. Pour the oil into a 4- or 5-quart Dutch oven. Add the beets and garlic cloves, stirring to coat them with the oil. Cover and bake until a knife easily pierces a beet, stirring occasionally, about 1¼ hours. Cool to room temperature.

Peel and quarter the beets. Squeeze the garlic out of the peels. In a food processor combine the beets, garlic, butter, vinegar, sugar, salt, and pepper. Process until smooth, scraping down the sides of the workbowl once or twice. Taste and adjust the seasoning— depending on the sweetness of the beets you might want to add a bit more sugar, vinegar, or both. *The beets can be prepared to this point up to 1 day ahead. Cool completely cover, and refrigerate.*

In a heavy saucepan over low heat stir the puree until steaming.

*Serves 4*

## LENTILS WITH TUSCAN OLIVE OIL

◆◆◆◆◆◆◆◆◆

**U**SE YOUR BEST, greenest, and most luscious Italian olive oil for this exquisitely simple side dish.

In a strainer under running water rinse the lentils. In a small saucepan combine the lentils and a quart of cold water. Set over medium heat and bring just to a boil. Lower the heat and cook very gently, stirring once or twice, until the lentils are just tender, 20 to 25 minutes. Drain. *The lentils can be prepared to this point up to 3 hours ahead.*

In a large skillet over low heat warm the olive oil. Add the lentils and the salt and stir gently, once or twice. Add the pepper, toss gently, and serve.

━● *Serves 4*

1 cup brown lentils
5 tablespoons extra virgin
  olive oil
1/2 teaspoon salt
1/2 teaspoon freshly ground
  black pepper

# MENU

♦ ♦ ♦ ♦ ♦ ♦ ♦ ♦ ♦ ♦ ♦ ♦ ♦ ♦ ♦

HAM AND LIMA BEAN SALAD
WITH MAPLE-THYME DRESSING

♦

PERFECT CORN BREAD
*page 71*

♦

BOURBON, PEACH, AND
SHORTBREAD FOOLS

WHEN THE WEATHER gets hot the folks down South know how to stay cool. This menu has a bit of a southern flair, and it is designed to take the least amount of kitchen time on a sweltering day. If you'd rather not serve the dessert, and if your peach tree (or your produce man) cooperates, just set out a basket of perfect peaches instead. In any case, a tall glass of *real* iced tea, with a mint leaf, seems the perfect beverage.

▼▲▼▲▼▲▼▲▼▲▼▲▼▲▼▲▼▲▼▲▼▲▼▲▼▲▼▲▼▲▼▲

# HAM AND LIMA BEAN SALAD WITH MAPLE-THYME DRESSING

♦ ♦ ♦ ♦ ♦ ♦ ♦ ♦ ♦

**T**HIS HEARTY SALAD, with its flavor of sweet-and-sour baked beans, makes wonderful summer sense. It doesn't hurt that it involves relatively little cooking and, once assembled, can marinate overnight. Your last-minute labor is then reduced to arranging and garnishing the plates.

Dried limas are more widely available, but if fresh ones come your way, the recipe adapts easily to accommodate the windfall.

♦ ♦ ♦  ♦ ♦ ♦

In a large bowl combine the beans with cold water to cover them by at least three inches. Soak overnight.

Drain the beans and transfer them to a large, heavy pot. Add fresh cold water to cover them by at least three inches, set over medium heat, and bring to a boil. Lower the heat and simmer, uncovered, stirring once or twice, for 25 minutes. Stir in 2 teaspoons of the salt and continue to cook gently until the beans are just tender, 15 to 25 minutes longer. Drain and transfer to a bowl.

In a large skillet over medium heat combine the ham and 3 tablespoons of the corn oil. Cook, tossing and stirring often, until the ham is crisp and brown, 6 to 8 minutes. With a slotted spoon, transfer the ham to the bowl with the beans. Do not clean the pan.

Set the skillet over high heat and stir in the maple syrup, cider vinegar, and the remaining corn oil. Bring to a boil, stirring and scraping to dissolve any browned bits from the bottom of the skillet. Stir in the thyme, boil 1 minute, and pour the hot dressing over the ham and beans. Add the carrots and stir. Season with the remaining salt and a generous grind of black pepper and stir again. Cool to room temperature, cover, and refrigerate for several hours or overnight.

*1 pound dried lima beans,*
  *picked over*
*3½ teaspoons salt*
*1½ pounds lean, smoky,*
  *baked ham, trimmed*
  *and cut into ½-inch dice*
*1 cup corn oil*
*⅓ cup maple syrup*
  *(see Cook's Sources)*
*⅓ cup cider vinegar*
*3 tablespoons finely*
  *minced fresh thyme*
  *(see note)*
*5 medium carrots, peeled*
  *and sliced thin*
*Freshly ground black*
  *pepper*
*1 head red-leaf lettuce,*
  *separated into leaves,*
  *washed, and patted dry*
*1 medium red onion,*
  *peeled and sliced into*
  *thin rings*

Allow the salad to return to room temperature. Adjust the seasoning. Line plates with the lettuce leaves. Stir the salad and divide it among the plates, shaping each portion into a slight mound. Garnish each salad with the onion. Drizzle any remaining dressing over each salad and serve immediately.

NOTE If fresh thyme is unavailable, cook 2½ teaspoons of dried thyme in the water with the lima beans.

*Serves 6*

◆◆◆◆◆◆◆◆◆◆◆◆◆◆◆◆◆◆◆◆◆◆◆◆◆◆◆◆◆◆◆◆◆◆◆◆◆◆◆◆◆◆◆◆◆◆◆◆◆◆◆◆

## BOURBON, PEACH, AND SHORTBREAD FOOLS

◆◆◆◆◆◆◆◆◆

4 pounds fresh, ripe
  peaches
⅔ cup sugar
⅓ cup bourbon
1 package (5½ ounces)
  shortbread cookies,
  coarsely crumbled
¾ cup whipping cream,
  chilled and whipped to
  soft peaks
Additional fan-shaped
  shortbread cookies,
  optional

FOOLISHLY SIMPLE is the only way to describe this old-fashioned layered concoction of peach sauce, buttery cookies, and whipped cream. Packaged Scottish shortbread is an entirely acceptable summer timesaver and is widely available in cheese and gourmet shops. For the splashiest effect, serve the fools in tall wineglasses and garnish them with an additional fan-shaped (petticoat) shortbread.

◆◆◆ ◆◆◆

Bring a pot of water to a boil. Two at a time, lower the peaches into the water, leave them for 30 seconds, and transfer them, using a slotted spoon, to a bowl of cold water. Peel the peaches (the skins will slip off easily), pit them, and transfer to a heavy saucepan. Stir in the sugar and bourbon and set over low heat. Bring to a simmer, stirring often. Cover and cook until the peaches are very tender, about 15 minutes. Cool to room temperature, cover, and refrigerate until well chilled.

Drain the peaches, reserving the syrup. Coarsely mash the peaches. Add enough reserved syrup to the peaches to make a juicy puree (you may not need all of the syrup). Divide half the peach puree among 6 stemmed glasses. Divide the crumbled cookies among the glasses. Top with the remaining peach puree, cover, and refrigerate about 1 hour, to mellow.

Top each fool with a dollop of whipped cream, garnish with a shortbread fan, if desired, and serve.

➡● *Serves 6*

◆ ◆ ◆ ◆ ◆ ◆ ◆ ◆ ◆ ◆ ◆ ◆ ◆ ◆ ◆ ◆ ◆ ◆ ◆ ◆ ◆ ◆ ◆ ◆ ◆ ◆ ◆ ◆ ◆ ◆ ◆ ◆ ◆ ◆ ◆ ◆ ◆ ◆ ◆ ◆

# MENU

◆ ◆ ◆ ◆ ◆ ◆ ◆ ◆ ◆ ◆ ◆ ◆ ◆ ◆

GRILLED BLUEFISH, SLICED
TOMATOES, AND NEW POTATOES WITH
MUSTARD-MINT VINAIGRETTE

◆

GRILL-TOASTED COUNTRY BREAD
*page 175*

◆

FRESH BERRIES WITH
ORANGE CUSTARD
*page 23*

*or*

BROWN SUGAR SAUCE
*page 313*

I DON'T HAVE a summer house, but occasionally I get to visit someone else's. This Friday-evening menu was developed to have six travel-weary people well fed and happy in the shortest possible time.

If you haven't brought the fish, tomatoes, potatoes, mint, and berries with you in a cooler, pick them up on arrival. After building the fire, whisk together the vinaigrette and boil the potatoes. If you've brought a batch of orange custard with you, so much the better. If not, the brown sugar sauce stirs together in minutes.

This is the sort of menu in which getting down to serious eating is a priority, so a starter is optional. If the roadside stand that sells you the berries and tomatoes has sweet corn, grill a few ears as an appetizer or buy tiny zucchini and other fresh vegetables and serve them raw to dip into olive oil and coarse salt.

# GRILLED BLUEFISH, SLICED TOMATOES, AND NEW POTATOES WITH MUSTARD-MINT VINAIGRETTE

♦♦♦♦♦♦♦♦♦

I GUESS THIS IS A SORT of warm salad; certainly it's one big, beautiful plate of food, and if your schedule gets crossed, it's as good cool as it is warm.

Soak the wood chips in water to cover for 30 minutes.

Scrub the potatoes. In a saucepan over medium heat cover them with cold, lightly salted water. Bring to a boil and cook until the potatoes are just tender, about 8 minutes after the water reaches a boil. Drain. When the potatoes are cool, cut them into thick slices.

Prepare a charcoal fire and let the coals burn until evenly white, or preheat a gas grill. Drain the wood chips and scatter them over the coals or grillstones. Brush the fillets lightly with the olive oil. Lay the fillets, or the basket, if you are using it, on the grill and cover. Cook, turning once, for a total of about 8 minutes. The fish should be almost fully cooked and just flaking except at the center of the fillets. (They will cook further as they stand.) Meanwhile, cut the tomatoes into thick slices.

Transfer the fillets to plates. Arrange the potatoes and tomatoes around the fish. Drizzle the Mustard-Mint Vinaigrette generously over the fish, potatoes, and tomatoes. Garnish each plate with a sprig of mint and serve hot or warm, passing a pepper mill.

NOTE The best fillets for grilling are cut from larger bluefish and should be about 1 inch thick. A hinged fish-grilling basket (see Cook's Sources) will make turning the fillets easier; if you are using a basket, fillets can be skinless. If you prefer to cook the fish directly on the grill, leave the skin on the fillets for

2 cups apple or other fruit-wood chips
12 to 18 small, red-skinned new potatoes
Salt
6 thick (about 2½ to 3 pounds) bluefish fillets, see note
½ cup (about) olive oil
3 ripe, red or yellow beefsteak tomatoes
Mustard-Mint Vinaigrette (recipe follows)
Sprigs of fresh mint, as garnish

easier turning. Also, to avoid transferring flavors to the grill-toasted bread, grill the bread first and keep warm.

*Serves 6*

♦♦♦♦♦♦♦♦♦♦♦♦♦♦♦♦♦♦♦♦♦♦♦♦♦♦♦♦♦♦♦♦♦♦♦♦♦♦♦♦♦♦♦

## MUSTARD-MINT VINAIGRETTE

♦♦♦♦♦♦♦♦♦

3 tablespoons sherry wine
  vinegar
3 tablespoons prepared
  Dijon-style mustard
½ teaspoon salt
1¼ cups corn oil
Freshly ground black
  pepper
½ cup minced fresh mint

THE VINAIGRETTE is also good when made with fresh basil, dill, or oregano. The rich, assertive taste of sherry vinegar works well with bluefish; with milder fish, substitute plain white wine vinegar and reduce the mustard, to taste.

♦♦♦  ♦♦♦

In a small bowl whisk together the vinegar, mustard, and salt. Slowly whisk in the corn oil. Season generously with fresh pepper. *The recipe can be prepared to this point up to 3 days in advance. Refrigerate, covered. Allow the dressing to come to room temperature before using.* Whisk in the mint and adjust the seasoning.

*Makes about 1½ cups*

♦♦♦♦♦♦♦♦♦♦♦♦♦♦♦♦♦♦♦♦♦♦♦♦♦♦♦♦♦♦♦♦♦♦♦♦♦♦♦♦♦♦

♦♦♦♦♦♦♦♦♦♦♦♦♦♦♦    ♦♦♦♦♦♦♦♦♦♦♦♦♦♦♦

**SERVING STRATEGY** Brown Sugar Sauce (page 313), a cool butterscotch sauce with a sour cream base, stirs together in minutes and is good over all sorts of summer berries. The Orange Custard (used as a tart filling on page 23) is another simple sauce that can turn merely perfect berries into a great dessert.

♦♦♦♦♦♦♦♦♦♦♦♦♦♦♦♦♦♦♦♦♦♦♦♦♦♦♦♦♦♦♦♦♦♦♦♦♦♦♦♦♦♦

# MENU

••••••••••••••••••

SUN-DRIED TOMATO
AND FONTINA TARTINES

•

HERBED SEAFOOD AND
BARLEY SALAD

•

NECTARINES POACHED
IN SPICED RED WINE

•

CORNMEAL BUTTER COOKIES
*page 113*

THIS SIMPLE SUMMER MENU illustrates a useful point: Even when most of the food is cool and done ahead, a touch of something hot and freshly prepared lends a welcoming note to a meal that can otherwise seemed canned or leftover.

In this case that welcome heat comes from the savory tartines. They make a rustic and tasty opener, and should be accompanied by a glass of uncomplicated cool white wine. The nectarine dessert is easy enough, but if you prefer, present an array of mixed plums and nectarines in a bowl of ice water for a satisfactory conclusion.

## SUN-DRIED TOMATO AND FONTINA TARTINES

8 slices crusty Italian
    bread, cut on the
    diagonal ½ inch thick
6 oil-packed, sun-dried
    tomatoes (see Cook's
    Sources), drained and
    julienned
6 ounces Fontina Val
    D'Aosta cheese (see
    Cook's Sources),
    trimmed and sliced into
    8 equal pieces
Freshly ground black
    pepper

IN THE SUMMERTIME, even this simple hot starter makes it seem like you've gone to great lengths as a cook and a host.

Position a rack in the upper third of the oven and preheat to 425 degrees F.

Lay the bread on a baking sheet. Divide the tomatoes evenly among the bread and top each with a piece of fontina. Bake about 5 minutes, or until the cheese is melted and the tartines are sizzling. Season generously with fresh pepper and serve immediately.

Serves 4

## HERBED SEAFOOD AND BARLEY SALAD

1⅓ cups pearl barley
Salt
¾ pound (about 20)
    medium shrimp, shelled
    and deveined
¾ pound small sea
    scallops
1 cup diced celery
⅔ cup diced red onion
1½ cups clean, loosely
    packed fresh basil leaves
    plus additional sprigs,
    as garnish

GRAINS LIKE BULGUR and barley, when served cool and dressed with a tart vinaigrette, seem light and refreshing and yet leave diners feeling well fed. This salad can be made with mint, parsley, or dill in place of the basil.

Bring a pot of water to a boil. Stir in the barley and 1 tablespoon of salt. Lower the heat and simmer, uncovered, stirring once or twice, until the barley is just tender, about 25 minutes. Drain (reserving the barley water for use in a soup if you wish), rinse briefly under running water, and drain thoroughly.

Bring a pot of water to a boil. Stir in 1 tablespoon of salt and the shrimp. After 1 minute stir in the scallops. After 1 more minute (the water need not even return to a boil), drain the seafood and cool to room temperature. In a large bowl combine the barley, the seafood, the celery, and onion.

In a food processor combine the basil, lemon juice and ½ teaspoon of salt and process until smooth. With the machine running dribble in the oil. Pour the dressing over the salad and toss. Season generously with pepper and toss again.

Place the salad in a mound on a serving platter. Scatter the olives over the salad and garnish with the sprigs of fresh basil. Serve at cool room temperature.

——● *Serves 4*

*2 tablespoons fresh lemon
  juice, strained*
*⅔ cup olive oil*
*Freshly ground black
  pepper*
*⅓ cup Niçoise olives (see
  Cook's Sources), drained*

◆◆◆◆◆◆◆◆◆◆◆◆◆◆◆◆◆◆◆◆◆◆◆◆◆◆◆◆◆◆◆◆◆◆◆◆◆◆◆◆◆◆◆◆◆◆◆◆

# NECTARINES POACHED
# IN SPICED RED WINE

◆◆◆◆◆◆◆◆◆◆

**T**HE RED WINE SYRUP enhances the taste of the nectarines, and since a day or two of refrigerated marination in the syrup is essential, what little work there is to this recipe gets done long before serving time. The cornmeal cookies are a nice accompaniment, but serving store-bought cookies works equally well.

◆◆◆  ◆◆◆

In a medium-size nonreactive saucepan combine the wine, sugar, allspice, peppercorns, cloves, and bay leaf. Bring the liquid to a boil over moderate heat, stirring until the sugar dissolves, about 2 minutes.

Add the nectarines and simmer, turning them once or twice in the syrup, until just tender, about 8 min-

*2 cups rich red wine, such
  as zinfandel or merlot*
*½ cup sugar*
*12 whole allspice*
*12 black peppercorns*
*2 whole cloves*
*1 imported bay leaf*
*6 large, ripe, firm
  nectarines, halved and
  pitted*

utes. With a slotted spoon, transfer the nectarines to a bowl, discarding any loosened peels. Set the pan over high heat, bring the syrup to a boil, and simmer briskly until it is reduced to 1 cup, about 6 minutes. Pour the syrup over the fruit, cool to room temperature, and refrigerate, covered, for 24 to 48 hours.

To serve, divide the nectarines among 4 chilled dessert bowls. Strain the syrup over the fruit and serve cold.

*Serves 4*

♦♦♦♦♦♦♦♦♦♦♦♦♦♦♦♦♦♦♦♦♦♦♦♦♦♦♦♦♦♦♦♦♦♦♦♦♦♦♦♦♦♦♦♦♦♦♦♦

# MENU

◆◆◆◆◆◆◆◆◆◆◆◆◆◆◆◆◆◆

SMALL FRESH GOAT AND SHEEP CHEESES
WITH HERBS
AND OLIVE OIL

◆

PEACH-GRILLED LOBSTERS
WITH ROASTED YELLOW
PEPPER–BASIL MAYONNAISE

◆

GRILLED CORN
WITH BACON-MUSTARD BUTTER

◆

GRILLED NEW POTATOES
*page 126*

◆

RED PLUM AND MARMALADE TART

WHEN I IMAGINE a menu that perfectly sums up what summer eating should be, this is the menu.

**SERVING STRATEGY** Fresh, rindless cheeses made from goat's and sheep's milk are full of the tang of the milk itself. The best cheeses are domestic or are flown in from France or Italy by conscientious cheesemongers. Naming a specific variety is difficult, but choose one or two fresh cheeses (see Cook's Sources) and set them on a white plate. Generously drizzle good olive oil over the cheeses, sprinkle them with minced fresh herbs—basil, thyme, oregano, or rosemary—and season generously with fresh black pepper. Offer a crusty whole-grain, plain, or walnut bread for scooping and spreading.

## PEACH-GRILLED LOBSTERS WITH ROASTED YELLOW PEPPER–BASIL MAYONNAISE

3 live lobsters (about 2
    pounds each)
2 cups peach or other wood
    chips
Roasted Yellow
    Pepper–Basil
    Mayonnaise (recipe
    follows)
Sprigs of fresh basil, as
    garnish

LOBSTERS GRILL WONDERFULLY, and the smoky edge produced by the combination of peach wood and slightly charred shell perfectly complements the sweet meat. Grill them first (they're particularly good lukewarm) and then grill the corn and potatoes.

Soak the wood chips in water to cover 30 minutes.

Kill the lobsters by inserting the point of a long knife into the top of the lobster where the head and body shell meet. Turn them over and, using the knife, split the lobsters. Remove the sac from the head. With the heavy butt of the knife blade, crack the claws.

Drain the wood chips. Prepare a charcoal fire and let it burn until the coals are evenly white, or preheat a gas grill. Scatter the wood chips over the coals or grillstones. When the chips are smoking arrange the lobster halves cut side up on the grill. Cover and cook 7 minutes, then turn the lobsters cut side down, cover, and grill another 7 to 10 minutes, or until just done.

Arrange the lobsters on 1 or 2 platters. Place a small bowl of Roasted Yellow Pepper–Basil Mayonnaise on each platter and garnish the platters with the sprigs of basil. Serve hot or lukewarm.

━━● *Serves 6*

◆ ◆ ◆ ◆ ◆ ◆ ◆ ◆ ◆ ◆ ◆ ◆ ◆ ◆ ◆ ◆ ◆ ◆ ◆ ◆ ◆ ◆ ◆ ◆ ◆ ◆ ◆ ◆ ◆ ◆ ◆ ◆ ◆ ◆ ◆ ◆ ◆ ◆ ◆ ◆

**SERVING STRATEGY** The Grilled New Potatoes (see page 126) are quick and easy when cooked along with the lobsters. They're also delicious with any extra Bacon-Mustard Butter, but the New Potato Salad with Peas and Mint (page 308) or the Lemon-Rice Salad (page 186) would also be good accompaniments.

◆ ◆ ◆ ◆ ◆ ◆ ◆ ◆ ◆ ◆ ◆ ◆ ◆ ◆ ◆ ◆ ◆ ◆ ◆ ◆ ◆ ◆ ◆ ◆ ◆ ◆ ◆ ◆ ◆ ◆ ◆ ◆ ◆ ◆ ◆ ◆ ◆ ◆ ◆ ◆

## ROASTED YELLOW PEPPER–BASIL MAYONNAISE

◆ ◆ ◆ ◆ ◆ ◆ ◆ ◆ ◆

**S**INCE YOUR GUESTS will like this mayonnaise as much as mine do, you may not have any leftovers; if you do, try it on chicken or turkey sandwiches or as a dip for cool poached shrimp. If you can't find a yellow pepper, a sweet orange or red one will work just as well.

◆ ◆ ◆  ◆ ◆ ◆

In the open flame of a gas burner, or under a preheated broiler, roast the pepper until the skin is charred. In a paper bag, or in a bowl covered with a plate, steam the pepper until cool. Peel the pepper and wipe with paper

*1 large, sweet yellow pepper*
*4 egg yolks*
*3 tablespoons lemon juice*
*½ teaspoon salt*
*½ cup olive oil*
*1 cup corn oil*
*⅓ cup finely minced fresh basil*
*Freshly ground black pepper*

towels. Cut away and discard the core and ribs. Chop the pepper.

In a food processor combine the pepper, the egg yolks, 1 tablespoon of the lemon juice, and ½ teaspoon of salt. Process until smooth. With the machine running, slowly dribble in the oils. Transfer the mayonnaise to a bowl and stir in the basil, a generous grind of pepper, and the remaining lemon juice, to taste. Adjust the seasoning with additional salt and pepper, if necessary. This mayonnaise is best served the day it is made.

*Makes about 2½ cups*

## GRILLED CORN WITH BACON-MUSTARD BUTTER

♦ ♦ ♦ ♦ ♦ ♦ ♦ ♦ ♦

¼ *pound smoky sliced bacon, minced*

*2 sticks unsalted butter, softened*

*3 tablespoons mild, prepared coarse-grained mustard*

*1 teaspoon freshly ground black pepper*

*12 ears of sweet corn, with husks*

CHOOSE YOUNG, SUPERSWEET corn hybrids, such as Cream and Sugar or Summer Sweet.

♦ ♦ ♦  ♦ ♦ ♦

In a skillet over medium heat cook the bacon until crisp but tender.

In a bowl cream together the butter, bacon, and mustard. Stir in the pepper. Transfer the butter to a bowl or small crock. *The butter can be refrigerated for up to 3 days, covered, or frozen for 1 month. Soften to room temperature before using.*

Do not remove the husks or silks from the corn. Lay the ears on the grill rack and cook them, turning once or twice, until the outer husks are charred, 5 to 7 minutes.

Peel the corn (or let the guests peel their own) and serve immediately, accompanied by the Bacon-Mustard Butter and a pepper mill.

*Serves 6*

# RED PLUM
# AND MARMALADE TART

♦ ♦ ♦ ♦ ♦ ♦ ♦ ♦ ♦

**W**HILE EVERYONE ELSE is taking it easy, a bit of simple baking—like this colorful plum tart—can earn you kitchen kudos.

For best color and flavor, select a firm, sweet plum with a tart red skin, such as the widely available Santa Rosa variety. Serve the dessert plain or with a dollop of sour or whipped cream.

*For the crust* In a small bowl whisk together the egg, egg yolk, and vanilla.

In a medium-size bowl combine the flour, sugar, and salt. Cut in the chilled butter and vegetable shortening until the mixture resembles coarse meal. Stir in the egg mixture. The dough will be loose and crumbly.

Transfer the dough to a fluted, 11-inch, loose-bottomed tart pan and pat it firmly and evenly into place. Chill 1 hour.

Position a rack in the upper third of the oven and preheat to 350 degrees F.

*For the topping* Quarter and pit the plums and slice each quarter in half. Beginning at the edge of the crust, arrange the plums in close-fitting concentric circles, until the crust is completely covered. Sprinkle the plums with the sugar. Bake the tart for 45 to 50 minutes, or until the crust is firm and golden and the plums are oozing juices. Cool to room temperature on a rack.

In a small pan over low heat, melt the marmalade. Cool slightly, then brush generously and evenly over the surface of the tart, using all the marmalade. Cool completely before cutting.

━● *Serves 8*

♦ ♦ ♦ ♦ ♦ ♦ ♦ ♦ ♦ ♦ ♦ ♦ ♦ ♦ ♦ ♦ ♦ ♦ ♦ ♦ ♦ ♦ ♦ ♦ ♦ ♦ ♦ ♦ ♦ ♦ ♦ ♦ ♦ ♦ ♦ ♦ ♦ ♦ ♦ ♦ ♦

COOKIE CRUST

*1 egg*

*1 egg yolk*

*1 teaspoon vanilla*

*1½ cups unbleached all-purpose flour*

*⅓ cup sugar*

*Pinch of salt*

*4 tablespoons unsalted butter, well chilled and cut into small pieces*

*2 tablespoons solid vegetable shortening, well chilled and cut into small pieces*

TOPPING

*2 pounds (about 12) medium red plums*

*2 tablespoons sugar*

*⅔ cup good-quality orange marmalade*

# MENU

◆ ◆ ◆ ◆ ◆ ◆ ◆ ◆ ◆ ◆ ◆ ◆ ◆ ◆

HARD SAUSAGE AND CHEESE
SALAD WITH BALSAMIC–MUSTARD
SEED DRESSING

◆

PESTO BREAD
*page 68*

◆

STRAWBERRIES WITH
BROWN SUGAR SAUCE
*page 313*

ON-CALL FOOD, ready when you are, is a plus any time of the year, and particularly in the summer. The sturdy, mayonnaise-free salad is portable, if you're picnicking; the pesto bread is ready in minutes if you're near a stove (if you're not, any good crusty bread will do), and the dessert is old-fashioned summer simplicity—and just as good when made with blueberries, blackberries, or raspberries.

# HARD SAUSAGE AND CHEESE SALAD WITH BALSAMIC–MUSTARD SEED DRESSING

♦♦♦♦♦♦♦♦♦♦

**T**HE GREATEST VIRTUE of this salad—aside from its requiring virtually no cooking—is the speed with which it goes together. Salami, soppressata, or a hot and spicy hard sausage will all work well here.

♦♦♦  ♦♦♦

In a small bowl combine the balsamic vinegar and mustard seeds and let stand at room temperature for 30 minutes. Whisk the oil into the vinegar.

In a pan of boiling water cook the corn for 3 minutes. Drain and cool slightly. Cut the kernels from the corn.

In a large bowl combine the corn, sausage, cheese, peppers, and onions and toss. Add the vinegar dressing and toss again. Adjust the seasoning with a pinch of salt and a generous grind of pepper. *The salad can be assembled to this point up to 3 hours ahead. Cover and refrigerate, bringing fully to room temperature before serving.*

Line the serving plates with the lettuce leaves. Toss the salad and spoon it onto the lined plates, forming a slight mound.

NOTE Fresh summer corn, tender and delicious though it is, can get lost in this robust salad. You may wish to substitute a 10-ounce package of frozen kernel corn, well drained (it requires no cooking), and save the prime ears of sweet corn for eating whole with butter at another meal.

➥ *Serves 4*

♦♦♦♦♦♦♦♦♦♦♦♦♦♦♦♦♦♦♦♦♦♦♦♦♦♦♦♦♦♦♦♦♦♦♦♦♦♦♦♦♦

*1/3 cup balsamic vinegar*

*1 tablespoon yellow mustard seeds*

*3/4 cup olive oil*

*5 ears of sweet, very tender corn ( see note )*

*1 pound hard sausage, trimmed and cut into 1/2-inch cubes*

*3/4 pound hard cheese, such as mild provolone, Gruyère, or cheddar*

*2 sweet red or orange peppers, stemmed, cored, and cut into 1/4-inch dice*

*4 green onions, trimmed and sliced thin*

*Pinch of salt*

*Freshly ground black pepper*

*1 head romaine lettuce, separated, washed, and patted dry*

# MENU

◆◆◆◆◆◆◆◆◆◆◆◆◆◆

CHUNKY GUACAMOLE
*see page 30*

◆

GRILLED CUMIN SHRIMP ON
BLACK BEAN SALAD

◆

FLOUR TORTILLAS
WARMED ON THE GRILL
*or*
PERFECT CORN BREAD
*page 71*

◆

FRESH PINEAPPLE
WITH HONEY AND LIME JUICE

MANY OF MY FAVORITE summertime main courses really consist of two contrasting elements in a single recipe. There is at least the illusion of less kitchen time, and the forgiving nature of the best of these meals, which can be partially prepared in advance or which taste good cool if your schedule gets disrupted, fit the casual summer mood—even when the results are showstopping. The shrimp and black bean dish in particular makes for spectacular hot weather eating.

# GRILLED CUMIN SHRIMP
# ON BLACK BEAN SALAD

♦♦♦♦♦♦♦♦♦

**W**HERE DO IDEAS for recipes come from? This one began with an image, nothing more, of pink and brown grilled shrimp on a mound of black beans. It went through several incarnations before coming together in this toothsome form.

♦♦♦  ♦♦♦

*For the bean salad* In a large bowl cover the beans with cold water and soak overnight. Drain the beans and transfer them to a heavy pot. Cover the beans with fresh cold water, set the pan over medium heat, and bring to a boil. Partially cover, lower the heat, and simmer for 30 minutes. Stir in 1 tablespoon of salt and continue to cook until the beans are just tender, another 20 to 30 minutes. Drain and transfer to a bowl.

In a small bowl whisk together the olive oil, sherry vinegar, mustard, and 1 teaspoon of salt. Pour the dressing over the warm beans and let them stand, stirring once or twice, until cool. *The recipe can be prepared to this point up to 1 day ahead. Cover and refrigerate. Let the beans come to room temperature before proceeding.*

Stir in the peppers, onions, and basil. Add a generous grind of pepper and adjust the seasoning.

*For the shrimp* In a blender or small food processor combine the olive oil, lime juice, cumin, garlic, jalapeño, and salt and process until smooth. In a large, nonreactive bowl, combine the puree with the shrimp and marinate at least 4 hours. *The shrimp can be covered and marinated in the refrigerator overnight. Return them to room temperature before grilling.*

Soak the wood chips in water for 30 minutes. Prepare a charcoal fire and let it burn until the coals are evenly white, or preheat a gas grill. Thread the shrimp

BLACK BEAN SALAD

*1 pound dried black beans,
    picked over*
*Salt*
*¾ cup olive oil*
*⅓ cup sherry vinegar*
*1 tablespoon prepared
    Dijon-style mustard*
*2 sweet peppers (1 yellow
    and 1 red), stemmed,
    seeded, and cut into
    ½-inch dice*
*1 bunch green onions,
    trimmed and sliced*
*½ cup finely chopped basil*
*Freshly ground black
    pepper*

GRILLED CUMIN SHRIMP

*¼ cup olive oil*
*3 tablespoons fresh lime
    juice*
*1 tablespoon ground
    cumin, from toasted
    seeds (page 66)*
*2 garlic cloves, peeled*
*1 fresh jalapeño, stemmed*
*¾ teaspoon salt*
*2 pounds (about 36) large
    shrimp, shelled and
    deveined*
*2 cups mesquite or other
    hardwood chips*
*1 medium head romaine
    lettuce, leaves separated,
    washed, and patted dry*
*Sprigs of fresh basil, as
    garnish*

on skewers, fitting them closely together. Smear any remaining marinade over the shrimp. Drain the chips and scatter them over the coals or grillstones. When the chips are smoking, lay the skewers on the grill. Cover the grill and cook, turning the shrimp once, until they are lightly browned and just done, 4 to 5 minutes.

To serve, slide the shrimp off the skewers. Line plates with the lettuce. Spoon the bean salad onto the lettuce. Arrange the shrimp over each portion of bean salad and garnish each plate with a sprig of the basil.

*Serves 6 to 8*

**SERVING STRATEGY** Quarter the pineapples vertically, leaving the leaves as intact as possible. Cut away the hard core, then cut between the pineapple flesh and rind, releasing it in one wedge. Cut the wedge into bite-size pieces and reassemble them on the rind. Cover and chill. Just before serving, drizzle the pineapple with honey. Serve, accompanied by wedges of fresh lime.

# MENU

◆ ◆ ◆ ◆ ◆ ◆ ◆ ◆ ◆ ◆ ◆ ◆ ◆ ◆

VEAL AND CHICKEN LOAF
WITH ARUGULA MAYONNAISE

◆

CARROT AND RED PEPPER SLAW
*page 39*

◆

HERBED PROSCIUTTO FLATBREAD

◆

ICED SWEET CHERRIES

◆

CORNMEAL BUTTER COOKIES
*page 113*
*or*
LEMON SUGAR COOKIES
*page 93*

I HAVE THIS LISTED in my original notes as a menu for a "pool party," and though I've never had the chance to enjoy it by a pool, it is the sort of ready-when-you-are menu that is suited to casual summer entertaining.

## VEAL AND CHICKEN LOAF WITH ARUGULA MAYONNAISE

♦♦♦♦♦♦♦♦♦♦

2 cups canned chicken
  broth or homemade stock
3 teaspoons salt
4 ounces (1 stick) unsalted
  butter
2 cups unbleached
  all-purpose flour (to
  measure, sift into
  measuring cups and
  sweep level)
4 eggs, at room
  temperature
4 egg whites, at room
  temperature
1 pound veal, trimmed and
  cut into ½-inch pieces
1 pound boneless, skinless
  chicken breast, trimmed
  and cut into ½-inch
  pieces
3 medium leeks, white part
  only, cleaned thoroughly
  and chopped
1 teaspoon dried thyme,
  crumbled
½ teaspoon freshly grated
  nutmeg
¼ teaspoon cayenne pepper
1 cup whipping cream,
  well chilled
4 ripe beefsteak tomatoes,
  sliced into thick rounds
Arugula Mayonnaise
  (recipe follows)
Arugula leaves, as garnish

**C**OOL, RICH AND MEATY, this moist, do-ahead loaf makes splendid hot weather eating. It is served in thick slices, garnished with slabs of ripe, red beefsteak tomatoes, and topped with a peppery arugula mayonnaise. Leftovers make good sandwiches.

♦♦♦  ♦♦♦

In a medium-size, heavy saucepan combine the broth, 2 teaspoons of the salt, and the butter. Set over medium heat and cook just until the liquid boils and the butter melts. Remove from the heat and add the flour all at once, whisking vigorously to prevent lumping. Set the pan over low heat and cook, stirring with a heavy spoon, until the dough is thick and pulls away from the sides of the pan, about 5 minutes.

Remove from the heat and beat in the eggs, one at a time. Add the egg whites and beat until shiny and smooth, about 5 minutes. Cover the dough and let it stand at room temperature.

Position a rack in the center of the oven and preheat to 350 degrees F. Generously butter a 12-cup loaf pan. In a food processor coarsely chop the veal using 4 to 5 brief bursts of power. Add the chicken and coarsely chop using 4 to 5 brief bursts of power. Add the remaining salt, the leeks, thyme, nutmeg, and pepper and blend 1 minute. With the machine running, add the cream through the feed tube in a thin stream, stopping once to scrape down the sides of the bowl. Add the meat mixture to the dough and blend well. Spoon the mixture into the prepared pan. Smooth the top using the back of a metal spoon dipped in cold water. Tap the pan on the work surface several times to eliminate air bubbles. Wrap the pan tightly in buttered foil. Set the loaf pan in a shallow roasting pan. Add enough boiling wa-

ter to the roasting pan to come halfway up the sides of
the loaf pan. Bake about 1½ hours, or until a tester
inserted in the loaf comes out *almost* clean. An instant-
reading thermometer inserted in the center of the loaf
should register 180 degrees F.

Remove the loaf pan from the water bath. Remove
the foil and cool the loaf to room temperature. Wrap
well and refrigerate until cold and firm, preferably
overnight. *The loaf can be prepared to this point up to
three days ahead.*

To unmold, run a thin, sharp knife around the edge
of the pan. Dip the bottom of the pan in hot water for 2
minutes. Invert the pan onto a cutting board and tap
the bottom; the loaf will drop out.

To serve, cut the loaf into thick slices. On a platter
alternate slices of the loaf and the tomatoes. Drizzle
half of the Arugula Mayonnaise over the sliced food,
and garnish with the arugula leaves. Pass the remaining mayonnaise at the table.

*Serves 10 to 12*

## ARUGULA MAYONNAISE

T HIS TART, green mayonnaise is also good on cold
poached seafood or chicken, and it makes a fine dip for
crudités.

Bring a pan of lightly salted water to a boil. Remove
from the heat. Stir in the arugula. Drain immediately
and at once plunge the arugula into a bowl of ice water.
Cool completely. Drain well and squeeze dry. Coarsely
chop the arugula.

In a food processor combine the arugula, eggs, egg
yolk, vinegar, mustard, salt, and a generous grind of

4 cups (about 3 medium
  bunches) clean, packed,
  trimmed arugula
2 eggs
1 egg yolk
⅓ cup white wine vinegar
1 tablespoon prepared
  Dijon-style mustard
1 teaspoon salt
Freshly ground black
  pepper
1 cup olive oil
1 cup corn oil

pepper. Process 1 minute. With the motor running add the oils through the feed tube in a slow stream. Adjust the seasoning and transfer the mayonnaise to a bowl. Cover and refrigerate until use. *The mayonnaise can be prepared up to 4 hours in advance.*

━━● *Makes about 3 cups*

◆◆◆◆◆◆◆◆◆◆◆◆◆◆◆◆◆◆◆◆◆◆◆◆◆◆◆◆◆◆◆◆◆◆◆◆◆◆◆◆◆◆◆◆◆◆◆

## HERBED PROSCIUTTO FLATBREAD

◆◆◆◆◆◆◆◆◆◆

1 envelope dry yeast

2 cups warm water (105 to 115 degrees F)

5½ cups (about) unbleached all-purpose flour

1 tablespoon freshly ground black pepper

2 teaspoons salt

½-pound slab prosciutto, trimmed and cut into ¼-inch dice

¼ cup minced fresh rosemary

¼ cup minced fresh oregano or marjoram

4 tablespoons olive oil

¼ cup cornmeal

T HE SLOW SPONGE-RISING method used here produces a moist, flavorful loaf. Baked immediately after it is spread in the pan, the bread will be thin and relatively crisp. Left to rise for 30 minutes before baking will produce a thicker, more traditional *foccacia*. Serve it warm, at room temperature, or brush generously with olive oil and toast on the grill.

◆◆◆  ◆◆◆

In a large bowl combine the yeast and water. Stir to dissolve. Let stand until foamy, about 10 minutes. Whisk in 2 cups of the flour and the pepper and salt. Cover the batter loosely with plastic wrap or foil and refrigerate 12 hours.

Stir 2 cups of the flour into the batter. Sprinkle the work surface with ½ cup of the flour. Turn the dough onto the surface. Sprinkle the dough with ½ cup of the flour. Knead until the flour is incorporated, about 5 minutes. Pat the dough onto a 12-inch circle. Sprinkle the prosciutto, rosemary, and oregano over the dough. Gather the dough into a ball and knead until the prosciutto and herbs are evenly distributed, about 5 minutes. Coat a large bowl with 2 tablespoons of the oil. Add the dough, turning to coat its entire surface. Cover loosely with plastic wrap or foil and refrigerate 4 hours.

Position a rack in the upper third of the oven and preheat to 475 degrees F. Sprinkle a 12 × 18-inch jelly-roll pan or baking sheet with the cornmeal. Flour the work surface and your hands with the remaining flour. Turn the dough out onto the surface. Pat the dough into a 12 × 18-inch rectangle. Transfer to the prepared pan; stretch and pat the dough to fit. Drizzle the remaining olive oil over the dough. Bake immediately, or let the dough rise, uncovered, at room temperature, for 30 minutes. Bake until golden, 20 to 25 minutes. Cool on a rack.

*Serves 8*

◆ ◆ ◆ ◆ ◆ ◆ ◆ ◆ ◆ ◆ ◆ ◆ ◆ ◆ ◆ ◆ ◆ ◆ ◆ ◆ ◆ ◆ ◆ ◆ ◆ ◆ ◆ ◆ ◆ ◆ ◆ ◆ ◆ ◆ ◆ ◆ ◆ ◆ ◆ ◆ ◆ ◆ ◆

**SERVING STRATEGY** In a heavy crockery bowl cover sweet, dark summer cherries (Bing, Lambert, Rainier, and Royal Anne) with water and refrigerate. Just before serving, add a tray of ice cubes to the chilled water and set the bowl on the table. Encourage guests to enjoy the cold, clean, crisp cherries directly from the icy bath. Either the Cornmeal Butter Cookies (page 113) or the Lemon Sugar Cookies (page 93) are a good but optional accompaniment.

◆ ◆ ◆ ◆ ◆ ◆ ◆ ◆ ◆ ◆ ◆ ◆ ◆ ◆ ◆ ◆ ◆ ◆ ◆ ◆ ◆ ◆ ◆ ◆ ◆ ◆ ◆ ◆ ◆ ◆ ◆ ◆ ◆ ◆ ◆ ◆ ◆ ◆ ◆ ◆ ◆ ◆ ◆ ◆

# MENU

◆ ◆ ◆ ◆ ◆ ◆ ◆ ◆ ◆ ◆ ◆ ◆ ◆ ◆

SMALL PIZZAS WITH CLAMS, BACON,
JALAPEÑOS, AND OREGANO

◆

GRILLED TUNA STEAKS WITH
MINT AND LEMON BUTTER

◆

RATATOUILLE VINAIGRETTE

◆

FRESH POTATO CHIPS
*page 40*
*or*
GRILLED NEW POTATOES
*page 126*

◆

PINEAPPLE-MACADAMIA
PRALINE TART

THIS IS A LITTLE summer grill supper for four, inspired by the cooking of the new American cafés. Instead of dinner at Spago or Stars, cook this up at home. Since your kitchen brigade (like mine) is probably smaller than Wolfgang's or Jeremiah's, the menu has plenty of do-ahead steps, so you'll stay cool and calm.

▼▼▼▼▼▼▼▼▼▼▼▼▼▼▼▼▼▼▼▼▼▼▼▼▼▼▼▼▼▼▼▼▼▼

## SMALL PIZZAS WITH CLAMS, BACON, JALAPEÑOS, AND OREGANO

♦♦♦♦♦♦♦♦♦

**T**HIS METHOD OF PREPARING and refrigerating the dough before rolling duplicates what I see at my neighborhood pizza parlor. Pliable and easy to handle, the chilled dough bakes into a tidy eye-appealing crust that is crisp and tasty.

I thought I had made up this topping combination, but in her comprehensive pizza treatise, *The Pizza Book* (Times Books), Evelyn Sloman says it is a New England speciality. It's also good when made with coarsely diced sea scallops in place of the clams, and other fresh herbs—rosemary, marjoram, or basil—can be substituted.

♦♦♦  ♦♦♦

*For the dough* In a medium-size bowl sprinkle the yeast over the water. Let stand 5 minutes; stir to dissolve. Add the salt, then stir in 2 to 2½ cups of the flour to form a soft dough. Dust the work surface with ¼ cup of the flour. Turn the dough out onto the prepared surface. Knead until smooth and elastic, about 5 minutes, adding up to ½ cup more of the flour if the dough remains sticky. Divide the dough into 4 pieces. Dust each with flour and form into a ball. Divide the oil among 4 small bowls. Place 1 ball of dough in each bowl, turn to coat with oil, cover tightly with plastic, and refrigerate for *at least* 24 hours. *The dough can be prepared up to 48 hours before baking.*

*To assemble* Preheat the oven to 500 degrees F for at least 30 minutes. In a small, heavy skillet over medium heat fry the bacon, stirring, until crisp and brown, about 10 minutes. Drain.

Sprinkle the cornmeal evenly over 2 heavy 11 × 17-inch baking sheets, preferably of black metal. Lightly flour the work surface. Flatten each ball of

PIZZA DOUGH

*1½ teaspoons dry yeast*
*1¼ cups warm water (105 to 115 degrees F)*
*2 teaspoons salt*
*3¼ cups (about) unbleached all-purpose flour*
*4 teaspoons olive oil*

TOPPING

*½ pound slab bacon, trimmed and cut into ¼-inch dice*
*⅓ cup yellow cornmeal*
*¾ pound low-moisture mozzarella cheese (see note), cut into ⅛-inch slices*
*1 or 2 fresh jalapeños, stemmed and sliced into thin rounds*
*⅓ cup clean, loosely packed fresh oregano leaves*
*32 littleneck clams, shucked*

dough into a 7-inch round, creating a ⅜-inch raised rim around the edge. Transfer each round to the prepared baking sheets. Lay the mozzarella evenly over the dough. Sprinkle each pizza with the bacon, jalapeños, oregano, and clams. Bake until the crust is lightly browned and crisp, 12 to 15 minutes, reversing the position of the baking sheets in the oven halfway through.

NOTE For perfect melting on pizza and in baked pasta dishes, whole or skim milk mozzarella labeled "low moisture" is the one to buy. For eating uncooked, lightly salted, freshly made mozzarella, available in specialty cheese shops and Italian groceries, is the ideal choice.

*Serves 4*

♦ ♦ ♦ ♦ ♦ ♦ ♦ ♦ ♦ ♦ ♦ ♦ ♦ ♦ ♦ ♦ ♦ ♦ ♦ ♦ ♦ ♦ ♦ ♦ ♦ ♦ ♦ ♦ ♦ ♦ ♦ ♦ ♦ ♦ ♦ ♦ ♦ ♦ ♦ ♦

## GRILLED TUNA STEAKS WITH MINT AND LEMON BUTTER

♦ ♦ ♦ ♦ ♦ ♦ ♦ ♦ ♦

*2 cups mesquite or other hardwood chips*
*4 tuna steaks (each 6 to 8 ounces, cut about 1 inch thick)*
*2 tablespoons olive oil*
*Coarse salt*
*Mint and Lemon Butter (recipe follows)*
*Fresh mint, as garnish*

SWORDFISH, shark, or salmon steaks can be used in place of the tuna.

♦ ♦ ♦    ♦ ♦ ♦

Soak the wood chips in water for 30 minutes. Prepare a charcoal fire and let it die down to a bed of evenly white coals, or preheat a gas grill. Drain the wood chips and scatter them over the hot coals or grillstones. Brush the tuna steaks with the olive oil. When the wood chips are smoking, lay the tuna steaks on the grill, about 4 inches above the fire. Cover and cook, turning once, until the fish is lightly browned but still pink inside, about 4 minutes per side. Transfer the fish to plates, sprinkle with coarse salt, and top each steak with a ½-inch slice of Mint and Lemon Butter. Garnish with fresh mint and serve immediately.

*Serves 4*

♦ ♦ ♦ ♦ ♦ ♦ ♦ ♦ ♦ ♦ ♦ ♦ ♦ ♦ ♦ ♦ ♦ ♦ ♦ ♦ ♦ ♦ ♦ ♦ ♦ ♦ ♦ ♦ ♦ ♦ ♦ ♦ ♦ ♦ ♦ ♦ ♦ ♦ ♦ ♦

## MINT AND LEMON BUTTER

♦ ♦ ♦ ♦ ♦ ♦ ♦ ♦ ♦

In a small bowl blend the butter, mint, lemon zest, and pepper. Form the mixture into a cylinder 2 inches long. Wrap the butter in plastic and refrigerate. *The butter can be prepared up to 2 days ahead and refrigerated, or it can be prepared up to 1 month ahead and frozen.* Soften the butter at room temperature for 15 minutes before using.

●—● *Makes about ½ cup*

6 tablespoons (¾ stick) unsalted butter, at room temperature
¼ cup minced fresh mint
Zest of 1 medium lemon, minced
½ teaspoon freshly ground white pepper

## RATATOUILLE VINAIGRETTE

♦ ♦ ♦ ♦ ♦ ♦ ♦ ♦ ♦

Fennel makes this easy side dish particularly compatible with fish (especially a rich and oily fish), but celery can be substituted. Serve the ratatouille at room temperature.

Trim the eggplant and quarter it lengthwise. Cut each quarter crosswise into 1-inch pieces. Trim the zucchini and halve it lengthwise. Cut each half crosswise into 1-inch pieces. Combine the eggplant and zucchini in a colander. Sprinkle with 1 tablespoon of salt and let stand 1 hour, tossing once or twice.

Drain the eggplant and zucchini on paper towels and pat dry. Discard the tough outer layer of the fennel and peel away any strings. Core and trim the fennel and cut it into ½-inch pieces.

In a large heavy skillet heat ⅓ cup of the olive oil over high heat. Add the eggplant and zucchini and cook, stirring and tossing, until brown, about 5 minutes. With a slotted spoon, transfer the vegetables to a medium-size bowl. Lower the heat to medium. Add the fennel and the sweet pepper and cook, stirring, until

1 small eggplant (about ¾ pound)
1 medium zucchini (about ½ pound), scrubbed
Salt
1 small fennel bulb
⅔ cup olive oil
1 large, sweet red pepper, stemmed, trimmed, and cut into 1-inch squares
1 medium onion, peeled and sliced
3 garlic cloves, peeled and minced
5 large Italian plum tomatoes (about 1¼ pounds), peeled, seeded, and coarsely chopped
¼ cup red wine vinegar
Freshly ground black pepper

golden, about 5 minutes. With a slotted spoon transfer them to a large bowl. Add the remaining olive oil to the skillet. Stir in the onion and garlic and cook, covered, stirring once or twice, until the onion is very tender, about 15 minutes. Return the eggplant and zucchini to the skillet. Add the tomatoes. Season lightly with salt and bring to a simmer. Cook, uncovered, stirring occasionally, until the vegetables are tender, about 10 minutes. Transfer the contents of the skillet to the bowl containing the pepper and fennel. Stir in the vinegar and a generous grind of pepper. Cool completely. Adjust the seasoning, adding more vinegar if desired. *The ratatouille can be prepared up to 2 days in advance. Cover and refrigerate, returning it to room temperature before serving.*

*Serves 4*

♦ ♦ ♦ ♦ ♦ ♦ ♦ ♦ ♦ ♦ ♦ ♦ ♦ ♦ ♦ ♦ ♦ ♦ ♦ ♦ ♦ ♦ ♦ ♦ ♦ ♦ ♦ ♦ ♦ ♦ ♦ ♦ ♦ ♦ ♦ ♦ ♦ ♦ ♦ ♦ ♦ ♦ ♦

## PINEAPPLE-MACADAMIA PRALINE TART

♦ ♦ ♦ ♦ ♦ ♦ ♦ ♦ ♦

**T**HE BRIGHT TROPICAL flavors and colors of this fruit-and-praline tart conclude the menu with style. Though the tart should be assembled as close to serving time as possible, the various components can be prepared well in advance. Reserve the extra praline to sprinkle over your favorite ice cream.

♦ ♦ ♦  ♦ ♦ ♦

*For the pastry cream* In a medium-size bowl whisk the egg yolks and sugar to blend. Stir in the flour. In a small, heavy saucepan over medium heat bring the half-and-half to a boil. Slowly whisk the hot cream into the yolk mixture. Return the mixture to the saucepan, set it over medium-low heat, and whisk constantly until the mixture thickens and becomes lumpy, about 5 minutes. Whisk until smooth, lower the heat, and cook,

GINGER PASTRY CREAM

*3 egg yolks*

*⅓ cup sugar*

*⅓ cup unbleached all-purpose flour*

*1 cup half-and-half*

*2 tablespoons (¼ stick) unsalted butter, at room temperature*

*2 tablespoons finely minced crystallized ginger*

*¼ teaspoon vanilla extract*

stirring constantly, for 3 minutes. Transfer immediately to a small bowl and whisk in the butter, ginger, and vanilla. Cover the pastry cream with plastic wrap, pressing it onto the surface of the cream, and refrigerate. *The pastry cream can be prepared to this point up to 2 days ahead.*

*For the crust* In a bowl or food processor combine the flour, sugar, and salt. Cut in the butter and shortening until a coarse meal forms. Blend in the water 1 tablespoon at a time until a soft dough forms. Turn the dough out onto a lightly floured surface, flatten it into a disc, and wrap tightly in plastic. Refrigerate at least 45 minutes. *The crust can be prepared to this point up to 2 days ahead.*

On a lightly floured surface roll the dough out ⅛ inch thick. Fit it into a 9-inch tart shell with a loose bottom and trim the edges. Refrigerate 30 minutes. *The shell can be refrigerated, wrapped, for up to 1 day.*

Preheat the oven to 400 degrees F. Lightly prick the bottom of the shell with the tines of a fork. Line the pastry with foil or parchment and fill it with pie weights. Bake until the pastry is set, about 10 minutes. Remove the weights and foil. Bake until lightly brown, 10 to 12 minutes more. Cool the tart shell on a rack. *The shell can be baked up to 8 hours ahead.*

*For the glaze* In a small, heavy saucepan over low heat combine the marmalade and sugar. Stir to dissolve the sugar. Increase the heat and boil 3 minutes, stirring occasionally. Cool completely.

*To assemble* Set the tart shell on a flat plate. Spread the pastry cream in the shell. Arrange the pineapple slices in slightly overlapping circles atop the pastry cream, covering it completely. Brush the pineapple with the marmalade glaze, using it all. Sprinkle the glaze evenly with the praline. *The tart can be assembled up to 30 minutes before serving and refrigerated.* Cut the tart into wedges and serve.

*Serves 8*

PASTRY CRUST

*1½ cups unbleached
all-purpose flour*
*2 tablespoons sugar*
*Pinch of salt*
*6 tablespoons (¾ stick)
unsalted butter, well
chilled and cut into
small pieces*
*3 tablespoons solid
vegetable shortening,
well chilled and cut into
small pieces*
*3 to 4 tablespoons chilled
water*

GLAZE

*½ cup good-quality
marmalade*
*1 tablespoon sugar*

*½ large pineapple,
trimmed, cored, halved
lengthwise, and cut into
quarter rounds ⅛ inch
thick*
*⅓ cup chopped praline
(page 342), made with
macadamia nuts*

# MENU

◆◆◆◆◆◆◆◆◆◆◆◆◆◆

### MIXED GAME PÂTÉ
*page 317*

◆

### SHRIMP AND GREEN
### OLIVE PICNIC LOAF

◆

### CATFISH FRIED CHICKEN
*page 305*

◆

### SIMPLE ORANGE SLAW
*page 43*

◆

### BLUEBERRY CARROT CAKE

◆

### FRESH BLUEBERRIES

◆

### 32-LEMONADE
*page 312*
*or*
### PINK SANGRIA

NOT ALL FOOD is suitable for traveling, and not everyone wants to eat away from the comfort of home. For those who do, this menu is reasonably portable—solid food, *sans* mayonnaise, and most of it edible with the fingers. Of course it will be just as good if you do nothing more than take off your shoes and enjoy it on the front porch.

## SHRIMP AND GREEN OLIVE PICNIC LOAF

◆◆◆◆◆◆◆◆◆◆

**S**TUFFED FULL OF PINK SHRIMP and green olives, and dressed with rich sherry vinegar, the sandwich loaf doubles as a sturdy appetizer or a main course.

Bring a pan of lightly salted water to a boil. Stir in the shrimp and remove from the heat. Let the shrimp stand in the water, stirring twice, until they are opaque and curled and turn a bright pink, 1½ to 2 minutes. Drain immediately and cool completely.

Coarsely chop the shrimp. In a medium-size bowl combine the shrimp, olive oil, parsley, vinegar, olives, and celery. Season lightly with the salt and generously with the pepper, to taste.

Using a long serrated knife, cut the bread in half horizontally. Pull out the soft interior crumb, leaving a ½-inch shell. Crumble the soft bread into the shrimp mixture and stir well. Divide the shrimp mixture among the 4 shells, packing it firmly and using it all. Re-form the shells into 2 loaves. Wrap each loaf tightly in plastic. Set the loaves on a baking sheet. Top the loaves with a second baking sheet and weigh down with a small skillet or similar object.

Refrigerate 1 hour. Turn the loaves, weigh down again, and refrigerate them at least 1 hour and not more than 3.

Using a serrated knife, cut the loaves into slices (thin slices for appetizers, thick slices for a main course) and serve.

━● *Serves 8 to 12 as an appetizer, 4 to 6 as a main course*

*Salt*

*1 pound (about 24) medium shrimp, shelled and deveined*

*¾ cup olive oil*

*½ cup minced Italian parsley*

*¼ cup sherry wine vinegar*

*3 ounces pimiento-stuffed green olives, drained and coarsely chopped*

*2 medium celery ribs, finely diced*

*Freshly ground black pepper*

*2 loaves (each 13 inches long and 2 to 2½ inches in diameter) sturdy French or Italian bread*

## B L U E B E R R Y   C A R R O T   C A K E

♦ ♦ ♦ ♦ ♦ ♦ ♦ ♦ ♦

2 cups unbleached
   all-purpose flour
2 teaspoons baking powder
2 teaspoons ground
   cinnamon
1 teaspoon baking soda
1 teaspoon salt
1 cup sugar
½ cup light brown sugar,
   firmly packed
1 cup corn oil
¼ walnut oil
4 eggs
4 medium carrots, peeled
   and coarsely grated
2 cups fresh blueberries
   (see note), rinsed and
   picked over
1 cup coarsely chopped
   walnuts

THIS MOIST, FIRM CAKE is ideal for eating out of hand. It's also a good "keeper," just the sort of casual-to-make, easy-to-eat dessert to have on hand during a free-form summer weekend. Not too sweet, it can be served at brunch, but when gussied up with a dollop of whipped cream and a sprinkle of fresh berries, it's pretty enough for a dinnertime finale.

Preheat the oven to 350 degrees F. Butter and flour a 10-cup bundt or ring pan, preferably nonstick; tap out excess flour.

In a medium-size bowl combine the flour, baking powder, cinnamon, baking soda, and salt. In a large bowl combine the sugars. Whisk in the oils. Beat in the eggs, one at a time, whisking until smooth. Stir in the carrots, blueberries, and walnuts. Add the dry ingredients and fold until just combined; do not overmix. The batter will be thick. Spoon the batter into the prepared pan and bake until the cake begins to pull away from the sides of the pan and a tester inserted into the center of the cake comes out clean, about 1 hour.

Cool the cake, in the pan, on a rack for 15 minutes. Invert onto a plate and cool completely before serving. *If you wish, the cake can be topped with the Pineapple-Rum Glaze (page 273). Store the cake at room temperature.*

NOTE You may substitute unsweetened frozen blueberries. Stir them into the cake without defrosting them.

Serves 8

## PINK SANGRIA

♦ ♦ ♦ ♦ ♦ ♦ ♦ ♦ ♦

IMPROVISATION IS THE NAME of this game. Use the best seasonal fruit you can find to flavor the sangria and garnish it with a perfect berry or two.

In a large pitcher, jar, or bowl combine the wine, *framboise,* and orange juice. Wash the fruit. Pit the stone fruits and slice them. Stir the fruit into the wine, cover, and refrigerate for at least 3 days, and up to 1 week.

Strain the mixture, discarding the softened fruit. Pour the sangria over ice in tall glasses. Garnish with the fresh fruit and mint and serve.

━━● *Serves 6 to 8*

♦ ♦ ♦ ♦ ♦ ♦ ♦ ♦ ♦ ♦ ♦ ♦ ♦ ♦ ♦ ♦ ♦ ♦ ♦ ♦ ♦ ♦ ♦ ♦ ♦ ♦ ♦ ♦ ♦ ♦ ♦ ♦ ♦ ♦ ♦ ♦ ♦ ♦ ♦ ♦

*1½ liters dry white wine*
*¾ cup framboise*
*(raspberry eau-de-vie)*
*Juice (about ½ cup) of 1*
*large orange, strained*
*About 2 pounds assorted*
*ripe fruit (peaches,*
*plums, cherries,*
*nectarines, or berries)*
*Additional fresh fruit and*
*sprigs of mint, as*
*garnish*

# MENU

◆ ◆ ◆ ◆ ◆ ◆ ◆ ◆ ◆ ◆ ◆ ◆ ◆ ◆

TUNA AND ROASTED RED
PEPPER MOUSSE
*page 123*

◆

GRILL-TOASTED COUNTRY BREAD

◆

GRILLED SQUAB AND ARUGULA
SALAD WITH
BLACK OLIVE VINAIGRETTE

◆

PLUM AND ZINFANDEL ICE

◆

CORNMEAL BUTTER COOKIES
*page 113*

THE BEST SUMMER FOOD is pared down to basics—prime ingredients, strong colors, intense flavors, and simple presentations.

## GRILL-TOASTED COUNTRY BREAD

♦ ♦ ♦ ♦ ♦ ♦ ♦ ♦ ♦

**A**S LONG AS THE GRILL is hot, why not use it to toast some thick slabs of country bread? The bread comes off the grill crisp and smoky, qualities that improve even the best of loaves.

Brush the bread with the oil. (For an herbal flavor, crush the herbs and marinate them in the oil for 1 hour first.) Turn the bread on the grill (using wood chips soaked in water for 30 minutes, drained well, and spread over the coals, if you wish), until crisply browned, 3 to 5 minutes per side.

Rub the bread with the cut side of the garlic, if you wish, sprinkle each side generously with pepper, and serve immediately.

*Serves 4*

♦ ♦ ♦ ♦ ♦ ♦ ♦ ♦ ♦ ♦ ♦ ♦ ♦ ♦ ♦ ♦ ♦ ♦ ♦ ♦ ♦ ♦ ♦ ♦ ♦ ♦ ♦ ♦ ♦ ♦ ♦ ♦ ♦ ♦ ♦

*8 thick slices of crusty country-style bread*
*⅓ cup olive oil*
*Several sprigs of fresh herbs, such as rosemary, basil, or oregano (optional)*
*1 head of garlic, cut in half (optional)*
*Freshly ground black pepper*

## GRILLED SQUAB AND ARUGULA SALAD WITH BLACK OLIVE VINAIGRETTE

♦ ♦ ♦ ♦ ♦ ♦ ♦ ♦ ♦

**T**HIS SALAD IS A powerful argument that the simplest food can also be the most elegant. Use *poussins* or small Cornish hens, if you wish, although the rich, dark flesh of the squab is really ideal with the tangy vinaigrette. Serve more of that good grilled bread and pour an excellent Chardonnay.

Cut down each side of the squab backbones from neck to tail. Discard the backbones. Crack the breastbones

*4 dressed squabs, about 1 pound each (see Cook's Sources)*
*20 brine-cured, imported black olives, such as Calamata (see Cook's Sources), pitted and coarsely chopped*
*1¼ cups olive oil*
*¼ cup sherry wine vinegar*

*(ingredients continued)*

¼ teaspoon salt
Freshly ground black
  pepper
2 cups apple, cherry, or
  peach fruit-wood chips
8 cups (2 large bunches)
  arugula leaves
1 pint yellow cherry or
  pear tomatoes, rinsed
  and halved

and flatten the squabs with the heel of your hand. Set aside.

In a small bowl whisk together the olives, olive oil, vinegar, salt, and a generous grind of fresh pepper. Soak the wood chips in water for 30 minutes.

Prepare a charcoal fire and let it burn until the coals are evenly white, or preheat a gas grill. Drain the soaked chips and scatter them over the coals or grill-stones. When the chips are smoking, lay the squabs on the grill, skin side down, and cook, turning them once, until they are a crisp, dark brown, about 10 minutes on each side. The squabs should be slightly pink and juicy inside. Remove them from the grill and let stand while arranging the salads.

Line 4 plates generously with the arugula. Scatter the tomatoes over the arugula. Set 1 squab in the center of each plate. Re-whisk the dressing and spoon over the salad, using it all. Serve the salads while the squabs are still warm, passing a pepper mill at the table.

—● Serves 4

♦ ♦ ♦ ♦ ♦ ♦ ♦ ♦ ♦ ♦ ♦ ♦ ♦ ♦ ♦ ♦ ♦ ♦ ♦ ♦ ♦ ♦ ♦ ♦ ♦ ♦ ♦ ♦ ♦ ♦ ♦ ♦ ♦ ♦ ♦ ♦ ♦ ♦ ♦ ♦ ♦

## PLUM AND ZINFANDEL ICE

♦ ♦ ♦ ♦ ♦ ♦ ♦ ♦ ♦

2 pounds (about 9) firm
  red plums, such as
  Santa Rosa, pitted and
  coarsely chopped
1½ cups zinfandel or other
  hearty red wine
1 cup sugar
1 piece (2 inches)
  cinnamon stick
2 bay leaves

**A** RIPE PLUM TASTES like red wine, and some zinfandels taste to me like plums, hence this pairing. Ice-cold, rich in color, and lush in flavor, this dessert is particularly delicious after the tart and smoky salad.

♦ ♦ ♦ ◖ ♦ ♦ ♦

In a 4-quart, nonreactive saucepan combine the plums, wine, sugar, ½ cup water, cinnamon stick, and bay leaves. Set the pan over the medium heat and bring to a boil, stirring to dissolve the sugar. Lower the heat and simmer, partially covered, skimming any foam that may form, until the plums are very tender, about 25 minutes.

Cool slightly and discard the cinnamon stick and bay leaves. Force the mixture through the medium disc of a food mill placed over a mixing bowl. There will be about 5 cups of puree. Cool completely, cover and refrigerate at least 5 hours, or until very cold.

Transfer the chilled mixture to the canister of an ice-cream maker and churn according to manufacturer's directions. Store the finished ice in the freezer. *The recipe can be prepared up to 2 days ahead. Soften the ice slightly in the refrigerator.* Serve immediately.

——● *Makes about 1½ quarts*

♦ ♦ ♦ ♦ ♦ ♦ ♦ ♦ ♦ ♦ ♦ ♦ ♦ ♦ ♦ ♦ ♦ ♦ ♦ ♦ ♦ ♦ ♦ ♦ ♦ ♦ ♦ ♦ ♦ ♦ ♦ ♦ ♦ ♦ ♦ ♦ ♦ ♦ ♦ ♦

# MENU

MIXED GAME PÂTÉ
*page 317*

GRILLED SALMON STEAKS WITH
A CHOICE OF COLD SAUCES

GAZPACHO SALSA
*or*
PINEAPPLE-*TOMATILLO* SALSA
*or*
*CHIPOTLE* VINAIGRETTE

GRILLED NEW POTATOES
*page 126*

GRILLED ZUCCHINI
*page 124*

FRESH BERRIES WITH
RASPBERRY CUSTARD SAUCE

THE RULES DON'T CHANGE in summer. People still get hungry and people still must be fed. The problem, of course, is the weather: There's too much of it and it's all too nice to miss for even a minute by hanging around the kitchen.

This menu illustrates one approach to no-sweat summer entertaining. Both the meaty, satisfying appetizer and the beautiful, light and seasonal dessert are done well ahead (or you may use a pâté and dessert purchased from your handy gourmet shop). One—or more—of the zesty sauces sits awaiting the moment the thick salmon steaks, zucchini, and potatoes come off the grill.

## GRILLED SALMON STEAKS WITH A CHOICE OF COLD SAUCES

♦ ♦ ♦ ♦ ♦ ♦ ♦ ♦ ♦

**N**O SEAFOOD GRILLS more satisfactorily than salmon. The rich, orange flesh comes from the grill crisp and smoky on the outside and wonderfully moist and flavorful on the inside. Firm steaks hold together better on the grill, but fillets will work well too. (If you plan to do a lot of outdoor fish cookery, consider purchasing a hinged grill basket—see Cook's Sources. It will make grilling a lot easier.)

Any of the three raw sauces below will enhance the fish; if you're feeding a crowd prepare more than one sauce and offer a choice.

♦ ♦ ♦  ♦ ♦ ♦

Soak the wood chips in water for 30 minutes. Prepare a charcoal fire and let it burn until the coals are evenly white, or preheat a gas grill. Drain the chips and scatter them over the coals or grillstones.

When the chips are smoking, brush the salmon steaks with the olive oil and place them on the grill 4 inches above the coals. Grill them, turning once, until crisply browned and just cooked through, about 4 minutes per side. Transfer the salmon to plates and season to taste with coarse salt and fresh pepper. Garnish each steak with a generous dollop of one of the following sauces and serve immediately.

—● *Serves 4*

♦ ♦ ♦ ♦ ♦ ♦ ♦ ♦ ♦ ♦ ♦ ♦ ♦ ♦ ♦ ♦ ♦ ♦ ♦ ♦ ♦ ♦ ♦ ♦ ♦ ♦ ♦ ♦ ♦ ♦ ♦ ♦ ♦ ♦ ♦ ♦ ♦ ♦ ♦ ♦

*2 cups mesquite or other hardwood chips*
*4 salmon steaks (each 6 to 8 ounces, cut about 1 inch thick)*
*2 tablespoons olive oil*
*Coarse salt and freshly ground pepper*
*Gazpacho Salsa, Pineapple-Tomatillo Salsa, or Chipotle Vinaigrette (recipes follow)*

1 medium cucumber,
   peeled, seeded, and cut
   into ¼-inch dice
1 large, sweet red pepper,
   stemmed, seeded, and
   cut into ¼-inch dice
1 medium red onion,
   peeled and cut into
   ¼-inch dice
2 large, ripe beefsteak
   tomatoes, seeded, juiced,
   and cut into ¼-inch dice
3 tablespoons red wine
   vinegar
1 tablespoon
   Worcestershire sauce
1 teaspoon hot pepper
   sauce
1 teaspoon salt
¼ cup olive oil

## GAZPACHO SALSA

**T**HIS CHUNKY AND ABUNDANT gazpacho-flavored salsa can serve as both sauce and vegetable garnish in a casual supper menu.

In a medium-size bowl, combine the cucumber, sweet pepper, onion, tomatoes, vinegar, Worcestershire sauce, pepper sauce, salt, and olive oil. In a blender or food processor puree one-third of the mixture. Stir the puree back into the remaining salsa ingredients and let stand, covered, at room temperature, for 1 hour. Adjust the seasoning.

*Makes about 2 cups*

½ large, ripe pineapple,
   peeled, cored, and cut
   into ½-inch dice (about
   2¾ cups)
5 small, fresh tomatillos,
   husked, rinsed in warm
   water, and coarsely
   chopped
½ fresh jalapeño or 1
   serrano chile, stemmed,
   seeded, and minced (see
   note)
3 tablespoons fresh lime
   juice
¼ teaspoon salt
¼ cup minced cilantro

## PINEAPPLE-*TOMATILLO* SALSA

**A** ZESTY, UNCOOKED SALSA that manages to taste southwestern without being at all familiar, this is good with other flavorful, oily fish such as swordfish, shark, tuna, or bluefish, as well as with chicken or pork. The smokiness of the wood paired with the sweet heat of the salsa provides for a spectacular balance of flavors.

Canned *tomatillos* are unacceptably sour and slippery for this recipe, and while fresh *tomatillos* are not common, they keep well; buy them when you find them and then schedule this salsa in the following week or two.

In a food processor combine half of the pineapple, the *tomatillos*, the jalapeño, 2 tablespoons of the lime juice, and the salt. Process until smooth. Scrape the salsa into a bowl and stir in the remaining pineapple and the cilantro. Adjust the seasoning and add more lime juice if you wish. Cover and let stand 1 hour at room temperature. The salsa is best when used the day it is made.

NOTE The seeds, and more especially the white ribs, hold capsaicin, the fiery alkaloid that causes chiles to feel "hot." When the seeds and ribs are removed, the remaining chile lends only a touch of heat and a fresh green flavor to the dish. For a spicier version of salsa, do not cut away the white ribs.

—• *Makes about 1½ cups*

## CHIPOTLE
## VINAIGRETTE

CHIPOTLES ARE ripe, red jalapeños, smoked and canned in a thick tomato-vinegar sauce (*adobo*). If you like the preserved intensity of sun-dried tomatoes, and if you appreciate the smoky quality of good barbecue, blackened fish, or grilled anything, you'll love the flavor of *chipotles*. They're habit-forming.

*Chipotles* vary in style and quality from brand to brand. I prefer to use the Embassa brand (see Cook's Sources) because the chiles are consistently plump and red and the *adobo* thick and flavorful.

1½ teaspoons prepared Dijon-style mustard

1 egg yolk

2 chipotles, *with clinging* adobo, *stemmed and minced*

2 tablespoons white wine vinegar

¼ teaspoon salt

½ cup olive oil

In a medium-size bowl whisk together the mustard, egg yolk, *chipotles,* vinegar, and salt. Gradually whisk in the oil. The dressing will thicken. Adjust the seasoning, and add additional *adobo* if you want the vinaigrette spicier. Serve at room temperature.

*Makes about ¾ cup*

♦♦♦♦♦♦♦♦♦♦♦♦♦♦♦♦♦♦♦♦♦♦♦♦♦♦♦♦♦♦♦♦♦♦♦♦♦♦♦♦♦♦♦

## RASPBERRY CUSTARD SAUCE

SERVE THIS chilled raspberry-flavored crème anglaise over an array of perfect summer berries.

4 egg yolks
⅓ cup sugar
1¾ cups half-and-half
3 tablespoons framboise
  (*raspberry* eau-de-vie)
¼ teaspoon vanilla extract

In a medium-size bowl whisk together the egg yolks and sugar. In a heavy, medium-size, nonreactive saucepan over medium heat bring the half-and-half to a boil. Whisk the hot cream into the yolk mixture. Return the mixture to the saucepan, set it over low heat, and cook, stirring constantly with a wooden spoon, until the mixture is thick and silky, about 5 minutes. Return the custard to the bowl, stir in the *framboise* and vanilla, and cool to room temperature. Cover the custard, pressing the plastic wrap onto the surface, and refrigerate until cold, at least 5 hours, or overnight.

*Makes about 2½ cups*

♦♦♦♦♦♦♦♦♦♦♦♦♦♦♦♦♦♦♦♦♦♦♦♦♦♦♦♦♦♦♦♦♦♦♦♦♦♦♦♦♦♦♦

# MENU

◆◆◆◆◆◆◆◆◆◆◆◆◆◆◆◆

BASIL VICHYSSOISE
WITH GARDEN TOMATOES AND
ROASTED SWEET PEPPERS

◆

GLAZED PICNIC CHICKENS
WITH BLUEBERRY-NECTARINE
STUFFING

◆

LEMON-RICE SALAD

◆

MEXICAN CHOCOLATE
ICE CREAM

THIS FOOD IS COOL, done in advance, and eaten when the flavors are at their respective peaks.

## BASIL VICHYSSOISE WITH GARDEN TOMATOES AND ROASTED SWEET PEPPERS

3 tablespoons unsalted
butter

5 medium leeks, white part
only, well cleaned and
sliced

2 garlic cloves, peeled and
chopped

6 cups canned chicken
broth or homemade stock

1 pound potatoes, peeled
and cut into coarse
chunks

1 teaspoon salt

2 cups clean, loosely
packed basil leaves plus
additional sprigs, as
garnish

½ cup whipping cream

1 yellow or orange sweet
pepper

1 large, ripe beefsteak
tomato

T HE COOL, CREAMY, basil-scented vichyssoise base can support any number of other summery garnishes—diced grilled zucchini, for example, with or without poached shrimp, or a dollop of black olive puree.

In a heavy pan over medium heat melt the butter. Stir in the leeks and garlic, lower the heat, and cook, covered, stirring once or twice, until the leeks are tender, about 15 minutes.

Add the broth and potatoes, stir in the salt, and bring to a boil. Lower the heat and simmer, partially covered, until the potatoes are very tender, about 40 minutes.

Stir in the basil, remove the soup from the heat, and let it stand, covered, until cool.

Pour the soup through a strainer placed over a bowl. Transfer the solids to a food processor, add 1 cup of the soup liquid, and process until smooth. Stir the puree back into the remaining liquid, stir in the heavy cream, and refrigerate, covered, until very cold, at least 5 hours, or overnight.

In the open flame of a gas burner, or under a preheated broiler, roast the pepper, turning it often, until the skin is charred. In a paper bag, or a bowl covered by a plate, steam the pepper until cool. Rub away the burnt peel, stem and core the pepper, and wipe it with paper towels. Cut the pepper into ½-inch dice.

Halve the tomato, squeeze out the seeds and juice, and cut the tomato into ½-inch dice. Taste the soup and adjust the seasoning. Ladle the soup into chilled bowls and garnish each portion with a sprinkling of the roasted pepper, tomato, and a sprig of basil.

◗ *Serves 6 to 8*

# GLAZED PICNIC CHICKENS
## WITH
## BLUEBERRY-NECTARINE
## STUFFING

♦♦♦♦♦♦♦♦♦

**I** HAD SIMILAR fruit-stuffed chickens at a rollicking Christmas party many years ago. The host encouraged us to eat the chickens with our fingers; since he provided no utensils there was no argument. Even in December, standing around a holly-decked groaning board, it seemed like a picnic, hence the name for these fruit-stuffed, brandy- and honey-glazed birds. Eat them with your fingers, if you wish, and serve them lukewarm to appreciate the juicy, flavorful results.

♦♦♦  ♦♦♦

In a heavy skillet over medium heat melt 3 tablespoons of the butter. Stir in the thyme. Raise the heat, add the nectarines, and sauté 6 minutes, turning them twice, or until they are lightly colored. Transfer to a bowl and cool.

Preheat the oven to 400 degrees F. Combine the sautéed nectarines and the blueberries. Spoon the fruit into the chickens and truss or skewer the birds closed. Set the chickens breast side up in a shallow roasting pan. Rub each with 1 tablespoon of the butter and season with salt and pepper to taste. Roast the chickens 15 minutes.

Meanwhile, in a bowl stir together the brandy, honey, and lemon juice. Turn the chickens on their sides and baste with one-third of the brandy mixture. Lower the oven temperature to 350 degrees F. Roast the chickens 15 minutes. Turn them on the other side and baste with half of the remaining brandy mixture. Roast 15 minutes. Mix the lemon zest with the remaining brandy mixture. Turn the chickens breast side up. Baste them with the remaining mixture. Continue to

*5 tablespoons unsalted butter, at room temperature*

*1 tablespoon minced fresh thyme*

*4 medium, ripe, firm nectarines, pitted and cut into eighths*

*1½ cups fresh blueberries, rinsed and picked over*

*2 chickens (about 3 pounds each), rinsed and patted dry*

*Salt and freshly ground black pepper*

*½ cup brandy*

*⅓ cup dark honey, such as thyme, buckwheat, or orange*

*¼ cup fresh lemon juice, strained*

*Zest of 2 lemons, finely julienned*

*Fresh watercress, as garnish*

roast and baste until the juices run clear when the thighs are pierced, about 20 minutes.

Spoon the stuffing into the center of a platter. Cool the chickens to room temperature, basting occasionally with the pan juices. Carve the chickens and arrange the meat around the stuffing. Garnish with the watercress. Degrease and strain the pan juices. Drizzle the juices over the chickens and stuffing and serve at room temperature.

*Serves 6 to 8*

♦♦♦♦♦♦♦♦♦♦♦♦♦♦♦♦♦♦♦♦♦♦♦♦♦♦♦♦♦♦♦♦♦♦♦♦♦♦♦♦♦♦♦

## LEMON-RICE SALAD

♦♦♦♦♦♦♦♦♦♦

3 cups cold water

1½ cups long-grain white rice

2½ teaspoons salt

¾ cup best-quality extra virgin olive oil

½ cup (about) strained fresh lemon juice

4 ounces cremini (see Cook's Sources) or cultivated white mushrooms, wiped, trimmed, and sliced

3 green onions, trimmed and sliced

3 ribs of celery, trimmed and sliced

½ cup finely chopped Italian parsley

⅓ cup finely chopped fresh mint

THIS WAS PROBABLY the first recipe I ever set to paper, and it was developed years ago to showcase the first extravagantly expensive bottle of Tuscan extra virgin olive oil I ever owned. There's been a lot more of that luscious green oil under the bridge since, and the salad remains in my repertoire.

It survives through the strength of its versatility, by accommodating shrimp, ham, or asparagus (or all three), to become a summertime main course; by allowing for a change in herbs and citrus zest (basil with orange is nice), depending on market availability and my mood; and by accompanying cold roast chicken and icy chablis whenever the weather's too hot for me to feel "creative."

The salad tastes best if never refrigerated and served at room temperature the day it's made.

In a medium-size, heavy saucepan bring the water to a boil. Stir in the rice and salt, cover, and turn the heat to very low. Cook undisturbed for 22 minutes, or until

the rice has absorbed all the water and steam holes appear. Remove the pan from the heat and let the rice stand, covered, 5 minutes.

Transfer the rice to a wide, shallow bowl. Add the olive oil and ¼ cup of the lemon juice and let the rice stand, stirring it once or twice, until cool. Stir in the mushrooms, onions, celery, parsley, mint, olives, and lemon zest. Season generously with fresh black pepper and add additional lemon juice to taste. Serve at room temperature.

— *Serves 6 to 8*

♦♦♦♦♦♦♦♦♦♦♦♦♦♦♦♦♦♦♦♦♦♦♦♦♦♦♦♦♦♦♦♦♦♦♦♦♦♦♦♦♦♦♦♦

*12 Calamata or other
    brine-cured, imported
    black olives, pitted and
    chopped*
*Zest of 2 lemons, finely
    julienned*
*Freshly ground black
    pepper*

## MEXICAN CHOCOLATE ICE CREAM

♦♦♦♦♦♦♦♦♦♦

**T**HERE *IS* SOMETHING CALLED Mexican chocolate. Sweet and gritty with stale almonds and too much cinnamon, it remains in many cupboards as the inedible souvenir from a trip across the border. Nonetheless, it served as the inspiration for this cool, sweet treat, in which I recommend you use the best-quality imported milk or dark chocolate (see Cook's Sources). Offer the ice cream with plain sugar cookies or Cornmeal Butter Cookies (page 113) and garnish each serving with a strawberry.

Preheat the oven to 400 degrees F. Spread the almonds in a single layer in a shallow, metal pan and bake, stirring occasionally, until they are a rich brown, 10 to 12 minutes. Remove them from the pen and cool completely.

In the top of a double boiler over gently simmering water, melt the chocolate, stirring occasionally. Remove from the heat, but leave the chocolate sitting over the hot water.

*1 cup (about 4 ounces)
    whole, unblanched
    almonds*
*½ pound imported milk or
    dark chocolate (see
    Cook's Sources), or a
    combination of the two,
    chopped*
*4 egg yolks*
*¾ cup sugar*
*1 teaspoon cinnamon*
*3 cups half-and-half*
*1 cup whipping cream*
*1½ tablespoons vanilla
    extract*

In a mixing bowl whisk the egg yolks until foamy. Combine the sugar and cinnamon and slowly whisk them into the yolks until the mixture is thick.

In a medium-size, heavy-bottomed saucepan bring the half-and-half and whipping cream to a boil. Dribble the hot cream slowly into the yolk mixture, whisking constantly. Return this mixture to the saucepan, set it over low heat, and cook, stirring constantly with a wooden spoon, until the mixture thickly coats the back of the spoon, about 5 minutes.

Remove the custard from the heat and immediately transfer it to a bowl. Scrape the melted chocolate into the custard. Stir in the vanilla extract and whisk vigorously; the mixture may appear grainy. Cool completely, cover by pressing plastic wrap onto the surface of the mixture, and refrigerate until very cold, at least 5 hours, and preferably overnight.

Pour the chilled mixture into an ice-cream maker and churn according to the manufacturer's instructions. Chop the almonds coarsely and fold them into the ice cream. Transfer to a covered storage container and freeze until use. *The ice cream can be prepared up to 24 hours in advance. Let it soften slightly in the refrigerator.* Serve immediately.

*Makes 1½ to 2 quarts*

# MENU

◆ ◆ ◆ ◆ ◆ ◆ ◆ ◆ ◆ ◆ ◆ ◆ ◆ ◆ ◆ ◆

GRILLED CHICKEN PITAS

◆

BUCKWHEAT AND
RAISIN–STUFFED GRAPE
LEAVES

◆

GRILLED EGGPLANT SALAD
*or*
RATATOUILLE VINAIGRETTE
*page 167*

◆

RASPBERRY-BUTTERMILK ICE CREAM

THE TACTILE CHARM of eating something tucked into a warm pita bread is only amplified when that something is grilled. This menu celebrates the charm, embellishes it with Middle Eastern flourishes, and concludes with a bright, cooling, and colorful ice cream.

## GRILLED CHICKEN PITAS

◆◆◆◆◆◆◆◆◆

¼ cup olive oil

3 tablespoons lemon juice

2 garlic cloves, peeled

1 fresh jalapeño, stemmed

1 teaspoon ground cumin,
   from toasted seeds (page
   66)

¾ teaspoon oregano,
   crumbled

½ teaspoon ground
   cinnamon

3 whole, boneless chicken
   breasts, halved,
   connective tissues and
   fat removed

2 cups fruit or mesquite
   wood chips

6 medium pita breads,
   trimmed to open the
   pockets

2 cups shredded fresh
   spinach

2 medium carrots, peeled
   and coarsely grated

Herbed Yogurt Sauce
   (recipe follows)

IT'S EASY FOR SOMEONE like me, who cooks a lot, writes many recipes, and loves rich, assertive food, to think of chicken as a bore. Still, it's hard to beat for its nutritional and economic virtues and culinary versatility. This tasty summer sandwich manages to celebrate the best of chicken's modest plusses while investing it, through a zesty marinade and a subsequent grilling over savory wood, with more character than you might think possible.

◆◆◆  ◆◆◆

In a food processor or blender combine the olive oil, lemon juice, garlic, jalapeño, cumin, oregano, and cinnamon and process until smooth. In a shallow dish combine the puree and the chicken breasts and marinate at room temperature, turning once or twice, 2 hours.

Soak the wood chips in water for 30 minutes. Prepare a charcoal fire and allow it to burn until the coals are evenly white, or preheat a gas grill. Drain the chips and scatter them over the coals or the grillstones. When the chips are smoking, arrange the chicken breasts on the grill. Baste them with any marinade remaining in the dish and grill, turning once, until just done through, 6 to 8 minutes. Transfer to a plate.

Lay the pitas on the grill and toast them briefly, turning once, about 2 minutes, or until lightly marked and heated through.

Tuck a chicken breast into each pita. Tuck the spinach and carrots into the pitas and spoon in the Herbed Yogurt Sauce. Serve at once.

━● *Makes 6 sandwiches*

## HERBED  YOGURT  SAUCE

♦ ♦ ♦ ♦ ♦ ♦ ♦ ♦ ♦

Whisk together all the ingredients and let the sauce stand 1 hour at room temperature before using.

━━● *Makes about 1¼ cups*

♦ ♦ ♦ ♦ ♦ ♦ ♦ ♦ ♦ ♦ ♦ ♦ ♦ ♦ ♦ ♦ ♦ ♦ ♦ ♦ ♦ ♦ ♦ ♦ ♦ ♦ ♦ ♦ ♦ ♦ ♦ ♦ ♦ ♦ ♦ ♦ ♦ ♦ ♦ ♦ ♦ ♦ ♦ ♦

*1 cup plain yogurt*
*¼ cup minced fresh mint*
*  or cilantro, or a*
*  combination of the two*
*3 tablespoons lemon juice*
*¼ teaspoon salt*

## BUCKWHEAT  AND RAISIN–STUFFED  GRAPE LEAVES

♦ ♦ ♦ ♦ ♦ ♦ ♦ ♦ ♦

**A**LTHOUGH TYPICALLY FILLED with white rice, stuffed grape leaves gain fiber and distinction when the filling is nutty buckwheat and raisins plus a touch of lemon and mint. If the fire lingers after the chicken is grilled, turn the stuffed grape leaves on the grill until just heated through and crisp, about 7 minutes.

♦ ♦ ♦  ♦ ♦ ♦

In a medium-size bowl combine the groats, onions, mint, tomatoes, raisins, oil, and lemon zest. Season generously with the pepper.

Lay a grape leaf vein side up, stem toward you, on the work surface. Place a tablespoon of buckwheat filling on the leaf, just above the stem. Fold in the sides over the filling and roll the stem end of the leaf up over the filling to form a rectangular bundle. Set the stuffed leaf seam side down in a heavy, 3-quart saucepan. Repeat with the remaining leaves.

Pour the broth evenly over the leaves and set the pan over low heat. Bring the broth just to a simmer,

*1 cup buckwheat groats,*
*  available in health food*
*  stores and some*
*  supermarkets*
*1 bunch green onions,*
*  trimmed and sliced*
*½ cup chopped fresh mint*
*1 can (14 ounces)*
*  Italian-style plum*
*  tomatoes, crushed and*
*  drained*
*½ cup golden raisins*
*¼ cup olive oil*
*Zest of 2 lemons, minced*
*Freshly ground black*
*  pepper*
*25 medium-sized,*
*  preserved grape leaves,*
*  rinsed and patted dry*
*3½ cups canned chicken*
*  broth or homemade stock*

then weigh down the leaves with a small plate that will just fit inside the pan. Cover and simmer until the buckwheat is tender and most of the broth is absorbed, about 50 minutes. Remove from the heat, cool, and refrigerate. *The grape leaves can be prepared up to 3 days ahead.*

Remove the leaves from any remaining broth and let them come to room temperature before serving.

*Makes 25 grape leaves, serving 4 to 6*

## GRILLED EGGPLANT SALAD

3 eggplants, about 1 pound
  each
Salt
½ cup minced fresh basil
⅓ cup olive oil
¼ cup (about) lemon juice
2 garlic cloves, peeled and
  forced through a press
Freshly ground black
  pepper

Grilling POTENTIATES the smoky taste of eggplant like no other cooking method. Those using gas grills will find it easy to prepare the eggplant early on the day the salad is being served. Those using charcoal may find it more convenient to take advantage of existing coals from a previous cookout and grill the eggplants a day or two in advance. The eggplant will keep well in the refrigerator. Complete the salad shortly before serving.

Cut the eggplants into 1-inch slices. In a colander salt the slices heavily on both sides and let stand 1 hour.

Shake off any clinging salt and pat the eggplant slices dry. Over hot coals, or on a preheated gas grill, using wood chips soaked in water for 30 minutes, drained, and spread over the coals, if desired, grill the eggplant slices, turning them once or twice, until very brown and tender, 5 to 7 minutes. (If the eggplant shows a tendency to stick to the grill, brush the slices very lightly with additional olive oil.)

Transfer the eggplant to a bowl, cover, and let stand until cool. Chop the eggplant. In a medium-size bowl mix the eggplant with the basil, olive oil, half of the lemon juice, and the garlic. Season generously with the pepper and adjust the seasoning, adding more lemon juice if desired. Serve the salad at room temperature.

*Serves 6 to 8*

## RASPBERRY-BUTTERMILK ICE CREAM

ICE CREAMS NOT BASED on cooked custards rarely have the sophisticated texture of those that are. In this recipe, though, the tangy thickness of the buttermilk contributes a velvety quality that is completely unexpected. Since buttermilk is low in fat, you can eat the ice cream without feeling too guilty—a perfect summer dessert.

*3 eggs*
*1¾ cups sugar*
*3 cups buttermilk*
*1 cup whipping cream*
*¼ cup fresh lemon juice, strained*
*1 teaspoon vanilla extract*
*2 baskets fresh raspberries, picked over, rinsed, and dried*

In a medium-size bowl beat the eggs until creamy and yellow. Whisk in 1¼ cups of the sugar. Whisk in the buttermilk, whipping cream, lemon juice, and vanilla. Cover and chill the mixture about 5 hours, or until very cold.

In a medium-size bowl roughly crush the raspberries. Stir in the remaining sugar and let stand 15 minutes. Stir the raspberry mixture into the buttermilk mixture and churn in an ice-cream maker according to the manufacturer's instructions. Store the ice cream in the freezer. *The ice cream can be prepared up to 2 days in advance.* Soften slightly in the refrigerator before serving.

*Makes about 1½ quarts*

# ONE GREAT DISH

GIVEN THE RIGHT DISH (one is enough)—a big, rich, earthy, and overstuffed main course plus a few basic accompaniments, purchased or easily assembled—your kitchen time can be cut in half and you can remain calm. Ordinarily, feeding a crowd can require a great many final flourishes, but with these menus there are fewer last-minute details requiring your attention, and the impact of that single, steaming, and splendid dish of food will spell instant welcome and abundance. The old saw, When the host enjoys the party, the guests have a better time, is utterly true, and the one-dish menu is the ultimate solution to feeding a modest crowd simply and successfully.

Entertaining, as I've said before, doesn't start and end with puff-paste-and-caviar shindigs but includes gatherings of an intimate few, celebrating friendship and kinship and nourishing the body as well as the soul—simple stuff that we need to be reminded of from time to time. A pot of chili or a deep casserole of sauced and baked pasta ought to be just as celebratory as the most extravagant shellfish-studded paella, and this chapter is an eclectic mix of both small and large menus, starring my favorite one-dish main courses.

# M E N U

◆ ◆ ◆ ◆ ◆ ◆ ◆ ◆ ◆ ◆ ◆ ◆ ◆

SUMMER NACHOS
*or*
CHUNKY GUACAMOLE
*page 30*
◆

RED PORK CHILI WITH BLACK BEANS
◆

WHITE RICE
◆

BLUE CORN STICKS
◆

JACK DANIEL'S CHOCOLATE
WHISKEY CAKE

THIS CHAPTER BEGINS with a menu featuring chili since to me, chili is *the* great, single dish around which to build a memorable meal. A straightforward chili supper, this is without gimcrackery or unnecessary adornment, which only clashes with chili's no-nonsense appeal. Pour lots of good cold beer—of Mexican (or other) background—or serve a rich and fruity red zinfandel, slightly chilled.

## SUMMER NACHOS

◆ ◆ ◆ ◆ ◆ ◆ ◆ ◆ ◆

**T**HESE COLD AND CRUNCHY nachos are reconstructed from a version I enjoyed years ago at a now defunct Boulder, Colorado, restaurant called Tico's. Although they take more fussing to assemble than hot nachos, the oven—and the cook—stay cool. Arrange them on one or two big white platters and consider drinking white or pink wine instead of margaritas or beer with these cool salad nachos.

In a small bowl stir together the refried beans and jalapeños.

In a separate bowl whisk together the egg yolk, lime juice, and mustard. Whisk in a pinch of salt and a grind of black pepper. Slowly whisk in the corn oil. Adjust the seasoning.

Pit the avocados. Scoop the flesh into a bowl and mash roughly. Stir in ¼ teaspoon of salt, the onions, and the cilantro. Adjust the seasoning.

Spread each of the corn tortilla chips with a thin layer—about 1 teaspoon—of the bean mixture. Top the bean layer with a slightly thicker layer of the avocado mixture, arranging the nachos on 1 or 2 serving platters as you go.

Sprinkle the cheese evenly over the nachos. Sprinkle the lettuce evenly over the cheese. Scatter the radishes over the lettuce. Drizzle the dressing evenly over the nachos, using it all. Serve immediately.

*Makes 36 nachos, serving 6 to 8*

¾ cup refried beans

3 pickled jalapeños, stemmed and minced

1 egg yolk

2 tablespoons fresh lime juice

1 teaspoon prepared Dijon-style mustard

Salt

Freshly ground black pepper

⅓ cup corn oil

1½ Hass avocados

⅓ cup finely diced red onion

¼ cup minced cilantro

36 unsalted, unspiced, round corn tortilla chips

4 ounces medium-sharp cheddar cheese, grated

2 cups finely shredded inner leaves of romaine lettuce

4 medium radishes, trimmed and sliced very thin (about ½ cup)

## RED PORK CHILI
## WITH BLACK BEANS

♦ ♦ ♦ ♦ ♦ ♦ ♦ ♦ ♦ ♦

6 tablespoons olive oil

2 large yellow onions,
   peeled and diced

8 garlic cloves, peeled and
   minced

5 pounds boneless pork
   butt or shoulder, cut into
   ½-inch cubes

⅔ cup mild, plain chile
   powder (see Cook's
   Sources)

3 tablespoons ground
   cumin, from toasted
   seeds (see page 66)

3 tablespoons oregano

2 teaspoons cayenne pepper

4 teaspoons salt

1 can (28 ounces)
   Italian-style plum
   tomatoes, crushed and
   with their juices

7 cups canned chicken
   broth or homemade stock

4 cans (16 ounces each)
   black beans, drained
   and rinsed

Sour cream and minced
   cilantro, as garnish

I'VE PUT TOGETHER some busy and ambitious chilies in my time, and I've eaten them all with gusto. But, as with many things I've learned, less is more. This uncluttered rendition of the great American dish features cubed pork in a rich but simple red chili, given distinction by the inclusion of black beans. Lamb is a delicious substitute, or if you're the traditional type, so is beef.

In a skillet over medium heat warm 3 tablespoons of the olive oil. Add the onions and garlic, lower the heat, and cook covered, stirring once or twice, until very tender, about 20 minutes.

In an 8-quart Dutch oven or flameproof casserole over medium heat warm the remaining oil. Add the pork and cook, without browning, stirring occasionally, until the meat is uniformly colored, about 20 minutes. Stir in the chili powder, cumin, oregano, pepper, and salt and cook 5 minutes. Stir in the onions and garlic, the tomatoes, their juices, and the chicken broth. Bring the chili to a boil, lower the heat, and simmer, uncovered, stirring occasionally, for 1 hour.

Adjust the seasoning and simmer the chili for another 35 to 45 minutes, or until the chili is thick and the pork is tender. *The chili can be made to this point up to 3 days in advance. Cover and refrigerate. Warm over low heat, stirring often, until simmering, before proceeding.*

Stir in the beans and simmer another 3 to 5 minutes, or until the beans are heated through. Serve immediately, accompanied by the sour cream and cilantro.

*Serves 8*

## BLUE CORN STICKS

♦ ♦ ♦ ♦ ♦ ♦ ♦ ♦ ♦

**Y**OU MAY BE GETTING a little tired of hearing about blue corn, but don't dismiss this southwestern staple as trendy; Indians have been grinding and cooking with the indigenous blue corn almost as long as there has been cultivation in the Americas. The cornmeal, more gray than blue, is difficult to turn into tortillas (unless you're a real expert) but makes tasty, easy, and distinctive-looking corn sticks. Serve them, if you like, with Black Olive Butter (page 26).

Position a rack in the middle of the oven and preheat to 425 degrees F.

In a large bowl combine the cornmeal, flour, sugar, baking powder, and salt. In a separate bowl whisk together the half-and-half, butter, and egg. Stir the half-and-half into the dry ingredients until just combined.

Brush cast-iron corn-stick pans with the vegetable oil. Heat the pans in the oven until the oil smokes slightly, 8 to 10 minutes. Pour off excess oil. Spoon the batter into the molds, filling each about three-quarters full. Bake until puffed and golden, about 15 minutes. Remove from the pan and serve hot.

━● *Makes 12 to 14 corn sticks*

♦ ♦ ♦ ♦ ♦ ♦ ♦ ♦ ♦ ♦ ♦ ♦ ♦ ♦ ♦ ♦ ♦ ♦ ♦ ♦ ♦ ♦ ♦ ♦ ♦ ♦ ♦ ♦ ♦ ♦ ♦ ♦ ♦ ♦ ♦ ♦ ♦ ♦ ♦ ♦ ♦

*1 cup blue cornmeal (see Cook's Sources)*
*1 cup unbleached all-purpose flour*
*2 tablespoons sugar*
*2 teaspoons baking powder*
*¼ teaspoon salt*
*⅔ cup half-and-half, at room temperature*
*6 tablespoons (¾ stick) unsalted butter, melted*
*1 egg, at room temperature*
*Vegetable oil*

▼▲▼▲▼▲▼▲▼▲▼▲▼▲▼▲▼▲▼▲▼▲▼▲▼▲▼▲▼▲▼

# JACK DANIEL'S
# CHOCOLATE WHISKEY CAKE

♦ ♦ ♦ ♦ ♦ ♦ ♦ ♦ ♦

2 cups unbleached
  all-purpose flour
2 teaspoons baking powder
⅛ teaspoon salt
1½ cups cold water
10 ounces (2½ sticks)
  unsalted butter
1 cup unsweetened cocoa
  powder
4 ounces semisweet
  chocolate, chopped
½ cup plus 2 tablespoons
  Jack Daniel's Tennessee
  Sour Mash Whiskey
1 tablespoon instant coffee
2 cups sugar
2 eggs, beaten
1 cup (about 4 ounces)
  chopped pecans
  (optional)
Unsweetened heavy cream,
  whipped to soft peaks, as
  garnish

**M**Y THANKS GO TO SUZANNE HAMLIN, the intelligent and earthy food writer for the New York *Daily News,* who discovered and printed this recipe from the Jack Daniel's test kitchens. In Lynchburg, a new bourbon cake is created each year to honor Jack's birthday, and Hamlin—a Kentuckian who knows from bourbon *and* chocolate—spotted this moist, dark, and chocolaty offering for the winner it is.

I've increased the chocolate ("Too much of a good thing is just right," said Mae West), but the cake remains simple to prepare and is an excellent conclusion to a chili supper. In a different menu substitute *framboise* for the bourbon (Don't tell Jack!) and serve the cake garnished with fresh raspberries.

•••  •••

Preheat the oven to 325 degrees F. Grease a 9- or 10-inch tube or bundt pan. In a bowl combine the flour, baking powder, and salt. In a saucepan combine the water, butter, cocoa, semisweet chocolate, ½ cup of the whiskey, and the coffee and set over medium heat. Stir just until the butter and chocolate are melted. Remove from the heat and whisk in the sugar. Cool to room temperature and whisk in the eggs. Fold in the dry ingredients and the pecans until just combined. Pour the batter into the prepared pan and bake 40 to 50 minutes, or until a tester inserted in the center of the cake comes out clean.

Cool 5 minutes in the pan on a rack. Invert and unmold onto a plate. Drizzle the remaining whiskey over the cake. Cool completely and garnish with the whipped cream.

━● *Serves 10*

♦ ♦ ♦ ♦ ♦ ♦ ♦ ♦ ♦ ♦ ♦ ♦ ♦ ♦ ♦ ♦ ♦ ♦ ♦ ♦ ♦ ♦ ♦ ♦ ♦ ♦ ♦ ♦ ♦ ♦ ♦ ♦ ♦ ♦ ♦ ♦ ♦ ♦ ♦ ♦

# MENU

◆ ◆ ◆ ◆ ◆ ◆ ◆ ◆ ◆ ◆ ◆ ◆ ◆ ◆ ◆ ◆ ◆

RIGATONI BAKED WITH
BRAISED BEEF SAUCE

◆

BROCCOLI AND TOMATO SALAD WITH
SHERRY–BLACK PEPPER DRESSING

◆

PESTO BREAD
*page 68*

◆

CANDY-COUNTER COOKIES

◆

FRESH FRUIT

A GREAT BIG DISH of baked pasta makes a splendid buffet for a crowd's main course. This one, with its sturdy accompanying salad and pesto-lavish garlic bread, is food for a voracious, happy group. Try it at a ski-lodge supper, a tree-trimming party, or any gathering where large quantities of hearty, delicious, uncomplicated food are needed.

▼▲▼▲▼▲▼▲▼▲▼▲▼▲▼▲▼▲▼▲▼▲▼▲▼▲▼▲▼▲▼▲

## RIGATONI BAKED WITH BRAISED BEEF SAUCE

♦ ♦ ♦ ♦ ♦ ♦ ♦ ♦ ♦ ♦

THIS DISH IS INSPIRED by both the Italian practice of saucing pasta using leftover pot roast juices and the traditional French *macaronnade*—pasta sauced with braised beef juices to accompany or precede the meat. The dish has big, simple, and endearing flavors and will be sure to appeal to anyone who has worked up an appetite. Most of the effort comes days before the guests arrive, making the job of feeding a dozen or so people a positive pleasure.

♦ ♦ ♦  ♦ ♦ ♦

1 boneless chuck or other pot roast (4 pounds)

2 large onions, peeled and chopped

3 medium carrots, peeled and sliced

8 garlic cloves, peeled and chopped

2 cans (28 ounces each), Italian-style plum tomatoes, crushed and with their juices

1 cup dry red wine

1 cup canned beef broth or homemade stock

1½ tablespoons dry thyme, crumbled

1½ tablespoons dry marjoram, crumbled

1½ tablespoons dry basil, crumbled

3 bay leaves

Salt

2 pounds rigatoni

3 tablespoons olive oil

36 Calamata or other brine-cured, imported black olives, pitted and coarsely chopped

1 cup freshly grated Parmesan cheese

1 cup finely chopped Italian parsley

2 pounds low-moisture mozzarella cheese cut into ½-inch dice (see note, page 166)

2 teaspoons freshly ground black pepper

Preheat the oven to 350 degrees F. Set the roast in a 5-quart ovenproof casserole and surround it with the onions, carrots, and garlic. Add the tomatoes, their juices, wine, broth, thyme, marjoram, basil, bay leaves, and 1 teaspoon of salt. Bake, covered, for 2 hours. Turn the roast over and bake, covered, until tender, another 1½ to 2 hours. Cool the roast to room temperature in the braising liquid. Cover and refrigerate overnight.

Remove the hardened fats from the surface of the braising liquid and discard the bay leaves. Transfer the roast to a cutting board. Trim away any strings or surface fat and cut the meat into ¼-inch dice. Stir the beef back into the braising liquid. *The sauce can be prepared to this point up to 2 days ahead. Cover and refrigerate.*

Bring a very large pot of water to a boil. Stir in 2 tablespoons of salt. When the water returns to a boil add the rigatoni. Cook, stirring occasionally, until just tender, 8 to 10 minutes. Drain immediately, rinse with cold water, and drain again. Toss the pasta with the olive oil and reserve, covered, at room temperature. *The recipe can be completed to this point up to 3 hours ahead.*

Preheat the oven to 375 degrees F. Reheat the beef sauce. Stir in the olives, grated cheese, and parsley.

In a large bowl toss together the beef sauce, the mozzarella, and the pasta. Add the pepper and toss again. Transfer the pasta to a large, ovenproof casserole and bake uncovered until the top is well browned and the cheese is melted throughout, about 50 minutes. Let stand on a rack for 10 minutes before serving.

➼● *Serves 12*

◆◆◆◆◆◆◆◆◆◆◆◆◆◆◆◆◆◆◆◆◆◆◆◆◆◆◆◆◆◆◆◆◆◆◆◆◆◆◆◆◆

## BROCCOLI AND TOMATO SALAD WITH SHERRY–BLACK PEPPER DRESSING

◆◆◆◆◆◆◆◆◆

**T**HE SALAD HOLDS UP on the buffet better than a leafy green one would, and the solid crunch of broccoli and the peppery sherry-vinegar dressing make it a vibrant accompaniment to the pasta. If large, red, ripe tomatoes are unavailable, substitute cherry tomatoes.

◆◆◆  ◆◆◆

Separate the broccoli into large florets. Bring a large pot of water to a boil. Stir in 1 tablespoon of salt and the broccoli. Cook until crisp but tender, about 4 minutes. Drain immediately and transfer at once to a large bowl of ice water. Cool completely and drain well. *The salad can be prepared to this point up to 1 day ahead. Wrap well in plastic bags and refrigerate.*

Arrange the broccoli on one side of a platter. Wash and stem the tomatoes and cut them into sixths. Arrange the tomato wedges on the other side of the platter. Drizzle the dressing generously over the broccoli and tomatoes. Scatter the onion over the salad and serve, passing the remaining dressing at the table.

➼● *Serves 12*

◆◆◆◆◆◆◆◆◆◆◆◆◆◆◆◆◆◆◆◆◆◆◆◆◆◆◆◆◆◆◆◆◆◆◆◆◆◆◆◆◆

*2 large bunches (3 to 3½ pounds) broccoli*
*Salt*
*4 large, red, ripe tomatoes*
*Sherry–Black Pepper Dressing (recipe follows)*
*1 medium red onion, peeled and cut into thin rings*

## SHERRY–BLACK PEPPER DRESSING

1 egg
2 egg yolks
⅓ cup sherry wine vinegar
3 tablespoons mild,
    prepared coarse-grained
    mustard
2 teaspoons freshly ground
    black pepper
1 teaspoon salt
2 cups olive oil

In a food processor fitted with the steel blade combine the egg, egg yolks, vinegar, mustard, pepper, and salt and process briefly to blend. With the machine running add the oil in a quick stream. Adjust the seasoning and transfer the dressing to a covered container. *The dressing can be prepared up to 3 days ahead and refrigerated. Bring it to room temperature before using.*

━● *Makes about 3 cups*

## CANDY-COUNTER COOKIES

1 cup unbleached
    all-purpose flour
1 cup regular-cooking
    rolled oats
½ cup plain M&M's
½ cup Reese's Pieces
½ cup golden raisins
½ cup peanuts
½ teaspoon salt
½ teaspoon baking soda
½ teaspoon baking powder
1 stick (½ cup) unsalted
    butter, softened
½ cup light brown sugar,
    packed
⅓ cup sugar
1 egg

**B**IG COOKIES, for big kids, studded with movie candies. Never has so little kitchen time afforded so much sweet satisfaction.

Preheat the oven to 350 degrees F. Grease 2 baking sheets.

In a medium-size bowl stir together the flour, oats, M&M's, Reese's Pieces, raisins, peanuts, salt, baking soda, and baking powder.

In a large bowl cream the butter and sugars. Whisk in the egg. Stir in the dry ingredients until just combined. By quarter cupfuls, drop the batter onto the prepared sheets, spacing about 2 inches apart. Flatten each ball of dough slightly. Bake, reversing the position of the sheets in the oven once, until the cookies are crisp and golden brown, about 11 minutes. Cool the cookies 5 minutes on the sheets, then transfer them to parchment paper, and cool completely. *The cookies can be baked up to 1 day ahead. Wrap them airtight and store at room temperature.*

➼ *Makes about 24 large cookies*

*Variation* Chill 20 Candy Counter Cookies for 1 hour. Soften 2 pints of premium vanilla ice cream slightly in the refrigerator. Place ⅓ cup of ice cream between 2 cookies, pressing slightly to bring the ice cream just to the edges of the cookies. Lay the cookie sandwich on a baking sheet in the freezer. Repeat with the remaining cookies and ice cream, transferring each completed sandwich to the freezer as it is assembled. When frozen solid, about 1 hour, wrap the cookie sandwiches individually in plastic wrap and store them in the freezer. *The sandwiches can be prepared up to 3 days ahead.* Soften the cookie sandwiches in the refrigerator for 15 minutes before serving.

➼ *Makes 10 ice cream sandwiches*

✦ ✦ ✦ ✦ ✦ ✦ ✦ ✦ ✦ ✦ ✦ ✦ ✦ ✦ ✦ ✦ ✦ ✦ ✦ ✦ ✦ ✦ ✦ ✦ ✦ ✦ ✦ ✦ ✦ ✦ ✦ ✦ ✦ ✦ ✦ ✦ ✦ ✦ ✦ ✦

# MENU

♦♦♦♦♦♦♦♦♦♦♦♦♦♦♦♦♦

MOZZARELLA WITH ROASTED
PEPPERS AND BASIL

♦

CHICKEN AND SWEET SAUSAGE STEW
WITH PARSLEY AND LEMON

♦

ARBORIO RICE CAKE
*page 278*
*or*
BUTTERED ORZO

♦

PEARS, WALNUTS, AND PARMESAN
*or*
SONOMA DRY JACK

THE STEW THAT THIS MENU is built around has a heartiness that makes it a crowd pleaser. Since it can be made entirely in advance, except for the sprightly sprinkle of fresh parsley and lemon zest that is added just before serving, it's convenient, too, and the rest of the down-scaled accompaniments can be assembled while the stew is reheating. As with most food of such friendly simplicity, the wine need not be the finest, but there should be plenty of it—Bardolino or one of the lighter California zinfandels would be ideal.

## MOZZARELLA WITH ROASTED PEPPERS AND BASIL

♦ ♦ ♦ ♦ ♦ ♦ ♦ ♦ ♦

THIS COMBINATION is easy, colorful, and pleasing but pointless if you don't have good, fresh mozzarella.

In the open flame of a gas burner, or under a preheated broiler, roast the peppers, turning them, until the skins are charred. In a paper bag, or in a bowl covered by a plate, let the peppers steam until cool. Rub off the charred peel and wipe with paper towels. Stem and core the peppers and cut into thin julienne strips.

In a small bowl combine the pepper strips, oil, vinegar, garlic, salt, and a generous grind of pepper. Let stand at room temperature for 30 minutes. *The peppers can be marinated, covered and refrigerated, up to 24 hours ahead. Return them to room temperature before proceeding.*

Cut the mozzarella into 12 equal pieces. Arrange the cheese on 6 plates. Top each portion with the marinated peppers, dividing them evenly and using them all. Spoon any of the juices remaining in the bowl over the peppers. Sprinkle with the basil and serve immediately passing a peppermill.

—● *Serves 6*

2 large sweet peppers (1 red and 1 yellow)
¼ cup olive oil
1½ tablespoons balsamic vinegar
1 garlic clove, peeled and forced through a press
½ teaspoon salt
Freshly ground black pepper
1 pound lightly salted fresh mozzarella (see Cook's Sources), at room temperature
½ cup loosely packed, julienned fresh basil leaves

# CHICKEN AND SWEET SAUSAGE STEW WITH PARSLEY AND LEMON

◆◆◆◆◆◆◆◆◆

*8 tablespoons olive oil*

*1 pound sweet Italian-style sweet sausage, pricked all over*

*1 chicken (about 3 pounds) cut into serving pieces, giblets reserved*

*2 medium onions, peeled and finely chopped*

*3 celery ribs, cut on the diagonal into 1-inch pieces*

*4 garlic cloves, peeled and minced*

*1½ teaspoons dried oregano, crumbled*

*1 teaspoon dried thyme, crumbled*

*1 bay leaf*

*3 tablespoons unbleached all-purpose flour*

*1 cup dry white wine*

*2 cups canned chicken broth or homemade stock*

*1 can (28 ounces) Italian-style plum tomatoes, crushed and with their juices*

*Salt*

*Freshly ground black pepper*

*1 pound medium fresh white mushrooms or cremini mushrooms (see Cook's Sources), wiped and trimmed*

**T**HE STEW IS GENEROUSLY liquid by intent: Even with a starchy accompaniment you'll need plenty of crusty bread for mopping up. If you have a big copper (or otherwise eye-appealing) skillet or casserole, serve the stew from it at the table.

•••  •••

In a large, nonreactive, flameproof casserole or deep skillet heat 2 tablespoons of the oil. Add the sausage and chicken giblets, discarding the liver, and cook, stirring and turning, until well browned, about 10 minutes. Transfer the sausage to a bowl, leaving the giblets in the casserole.

Pat the chicken dry, add it to the skillet, skin side down, and cook, turning once, until golden, about 5 minutes per side. Transfer to the bowl with the sausage. Discard the giblets and oil, but do not clean the casserole.

Return the casserole to moderate heat. Add 3 tablespoons of the oil, the onions, celery, garlic, oregano, thyme, and bay leaf. Lower the heat, cover, and cook, stirring occasionally and scraping browned deposits from the bottom of the casserole, until the onions are tender, about 15 minutes. Sprinkle the flour over the onions and cook, stirring often, for 5 minutes.

Whisk in the wine and then the broth. Add the tomatoes, their juices, 1 teaspoon of salt, and ½ teaspoon of pepper. Raise the heat and bring to a boil. Lower the heat and simmer, partially covered, for 30 minutes.

Cut the sausage on the diagonal into 1-inch pieces. Add the sausage, chicken, and any juices from the bowl to the casserole. Simmer, uncovered, turning the chicken occasionally, until it is tender, about 30 minutes.

Meanwhile, in a large skillet heat the remaining olive oil. Add the mushrooms and sauté them over moderately high heat for 5 minutes. Season them lightly with salt and pepper and remove from the heat. Stir the mushrooms, their juices, and the olives into the casserole. *The stew can be prepared to this point up to 1 day ahead. Cool to room temperature. Cover and refrigerate.*

Warm the stew over low heat, stirring often and basting the chicken with the sauce, until hot, before proceeding. Adjust the seasoning. Stir the parsley into the stew and sprinkle the lemon zest on top and serve.

*Serves 6*

1 cup brine-cured, imported black olives, such as Calamata (see Cook's Sources), rinsed and drained

1/2 cup finely chopped Italian parsley

1 tablespoon finely minced lemon zest

**SERVING STRATEGY** Though the rustic peel, shell, and munch approach is right in character with this simple menu, the dessert can be made more dramatic if you wish. Try slicing and fanning the pears onto the dessert plates and serving them sprinkled with the walnuts and shards of aged Sonoma Jack cheese. Bread, sweet butter, and a glass of wine are sound partners for the fruit, nuts, and cheese.

# M E N U

♦ ♦ ♦ ♦ ♦ ♦ ♦ ♦ ♦ ♦ ♦ ♦ ♦ ♦

GREEN OLIVES WITH MUSTARD SEED
AND SHERRY VINEGAR
*page 294*

♦

BLACK OLIVES WITH CILANTRO,
GARLIC, AND LEMON RIND
*page 294*

♦

TANGY GOAT'S OR SHEEP'S
MILK CHEESES

♦

SHELLFISH PAELLA WITH
ARTICHOKES AND FENNEL

♦

PARSLIED GARLIC BREAD
*page 67*

♦

FRESH RASPBERRIES, STRAWBERRIES,
AND BLUEBERRIES

♦

LEMON CURD MOUSSE
*page 302*

♦

CORNMEAL BUTTER COOKIES
*page 113*

PAELLA, THE SPANISH DISH of rice with a multitude of colorful components, is such a spectacular one-dish meal that the simplest of accompaniments—cheese, olives, and bread—are all the host needs for a truly festive meal. I like to personalize store-bought olives by marinating or garnishing them, but even that subtle touch is really not necessary when time is short. Serve plenty of good bread (hot garlic bread if you wish), and let the dessert be as simple or elaborate as time allows.

## SHELLFISH PAELLA WITH ARTICHOKES AND FENNEL

♦ ♦ ♦ ♦ ♦ ♦ ♦ ♦ ♦

ONE SURE SIGN that a dish has entered classic status is the appearance of ersatz restaurant versions that only echo the real thing. If you've ordered paella lately and been served converted rice, dyed yellow, garnished with odds and ends of seafood and chicken, and generously topped with canned peas, you may not immediately think of serving it to guests.

The version below will change your mind. Please remember that in Spain the garnishing elements can vary from cook to cook and region to region, but the rice remains the essential ingredient. Short-grain rice from the marshy Valencia area of Spain is unique, and because it is hard to locate in this country the more widely available Italian superfino arborio rice (see Cook's Sources) will substitute nicely. Long-grain and converted rice do not begin to equal the texture of these European grains and are not acceptable in paella.

For my party paella I've chosen to concentrate on shellfish, which makes for a truly festive dish. Be flexible at the market, though, remembering to balance freshness, variety, and color.

To make this paella for a crowd, use the bottom of a large turkey roaster placed across two burners, or divide the recipe between two of the traditional flat metal paella pans. Transfer the paella to a large, deep platter or terra-cotta serving dish just before taking it to the table.

♦ ♦ ♦  ♦ ♦ ♦

In a heavy saucepan over medium-high heat bring the wine to a simmer. Add the mussels and clams, cover, and cook, stirring and shaking the pan, removing them with a slotted spoon as the shells open. Discard those which do not open after 5 minutes. Cool the wine slightly, then decant it into a measuring cup, discarding the sandy residue. Add enough of the broth to the wine to equal 7 cups. In a saucepan over high heat

*1½ cups dry white wine*

*12 mussels, scrubbed and debearded*

*12 small clams, scrubbed*

*6½ cups (about) canned chicken broth or homemade stock*

*1 teaspoon (¼ gram) saffron thread (see Cook's Sources)*

*¾ cup olive oil*

*9 baby artichokes, stems and tough outer leaves trimmed, halved*

*2 lobsters (1 pound each) claws removed and cracked, bodies halved lengthwise, and cut crosswise into thirds (page 150)*

*½ pound* chorizo, andouille, *or other spicy, smoked pork sausage (see Cook's Sources), sliced into ¼-inch rounds*

*1 medium onion, peeled and chopped*

*1 small fennel bulb, tough outer layer removed, inner layers sliced thin, plus fronds, as garnish*

*6 garlic cloves, peeled and minced*

*3 bay leaves*

*(ingredients continued)*

*3 large sweet peppers (1 red, 1 yellow, and 1 orange), stemmed, cored, and cut into sixths*

*3½ cups Italian short-grain rice (see Cook's Sources)*

*1½ pounds (about 15) jumbo shrimp, shelled and deveined*

*1 pound sea scallops, small side muscles removed*

*1½ teaspoons salt*

*1 teaspoon freshly ground black pepper*

*3 green onions, trimmed and sliced thin*

*½ cup finely chopped Italian parsley*

bring the wine mixture to a boil. Stir in the saffron, remove from the heat, and let stand until cool.

In a medium-size skillet over moderate heat warm 3 tablespoons of the olive oil. Add the artichokes and cook, tossing and stirring, until lightly colored, about 5 minutes. Add ½ cup of the remaining chicken broth, partially cover the pan, lower the heat, and simmer until just tender, 5 to 7 minutes. Remove from the heat and reserve.

In a wide, 7-quart, flameproof casserole or metal roasting pan placed over 2 burners heat the remaining olive oil. When it is hot add the lobster pieces and cook, turning once, until the shells are bright red, about 5 minutes. Using tongs, remove the lobster. Add the *chorizo* to the casserole and cook, tossing and stirring, until lightly colored, about 10 minutes. Add the onion, fennel, garlic, and bay leaves, lower the heat, and continue to cook, stirring occasionally, until the vegetables are tender, about 15 minutes. *The recipe can be prepared to this point up to 3 hours before serving. Refrigerate the clams, mussels, and lobster. Reheat the onions in the casserole over medium heat before proceeding.*

Position a rack in the middle of the oven and preheat to 325 degrees F. Bring the wine stock to a boil. Stir the sweet peppers and rice into the *chorizo* and vegetable mixture in the casserole and cook, stirring constantly, until the rice is well coated with oil and slightly translucent, about 4 minutes. Stir in the boiling stock and bring the entire mixture to a boil. Lower the heat slightly and cook, stirring occasionally, for 10 minutes. Stir in the artichokes, their cooking liquid, the shrimp, scallops, salt, and pepper. Arrange the lobster pieces over the rice and bake, uncovered, for 20 minutes. Remove the casserole from the oven, arrange the mussels and clams over the paella, and cover the pan tightly. Let the paella stand for 10 minutes.

Transfer the paella to a serving dish. Mince the fennel fronds, combine them with the green onions and parsley, and sprinkle over the paella. Serve immediately.

━● *Serves 12*

◆◆◆◆◆◆◆◆◆◆◆◆◆◆◆◆◆◆◆◆◆◆◆◆◆◆◆◆◆◆◆◆◆◆◆◆◆◆◆◆◆◆◆

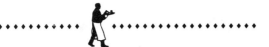

**SERVING STRATEGY** Because the Lemon Curd Mousse (page 302) is soft and spoonable, it makes a good topping for sweet, fresh berries. The combination (I like it served in my footed, ice-cream sundae dishes) is light and colorful but rich enough to end the meal on a big note. If time is short, serve store-bought butter cookies or Amaretti instead of the Cornmeal Butter Cookies (page 113).

# MENU

◆ ◆ ◆ ◆ ◆ ◆ ◆ ◆ ◆ ◆ ◆ ◆ ◆ ◆ ◆

CASSEROLE OF PORK, CARROTS,
AND BULGUR WITH MORELS

◆

MIXED GREENS WITH RED WINE
VINAIGRETTE AND CHEESE TOASTS
*page 50*

◆

BOURBON–BUTTERSCOTCH
BAKED APPLES
*page 36*

CASSEROLE IS A WORD that can strike fear in the hearts of otherwise strong folks, but just because food is combined and baked together in a single dish doesn't mean it contains canned soup, potato chips, and mysterious meat. This simple, hearty fall or winter menu features a casserole made fresh from scratch, that, with a salad and a homespun apple dessert, won't remind anyone in the least of cafeteria cuisine.

Spread the cheese toasts for the salad with a good, ripe Camembert (see Cook's Sources) and drink a light but well-balanced Oregon Pinot Noir.

▼▲▼▲▼▲▼▲▼▲▼▲▼▲▼▲▼▲▼▲▼▲▼▲▼▲▼▲▼▲▼▲▼▲▼

## CASSEROLE OF PORK, CARROTS, AND BULGUR WITH MORELS

♦ ♦ ♦ ♦ ♦ ♦ ♦ ♦ ♦

THIS DISH COMBINES the richness of pork with sweet carrots, nutty bulgur, and the earthy intensity of wild mushrooms in a sturdy but sophisticated casserole suitable for family and company alike.

♦ ♦ ♦  ♦ ♦ ♦

In a strainer under cold water rinse the morels. In a saucepan bring 2 cups of the broth to a boil. In a small, heatproof dish pour the broth over the mushrooms and let stand covered, stirring once or twice, until cool.

Set a 4½- or 5-quart, nonreactive flameproof casserole over medium-high heat. Add 3 tablespoons of the olive oil and when it is hot, add one-third of the pork. Cook, turning occasionally, until browned, about 7 minutes. With a slotted spoon, transfer the pork to a bowl. Repeat, in 2 batches, with the remaining pork; add oil to the casserole sparingly if necessary.

Do not clean the casserole. Add any remaining oil and set the casserole over low heat. Add the carrots, leeks, onion, thyme, and bay leaf and cook, covered, stirring occasionally and scraping browned deposits from the pan, until the vegetables are tender, about 15 minutes.

Position a rack in the lower third of the oven and preheat to 350 degrees F.

With a slotted spoon lift the morels gently from their soaking liquid. Let the liquid settle, then carefully decant it into a measuring cup, leaving behind any sandy residue. Add the wine to the soaking liquid, then add additional broth to bring the liquid to a total of 4½ cups. Add the liquid to the casserole.

Stir in the pork, with any juices from the bowl, the salt, and the pepper and bring to a simmer, skimming

*1 ounce (about 1 cup) dry morel or porcini mushrooms (see Cook's Sources)*

*5 cups (about) canned chicken broth or homemade stock*

*⅓ cup olive oil*

*3 pounds boneless pork shoulder, cut into 1-inch cubes*

*4 carrots, trimmed, peeled, and sliced on the diagonal ½ inch thick*

*2 large leeks, white part only, well cleaned and chopped*

*1 medium onion, peeled and chopped*

*1 teaspoon dry thyme, crumbled*

*1 bay leaf*

*1 cup dry white wine*

*1½ teaspoons salt*

*½ teaspoon freshly ground black pepper*

*2 cups medium-grain bulgur (see Cook's Sources)*

*⅓ cup finely chopped Italian parsley*

any surface scum that may form. Cover the casserole and bake 45 minutes.

Stir in the morels and the bulgur. Bake, covered, 30 minutes. Stir in the parsley and bake uncovered until the bulgur has absorbed all the cooking liquid and is lightly browned, 10 to 15 minutes. Serve directly from the casserole.

 *Serves 6*

♦♦♦♦♦♦♦♦♦♦♦♦♦♦♦♦♦♦♦♦♦♦♦♦♦♦♦♦♦♦♦♦♦♦♦♦♦♦♦♦♦♦♦♦♦♦♦

# MENU

◆ ◆ ◆ ◆ ◆ ◆ ◆ ◆ ◆ ◆ ◆ ◆ ◆ ◆ ◆

PLATTER OF FRESH GOAT'S AND
SHEEP'S MILK CHEESES,
SLICED RIPE TOMATOES, AND OLIVES

◆

HERBED PROSCIUTTO FLATBREAD
*page 162*

◆

SHRIMP AND VEGETABLE SPAGHETTI

◆

DEEP-DISH PLUM PIE

THIS LAZY SUMMER weekend menu is composed of a purchased and arranged starter, a colorful and zesty seafood pasta, a good bread, and a simple seasonal baked fruit dessert. The total effect is relaxed and rather earthy—perfect summer fare.

# SHRIMP AND VEGETABLE SPAGHETTI

◆◆◆◆◆◆◆◆◆◆

Salt
12 ounces dried spaghetti
    or linguine
2 tablespoons unsalted
    butter
2 tablespoons olive oil
3 medium carrots, peeled
    and julienned
2 large sweet peppers (1
    red and 1 green),
    stemmed, cored, and
    julienned
4 garlic cloves, peeled and
    minced
1 yellow summer squash,
    trimmed, scrubbed, and
    julienned
1 zucchini, trimmed,
    scrubbed, and julienned
2 pounds (about 24)
    jumbo shrimp, shelled
    and deveined
½ cup fish stock or bottled
    clam juice
⅔ cup whipping cream
2 cups clean, loosely
    packed fresh basil
    leaves, minced
½ teaspoon freshly ground
    black pepper

THIS BIG, COLORFUL MÉLANGE of jumbo shrimp, vegetables, and pasta is precisely the kind of eye-pleasing, palate-pleasing meal that successfully belies how little work is actually involved. If you've done any wok cookery, you'll recognize the game plan: With all the chopping, peeling, and mincing out of the way in advance, the actual cooking time is slightly less than 20 minutes.

Bring a large pot of water to a boil. Stir in 1 tablespoon of salt. When the water returns to a boil add the spaghetti. Cook, stirring once or twice, until the pasta is just tender, about 8 minutes. Drain immediately, rinse thoroughly with cold water, and drain again. *The recipe can be prepared to this point up to 3 hours before final cooking.*

In a large skillet over medium-high heat melt together the butter and olive oil. Add the carrots and cook, stirring, for 2 minutes. Add the sweet peppers and the garlic and cook, stirring, until the vegetables are slightly soft, about 3 minutes. Stir in the squash and zucchini and cook until they are slightly soft, about 3 minutes. With a slotted spoon, transfer the vegetables to a bowl.

Add the shrimp to the hot skillet and sauté for 1 minute. Add the fish stock and cook, scraping the bottom and sides of the pan, 30 seconds. Add the cream, raise the heat, and bring the liquid to a boil. Cook, tossing and stirring the shrimp, until they are just cooked through, 2 or 3 minutes longer.

Remove the skillet from the heat. With a slotted spoon, transfer the shrimp to the bowl with the vegetables. Add the spaghetti to the skillet, set it over medium heat, and cook, tossing and stirring, until the pasta is heated through and has absorbed much of the liquid, about 2 minutes. Stir in the vegetables and shrimp. Add the basil, ½ teaspoon of salt, and the pepper and cook, stirring and tossing, until all the ingredients are hot and the basil is fragrant, about 1 minute. Toss again and serve.

*Serves 6*

# DEEP-DISH PLUM PIE

**T**HIS PIE IS BEST if you serve it slightly warm. Enjoy it unadorned, or you may add a drizzle of heavy cream, a dollop of crème fraîche or sour cream, or a scoop of good ice cream.

The best plums will be slightly underripe and on the tart side—the Santa Rosa is a good, all-purpose variety to use here.

*For the filling* In a medium-size bowl combine the plums, sugar, flour, and orange zest and let stand, stirring occasionally, for 30 minutes.

Position a rack in the center of the oven. On a lower rack set a baking sheet to catch possible drips. Preheat the oven to 375 degrees F.

Spoon the filling, including any juices, into a 10-cup baking dish about 2½ inches deep. Bake about 20 minutes, or until the juices are clear and bubbling gently.

*For the crust* In a food processor combine the flour, cornmeal, sugar, and salt and pulse briefly to blend. Add the butter and shortening and process until a coarse meal forms, about 10 seconds. With the machine running add the cream through the feed tube until a soft dough forms.

PLUM FILLING

*4 pounds of firm red plums, pitted and sliced into eighths*
*1½ cups sugar*
*⅓ cup unbleached all-purpose flour*
*Zest of 1 medium orange, finely grated*

PIE CRUST

*1½ cups unbleached all-purpose flour (to measure, sift the flour into a measuring cup and sweep level)*
*½ cup yellow cornmeal*
*2 tablespoons sugar*
*¼ teaspoon salt*
*5 tablespoons unsalted butter, well chilled and cut into small pieces*
*3 tablespoons solid vegetable shortening, well chilled and cut into small pieces*

*(ingredients continued)*

*3 tablespoons whipping cream*

*1 egg yolk beaten with 1 tablespoon of water*

Turn the dough onto a floured surface. With the heel of your hand, push small pieces of dough down onto the work surface and away from you. With a scraper, gather the dough into a ball and wrap it in plastic. Refrigerate 20 to 30 minutes.

Lightly flour a work surface. Roll the dough out ⅜ inch thick. Using a 2½-inch cutter, cut the dough into rounds.

*To assemble* With a spatula, arrange the rounds atop the hot plum filling, overlapping them slightly, leaving a ½-inch border of filling visible around the edge of the dish. Brush the crust with the egg glaze. Bake the pie until the crust is golden brown and the juices are thick, another 30 to 35 minutes. Serve warm.

*Serves 6 to 8*

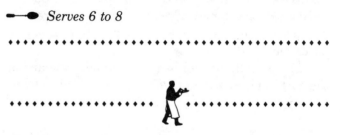

**SERVING STRATEGY** As I've said elsewhere, it's impossible for me to tell you which cheeses to buy, but they should be soft, fresh, and tangy. Add touches of sliced, ripe, red and yellow tomatoes and a mound or two of good olives, and the array will tantalize displayed on a big platter. Drizzle excellent olive oil over everything, sprinkle on minced fresh herbs, if you wish, and add a generous grind of black pepper. The flat-bread is simply one of my favorite things to eat, but of course you should feel free to serve a crusty store-bought loaf.

# M E N U

♦ ♦ ♦ ♦ ♦ ♦ ♦ ♦ ♦ ♦ ♦ ♦ ♦ ♦ ♦

CREAMED WILD MUSHROOMS WITH
BACON ON TOAST

♦

PORK RAGOUT WITH SWEET PEPPERS,
ANCHOVIES, AND OLIVES

♦

POTATO GRATIN
WITH ROSEMARY AND GARLIC

♦

SALAD OF WINTER GREENS WITH
BLUE GOAT CHEESE DRESSING

♦

SKILLET DESSERT OF PEARS,
CHESTNUTS, AND ARMAGNAC

NO SOONER HAD I finally gotten a dining room table than I began work on this book, and the computer and printer now sit where I had hoped to serve rustic dinners like this one. Fortunately the menu works well on the buffet, if you have one, or you can prepare the plates in the kitchen and serve the dinner as a lap meal.

## CREAMED WILD MUSHROOMS
## WITH BACON ON TOAST

◆◆◆◆◆◆◆◆◆◆

3 pounds assorted fresh
  mushrooms, such as
  shiitake, cremini,
  porcini (or cepes),
  oyster, morel, or
  chanterelle (see Cook's
  Sources)
½ pound smoky slab bacon
8 shallots, peeled and
  minced
1 teaspoon salt
¼ cup minced fresh
  marjoram plus
  additional sprigs, as
  garnish
2 cups canned chicken
  broth or homemade stock
1 cup (8 ounces) crème
  fraîche
Freshly ground black
  pepper
8 slices (1 inch thick)
  country-style bread,
  toasted

**F**OR THE BEST EFFECT of both taste and texture, combine at least two kinds of mushrooms—even if one of those is the ordinary cultivated white mushroom. Fresh marjoram and mushrooms are a flavor marriage made in heaven, but fresh thyme or oregano will do almost as well.

◆◆◆  ◆◆◆

Stem and trim the mushrooms. Wipe them with a damp towel. Cut the large mushrooms into thick slices. Quarter the medium mushrooms. Leave small, cultivated mushrooms whole. Cut away any tough rind from the bacon and slice the bacon crosswise into squares about ⅛ inch thick.

Lay the bacon squares in a single layer in a large skillet. Set the skillet over medium heat and cook, turning the bacon once or twice, until it is crisp and brown, 10 to 12 minutes. With a slotted spoon, transfer the bacon to a small bowl.

Remove the skillet from the heat and stir the shallots into the hot bacon fat. Return the skillet to medium heat and add the mushrooms. Cook, stirring occasionally, until the mushrooms begin to soften, about 5 minutes. Stir in the salt and cook, stirring occasionally, for another 5 to 7 minutes, or until the mushrooms just began to render their juices. Stir in the marjoram, chicken broth, and crème fraîche and bring just to a boil. Lower the heat and simmer, uncovered, stirring occasionally, until the mushrooms are tender, 7 to 10 minutes. Adjust the seasoning, adding fresh pepper to taste. *The recipe can be prepared to this point up to 3 hours ahead. Reheat over low heat, stirring often, until simmering, before proceeding.*

Stir the bacon into the mushroom mixture. Set the toast on plates. Spoon the mushrooms and sauce over the toast. Garnish with the sprigs of marjoram and serve immediately.

➤ *Serves 8*

◆ ◆ ◆ ◆ ◆ ◆ ◆ ◆ ◆ ◆ ◆ ◆ ◆ ◆ ◆ ◆ ◆ ◆ ◆ ◆ ◆ ◆ ◆ ◆ ◆ ◆ ◆ ◆ ◆ ◆ ◆ ◆ ◆ ◆ ◆ ◆ ◆ ◆ ◆ ◆

## PORK RAGOUT WITH SWEET PEPPERS, ANCHOVIES, AND OLIVES

◆ ◆ ◆ ◆ ◆ ◆ ◆ ◆

T HE BRIGHT, FRESH FLAVOR of this satisfying stew results from the combination of orange juice, Provençal herbs, and garlic. The peppers add a zesty sweetness and the anchovies contribute a rich, subtle background taste few will be able to identify. The ragout is just as good when made with lamb.

Preheat the oven to 350 degrees F.

Pat the pork dry. In a 4½- or 5-quart, flameproof casserole over medium-high heat warm 2 tablespoons of the oil. Add one-quarter of the pork and cook, turning the cubes occasionally, until well browned, about 7 minutes. Season lightly with salt and pepper. With a slotted spoon, transfer the pork to a bowl. Repeat, working in batches, with the remaining pork, adding oil to the pan as needed to prevent the pork from sticking.

Do not clean the pan. Add 3 tablespoons of the oil and set over medium heat. Stir in the onion, garlic, oregano, basil, thyme, and bay leaves. Cover and cook, stirring once or twice, until tender, about 15 minutes. Uncover, stir in the flour, and cook, stirring often, for 5 minutes. Stir in the chicken broth, wine, orange juice, anchovies, and browned pork, including any juices that have accumulated in the bowl.

*5 pounds boneless pork shoulder or Boston butt, trimmed and cut into 2-inch cubes*

*½ cup olive oil*

*Salt and freshly ground black pepper*

*4 cups chopped yellow onion*

*6 garlic cloves, peeled and minced*

*2 teaspoons dried oregano, crumbled*

*2 teaspoons dried basil, crumbled*

*2 teaspoons dried thyme, crumbled*

*2 bay leaves*

*⅓ cup flour*

*2½ cups canned chicken broth or homemade stock*

*1½ cups dry white wine*

*¾ cup fresh orange juice, strained*

*12 oil-packed anchovy fillets, minced*

*(ingredients continued)*

*3 large sweet peppers (1
red, 1 green, and 1
yellow), stemmed, cored,
and quartered*
*1 cup medium, imported
black olives, such as
Gaeta (see Cook's
Sources), rinsed*
*½ cup finely chopped
Italian parsley*

Bring the ragout to a boil, cover the casserole, and bake 45 minutes. Stir the ragout and continue to bake, uncovered, for 45 to 50 minutes, or until the pork is tender. *The dish can be prepared to this point up to 24 hours ahead. Cool to room temperature, cover, and refrigerate. Warm over low heat, stirring often, until simmering.*

In a medium-size skillet over high heat warm the remaining olive oil. Add the peppers and cook, tossing and stirring, until lightly browned, about 5 minutes. Adjust the seasoning. Stir the browned peppers, the olives, and the parsley into the ragout and simmer another 1 or 2 minutes, or until heated through. Serve immediately.

*Serves 8*

♦♦♦♦♦♦♦♦♦♦♦♦♦♦♦♦♦♦♦♦♦♦♦♦♦♦♦♦♦♦♦♦♦♦♦♦♦♦♦♦♦♦♦

▀▄▀▄▀▄▀▄▀▄▀▄▀▄▀▄▀▄▀▄▀▄▀▄▀▄▀▄▀▄▀▄▀▄▀▄▀▄

## POTATO GRATIN WITH ROSEMARY AND GARLIC

♦♦♦♦♦♦♦♦♦

*3 tablespoons olive oil*
*3½ pounds boiling
potatoes, peeled and
sliced thin*
*2 tablespoons minced fresh
rosemary*
*6 garlic cloves, peeled and
sliced thin*
*2 teaspoons salt*
*Freshly ground black
pepper*
*1½ cups canned chicken
broth or homemade stock*

I DON'T HAVE TO ARGUE that potatoes are a comfort. Anyone who has ever sought consolation with a pound or two on a lonely winter night knows that already. Instead, just let me say that this crisp and moist rendition, fragrant with fresh rosemary and loads of garlic, is not only a comfort but also a stylish and savory accompaniment to the pork ragout.

♦♦♦  ♦♦♦

Position a rack in the upper third of the oven and preheat to 375 degrees F. Brush the bottom of a 9 × 13-inch oval gratin dish with 1 tablespoon of the oil. Arrange one-third of the potato slices, overlapping them as necessary, in the baking dish. Sprinkle with 1 tablespoon of the rosemary, half of the garlic, and 1 teaspoon of the salt. Season generously with pepper.

Drizzle 1 tablespoon of the oil over the seasoned potatoes. Layer half of the remaining potato slices in the dish. Sprinkle with the remaining rosemary, garlic, and salt. Season with pepper and drizzle the remaining olive oil over the seasoned potatoes. Spread the remaining potato slices in the dish. Pour the chicken broth evenly over the potatoes.

Place the pan in the oven and bake until the potatoes are tender, the top layer is crisp and golden, and all the stock has been absorbed, about 1¼ hours. Let the gratin stand 10 minutes before serving.

━● *Serves 8*

◆ ◆ ◆ ◆ ◆ ◆ ◆ ◆ ◆ ◆ ◆ ◆ ◆ ◆ ◆ ◆ ◆ ◆ ◆ ◆ ◆ ◆ ◆ ◆ ◆ ◆ ◆ ◆ ◆ ◆ ◆ ◆ ◆ ◆ ◆ ◆ ◆ ◆

## SALAD OF WINTER GREENS WITH BLUE GOAT CHEESE DRESSING

◆ ◆ ◆ ◆ ◆ ◆ ◆ ◆

T HE BEST OF the blue-veined goat cheeses have the tang of regular chèvre, plus a moist texture, and a spectacular blue-veined flavor. The creamy vinaigrette employs a generous amount of blue chèvre and is spooned over a gutsy salad of winter greens. If you can't find the chèvre, use 3 ounces of ordinary goat cheese, pureed into the dressing, and 3 ounces of a good blue cheese, such as Roquefort, crumbled in at the end.

◆ ◆ ◆  ◆ ◆ ◆

*For the salad* Trim and wash the watercress and chicory and tear into bite-size pieces. Core the cabbage and cut into julienne strips. Trim the fennel and cut into julienne strips. Peel the onion and slice into thin rings. *The salad can be prepared up to 1 day ahead. Wrap separately in plastic bags and refrigerate.*

SALAD OF WINTER GREENS

*2 bunches watercress*
*2 heads French chicory*
  *(frisée) or escarole*
*⅓ head purple cabbage*
*1 large fennel bulb*
*1 medium red onion*

BLUE GOAT CHEESE DRESSING

*¼ cup red wine vinegar*
*1½ tablespoons prepared*
  *Dijon-style mustard*
*2 egg yolks*
*6 ounces blue-veined goat*
  *cheese*
*1 teaspoon freshly ground*
  *black pepper*
*¾ cup olive oil*
*¾ cup corn oil*

*For the dressing* In a food processor combine the vinegar, mustard, egg yolks, half of the cheese, and the pepper and process until smooth. With the motor running, quickly pour in the olive and corn oils. Transfer the dressing to a bowl. Crumble the remaining cheese and stir it into the dressing. *The dressing can be prepared 1 day ahead. Cover and refrigerate; return to room temperature before proceeding.*

*To assemble the salad* Arrange the greens on salad plates. Drizzle with the dressing and garnish with onion rings.

—● *Serves 8*

◆◆◆◆◆◆◆◆◆◆◆◆◆◆◆◆◆◆◆◆◆◆◆◆◆◆◆◆◆◆◆◆◆◆◆◆◆◆◆◆◆◆◆◆◆◆

## SKILLET DESSERT OF PEARS, CHESTNUTS, AND ARMAGNAC

◆◆◆◆◆◆◆◆◆◆

6 ripe, firm pears
6 tablespoons unsalted
   butter
24 whole roasted chestnuts
   (see note)
¼ cup sugar
¾ cup armagnac or
   brandy
¾ cup whipping cream

**S**OME LAST-MINUTE DESSERTS are worth the effort. This sauté, lavish with rich winter flavors, is one of them. While red-skinned Bartlett pears add visual appeal, any ripe but still fairly firm pear will do equally well. It is desirable that the pears darken, so don't bother fussing with lemon juice to keep them white.

◆◆◆  ◆◆◆

Peel the skins of the pears only if they are tough or spotty. Halve and core the pears. Slice each pear half into thirds.

In a large skillet over medium heat melt the butter. Add the pears and cook until lightly colored, about 5 minutes. Turn the pears and lower the heat. Stir in the chestnuts, sugar, and armagnac and simmer, basting the pears once or twice with the accumulated pan juices, until tender, about 4 minutes.

With a slotted spoon, transfer the pears and chestnuts to dessert plates. Add the whipping cream to the skillet, turn the heat to high, and bring the sauce to a boil. Cook hard for 3 minutes, stirring constantly, or until thickened. Spoon the sauce over the pears and chestnuts and serve while still warm.

NOTE Whole, peeled chestnuts, roasted and vacuum-packed without liquid or sugar, are available in specialty food shops or by mail (see Cook's Sources).

To roast fresh chestnuts, preheat the oven to 400 degrees F. Cut a shallow X in the flat side of the nuts, spread them in a single layer on a baking sheet, and bake for 10 minutes. Peel the chestnuts while still warm, being certain to remove both the outer and inner peels. Chestnuts prepared this way can be refrigerated, well wrapped, for 24 hours.

*Serves 8*

◆ ◆ ◆ ◆ ◆ ◆ ◆ ◆ ◆ ◆ ◆ ◆ ◆ ◆ ◆ ◆ ◆ ◆ ◆ ◆ ◆ ◆ ◆ ◆ ◆ ◆ ◆ ◆ ◆ ◆ ◆ ◆ ◆ ◆ ◆ ◆ ◆ ◆ ◆

# MENU

◆ ◆ ◆ ◆ ◆ ◆ ◆ ◆ ◆ ◆ ◆ ◆ ◆ ◆ ◆

BROTH WITH MIXED SALAD GREENS

◆

PARSLEY-PEPPER SKILLET BREAD

◆

HUNTER'S CHICKEN

◆

POTATO GRATIN WITH
ROSEMARY AND GARLIC
*page 224*

◆

APPLES POACHED IN CALVADOS

◆

CORNMEAL BUTTER COOKIES
*page 113*

THIS RUSTIC, COUNTRY MENU is one I would serve on an
evening in early fall. Warm days mean plenty of activ-
ity; cool evenings mean big appetites. The change of
the seasons brings an abundance of both summer and
autumn fruits and vegetables. The resulting food is
hearty and exciting to cook and to eat.

## BROTH WITH
## MIXED SALAD GREENS

♦ ♦ ♦ ♦ ♦ ♦ ♦ ♦ ♦

**A** SIMPLE SOUP, but good, this is little more than assorted assertive greens floating in a rich broth. Use one kind or as many as you'd like, and pass a bowl of grated Parmesan and a pepper mill at the table.

Heat the oil in a large, heavy pot over high heat. Pat the chicken dry. Add the chicken to the pot, in batches if necessary, and brown well on all sides, 10 to 15 minutes.

Add the onions, carrots, garlic, parsley stems, marjoram, thyme, and bay leaves to the pot. Turn the heat to low, cover the pot, and cook, stirring occasionally and scraping the bottom of the pot, until the vegetables are very tender and lightly colored, 20 to 25 minutes.

Add the chicken broth (plus water, if needed, to cover the solids) and peppercorns to the pot and bring to a boil. Lower the heat, cover, and simmer 2 hours, skimming and stirring occasionally.

Strain the broth, discarding the solids. Measure the broth and, if necessary, reduce it by boiling hard over high heat, to 2 quarts. *The soup can be prepared to this point up to 3 days ahead. Cool completely, cover, and refrigerate. Remove the hardened fats from the surface of the broth. In a medium-size saucepan bring the broth to a boil.*

Adjust the seasoning. Divide the shredded greens among soup bowls. Ladle the hot broth over the greens and serve at once.

━● *Serves 8*

¼ cup vegetable oil
3 pounds chicken backs, necks, and wings
3 medium onions, peeled and chopped
4 large carrots, peeled and chopped
8 whole, unpeeled garlic cloves
Stems from 1 bunch parsley
1 tablespoon dried marjoram, crumbled
1 teaspoon dried thyme, crumbled
2 bay leaves
12 cups canned chicken broth
12 black peppercorns
Salt
4 cups finely shredded mixed salad greens, such as romaine, watercress, escarole, arugula, or spinach

## PARSLEY-PEPPER SKILLET BREAD

♦ ♦ ♦ ♦ ♦ ♦ ♦ ♦ ♦

4 cups unbleached
all-purpose flour
1 cup finely chopped
Italian parsley
2 tablespoons baking
powder
1 tablespoon freshly
ground black pepper
¾ teaspoon salt
½ cup (1 stick) unsalted
butter, well chilled and
cut into small pieces
1½ cups heavy cream, well
chilled
1 tablespoon olive oil

**S**ERVE THIS PEPPERY quick bread piping hot from the oven in its cast-iron skillet, and accompany it with sweet butter, or, if you'd like, with Black Olive Butter (page 26). In this menu I like it best with the soup, but you might serve it with the entrée instead.

♦♦♦  ♦♦♦

Position a rack in the center of the oven and preheat to 425 degrees F. Generously butter a 10-inch cast-iron skillet.

In a food processor combine the flour, parsley, baking powder, pepper, and salt and process briefly to blend. Cut in the butter until the mixture resembles coarse meal. With the machine running add the cream through the feed tube; do not overprocess.

Turn the dough out onto a lightly floured surface. Pat it into a 10-inch disc. Transfer the dough to the prepared skillet. Drizzle the olive oil over the top. Bake the skillet bread until puffed, golden brown, and crisp around the edges, about 30 minutes. Cut into wedges and serve hot or warm.

➼ *Serves 8*

♦ ♦ ♦ ♦ ♦ ♦ ♦ ♦ ♦ ♦ ♦ ♦ ♦ ♦ ♦ ♦ ♦ ♦ ♦ ♦ ♦ ♦ ♦ ♦ ♦ ♦ ♦ ♦ ♦ ♦ ♦ ♦ ♦ ♦ ♦ ♦ ♦ ♦ ♦ ♦

## HUNTER'S CHICKEN

♦ ♦ ♦ ♦ ♦ ♦ ♦ ♦ ♦

**A** GREAT BIG BEAUTIFUL dish of chicken, sausages, sweet peppers, and wild mushrooms, the inspiration for this came from the chicken cacciatore recipe of an old friend, Victor Fabrizio. My first boss in the food business, he is now the owner of Victor's, a splendid if somewhat unexpected Italian restaurant located in Santa Fe, New Mexico.

In a strainer rinse the mushrooms under cold water. Transfer them to a small bowl. In a small pan bring the chicken broth to a boil. Pour it over the mushrooms and let stand 1 hour, stirring occasionally.

In a large, heavy skillet over medium-high heat warm ¼ cup of the oil. Add the peppers and cook, stirring and tossing, until lightly browned, about 5 minutes. With a slotted spoon, transfer the peppers to a bowl. Do not pour off the oil.

Pat the chicken pieces dry. In the skillet over medium heat sauté the chicken, in batches if necessary, until lightly browned on all sides, about 10 minutes. (Add additional oil if the skillet becomes dry.) Arrange the browned chicken skin side up in a single layer in a baking dish and lightly salt and pepper. Set aside.

Add the sausage to the skillet and brown well on all sides, about 15 minutes. Remove the sausage from the skillet and cut into 8 pieces. Scatter the sausage over the chicken. Pour off the fat but do not clean the skillet.

Drain the mushrooms, reserving the liquid. Strain the liquid through a strainer lined with several thicknesses of dampened cheesecloth. There should be about 1½ cups; add enough marsala to total 2 cups. Stir the liquid into the skillet, set it over medium heat, and bring to a boil, stirring and scraping to dissolve browned bits. Lower the heat and simmer 3 minutes.

Scatter the peppers and mushrooms over the chicken and sausage. Pour the liquid from the skillet over all. Season lightly with salt and pepper. *The chicken can be assembled, covered, and stored at room temperature to this point up to 3 hours ahead.*

Preheat the oven to 350 degrees F. Cover the baking dish tightly with foil and bake until the chicken is tender, basting every 15 minutes, about 1 hour.

Transfer the chicken, sausages, peppers, and mushrooms to a platter. Cover and keep warm. Degrease the pan juices and transfer them to a medium-size saucepan over high heat. Cook hard until the

*2 ounces dried porcini mushrooms (see Cook's Sources)*

*3 cups canned chicken broth or homemade stock*

*⅓ cup (about) olive oil*

*4 large, sweet red peppers, stemmed, cored, and cut into quarters*

*2 chickens (3 pounds each), quartered*

*Salt and freshly ground black pepper*

*1½ pounds Italian-style sweet sausage*

*½ cup (about) dry marsala*

liquid is reduced by one-third, about 15 minutes; adjust the seasoning. Spoon some of the juices over the chicken and pass the remainder separately.

━━● *Serves 8*

◆◆◆◆◆◆◆◆◆◆◆◆◆◆◆◆◆◆◆◆◆◆◆◆◆◆◆◆◆◆◆◆◆◆◆◆◆◆◆◆◆◆◆◆◆

## APPLES POACHED IN CALVADOS

◆◆◆◆◆◆◆◆◆◆

*1 can (12-ounce) frozen apple juice concentrate, thawed*
*¾ cup Calvados brandy or good-quality American applejack*
*½ cup sugar*
*3 cups cold water*
*1 vanilla bean, split*
*8 tart apples, peeled, cored, and quartered*
*½ cup crème fraîche*
*Fresh mint, as garnish*

**W**HEN IT COMES TO BOOZE, apples are easy-going, combining well with any number of spirits. Calvados suits the country mood of this menu, but at other times Scotch or bourbon will be equally tasty. This dessert is light but apple-intense.

◆◆◆  ◆◆◆

In a medium-size, heavy saucepan combine the apple concentrate, brandy, and sugar with the water. Scrape in the vanilla bean seeds, then add the pod. Set the pan over low heat and cook, stirring, until the sugar dissolves, about 2 minutes. Increase the heat to medium and simmer 10 minutes.

Add the apples to the liquid and bring it to a boil. Lower the heat and simmer until the apples are tender, stirring gently, about 10 minutes. With a slotted spoon, remove the apples and reserve. Transfer 1½ cups of the poaching liquid and the vanilla bean to a small, heavy saucepan. Whisk in the crème fraîche and set over high heat. Bring to a boil, lower the heat slightly, and cook hard for 15 minutes. *The dessert can be prepared and stored at room temperature to this point up to 3 hours ahead. Cool the poaching liquid, so the apples won't cook further, and pour it over the fruit.*

In a medium-size saucepan combine the apples and the sauce. Over low heat, baste the apples until warmed through, being careful not to overcook them.

━━● *Serves 8*

◆◆◆◆◆◆◆◆◆◆◆◆◆◆◆◆◆◆◆◆◆◆◆◆◆◆◆◆◆◆◆◆◆◆◆◆◆◆◆◆◆◆◆◆◆

# MENU

◆◆◆◆◆◆◆◆◆◆◆◆◆◆◆◆◆

OYSTERS ON THE HALF-SHELL
*page 99*

◆

CHOUCROUTE GARNIE

◆

ASSORTED MUSTARDS

◆

BUCKWHEAT
COUNTRY PUMPERNICKEL
BREAD
*page 56*

◆

APPLES, ROQUEFORT CHEESE,
AND CRISP, PLAIN CRACKERS

YOU KNOW A RECIPE truly qualifies for the one-dish Hall of Fame when you're stymied for accompaniments. I *tried* to gussy things up, but choucroute garnie is such a complex, overstuffed, and rib-sticking dish of food that almost anything except a fork, a beer, and a roomful of friends is superfluous. Start with a few cool oysters, raw clams, or poached shrimp and finish up with apples and cheese. That's it, that's the menu—and that's great eating.

5 pounds of sauerkraut
(see note)

6 tablespoons (¾ stick)
unsalted butter

½ pound lean, smoky ham,
cut into ¼-inch dice

¼ pound smoky slab
bacon, trimmed and cut
into ¼-inch dice

2 large yellow onions,
peeled and chopped

6 carrots, peeled and sliced

4 garlic cloves, peeled and
minced

3 large pears, such as
Bartlett, cored, peeled,
and chopped

6 juniper berries

1 teaspoon caraway seeds

1 teaspoon dry thyme,
crumbled

1 teaspoon freshly ground
black pepper

2 bay leaves

8 cups canned chicken
broth or homemade stock

2 cups Gewürztraminer or
Riesling wine

24 (about 3 pounds)
red-skinned new
potatoes

Salt

6 pounds assorted link
sausages, such as
bratwurst, knockwurst,
weisswurst, kielbasa,
andouille, or saucisson
de l'ail

⅔ cup finely chopped
Italian parsley

# CHOUCROUTE GARNIE

♦ ♦ ♦ ♦ ♦ ♦ ♦ ♦ ♦

**S**AUERKRAUT, SLOWLY BRAISED with broth, wine, ham, pears, carrots, and onions, becomes mellow, sweet, and user-friendly. When garnished with an array of succulent sausages and served with new potatoes, mustards, and hearty dark bread, kraut provides the basis for one of the most crowd-pleasing meals I know.

When it comes to selecting the sausages, variety is important. So, too, is quality, and if you find only one kind of truly excellent sausage—at the local butcher, famous for his bratwurst, for example, or in a care package of *andouille* from a friend in Louisiana—don't hesitate to star it solo in your choucroute. (Or, see Cook's Sources.)

You may choose to pour more of the same wine you cooked the kraut in, but I usually offer an array of good beers.

Drain the sauerkraut and soak it in a large bowl of cold water for 1 hour, changing the water once. Drain the sauerkraut and squeeze out all the moisture.

Position a rack in the lower third of the oven and preheat to 350 degrees F. In a large, wide, nonreactive, flameproof casserole or roaster over medium heat melt the butter. Add the ham and bacon and cook, stirring, for 10 to 12 minutes, or until crisp and brown. Stir in the onions, carrots, and garlic and cook, covered, stirring once or twice, until the vegetables are tender, about 15 minutes. Stir in the pears, juniper berries, caraway, thyme, pepper, and bay leaves. Cook 5 minutes. Add the chicken broth, wine, and sauerkraut and bring to a simmer. Lightly butter a piece of parchment paper and place it, butter side down, on the sauerkraut mixture. Cover the casserole and bake 4 to 4½ hours, or until most of the liquid has evaporated. Remove the casserole from the oven, uncover it, discard the parchment paper, and cool to room temperature. *The dish can be prepared to this point up to 3 days ahead. Cover and refrigerate.*

Scrub the potatoes. Peel a ½-inch strip around the middle of each. In a large pan cover the potatoes with cold, lightly salted water. Set the pan over high heat and bring to a boil. Lower the heat slightly and cook until the potatoes are just tender, about 8 minutes after the water returns to a boil. Drain.

Preheat the broiler. Place the sausages on a broiler-proof pan and broil them, turning often, until well browned, 3 to 5 minutes. Cut the sausages into 2-inch chunks. *The sausages and potatoes can be prepared to this point up to 3 hours before serving.*

Preheat the oven to 375 degrees F. Arrange the potatoes and sausages over the sauerkraut. Bake the choucroute garnie, covered, until the sauerkraut, potatoes, and sausages are steaming and fully heated, 30 to 40 minutes. Arrange the potatoes and sausages on a platter. Spoon the sauerkraut and any juices into a bowl. Sprinkle both with the parsley and serve immediately.

NOTE Use the refrigerated sauerkraut that comes in bags or jars. For excellent kraut by mail, see Cook's Sources. Canned sauerkraut is not acceptable in this recipe.

*Serves 12*

♦ ♦ ♦ ♦ ♦ ♦ ♦ ♦ ♦ ♦ ♦ ♦ ♦ ♦ ♦ ♦ ♦ ♦ ♦ ♦ ♦ ♦ ♦ ♦ ♦ ♦ ♦ ♦ ♦ ♦ ♦ ♦ ♦ ♦ ♦ ♦ ♦ ♦ ♦ ♦

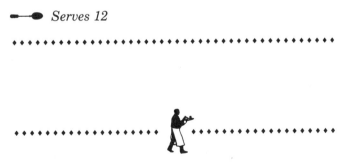

**SERVING STRATEGY** Roquefort produced for export is somewhat saltier than that consumed in France, and, of course, has spent a lot of prime time finding its way to your neighborhood store. It's important to look for a reliable brand (*Société B* is readily available and good; *Gabriel Coulet* is harder to find but preferable) and to buy it from a dealer whose turnover is brisk. The cheese should be creamy and ivory colored, veined with blue. If it is hard, yellow, or oozing liquid, it will be too strong to enjoy with dessert—or with anything else. If your cheese dealer consistently fails you in the Roquefort department, you may want to mail order the excellent American cow's milk blue cheese from Maytag Dairy Farms (see Cook's Sources). It's a nice idea to offer diners sweet butter, which, mixed with the cheese on a cracker, will mellow the Roquefort for those who like their cheese on the tamer side. Red wine is usually defeated by Roquefort; experts prefer port (vintage port if you can locate and afford it) or a complex and opulently sweet French sauternes.

◆ ◆ ◆ ◆ ◆ ◆ ◆ ◆ ◆ ◆ ◆ ◆ ◆ ◆ ◆ ◆ ◆ ◆ ◆ ◆ ◆ ◆ ◆ ◆ ◆ ◆ ◆ ◆ ◆ ◆ ◆ ◆ ◆ ◆ ◆ ◆ ◆ ◆ ◆ ◆ ◆

# SIX FRIENDS

◆◆◆◆◆◆◆◆◆◆◆◆◆◆◆◆◆◆◆◆◆◆◆◆◆◆◆◆◆◆◆◆◆◆◆◆◆◆◆◆◆◆◆

FORTUNATELY, I have more than six friends, but the title of this chapter still makes a point. These are dinner-party menus—formal, sit-down affairs, with a structured progression of courses—for six, which seems to be the most manageable number of people to feed. My pots and pans hold food to feed six, two bottles of wine pour six full glasses, and a standard-sized dining-room table seats six comfortably and with plenty of elbow-room. If you're a social strategist, conversation is carried on most easily with this size group, and the dynamics are lively without becoming raucous.

Despite the more formal approach, these menus are still on the zesty and colorful side. I like big flavors, vibrant colors, and food that is solidly filling. My inclination is toward big, deep terra-cotta plates, heavy restaurant silver, soft absorbent hand towels in place of linen, and sturdy, oversized bistro wineglasses that hold a generous pour. I find that hors d'oeuvres are fussy and unnecessary when entertaining a small number of people on this scale, and in my house we usually move directly to the table. Courses are well spaced for digestion and conversation, food is usually brought from the kitchen on plates for easy presentation, and a meal that lasts hours but seems much shorter is the norm.

I have at least one extra bottle of wine on hand for lingering over after every morsel is gone, and though I expect to offer coffee and after-dinner liqueurs of some kind, I just as often skip them when the mood of contentment around the table seems too complete to improve upon.

As I have tried to do throughout this book, I have included here do-ahead steps to simplify preparing these small dinner parties, along with some tips on creative rearranging of the typical meat/veg/starch planning approach to make things even simpler. On the other hand, feeding people well is never an effortless task (anyone who tries to sell you that notion is a fraud), and your guests' appreciation of the results on the plate is directly linked to their knowledge that you cared enough to cook for them.

▚▚▚▚▚▚▚▚▚▚▚▚▚▚▚▚▚▚▚▚▚▚▚▚▚▚▚▚▚▚▚▚▚▚▚▚▚▚

# MENU

◆◆◆◆◆◆◆◆◆◆◆◆◆◆◆◆

MUSSEL SALAD WITH
FRESH OREGANO DRESSING

◆

COUNTRY BEEF STEW

◆

HERBED CORNMEAL FETTUCCINE
*page 97*

◆

LEMON-GRAPPA TART

I DON'T COOK AS MUCH beef at home as I do other meats, not because I don't like it as well (on the contrary) but because when barbecued brisket, a grilled burger with the works, or an aged prime sirloin are on my mind. I gladly let restaurateurs do the work—I trust them to do a better job than I ever could.

Beef stew, on the other hand, I jealously guard as my own domain. I can't think of a restaurant where I would enjoy a stew quite as much as the one this menu is centered around. The fact that I like the process of making it as much as I like the actual eating of it is also a plus, and knowing that nearly all of the stew can be made completely in advance just makes the whole business that much sweeter.

## MUSSEL SALAD WITH FRESH OREGANO DRESSING

♦♦♦♦♦♦♦♦♦

**M**USSELS REMAIN downright cheap to buy (the culti-vated ones that come sealed in plastic bags are fre-quently past their prime: *caveat emptor*) but still have an aura of mystique signaling that great eating is on the way. For this light, easy, and colorful starter, the dressing can be prepared a day or two ahead and the mussels can be steamed open an hour or two in ad-vance. Assemble and dress the salad while the stew is reheating. No fresh oregano? Basil is a good substitute.

*1 large bunch arugula*
*48 fresh mussels*
*Fresh Oregano Dressing*
  *(page 80)*
*Salt*
*Freshly ground black*
  *pepper*
*Sprigs of fresh oregano, as*
  *garnish*

Trim and wash the arugula and pat it dry. *The arugula can be cleaned up to 1 day ahead and refrigerated, well wrapped in plastic bags.*

Sort through the mussels, discarding those that do not close when tapped or that are heavy. Scrub the mussels and remove the beards. In a large, deep skillet over medium heat bring 1 inch of water to a boil. Add the mussels and cover the skillet. Cook, tossing and stirring occasionally, removing the mussels as they open. After 5 minutes discard those that remain un-opened. Remove the mussels from their shells. *The mussels can be opened up to 3 hours in advance. Cover and refrigerate. Return the mussels to room tempera-ture before proceeding.*

Line 6 salad plates with the arugula. In a bowl toss the mussels with the dressing. Season lightly with salt and more generously with pepper. Divide the mussel salad among the 6 plates, forming a mound on the arug-ula leaves. Garnish the mussel salads with the sprigs of oregano.

—● *Serves 6*

♦♦♦♦♦♦♦♦♦♦♦♦♦♦♦♦♦♦♦♦♦♦♦♦♦♦♦♦♦♦♦♦♦♦♦♦♦♦♦♦

3 pounds lean, boneless
   beef stewing meat, cut
   into 1½-inch cubes
1 cup dry red wine
⅓ cup red wine vinegar
4 garlic cloves, peeled and
   minced, plus 24 whole
   and unpeeled cloves
2 teaspoons dried thyme,
   crumbled
2 bay leaves
8 tablespoons olive oil
Salt
Freshly ground black
   pepper
2 medium onions, peeled
   and chopped
¼ cup unbleached
   all-purpose flour
2 cups canned beef broth
   or homemade stock
1 cup canned crushed
   tomatoes
4 large carrots, peeled and
   cut on the bias into
   2-inch pieces
¾ cup finely chopped
   Italian parsley

## COUNTRY BEEF STEW

THIS IS ONE of the sturdiest, most satisfying dishes of food I know. Diners can mash the sweet and tender garlic cloves against the bowl, adding savor to the stew, or retrieve them and spread the pulp on bread. Serving the stew with herbed Cornmeal Fettuccine (page 97) makes for an especially festive presentation, but you could choose to omit the pasta and add nine new potatoes, scrubbed and halved, to cook in the stew with the carrots.

In a large, nonreactive bowl combine the meat, wine, vinegar, minced garlic, thyme, bay leaves, and 3 tablespoons of the oil and stir well. Marinate at room temperature, stirring once or twice, for 2 hours.

Drain the meat, reserving the marinade. In a large, nonreactive, flameproof casserole or Dutch oven over medium-high heat warm 3 tablespoons of the remaining oil until very hot. Working in batches, without crowding the pan, cook the meat, turning it frequently until brown, about 7 minutes. With a slotted spoon, transfer the meat to a bowl and season it lightly with salt and pepper. Repeat with the remaining meat, adding additional oil if the casserole becomes dry. Do not clean the casserole.

Position a rack in the lower third of the oven and preheat to 350 degrees F.

Set the casserole over low heat and warm all of the remaining oil. Add the onions and cook, covered, stirring occasionally, until tender, 15 minutes. Sprinkle the flour over the onions and continue to cook for 5 minutes, stirring often.

Add the marinade to the casserole, raise the heat, and bring it to a boil, stirring to scrape up any browned bits from the bottom of the pan.

Return the browned meat, along with any juices from the bowl, to the casserole. Stir in the beef broth, tomatoes, 1 teaspoon of salt, and ½ teaspoon of pepper. Over medium heat bring the stew to a simmer. Cover the casserole and bake it for 1 hour. *The stew can be prepared to this point up to 1 day ahead. Cool completely, cover, and refrigerate. Bring the stew to a simmer, stirring often, before proceeding.*

Add the carrots and whole garlic cloves and return the stew to the 350 degree F oven. Bake, uncovered, for 45 to 55 minutes, or until the carrots and meat are tender and the sauce is slightly thickened. Discard the bay leaves and stir in the parsley. Let the stew stand, covered, for 1 minute before serving.

*Serves 6*

## LEMON-GRAPPA TART

**G**RAPPA IS USUALLY A ROUGH and fiery Italian brandy, but there are smooth, aged versions, and restaurants often mellow a bottle of Grappa with the addition of lemon peel or raisins—the inspiration for this intensely lemony tart. The raisins can be soaked in ordinary brandy, dry sherry, or vodka, if you prefer.

¾ *cup golden raisins*
¾ *cup Grappa brandy*
*1 chilled, unbaked 9-inch tart shell (page 169)*
*3 eggs*
*3 egg yolks*
¾ *cup plus 1 tablespoon sugar*
⅔ *cup fresh lemon juice, strained*
*3 tablespoons minced lemon zest*

In a small saucepan over medium heat combine the raisins and brandy and bring just to a boil, stirring once or twice. Remove the pan from the heat and let the raisins stand at least 4 hours, or overnight.

Position a rack in the upper third of the oven and preheat to 400 degrees F. Prick the chilled shell *lightly* with a fork. Line the shell with foil or parchment, fill it with pie weights, and bake 10 minutes, or until the pastry is just set. Remove the pie weights and foil and bake the shell another 5 to 7 minutes, or until golden. Cool the shell on a rack. *The tart shell can be baked several hours ahead. Reserve, loosely covered, in the tart pan at room temperature.*

Lower the oven temperature to 350 degrees F. Drain the raisins, reserving any unabsorbed brandy. In a medium-size bowl whisk the eggs and egg yolks. Whisk in the brandy, sugar, lemon juice, and lemon zest. Scatter the raisins evenly over the tart shell.

Set the shell on the oven rack and pour the filling carefully and evenly over the raisins. Bake the tart until firm, 20 to 25 minutes. Cool to room temperature. *The tart can be baked up to 3 hours ahead. Cover loosely and hold at room temperature.* Cut into wedges and serve.

 *Serves 6*

# MENU

◆ ◆ ◆ ◆ ◆ ◆ ◆ ◆ ◆ ◆ ◆ ◆ ◆ ◆

RUSTIC PIZZA WITH
EXOTIC MUSHROOMS AND FONTINA

◆

SAFFRON SHELLFISH STEW
WITH LEEK AND
SWEET RED PEPPER MARMALADE

◆

GREEN SALAD TO FOLLOW SEAFOOD

◆

PLUM AND BLUEBERRY BETTY
*page 279*

HERE IS ANOTHER stew menu, but one that falls at the opposite end of the culinary spectrum. By now surely everyone realizes that a seafood entrée is not automatically delicate and subtle. In fact, in the right form, seafood can be enjoyed with the same hearty gusto as the beefiest stews.

This shellfish ragout is a good case in point. Despite its creamy, tranquil appearance, it's packed with flavor and good eating. The accompaniments don't tiptoe around either, and the entire meal is a rousing joy to cook and to eat.

## RUSTIC PIZZA WITH EXOTIC MUSHROOMS AND FONTINA

◆ ◆ ◆ ◆ ◆ ◆ ◆ ◆ ◆ ◆

*¾ pound assorted fresh
exotic mushrooms, such
as cremini, porcini, or
shiitake (see Cook's
Sources)*

*⅓ cup olive oil*

*6 garlic cloves, peeled and
minced*

*1 teaspoon salt*

*2 tablespoons minced fresh
marjoram*

*1 tablespoon minced fresh
thyme*

*3 tablespoons yellow
cornmeal*

*1 recipe Pizza Dough (page
165), formed into a
single ball and
refrigerated for 24 hours*

*⅓ pound Fontina* Val
D'Aosta *cheese, trimmed
and grated*

*Freshly ground black
pepper*

A GARLICKY, MIXED SAUTÉ of exotic mushrooms and fresh herbs is laid over a base of melting Italian Fontina *Val D'Aosta* (please accept no substitutes) in this hearty starter. The more varieties of mushrooms the better the pizza, but otherwise feel free to improvise, and if marjoram and thyme are not at hand, consider fresh oregano, sage, or basil.

◆ ◆ ◆  ◆ ◆ ◆

Trim the mushrooms and wipe them with a damp towel or a soft brush. Cut the mushrooms, including tender stems, into thin slices.

In a large skillet over low heat warm the olive oil. Add the garlic and cook over low heat for 3 minutes. Add the mushrooms, stir well to coat them with oil, and raise the heat to medium-high. Cook, stirring occasionally, until the mushrooms soften slightly, about 5 minutes. Stir in the salt and cook until the mushrooms begin to render their juices, 4 to 5 minutes. Raise the heat to high and cook, stirring and tossing frequently, until the mushrooms are dry, 1 or 2 minutes. Remove the mushrooms from the heat and cool to room temperature. Stir in the marjoram and thyme. *The mushrooms can be prepared to this point up to 1 day ahead. Cover and refrigerate. Bring to room temperature before proceeding.*

Position a rack in the upper third of the oven and preheat to 500 degrees F for at least 30 minutes. Evenly sprinkle the cornmeal over an 11 × 18-inch jelly-roll pan.

Without excessive handling (which will make it springy and difficult to work with) turn the dough onto an unfloured surface and pat it out, leaving a slight rim around the edge, into a rough oval that will just fit the prepared pan. Transfer the dough to the pan and stretch and shape it into place. Evenly sprinkle the dough with the fontina. Spoon the mushrooms evenly over the cheese. Season generously with the pepper.

Immediately bake the pizza until the crust is sizzling, about 15 minutes, rotating the pan in the oven once. Let the pizza settle for 2 or 3 minutes, cut into wedges, and serve.

—• *Serves 6 as an appetizer, 2 to 3 as a main course*

✦✦✦✦✦✦✦✦✦✦✦✦✦✦✦✦✦✦✦✦✦✦✦✦✦✦✦✦✦✦✦✦✦✦✦✦✦✦✦✦

## SAFFRON SHELLFISH STEW WITH LEEK AND SWEET RED PEPPER MARMALADE

✦✦✦✦✦✦✦✦✦

**S**ERVE THE STEW IN WIDE, shallow bowls, and encourage guests to stir the marmalade into the sauce after admiring the arrangement of shellfish and garnish.

✦✦✦  ✦✦✦

In a large, heavy saucepan over medium heat melt half the butter. Add the red pepper flakes and cook for 1 minute. Stir in the sweet peppers, 3 cups of the leeks, and ½ teaspoon of the salt. Lower the heat and cook, covered, stirring occasionally, until the vegetables are very tender but not browned, about 30 minutes.

Uncover, raise the heat to medium-high, and cook, stirring constantly, until any excess moisture is evaporated and the mixture is thick enough to make a mound in a spoon, about 15 minutes. Remove from the heat and cool slightly.

Transfer the mixture to a food processor and with brief pulses of power coarsely chop the vegetables. Scrape the marmalade into a bowl and cover. *The marmalade can be prepared up to 1 day ahead and refrigerated. Return it to room temperature before using.*

At least 30 minutes before beginning the stew, in a medium-size bowl whisk together the egg yolks and cream. Stir in the saffron and set aside to steep.

10 tablespoons (1¼ sticks) unsalted butter

½ teaspoon crushed red pepper flakes

4 cups (about 4 large) sweet red peppers, cut into ¼-inch dice

4 cups (about 4 large) coarsely chopped leeks, white part only

1 teaspoon salt

5 egg yolks

2 cups whipping cream

¼ teaspoon crumbled saffron threads (see Cook's Sources)

2 medium onions, peeled and chopped

3 carrots, peeled and chopped

2 small celery ribs, trimmed and chopped

6 sprigs Italian parsley

¼ teaspoon dried thyme, crumbled

*(ingredients continued)*

*2 bay leaves*

*1½ pounds (about 36) medium shrimp, cleaned and shells reserved*

*2 cups dry white wine*

*2 cups fish stock or bottled clam juice*

*¼ teaspoon freshly ground black pepper*

*1½ pounds sea scallops, side muscles removed*

*12 to 15 mussels, scrubbed and debearded*

*Sprigs of fresh basil, as garnish*

In a large, nonreactive saucepan over medium heat melt the remaining butter. Stir in the onions, carrots, celery, parsley, thyme, bay leaves, and the remaining cup of leeks. Lower the heat and cook, covered, stirring occasionally, for 10 minutes.

Add the reserved shrimp shells and cook 10 minutes. Add the wine, fish stock, the remaining salt, and the black pepper. Raise the heat and bring the mixture to a boil. Lower the heat, partially cover, and simmer, stirring and skimming occasionally, for 20 minutes. Strain the stock into a large saucepan, pressing hard with the back of a spoon to extract as much liquid as possible. Discard the solids.

Over high heat bring the stock to a boil. Add the shrimp and scallops all at once and remove the pan from the heat. Gently stir the shellfish until they are somewhat stiffened and slightly opaque, about 3 minutes; they should be only partially cooked. With a slotted spoon, remove the shellfish and transfer to a bowl.

Bring the stock to a simmer over moderate heat. Add the mussels, cover, and cook, turning the mussels and shaking the pan occasionally, until the mussels open, about 5 minutes. With a slotted spoon, remove the opened mussels and set aside, discarding any that have not opened. Pour the stock through a fine-mesh strainer or a strainer lined with a double thickness of dampened cheesecloth.

Rinse out the saucepan. Return the stock to the saucepan and boil it over high heat until it is reduced to 1 cup, about 20 minutes. *The recipe can be prepared to this point up to 1 hour before serving. Cover the shellfish, mussels, and stock and reserve at room temperature.*

Lower the heat and bring the stock to a simmer. Slowly whisk the hot stock into the cream mixture. Return this stew base to the saucepan. Add the reserved shrimp and scallops and cook very gently, without boiling, over low heat, stirring occasionally, until the stew is hot and slightly thickened and the seafood is done, about 5 minutes.

Remove the stew from the heat, stir in the mussels, and let the stew stand, covered, for 1 minute to warm the mussels. Adjust the seasoning.

Ladle the stew into soup plates, dividing the seafood evenly. Garnish each serving with a dollop of the red pepper marmalade and a sprig of the basil and serve immediately.

*Serves 6*

## GREEN SALAD
## TO FOLLOW SEAFOOD

THIS BRISK AND BRACING salad is expressly designed to clear the palate after rich and creamy seafood. Arugula can be used in place of the watercress.

Trim the watercress, removing any tough stems. Separate the fennel, discarding any tough outer layers. Cut the fennel into matchstick julienne. Wash and dry the watercress and fennel. *The greens can be prepared up to 1 day ahead. Store separately in plastic bags and refrigerate.*

In a salad bowl toss together the watercress and fennel. In a small bowl whisk together the vinegar, mustard, and salt. Continue whisking while slowly adding the oil. The dressing will thicken. Adjust the seasoning, adding a generous grind of pepper.

Pour the dressing over the greens and toss to coat them well. Transfer the salad to 6 plates and serve immediately, passing a pepper mill at the table.

*Serves 6*

2 medium bunches of
   watercress
1 medium fennel bulb
1½ tablespoons sherry
   wine vinegar
1 tablespoon prepared
   Dijon-style mustard
Pinch of salt
½ cup olive oil
Freshly ground black
   pepper

**SERVING STRATEGY** A sweet, tart fruit dessert always seems the right conclusion to a seafood meal. The Plum and Blueberry Betty (page 279) is my preferred choice in this menu (loosely inspired by many a lobster followed by many a slice of blueberry pie), but the Lattice-Topped Raspberry and Pear Pie (page 314) or the Sauce Apple Pie (page 328) would also be great finales.

# MENU

◆ ◆ ◆ ◆ ◆ ◆ ◆ ◆ ◆ ◆ ◆ ◆ ◆ ◆ ◆ ◆

WARM SALAD OF SCALLOPS,
CABBAGE, AND BACON

◆

RAGOUT OF CORNISH HENS
WITH MORELS

◆

CONFETTI CORN CAKES

◆

BEETS GLAZED WITH
RASPBERRY VINEGAR

◆

PUMPKIN CRÈME BRÛLÉE

POPULAR WITH STUDENTS in my cooking classes as well as guests in my home, this menu has stood the test of time. Like much of the food in this book (I hope), its virtues include easy preparation and hearty eating, plus a fresh twist or two.

## WARM SALAD OF SCALLOPS, CABBAGE, AND BACON

◆◆◆◆◆◆◆◆◆

6 ounces smoked slab
bacon, trimmed and cut
into ¼-inch cubes

1¼ pounds medium sea
scallops, of equal size
and weight

3 medium shallots, peeled
and minced

½ small green cabbage,
cored and shredded

¼ teaspoon salt

Freshly ground black
pepper

⅓ cup white wine tarragon
vinegar

1 tablespoon sugar

**A**N INTRIGUING COMBINATION of bold flavors, the salad can be made with shrimp in place of the scallops. The puckery smell of warm vinegar—which immediately excites appetites—makes the salad particularly appropriate as a starter, but I have also served it as a main course to four people, accompanied by black bread and a cold Gewürztraminer. If you have fresh tarragon, add 1 tablespoon, minced, to the cabbage as it sautés.

◆◆◆  ◆◆◆

In a large, nonreactive skillet over low heat cook the bacon, uncovered, stirring occasionally, until it is crisp and brown, about 10 minutes. With a slotted spoon, transfer the bacon to paper towels to drain, reserving the bacon fat in the skillet.

Remove the rectangular muscles from the sides of the scallops (they pull away easily with the fingers) and reserve any odd-sized or partial scallops for another use. *The recipe can be completed to this point up to 3 hours ahead. Refrigerate the scallops.*

Pat the scallops dry. Over medium-high heat warm the bacon fat. Add the scallops and cook, stirring and tossing, until they are just firm and becoming opaque, about 5 minutes. With a slotted spoon, transfer the scallops to a bowl and cover.

Return the skillet to low heat and add the shallots. Cook, stirring often, for 1 minute. Add the cabbage, stirring to coat it with the bacon fat, and cover the skillet. Cook, stirring once or twice, until the cabbage is just tender, about 5 minutes. Transfer the contents of the skillet to a bowl, stir in the salt, and season generously with pepper. Cover.

Return the skillet to low heat and add the vinegar and sugar. Stir well to dissolve the sugar and to scrape up any browned deposits remaining on the bottom of the skillet. Raise the heat. When the vinegar boils, remove the skillet from the heat.

Immediately pour the hot vinegar over the cabbage. Add the bacon and stir well. Divide the cabbage mixture among 6 plates. Arrange the scallops over the cabbage. Combine any juices from the 2 bowls, spoon them over the salads, and serve immediately.

*Serves 6*

◆◆◆◆◆◆◆◆◆◆◆◆◆◆◆◆◆◆◆◆◆◆◆◆◆◆◆◆◆◆◆◆◆◆◆◆◆◆◆◆◆◆◆

## RAGOUT OF CORNISH HENS WITH MORELS

◆◆◆◆◆◆◆◆◆

**F**RESH MORELS ARE WILD and costly springtime rarities, found only in certain areas of the United States or available in specialty produce shops. At other times of the year, or in dishes like this one, dried morels are reconstituted to add a more intense and slightly smoky flavor.

In a strainer under running water rinse the morels well. In a small saucepan bring 2 cups of the chicken broth to a boil. In a small, heatproof bowl pour the hot stock over the mushrooms. Cover and let stand until cool, stirring once or twice.

Chop the giblets and necks of the Cornish hens, discarding the livers or reserving them for another use. Quarter the hens and pat them dry.

In a large, deep, nonreactive skillet over high heat melt together 2 tablespoons of the butter and the oil. Add the hens, skin side down, and cook, turning them once, until browned, about 7 minutes per side. Season lightly with salt and pepper and transfer to a plate. Do not clean the skillet.

Set the skillet over medium-high heat. Add the giblets and necks and cook, stirring often, until

1 ounce dried morel mushrooms (see Cook's Sources)

7 cups (about) canned chicken broth or homemade stock

3 large Cornish hens (about 1¼ pounds each)

5 tablespoons unsalted butter, softened

1 tablespoon vegetable oil

Salt

Freshly ground black pepper

1 cup finely chopped onion

3 leeks, white part only, cleaned and chopped

2 carrots, peeled and chopped

1½ teaspoons dried thyme, crumbled

2 bay leaves

6 sprigs Italian parsley

¾ cup medium-dry (Sercial) madeira

3 tablespoons unbleached all-purpose flour

browned, about 10 minutes. Add the onion, leeks, carrots, thyme, bay leaves, and parsley, lower the heat, cover, and cook, stirring occasionally, until the vegetables are tender, about 15 minutes.

Meanwhile, with a slotted spoon, remove the morels from their soaking liquid. Let the liquid settle, then carefully decant it into a measuring cup, leaving any sandy residue behind. Add additional broth to the soaking liquid to total 5 cups.

Add this liquid to the skillet with the vegetables and bring it to a boil, skimming any surface scum that may form. Lower the heat, partially cover the skillet, and simmer 30 minutes. Pour the contents of the skillet into a strainer placed over a bowl. Press hard to extract as much liquid as possible and discard the solids. Wipe the skillet.

Return the strained liquid to the skillet. Add the madeira and the morels, bring to a boil, lower the heat, and simmer briskly, uncovered, for 15 minutes. Add the browned hens, including any juices that have accumulated in the bowl. *The recipe can be prepared to this point up to 1 day ahead. Cool completely, cover, and refrigerate.*

Bring the contents of the skillet to a simmer, basting the hens with the liquid. Partially cover the skillet and simmer about 20 minutes, or until the hens are tender. In a small bowl mash together the remaining butter and the flour.

Transfer the hens to a platter and keep them warm. Raise the heat to high and boil the liquid in the skillet hard for 5 minutes. Lower the heat, whisk in the butter and flour mixture, and simmer 5 minutes. Adjust the seasoning.

To serve, arrange Confetti Corn Cakes (recipe follows) on plates. Place the Cornish hens next to the corn cakes and spoon the sauce and morels partially over both.

*Serves 6*

## CONFETTI CORN CAKES

◆◆◆◆◆◆◆◆◆◆

THESE VEGETABLE-SPANGLED rounds of crisp, fried corn-meal are a delicious and colorful accompaniment to rich and saucy main courses like the ragout. Fry up the leftovers on another day to accompany eggs, omelets, and the like.

Line a 9 × 13-inch pan with foil. Grease the foil with 2 tablespoons of the butter and set aside.

In a small skillet over medium heat melt 3 table-spoons of the butter. Add the sweet pepper, lower the heat, and cook, covered, stirring once or twice, until very tender, about 15 minutes. Stir in the corn and parsley, season with ½ teaspoon of the salt and a generous grind of black pepper, and set aside.

In a heavy saucepan whisk the cold water into the cornmeal. Add the remaining salt and set the pan over low heat. Cook, stirring often, until the mixture reaches a boil. Lower the heat and simmer another 12 to 15 minutes, stirring constantly, or until the corn-meal is very thick and pulling away from the sides of the pan.

Remove from the heat and stir in the pepper and corn mixture. Pour the cornmeal into the prepared pan and spread it with a spatula to a thickness of about ½ inch. Cool completely, cover, and refrigerate until very cold and firm, preferably overnight.

In a large skillet over medium heat melt the re-maining butter and the olive oil together. Add the gar-lic, lower the heat, and cook, stirring occasionally, until the garlic is golden, about 15 minutes. Discard the gar-lic, reserving the oil.

With a sharp, 2-inch round cookie cutter, cut 12 rounds of the chilled cornmeal. Set the skillet with the oil over medium-high heat. Dredge the cornmeal rounds in the flour and shake off the excess. Cook the

7 tablespoons unsalted butter, softened
1 sweet red pepper, trimmed, cored, and cut into ¼-inch dice
1 cup frozen or canned corn kernels, well drained
½ cup finely chopped Italian parsley
2½ teaspoons salt
Freshly ground black pepper
5 cups cold water
2 cups stone-ground yellow cornmeal
1 tablespoon olive oil
4 garlic cloves, peeled
½ cup unbleached all-purpose flour

cornmeal cakes in the hot skillet, carefully turning them once with a spatula, until crisp and browned, about 4 minutes per side. Serve immediately.

➤ *Serves 6*

◆◆◆◆◆◆◆◆◆◆◆◆◆◆◆◆◆◆◆◆◆◆◆◆◆◆◆◆◆◆◆◆◆◆◆◆◆◆◆◆◆◆◆

▀▄▀▄▀▄▀▄▀▄▀▄▀▄▀▄▀▄▀▄▀▄▀▄▀▄▀▄▀▄▀▄▀▄▀▄▀

## BEETS GLAZED WITH RASPBERRY VINEGAR

◆◆◆◆◆◆◆◆◆◆

24 small beets (about 4 bunches), tops trimmed to ½ inch, rinsed, and patted dry

3 tablespoons vegetable oil

1 cup canned chicken broth or homemade stock

½ cup raspberry vinegar

6 tablespoons unsalted butter

2 tablespoons sugar

Freshly ground black pepper

I GREW UP EATING—and loving—the sweet-and-sour dish called Harvard beets, the origin of whose prestigious name is uncertain. As with many of my childhood favorites, I continue to enjoy Harvard beets, preparing them in only a slightly altered form in my grown-up culinary repertoire. Though homemade Raspberry-Thyme Vinegar (page 374) will make this dish particularly delicious, store-bought berry vinegars will work just fine. Baking the beets keeps the flavor and color intense, and a generous shower of black pepper adds savory emphasis. The result—beets at their best—makes a splendid accompaniment to game birds, pork, or ham.

◆◆◆ ➤ ◆◆◆

Preheat the oven to 375 degrees F. Pour the oil into a 5-quart Dutch oven. Add the beets and stir to coat them with the oil. Cover and bake, stirring occasionally, until a knife easily pierces a beet, about 1¼ hours. Cool to room temperature. Peel the beets. *The dish can be prepared to this point up to 1 day ahead. Refrigerate the beets, covered tightly. Bring to room temperature before proceeding.*

In a large, nonreactive skillet combine the chicken broth, vinegar, butter, and sugar and set over high heat. Bring to a boil, then lower the heat slightly, and simmer briskly until the liquid is reduced by half, 12 to

15 minutes. Add the beets and continue to cook, rolling the beets in the liquid, until the sauce is very thick and syrupy, about 7 minutes. Season generously with the pepper.

━━● *Serves 6*

◆ ◆ ◆ ◆ ◆ ◆ ◆ ◆ ◆ ◆ ◆ ◆ ◆ ◆ ◆ ◆ ◆ ◆ ◆ ◆ ◆ ◆ ◆ ◆ ◆ ◆ ◆ ◆ ◆ ◆ ◆ ◆ ◆ ◆ ◆ ◆ ◆ ◆ ◆

## PUMPKIN CRÈME BRÛLÉE

◆ ◆ ◆ ◆ ◆ ◆ ◆ ◆ ◆

**F**ASHION IS FICKLE; food fashion is *very* fickle. Still, the cycle of demand for a genuine classic will sooner or later bring it back into vogue. When that happens again to crème brûlée, as it did when it resurfaced a few years ago, this spicy pumpkin version will be part of the trend; until then, I suggest you make it anyway, flaunt fashion, and build your reputation as a reactionary, a tastemaker, or both.

◆ ◆ ◆  ◆ ◆ ◆

Preheat the oven to 325 degrees F.

In a mixing bowl whisk together the pumpkin and egg yolks. Whisk in the sugar, vanilla, cinnamon, cloves, ginger, and nutmeg.

In a saucepan over medium heat bring the cream to a boil. Whisk the hot cream into the pumpkin mixture. Divide the mixture among 8 broilerproof ramekins with a ¾-cup capacity. Set the ramekins into a shallow baking dish. Add enough boiling water to the baking dish to come halfway up the sides of the ramekins.

Bake 25 minutes. The custards will be a rich golden color but will not be firm. Do not overcook. The custards will thicken further as they cool. Remove them from the hot water bath and cool them to room temperature. Cover the ramekins (use a baking sheet or a piece of foil), being careful not to touch the cus-

*1 can (16 ounces) unsweetened solid pack pumpkin puree (not pie filling)*
*5 large egg yolks*
*⅔ cup sugar*
*1½ tablespoons vanilla*
*1½ teaspoons ground cinnamon*
*1 teaspoon ground cloves*
*½ teaspoon ground ginger*
*¼ teaspoon freshly grated nutmeg*
*3 cups whipping cream*
*½ cup light brown sugar, packed*

tards and mar the surfaces, and refrigerate them until very cold, preferably overnight. *The custards can be prepared up to 2 days ahead.*

Preheat the broiler. Force the brown sugar through a sieve onto the tops of the custards in an even, fluffy layer. Wipe any excess sugar from the rims of the ramekins. Set the custards, working in batches if necessary, under the broiler. The tops of the custards should be about 5 inches from the broiler unit or gas flame. Watch them carefully. The time will vary, but in 30 seconds to 3 minutes the sugar will liquefy and caramelize. When the topping is a rich brown remove the custards from the broiler and return them to the refrigerator. Repeat with the remaining custards. *The sugar-topped custards can be broiled up to 4 hours before serving.* Serve directly from the refrigerator.

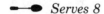 *Serves 8*

# MENU

◆ ◆ ◆ ◆ ◆ ◆ ◆ ◆ ◆ ◆ ◆ ◆ ◆ ◆ ◆

PICKLED PEPPER AND FONTINA
APPETIZER SANDWICHES

◆

RABBIT BRAISED IN DARK BEER
WITH GREEN OLIVES

◆

COUSCOUS WITH SWEET POTATOES,
ZUCCHINI, AND CHICK-PEAS

◆

BITTERSWEET CHOCOLATE–HAZELNUT
PRALINE MOUSSE

THIS MENU IS a pleasant jumble of influences from Italian trattorias to Parisian Algerian-French restaurants to modern bistros. Fortunately it all goes together in a hearty, eclectic meal that satisfies mightily. Drink Beaujolais, or pour more of the same beer you used for the rabbit.

## PICKLED PEPPER AND FONTINA APPETIZER SANDWICHES

♦ ♦ ♦ ♦ ♦ ♦ ♦ ♦ ♦ ♦

**G**OOEY AND PIQUANT, these cheese and pickled pepper sandwiches, with their rustic sauce, start things off on a savory note.

♦ ♦ ♦  ♦ ♦ ♦

½ cup half-and-half

3 eggs

3 tablespoons freshly grated Parmesan cheese

Freshly ground black pepper

1 loaf (13 × 3 inches) crusty semolina Italian bread

2 large, Italian pickled peppers (about 7 inches long), each cut lengthwise into 3 pieces

8 ounces Fontina Val D'Aosta, trimmed and sliced ⅛ inch thick

6 oil-packed anchovy fillets

¾ cup olive oil

2 tablespoons unsalted butter

2 garlic cloves, peeled and minced

2 tablespoons balsamic vinegar

1 tablespoon tomato paste

1 teaspoon minced fresh rosemary

Pinch of salt

6 sprigs of Italian parsley, as garnish

In a shallow bowl whisk together the half-and-half, eggs, grated cheese, and 1 teaspoon of pepper. With a serrated knife cut the bread, on the bias, into 12 slices ¼ inch thick. Trim the pickled peppers to fit the bread slices and set aside. Lay 6 slices of bread on the work surface. Divide the fontina evenly over the bread. Top the fontina with the anchovies and then lay the pieces of pepper over the anchovies. Top with the remaining bread slices.

In a large, heavy skillet over medium heat warm ¼ cup of the olive oil. Re-whisk the half-and-half batter. Dip each sandwich into the batter, coating it completely, and allowing it to absorb as much batter as possible. Set the sandwiches in the skillet and cook until golden brown, about 5 minutes. Carefully turn the sandwiches with a spatula and cook, pressing down as the cheese melts, until they are golden, about 5 minutes. Drain the sandwiches briefly on paper towels.

Meanwhile, combine the remaining olive oil, the butter, and the garlic in a small saucepan over low heat. Cook, stirring, for 5 minutes. Whisk in the vinegar, tomato paste, and rosemary. Season with a pinch of salt and a generous grind of black pepper. Simmer 5 minutes, stirring often.

Set each sandwich on a plate. Divide the sauce over the sandwiches, garnish each with a sprig of the parsley, and serve.

●➤ *Serves 6*

## RABBIT BRAISED IN DARK BEER WITH GREEN OLIVES

♦♦♦♦♦♦♦♦♦

THE NEGATIVE FUSS over serving rabbit mystifies me. Chickens are cute, too, but that doesn't stop us from eating many pounds per person per year. Rabbit is very chickenlike, a bit more flavorful and slightly more resistant to the tooth, but otherwise lean and reasonably affordable. One brand is available nationally, frozen, in many supermarkets. Good butcher shops stock (or will order) fresh rabbit, and in cities like New York one can still visit a live poulterer and select a plump rabbit, to be killed and dressed to order.

The delicious braise below, flavored with dark beer and studded with tart green olives, can be prepared in advance. Avoid English and Irish dark beers, which can become bitter when reduced, and look instead for dark Heineken, Beck's, or the mellow American beer, Double Dark Prior's.

♦♦♦  ♦♦♦

Pat the rabbit dry. In a large, heavy skillet over medium heat melt together the butter and 2 tablespoons of the olive oil. Working in batches, brown the rabbit lightly, turning it once, about 7 minutes on each side. Season lightly with salt and pepper and transfer to a bowl. Do not clean the skillet.

Add the remaining oil, the onions, leeks, carrots, garlic, thyme, and bay leaf to the skillet. Cover and cook over medium heat, stirring occasionally, until tender, 20 minutes. Stir in the flour and cook, stirring often, for 5 minutes, without browning. Stir in the chicken broth and the beer. Return the rabbit and any juices from the bowl to the skillet and bring to a boil. Lower the heat, cover, and simmer gently, turning occasionally, until the rabbit is tender, 50 to 60 minutes.

With a slotted spoon, transfer the rabbit to a bowl and cover. Strain the liquid, pressing hard with the back of a spoon to extract all the liquid from the solids.

*2 fresh rabbits (3 pounds each), cut into serving pieces*
*3 tablespoons unsalted butter*
*3 tablespoons olive oil*
*Salt*
*Freshly ground black pepper*
*2 medium onions, peeled and chopped*
*4 medium leeks, white part only, well cleaned and chopped*
*3 medium carrots, peeled and chopped*
*2 garlic cloves, peeled and minced*
*1½ teaspoons dried thyme, crumbled*
*1 bay leaf*
*3 tablespoons unbleached all-purpose flour*
*2 cups canned chicken broth or homemade stock*
*1 bottle (12 ounces) dark beer*
*24 medium green olives, such as picholines (see Cook's Sources), unpitted*

Return the liquid to the skillet, set over high heat, and boil until reduced to 2 cups, 10 to 12 minutes. Correct the seasoning. Rinse the olives and add them, the rabbit, and any juices from the bowl to the skillet. *The recipe can be prepared to this point up to 1 day ahead. Cool, cover, and refrigerate. Return to room temperature before proceeding.*

Warm the rabbit over low heat, basting frequently with the sauce, until steaming, and serve.

**━● *Serves 6***

❖❖❖❖❖❖❖❖❖❖❖❖❖❖❖❖❖❖❖❖❖❖❖❖❖❖❖❖❖❖❖❖❖❖❖❖❖❖❖❖

## COUSCOUS WITH ZUCCHINI, SWEET POTATOES, AND CHICK-PEAS

◆◆◆◆◆◆◆◆◆

*Salt*

*1½ pounds (about 3 medium) sweet potatoes, peeled and cut into ¾-inch cubes*

*10 tablespoons (about) unsalted butter*

*2 tablespoons olive oil*

*1 pound (about 3 medium) zucchini, scrubbed, trimmed, and sliced ¾ inch thick*

*½ teaspoon dried red pepper flakes*

*1 pound (2 cups) medium-grain quick-cooking couscous, see Cook's Sources*

*2 cups canned chicken broth or homemade stock*

*1 can (16 ounces) chick-peas, rinsed and drained*

**T**HE TECHNIQUE for preparing authentic couscous is a complex and wonderful one, and you can read all about it in Paula Wolfert's *Couscous and Other Good Food from Morocco.* This side dish, using quick-cooking couscous, is not meant to be authentic, but it does produce a speedy, colorful, and sauce-absorbing accompaniment to the braised rabbit.

◆◆◆  ◆◆◆

Bring a large pan of lightly salted water to a boil. Add the sweet potatoes and cook until just tender, about 10 minutes. Drain.

In a large, heavy skillet over high heat melt 2 tablespoons of the butter with the olive oil. Add the zucchini and cook, stirring occasionally, until browned, about 7 minutes. Remove from the skillet with a slotted spoon. Do not clean the skillet.

In a medium-size, heavy saucepan over moderate heat melt 6 tablespoons of the butter. Add the pepper flakes and cook 5 minutes. Stir in the couscous, coating the grains with butter, and then the chicken broth. Lower the heat, cover, and cook until the liquid is absorbed, about 10 minutes. Fluff the couscous with a fork.

Meanwhile, set the large skillet over medium heat. Add additional butter, if necessary, and stir in the sweet potatoes, zucchini, and chick-peas. Season to taste with salt, cover, and cook until just warmed through, stirring once or twice, about 5 minutes.

Divide the couscous among plates. Spoon the sweet potato mixture over the couscous and serve.

**━━●** *Serves 6 to 8*

♦ ♦ ♦ ♦ ♦ ♦ ♦ ♦ ♦ ♦ ♦ ♦ ♦ ♦ ♦ ♦ ♦ ♦ ♦ ♦ ♦ ♦ ♦ ♦ ♦ ♦ ♦ ♦ ♦ ♦ ♦ ♦ ♦ ♦ ♦ ♦ ♦ ♦ ♦ ♦ ♦ ♦ ♦ ♦

# BITTERSWEET CHOCOLATE–HAZELNUT PRALINE MOUSSE

♦ ♦ ♦ ♦ ♦ ♦ ♦ ♦ ♦

**T**HIS IS CLASSIC chocolate mousse, dark, sticky, spiked with hazelnut liqueur, and topped by the crunch of hazelnut praline.

♦ ♦ ♦  ♦ ♦ ♦

Make a modified double boiler by setting a large, heavy ceramic bowl over a saucepan of water. The bottom of the bowl should just touch the water.

Place the chopped chocolate and butter in the bowl and set the double boiler over low heat. Stir occasionally as the chocolate melts, about 10 minutes. Do not let the water boil.

Meanwhile, whip the cream to the point *just before* it will hold soft peaks. Refrigerate.

Separate the eggs, placing the egg yolks in a small bowl and the whites in a medium-size bowl. Whisk the yolks briefly, stir in the hazelnut liqueur, and set aside.

10 ounces best-quality imported bittersweet chocolate (see Cook's Sources), coarsely chopped

4 tablespoons unsalted butter

1 cup whipping cream

3 large eggs, at room temperature

5 tablespoons hazelnut liqueur, such as Frangelico

Whipped cream, as garnish

1 cup Praline (page 342), made with hazelnuts, chopped

Whisk the egg whites to the point *just before* they will hold soft peaks.

Transfer the bowl with the melted chocolate to the work surface. Stir in the yolk mixture all at once. Stir in the whipped cream. Fold in the egg whites until just incorporated. Spoon the mousse into a large bowl or into individual serving cups and chill until firm, 2 hours for individual cups and 6 hours for the large bowl.

To serve, garnish the mousse with whipped cream and a generous sprinkling of chopped praline.

*Makes about 1 quart, serving 8 to 10*

♦ ♦ ♦ ♦ ♦ ♦ ♦ ♦ ♦ ♦ ♦ ♦ ♦ ♦ ♦ ♦ ♦ ♦ ♦ ♦ ♦ ♦ ♦ ♦ ♦ ♦ ♦ ♦ ♦ ♦ ♦ ♦ ♦ ♦ ♦ ♦ ♦ ♦ ♦ ♦ ♦ ♦

# MENU

◆ ◆ ◆ ◆ ◆ ◆ ◆ ◆ ◆ ◆ ◆ ◆ ◆ ◆ ◆ ◆

ARUGULA AND CREMINI MUSHROOM
SALAD WITH WALNUTS AND
SONOMA DRY JACK CHEESE

◆

RABBIT BRAISED WITH *ANCHO* CHILES,
RAISINS, AND GARLIC

◆

OAT AND VEGETABLE PILAF

◆

SWEET POTATO CORN STICKS

◆

JACK DANIEL'S
CHOCOLATE WHISKEY CAKE
*page 200*

NOT ONLY ARE THERE more and more varied ingredients available to the cook than ever before, but when they are combined with an informed sense of adventure the results can be delicious. This is another menu starring rabbit, this time braised in a sauce with, among other things, Mexican *ancho* chiles. The accompaniments include a salad with Italian mushrooms and California cheese, a grain side dish of Irish oatmeal, and a dessert with Tennessee sour-mash whiskey. The menu may sound like it's all over the map, but the new American kitchen is the only place you'll ever find this sensationally attractive meal being prepared.

# ARUGULA AND CREMINI MUSHROOM SALAD WITH WALNUTS AND SONOMA DRY JACK CHEESE

2 medium bunches
arugula
1 medium head frisée
½ pound cremini (see
Cook's Sources) or
cultivated white
mushrooms, wiped,
trimmed, and sliced
1 cup walnut pieces,
toasted (see page 65)
¼ cup olive oil
¼ cup walnut oil
Generous pinch of salt
¼ cup balsamic vinegar
⅓ pound Vella Sonoma
Dry Jack cheese (see
Cook's Sources) or a
young parmigiano
reggiano, trimmed and
cut into thin slices

VELLA SONOMA DRY JACK, made in California for many years, is possibly the best American cheese. Made in the Parmesan tradition, it's available by mail (see Cook's Sources), and though it comes in a rather generously sized wheel, under its coating of cocoa, pepper, and oil (meant to simulate the lampblack used years ago), it keeps well and only gets better as it gets harder and sharper. As a grating cheese on pasta or risotto or as an eating cheese scattered in shards over a salad like the one below, it's hard to beat.

Trim and wash the arugula. Core and wash the frisée. Tear the greens into bite-size pieces, wrap, and refrigerate. *The greens can be cleaned up to 1 day ahead.*

In a large bowl combine the greens, mushrooms, and walnuts and toss. Add the oils, season with a generous pinch of salt, and toss again. Add the vinegar and toss well.

Divide the salads among 6 plates. Scatter the slices of cheese over the salads and serve immediately, passing a pepper mill at the table.

*Serves 6*

## RABBIT BRAISED WITH *ANCHO* CHILES, RAISINS, AND GARLIC

♦ ♦ ♦ ♦ ♦ ♦ ♦ ♦ ♦

*A*NCHO CHILES—CRINKLED, reddish brown beauties—have a rich, almost chocolaty taste that wonderfully complements the full-flavored rabbit while the raisins and garlic cloves add savory emphasis. I encourage you to make this moist braise, with its abundant brick-red sauce, in advance; it will taste even better when reheated the next day.

♦ ♦ ♦  ♦ ♦ ♦

Lay the chiles in a single layer in a large, heavy skillet and set it over medium heat. Toast the chiles, turning them occasionally, until they are fragrant and flexible, 5 to 6 minutes. Remove them from the heat. When they are cool enough to handle, remove the stems, seeds, and veins. Tear the chiles into 1-inch pieces and place them in a medium-size heatproof bowl.

In a medium-size saucepan bring the chicken broth to a boil. Pour 3 cups of it over the chiles. In a small heatproof bowl combine the remaining broth with the raisins. Let the chiles and raisins stand 1 hour, stirring occasionally.

Pat the rabbit pieces dry. In a large, flameproof casserole or deep, heavy skillet over medium-high heat warm 4 tablespoons of the olive oil. Working in batches, sauté the rabbit, turning it once, until it is lightly browned, about 7 minutes per side. Transfer the rabbit to a bowl and season lightly with salt and pepper. Do not clean the casserole.

Add the remaining olive oil to the casserole and set it over low heat. Add the garlic cloves and cook, stirring occasionally, until the garlic is tender and lightly colored, about 20 minutes. With a slotted spoon, transfer the garlic to a small bowl.

Add the onion, oregano, and cumin to the casse-

*4 ounces (6 to 8) dried ancho chiles (see Cook's Sources)*

*3½ cups canned chicken broth or homemade stock*

*½ cup raisins*

*2 fresh rabbits (3 pounds each), cut into serving pieces*

*6 tablespoons olive oil*

*Salt*

*Freshly ground black pepper*

*24 garlic cloves, peeled*

*3 cups chopped yellow onion*

*2 teaspoons oregano*

*1½ teaspoons ground cumin, from toasted seeds (see page 66)*

*1 cup amber beer, such as Dos Equis or New Amsterdam*

*1 can (28 ounces) Italian-style plum tomatoes, crushed and drained*

role. Cover it and cook, stirring occasionally and scraping browned deposits from the bottom of the pan, until the onions are tender, about 15 minutes. Stir in the beer, the tomatoes, and the chiles with their soaking liquid. Return the rabbit and any accumulated juices to the casserole. Stir in 1½ teaspoons of salt and ½ teaspoon of pepper and bring to a boil. Lower the heat and simmer, uncovered, turning the rabbit occasionally, until it is tender, 50 to 60 minutes. Transfer the rabbit to a bowl. Cool the sauce slightly.

In a food processor, in batches, puree the sauce. Return the sauce to the casserole and stir in the raisins, their soaking liquid, and the garlic cloves. Set the casserole over medium heat, bring to a boil, and cook, stirring often, for 5 minutes. Return the rabbit to the sauce. *The recipe can be prepared to this point up to 1 day ahead. Cool, cover, and refrigerate.*

Warm the rabbit over low heat, basting frequently with the sauce, until heated through and steaming and serve.

*Serves 6*

## OAT AND VEGETABLE PILAF

⅓ cup olive oil

2 carrots, trimmed, peeled, and sliced thin

2 ribs of celery, trimmed and sliced thin

1 sweet red pepper, stemmed, cored, and cut into ¼-inch dice

1 teaspoon dried thyme, crumbled

STEEL-CUT IRISH OATS (see Cook's Sources) are a breakfast staple in my house, their nutty taste and satisfying texture a comforting way to stoke up for the day ahead. As a grain, though, oats also deserve to be remembered when you're looking for an offbeat starch to serve alongside a main course. This pilaf will probably leave guests mystified as to what its base is, but they'll have little doubt that the color, taste, and texture are deliciously at home in the eclectic menu.

In a medium-size, heavy saucepan over low heat warm the olive oil. Stir the carrots, celery, sweet pepper, thyme, pepper flakes, and bay leaf and cook, covered, 15 minutes.

Raise the heat to high. Add the oats to the pan and stir to coat them with the contents of the saucepan. Cook, stirring often (the oats will tend to stick slightly), until lightly colored, about 3 minutes. Stir in the chicken broth and salt and bring the oats to a boil. Lower the heat and simmer, uncovered, stirring occasionally, until the oats are just tender and have absorbed the stock, about 25 minutes.

Remove the pan from the heat and stir in the onion and parsley. Cover and let the pilaf stand 5 minutes before serving.

*Serves 6*

*½ teaspoon crushed red pepper flakes*
*1 bay leaf*
*1 cup Irish or steel-cut Irish oats (see Cook's Sources)*
*3 cups canned chicken broth or homemade stock*
*1 teaspoon salt*
*¼ cup sliced green onion*
*¼ cup finely minced Italian parsley*

## SWEET POTATO CORN STICKS

**F**OR THE CRISPEST, crustiest corn sticks, use cast-iron pans. Serve the corn sticks, if you wish, with Black Olive Butter (page 26) or Orange Butter (page 62).

Position a rack in the center of the oven and preheat to 400 degrees F. Bake the potatoes until a knife easily pierces the center, about 1 hour. Cool, peel, and mash them, measuring out and reserving 1½ cups of the puree. *The potatoes can be prepared up to 1 day ahead. Cover and refrigerate, returning the puree to room temperature before proceeding.*

*2 medium sweet potatoes (about 1¼ pounds)*
*Vegetable oil*
*½ cup buttermilk, at room temperature*
*6 tablespoons (¾ stick) unsalted butter, melted*
*2 eggs*
*1 cup yellow cornmeal*
*1 cup unbleached all-purpose flour*
*½ cup sugar*
*2½ teaspoons baking powder*
*½ teaspoon salt*

Meanwhile, generously brush 2 corn-stick pans with the vegetable oil. Heat the pans in the 400-degree F oven until the oil smokes slightly.

In a mixing bowl whisk together the puree, buttermilk, butter, and eggs. In a smaller bowl combine the cornmeal, flour, sugar, baking powder, and salt. Stir the dry ingredients into the potato mixture. Do not overmix.

Pour any excess hot oil out of the cornstick pans. Spoon the batter into the hot pans, filling each depression three-fourths full and spreading the batter evenly along the length of each depression. Bake until the corn sticks are crisp and golden brown, 15 to 20 minutes. Cool the corn sticks in the pans for 5 minutes before serving.

*Makes 10 to 14*

# MENU

◆ ◆ ◆ ◆ ◆ ◆ ◆ ◆ ◆ ◆ ◆ ◆ ◆ ◆ ◆ ◆

SHRIMP AND CELERY SALAD
WITH WARM DILL DRESSING

◆

DUCK AND WHITE BEAN
RAGOUT WITH CRACKLINGS

◆

BROCCOLI WITH
ORANGE-SHALLOT BUTTER
*page 277*

◆

WHOLE-GRAIN
PINEAPPLE SPICE CAKE

A LITTLE SOMETHING light and tart is provided by the shrimp and celery salad, and it's needed, since the entrée is meaty, rich, and powerfully garlicked. The meal concludes with a simple dried fruit and spice cake. Pour a generous amount of slightly cool Beaujolais or other easy-drinking red wine.

1 head Bibb or Boston
    lettuce, separated
Salt
1½ pounds (about 36)
    medium shrimp, shelled
    and deveined
6 celery stalks, cut on the
    diagonal into 1-inch
    pieces
3 tablespoons white wine
    vinegar
2 tablespoons prepared
    Dijon-style mustard
1 teaspoon sugar
⅓ cup whipping cream
¼ cup minced fresh dill
⅓ cup corn oil
1 medium red onion,
    peeled and sliced in thin
    rings
Freshly ground black
    pepper

## SHRIMP AND CELERY SALAD WITH WARM DILL DRESSING

THIS PRETTY PINK and green salad is just the kind of palate awakener the sturdy entrée requires. It's equally good, if not quite as pretty, when made with scallops.

Wash and dry the lettuce. *The lettuce can be prepared up to 1 day ahead. Store in plastic bags and refrigerate.*

Bring a pot of lightly salted water to a boil. Add the shrimp and celery and cook 1 minute, stirring. Drain immediately and cool to room temperature.

In a small, nonreactive saucepan blend the vinegar, mustard, sugar, and a pinch of salt. Whisk in the cream. Set the pan over medium heat and bring just to a simmer, stirring constantly. Stir in the dill and remove from the heat. Slowly whisk in the oil. Cover and keep warm.

Line 6 salad plates with the lettuce leaves. Place a mound of the shrimp and celery on the lettuce and garnish with the red onion. Re-whisk the dressing and spoon it over the salads. Season with the pepper and serve immediately.

*Serves 6*

## DUCK AND WHITE BEAN RAGOUT WITH CRACKLINGS

CONSIDERABLY LESS WORK than a full-scale cassoulet, this ragout is nonetheless as deeply flavored and satisfying to eat.

In a bowl generously cover the beans with cold water and soak for 24 hours.

Cut off the duck wings and reserve them. Skin the ducks, reserving the skin from the breast. Cut the skin into 1-inch squares. Bone the ducks and cut the meat into 1-inch chunks.

In a small, heavy skillet combine the duck skin and the water. Set over medium heat and bring to a boil. Lower the heat and simmer until the water has evaporated and the skin is crisp and brown, 40 to 50 minutes. With a slotted spoon, transfer the cracklings to paper towels to drain.

In a heavy 4½- or 5-quart pot over medium heat cook the bacon until crisp and brown, about 10 minutes. With a slotted spoon, transfer the bacon to paper towels to drain. Pour off all but ¼ cup of the rendered bacon fat.

Set the pan over medium-high heat. Pat the duck pieces dry and cook, working in batches, until well browned on all sides, 7 to 10 minutes. Using a slotted spoon, transfer the duck to a bowl. Add the giblets (discarding the liver) and wings to the pan and cook until very brown, about 15 minutes. Stir in the leeks, onions, chopped carrots, half of the garlic, the parsley sprigs, the thyme, and the bay leaves. Lower the heat, cover, and cook, stirring occasionally, until very tender, about 15 minutes.

Stir in the chicken broth and wine, scraping up the browned bits from the bottom of the pan, and bring to a boil. Lower the heat, cover, and simmer 30 minutes, stirring occasionally and skimming the foam from the surface of the stock.

Strain the stock into a bowl, pressing hard with the back of a spoon to extract as much liquid as possible. Discard the solids. Wipe out the pan and return the stock to it. Drain and stir in the beans, the pound of sliced carrots, and the crushed tomatoes and, over medium heat, bring to a boil. Lower the heat, partially cover, and simmer 30 minutes.

1 pound dried Great Northern beans, picked over

2 ducks (5 pounds each), giblets reserved

1 cup cold water

1 pound smoky slab bacon, rind removed, cut into ½-inch cubes

2 large leeks, white part only, cleaned and chopped

2 medium onions, peeled and chopped

2 medium carrots, peeled and chopped, plus 1 pound carrots, peeled and cut on the diagonal into 1-inch pieces

10 garlic cloves, peeled and minced

6 sprigs Italian parsley plus 1 cup finely chopped Italian parsley leaves

1 tablespoon dried thyme, crumbled

2 bay leaves

3 cups canned chicken broth or homemade stock

2 cups dry white wine

1 cup canned crushed tomatoes

2 teaspoons salt

Freshly ground black pepper

Stir in the duck meat, salt, and pepper and simmer, uncovered, stirring occasionally, until the beans are very tender, about 1 hour. *The recipe can be prepared to this point up to 48 hours ahead. Cool the ragout to room temperature, cover, and refrigerate. Wrap the cracklings and bacon airtight and refrigerate. Return cracklings and bacon to room temperature and reheat the ragout until simmering, thinning it with water as needed, before proceeding.*

In a food processor combine 1 cup of the beans and 1 cup of the cooking liquid with the remaining garlic and the chopped parsley. Process until smooth. Stir the puree back into the ragout, remove from the heat, cover, and let it stand 1 minute before serving. Garnish with the cracklings and bacon and serve.

*Serves 6*

## WHOLE-GRAIN PINEAPPLE SPICE CAKE

8 ounces dried pineapple, cut into ¼-inch dice

1¼ cups corn oil

1 cup sugar

½ cup light brown sugar, packed

4 eggs

1 cup unbleached all-purpose flour

½ cup stone-ground whole wheat flour

½ cup medium rye flour

1 tablespoon baking powder

1 teaspoon salt

1 teaspoon cinnamon

½ teaspoon freshly grated nutmeg

¼ teaspoon ground ginger

THIS KIND OF OLD-FASHIONED cake seems the right conclusion to such a country-style menu, and the spices clear the palate after the rich entrée.

Bring a quart of water to a boil. In a medium-size heat-proof bowl pour the water over the pineapple and let stand 2 hours. Drain.

Position a rack in the center of the oven and preheat to 350 degrees F. Butter and flour a 10-cup ring pan, tapping out the excess.

In a large bowl whisk together the oil and sugars. Whisk in the eggs, one at a time. In a separate bowl combine the unbleached, whole wheat, and rye flours, baking powder, salt, cinnamon, nutmeg, ginger, allspice, and cloves. Add the pineapple, dry ingredients, and black walnuts to the oil mixture and stir until just combined. Pour the batter into the prepared pan and bake until the cake is puffed and golden and just pulling away from the sides of the pan, 50 to 60 minutes. Cool 10 minutes in the pan on a rack. Invert the cake onto a platter and cool completely. Drizzle the cake with Pineapple-Rum Glaze and serve with the whipped cream.

*¼ teaspoon ground allspice*
*¼ teaspoon ground cloves*
*1 cup coarsely chopped black walnuts (see Cook's Sources) or pecans or English walnuts*
*Pineapple-Rum Glaze (recipe follows)*
*Unsweetened whipped cream, as garnish*

━● *Serves 8*

# PINEAPPLE-RUM GLAZE

In a small, heavy saucepan combine all the ingredients. Set over medium heat and bring to a boil, stirring. Lower the heat and simmer briskly until bubbly and caramel colored, about 7 minutes. Cool to room temperature.

*⅓ cup pineapple juice*
*¼ cup (½ stick) unsalted butter*
*¼ cup sugar*
*¼ cup light brown sugar, firmly packed*
*¼ cup dark rum*

━● *Makes about ¾ cup*

# MENU

◆◆◆◆◆◆◆◆◆◆◆◆◆◆

TOMATO, WATERCRESS,
AND ENDIVE SALAD

◆

SEA SCALLOPS
IN RED PEPPER CREAM

◆

BROCCOLI WITH
ORANGE-SHALLOT BUTTER

◆

ARBORIO RICE CAKE

◆

PLUM AND BLUEBERRY BETTY

THINK OF THIS as an Indian-summer seafood menu, capturing the last tomatoes, red peppers, plums, and blueberries of summer, and celebrating the first fat, sweet scallops from icy northern waters. A well-balanced California Chardonnay, combining fruit, acid, and a touch of oak, will nicely complement the red pepper sauce.

## TOMATO, WATERCRESS, AND ENDIVE SALAD

♦ ♦ ♦ ♦ ♦ ♦ ♦ ♦ ♦

**P**EPPERY WATERCRESS provides the herbal seasoning in this colorful salad. The dark, rich vinegar made from good Spanish sherry is my favorite (in this recipe and almost everywhere else), but if your tomatoes lack the proper sweet-and-sour ripeness, substitute balsamic vinegar for a flavor boost.

♦ ♦ ♦  ♦ ♦ ♦

Combine the diced tomatoes and 1 teaspoon of the salt in a strainer placed over a bowl and let drain 30 minutes.

In a bowl whisk together the vinegar, the mustard, and the remaining salt. Slowly whisk in the oil. Shake the tomatoes to remove excess liquid. In a medium-size bowl combine the tomatoes, the watercress, and ½ cup of the dressing. Season generously with pepper.

Arrange the endive in a starburst pattern on plates, placing a mound of the tomato salad in the center. Serve, passing the remaining vinaigrette at the table.

**—●** *Serves 6*

♦ ♦ ♦ ♦ ♦ ♦ ♦ ♦ ♦ ♦ ♦ ♦ ♦ ♦ ♦ ♦ ♦ ♦ ♦ ♦ ♦ ♦ ♦ ♦ ♦ ♦ ♦ ♦ ♦ ♦ ♦ ♦ ♦ ♦ ♦ ♦ ♦ ♦ ♦ ♦ ♦ ♦ ♦

*1½ pounds (3 large) tomatoes, seeded and diced*
*1⅛ teaspoons salt*
*2 tablespoons sherry wine vinegar*
*2 teaspoons prepared Dijon-style mustard*
*¾ cup olive oil*
*½ cup chopped watercress leaves*
*Freshly ground black pepper*
*18 large Belgian endive leaves*

## SEA SCALLOPS IN RED PEPPER CREAM

♦ ♦ ♦ ♦ ♦ ♦ ♦ ♦ ♦

**S**AUCE-MAKING NEED NOT always depend on complex, long-simmered assemblages of hard-to-find ingredients. Easy-to-find flavor makers are available to us, as this recipe illustrates. The red pepper puree, enhanced with a touch of heat from the paprika and hot pepper,

2½ *pounds large sea*
  *scallops, of equal size*
  *and weight*
2 *tablespoons unsalted*
  *butter*
*Salt and freshly ground*
  *black pepper*
1 *cup dry white wine*
¼ *cup medium-dry sherry*
1 *cup whipping cream*
½ *cup Red Pepper Puree*
  (*recipe follows*)

and its natural sweetness and acidity heightened by a touch of sugar and vinegar, combines with the scallops, white wine, sherry, and cream to produce a lush—and very quick—sauce. Leftover puree refrigerates for up to 1 week and freezes well for several months. This recipe can easily be modified to feature shrimp or boneless chicken breasts.

Remove and discard the tiny side muscles from the scallops. (They pull away easily using your fingers.) Rinse the scallops well and pat dry.

In a large, heavy skillet over high heat melt the butter. Add the scallops, season lightly with salt and pepper, and cook, tossing and stirring, until just opaque, about 4 minutes. With a slotted spoon, transfer the scallops to a bowl and reserve. Add the wine and sherry to the skillet, bring to a boil, and cook, stirring often, until reduced to a few syrupy spoonfuls, about 7 minutes. Whisk in the cream and any accumulated juices from the bowl of scallops, bring to a boil, and cook another 5 minutes, or until slightly reduced and thickened. Whisk in the Red Pepper Puree, then stir in the scallops, and simmer about 3 minutes, or until heated through. Adjust the seasoning and serve immediately.

*Serves 6*

## RED PEPPER PUREE

4 *tablespoons unsalted*
  *butter*
2 *pounds sweet red*
  *peppers, stemmed, cored,*
  *and diced*
2 *tablespoons sugar*
2 *tablespoons cider vinegar*

In a small, heavy saucepan over medium heat melt the butter. Stir in the remaining ingredients, lower the heat, and cover. Cook, stirring once or twice, for 50 minutes. Uncover the pan, raise the heat to medium, and stir until all liquid evaporates and the peppers just begin to brown, about 10 minutes. Cool, then force the peppers through the medium blade of a food mill, discarding the skins. Cover and refrigerate or freeze until use.

*1 teaspoon Hungarian
sweet paprika (see
Cook's Sources)*
*½ teaspoon dried hot
pepper flakes*
*Pinch of salt*

━● *Makes about 1 cup*

◆ ◆ ◆ ◆ ◆ ◆ ◆ ◆ ◆ ◆ ◆ ◆ ◆ ◆ ◆ ◆ ◆ ◆ ◆ ◆ ◆ ◆ ◆ ◆ ◆ ◆ ◆ ◆ ◆ ◆ ◆ ◆ ◆ ◆ ◆ ◆ ◆ ◆ ◆ ◆ ◆

## BROCCOLI WITH ORANGE-SHALLOT BUTTER

◆ ◆ ◆ ◆ ◆ ◆ ◆ ◆

**B**ROCCOLI, LIKE ANY old friend, can sometimes become a bore. Reliability, compatibility, and comfort are all solid virtues, however, and with this simple sauce to perk things up, even the oldest of friends makes a boon dining companion.

*2 pounds broccoli*
*Salt*
*½ cup fresh orange juice*
*1 stick unsalted butter*
*⅓ cup minced shallot*
*1½ tablespoons minced
orange zest*

◆ ◆ ◆  ◆ ◆ ◆

Trim the broccoli into serving-size pieces, reserving the stems for another use. Bring a large pot of lightly salted water to a boil, add the broccoli, and cook until just tender, about 5 minutes. Drain and plunge the broccoli immediately into ice water. When cool, drain well. *The broccoli can be prepared to this point up to 1 day ahead. Cover and refrigerate; return to room temperature before proceeding.*

In a small, heavy saucepan over medium heat simmer the orange juice until reduced to 2 tablespoons, about 10 minutes. In a large skillet over low heat melt the butter. Add the shallot, cover, and cook, stirring occasionally, until tender, about 10 minutes. Stir in the orange zest, the reduced orange juice, and ½ teaspoon of salt. Add the broccoli and raise the heat to medium. Toss the broccoli until just heated through, about 3 minutes. Serve immediately.

━● *Serves 6*

◆ ◆ ◆ ◆ ◆ ◆ ◆ ◆ ◆ ◆ ◆ ◆ ◆ ◆ ◆ ◆ ◆ ◆ ◆ ◆ ◆ ◆ ◆ ◆ ◆ ◆ ◆ ◆ ◆ ◆ ◆ ◆ ◆ ◆ ◆ ◆ ◆ ◆ ◆ ◆ ◆

## A R B O R I O   R I C E   C A K E

◆◆◆◆◆◆◆◆◆

9 tablespoons unsalted
    butter
½ cup minced yellow
    onion
1 garlic clove, peeled and
    minced
1 cup Arborio rice (see
    Cook's Sources)
3 cups canned chicken
    broth or homemade stock
¾ teaspoon salt
½ cup finely chopped
    Italian parsley
2 tablespoons freshly
    grated Parmesan cheese
Freshly ground black
    pepper

**A**RBORIO—THE ITALIAN short-grain rice that is the star of risotto—cooks into soft, tender nuggets. In this skillet cake, crusty outside and creamy inside, the rice is a perfect foil for rich sauces.

◆◆◆  ◆◆◆

In a heavy saucepan over low heat melt 3 tablespoons of the butter. Add the onion and garlic and cook, stirring once or twice, 5 minutes. Add the rice and cook until it is a pale golden color and crackles audibly, about 4 minutes. Stir in the chicken broth and salt and bring to a boil. Reduce the heat to low, cover, and cook, without stirring, until the rice is tender and the broth is absorbed, 20 to 22 minutes. Remove from the heat, stir in the parsley and cheese, and season generously with pepper. Cool completely. *The recipe can be prepared to this point up to 1 day ahead. Cover and refrigerate, returning the rice to room temperature before proceeding.*

Butter a baking sheet with 1 tablespoon of the butter. In a 10-inch, nonstick skillet over medium heat melt 2½ tablespoons of the butter. Add the rice and flatten it with a spatula into a disc ¾ inch thick. Cook until golden brown, shaking the rice cake occasionally, 7 to 8 minutes. If it sticks to the bottom or sides of the pan, release it gently with the spatula. At this point, the cake will not cohere; continue to press it together with the spatula.

Place the prepared baking sheet over the skillet and invert the cake onto the sheet. Melt the remaining butter in the skillet. Using the spatula, slide the cake back into the skillet and cook until golden brown, about 8 to 9 minutes, again keeping the cake from sticking, as necessary, and shaking the pan occasionally.

Slide the cake onto a serving plate and cut into wedges.

*Serves 4 to 6*

♦ ♦ ♦ ♦ ♦ ♦ ♦ ♦ ♦ ♦ ♦ ♦ ♦ ♦ ♦ ♦ ♦ ♦ ♦ ♦ ♦ ♦ ♦ ♦ ♦ ♦ ♦ ♦ ♦ ♦ ♦ ♦ ♦ ♦ ♦ ♦ ♦ ♦ ♦ ♦ ♦ ♦ ♦ ♦

## PLUM AND BLUEBERRY BETTY

♦ ♦ ♦ ♦ ♦ ♦ ♦ ♦ ♦

TWO RIPE AND PERFECT FRUITS, when combined, always seem to create a whole that is much greater than the mere sum of the parts. Plums and blueberries are particularly compatible, and combined, their taste and color are spectacular. Serve the crisp drizzled with heavy cream or a dollop of sour cream.

*For the topping* In a food processor in the order listed, combine the flour, almonds, brown sugar, and butter. Process until a lumpy dough forms. The mixture should be somewhat crumbly and dry. Do not overprocess. Transfer to a bowl and refrigerate at least 30 minutes.

*For the filling* In a large bowl combine the plums, blueberries, sugar, flour, vanilla, and cinnamon and let stand 30 minutes, stirring occasionally.

*To assemble* Position a rack in the upper third of the oven and preheat to 400 degrees F. Spoon the fruit mixture into a shallow 1½- or 2-quart baking dish. Break up any large chunks of topping with a fork and scatter it evenly over the fruit. Bake until well browned and bubbly, about 40 minutes. Serve warm or cool.

*Serves 6 to 8*

♦ ♦ ♦ ♦ ♦ ♦ ♦ ♦ ♦ ♦ ♦ ♦ ♦ ♦ ♦ ♦ ♦ ♦ ♦ ♦ ♦ ♦ ♦ ♦ ♦ ♦ ♦ ♦ ♦ ♦ ♦ ♦ ♦ ♦ ♦ ♦ ♦ ♦ ♦ ♦ ♦ ♦ ♦ ♦

TOPPING

*1 cup flour*
*4 ounces (about 1 cup) whole, unblanched almonds*
*¾ cup brown sugar, packed*
*12 tablespoons unsalted butter, well chilled and cut into small pieces*

FILLING

*2½ pounds slightly underripe, red plums, pitted and cut into ½-inch chunks*
*3 cups blueberries, rinsed and picked over*
*¾ cup sugar*
*3 tablespoons flour*
*2 tablespoons vanilla*
*2 teaspoons cinnamon*

# M E N U

◆ ◆ ◆ ◆ ◆ ◆ ◆ ◆ ◆ ◆ ◆ ◆ ◆ ◆

CREAMY VEGETABLE BISQUE

◆

ROAST LOIN OF PORK
IN LEMON-GARLIC MARINADE

◆

APPLE-BASIL COMPOTE

◆

PARMESAN MASHED POTATOES

◆

RASPBERRY-APRICOT JAM PIES

THIS MENU BELONGS to Indian summer, designed to take advantage of the season in which summer abundance merges into the opulence of autumn. In the crossover the cook has the chance to blend two rich seasons into one short but unique eating experience.

## CREAMY VEGETABLE BISQUE

♦ ♦ ♦ ♦ ♦ ♦ ♦ ♦ ♦

**H**ERE IS A SOUP that will utilize the last of the garden's (or market's) produce before frost puts an end to summer. Freely substitute whatever vegetables you wish, always cutting them into regular dice to promote even cooking. Any herb that is compatible with tomatoes (most are) will do as the final garnish.

♦ ♦ ♦  ♦ ♦ ♦

In a medium-size pan over moderate heat melt the butter. Stir in the onions, chopped carrot, celery, parsley stems, garlic, and thyme. Lower the heat, cover, and cook, stirring occasionally, until the vegetables are tender and lightly colored, about 20 minutes.

Add the broth, stir in the salt, and bring to a boil. Lower the heat, partially cover, and simmer until the vegetables are very tender, about 30 minutes. Cool slightly and strain, discarding the solids. *The soup base can be prepared up to 1 day ahead. Cool completely, cover, and refrigerate.*

Hold the corn over a medium-size bowl and, using a sharp knife, scrape the kernels and juices into the bowl.

Set the soup base over medium heat and bring it to a simmer. Add the diced carrots and simmer 5 minutes. Add the green beans and sweet pepper and simmer 5 minutes. Add the zucchini and simmer 5 minutes. Add the corn, its juices, and the tomatoes and simmer 1 minute. Stir in the cream and season generously with pepper. Adjust the seasoning and simmer another 3 to 5 minutes, or until the soup is just heated through. Ladle the soup into bowls, sprinkle with the herbs, and serve immediately.

*Serves 6*

4 tablespoons unsalted
  butter
2 medium yellow onions,
  peeled and chopped
1 large carrot, peeled and
  coarsely chopped, plus 3
  large carrots cut into
  1/3-inch dice
2 ribs celery, leaves
  included, chopped
Stems from 1 bunch
  parsley
3 garlic cloves, peeled and
  minced
1 1/2 teaspoons dried thyme,
  crumbled
4 cups canned chicken
  broth or homemade stock
1 teaspoon salt
3 ears of corn, husked
1/4 pound green beans,
  trimmed and cut into
  1/3-inch pieces
1 large, sweet red pepper,
  stemmed, cored, and cut
  into 1/3-inch dice
1 medium zucchini,
  scrubbed, trimmed, and
  cut into 1/3-inch dice
2 medium tomatoes, seeded
  and cut into 1/3-inch dice
1/3 cup whipping cream
Freshly ground black
  pepper
1/4 cup minced fresh herbs,
  such as mint, oregano,
  marjoram, thyme, or dill

# ROAST LOIN OF PORK IN LEMON-GARLIC MARINADE

1 boneless pork loin roast
  (2½ to 3 pounds), fat
  trimmed to a thin layer,
  roast-tied, and rib bones
  reserved in one piece
½ cup olive oil
½ cup strained fresh
  lemon juice (from 2 or 3
  lemons)
3 garlic cloves, forced
  through a press
Freshly ground black
  pepper
Salt

THE SIMPLE MARINADE helps keep the roast moist and adds just the right edge to the pork's rich flavor. Including the riblets gives guests crusty bones to nibble on—miniature spareribs. If the night unexpectedly turns warm, the roast and ribs can be served cooled just to room temperature.

Set the roast and ribs in a shallow, nonreactive bowl. In a small bowl whisk together the oil, lemon juice, and garlic. Pour the marinade over the roast, cover, and refrigerate 24 hours, turning occasionally.

Preheat the oven to 325 degrees F. Arrange the rack of ribs meaty side up in a roasting pan just large enough to accommodate it. Season generously with pepper and lightly with salt. Set the roast, fat side up, atop the ribs (in effect, reassembling the roast as it was before boning). Season the loin generously with pepper and lightly with salt. Roast about 2 hours, or until an instant-reading thermometer inserted into the center of the roast registers 165 to 170 degrees F, basting frequently with the marinade and the accumulated pan juices. Transfer the roast to a cutting board and keep it warm. Continue to bake the ribs until they are crisp and brown, another 20 minutes.

Slice the pork. Cut the ribs apart and serve with the roast.

Serves 6

## APPLE-BASIL COMPOTE

**T**HIS DISH PERFECTLY symbolizes the culinary possibilities of the changing of the seasons. While frost may not yet have claimed the basil crop (indeed it may sometimes be had at bargain prices as farmers hurry to unload the last of it), the crisp nip in the air has us thinking of apples. Of course, even culinary possibilities must taste good, and though you may think of roast pork and applesauce as old-fashioned, the lemon, garlic, and basil give the duo a fresh—and delicious—twist.

6 cups cold water

½ cup strained fresh lemon juice (from 2 or 3 lemons)

2 pounds firm, tart apples, such as McIntosh or Jonathan

2 cups dry white wine

⅓ cup sugar

1 cup loosely packed fresh basil leaves

In a large bowl combine the water and half of the lemon juice. Peel and core the apples, cutting them into 1-inch chunks. Transfer them to the acidulated water.

In a large, heavy, nonreactive saucepan combine the remaining lemon juice, the wine, and the sugar and set over low heat. Cook, stirring, until the sugar dissolves. Bring to a boil. Drain the apples and add them to the saucepan. Lower the heat, partially cover, and simmer until the apples are just tender, 7 to 15 minutes.

With a slotted spoon, transfer the apples to a bowl. Increase the heat and boil the liquid hard until it is reduced by half, about 10 minutes. Mince the basil. Stir the basil into the hot liquid, pour it over the apples, and cool to room temperature. Cover and refrigerate at least 4 hours. *The compote can be prepared up to 1 day ahead. Let it come to cool room temperature before serving.*

*Serves 6*

## PARMESAN
## MASHED POTATOES

4 tablespoons unsalted
   butter
8 garlic cloves, peeled and
   chopped
1 cup whipping cream
Salt
3 pounds baking potatoes,
   peeled and quartered
¾ cup grated Parmesan
   cheese
½ cup finely chopped
   Italian parsley

THESE ARE NOT EXACTLY the ones that Mom makes, but they are rich and deliciously comfy all the same. Although it sounds unlikely, for the best texture use Idaho baking potatoes. Pass additional unsalted butter and the pepper mill at the table.

In a small saucepan over low heat melt the butter. Add the garlic, cover, and cook without browning, stirring occasionally, until very tender, about 20 minutes. Add the cream and 1 teaspoon of salt. Bring the mixture to a boil, lower the heat, and simmer, partially covered, for 10 minutes. Remove from the heat and keep warm.

Meanwhile, in a medium-size saucepan, cover the potatoes with cold, lightly salted water. Set the pan over medium heat and bring to a boil. Lower the heat and simmer until the potatoes are very tender, about 20 minutes. Drain.

Force the potatoes through a ricer or the medium blade of a food mill or mash them by hand (do not use a food processor). Return the potatoes to the pan and set it over very low heat. Strain the warm garlic cream into the potatoes (for a garlic booster you may also force the garlic cloves through the strainer into the potatoes if you wish). Stir in the cheese and parsley and whip the potatoes until fluffy. Serve immediately.

Serves 6

# RASPBERRY-APRICOT
# JAM PIES

♦ ♦ ♦ ♦ ♦ ♦ ♦ ♦ ♦

**T**HESE PORTABLE PIES were inspired by my love of cold, leftover fruit pie, usually eaten out of hand while standing over the kitchen sink and washed down with a glass of icy milk.

They *are* a great finger dessert (take them along on a picnic), but if you're not standing around the sink with your dinner guests, consider serving the pies on plates, accompanied by a scoop of vanilla ice cream.

♦ ♦ ♦  ♦ ♦ ♦

*For the filling* In a bowl stir together the apricot and raspberry preserves. Stir in the Amaretto. Stir in the bread crumbs, cover, and refrigerate until cold and very thick, at least overnight.

*For the crust* In a food processor combine the flour, pecans, sugar, and salt and process until the pecans are coarsely chopped. Add the butter and process until a coarse meal forms. With the motor running, add enough of the cream, 1 tablespoon at a time, to form a soft, crumbly dough. Lightly flour the work surface. Turn the dough out onto the surface, knead it briefly, until it just coheres, divide it in half, and form each half into a disc. Wrap each piece of dough well in plastic and refrigerate 45 minutes. *The dough can be prepared up to 2 days ahead. It may be necessary to let it soften slightly at room temperature before proceeding.*

*To assemble* Position a rack in the upper level of the oven and preheat to 350 degrees F. Lightly flour the work surface. Roll out 1 disc of dough into a rectangle slightly larger than 8 × 12 inches. Cut the dough into 6 squares, of 4 inches each. Spoon a slightly mounded tablespoon of the chilled filling into the center of each square. Brush 2 edges of the square lightly with the

FILLING

*½ cup thick apricot preserves*

*½ cup thick raspberry preserves*

*2 tablespoons Amaretto*

*¼ cup fine, dry bread crumbs*

PECAN PASTRY II

*2½ cups unbleached all-purpose flour*

*¾ cup pecans*

*3 tablespoons sugar*

*¼ teaspoon salt*

*12 tablespoons (1½ sticks) unsalted butter, well chilled and cut into small pieces*

*½ cup (about) chilled whipping cream*

*1 egg, beaten to blend*

*1½ pints vanilla ice cream, softened slightly*

*Confectioners' sugar*

beaten egg. Fold the dough over to form a triangle. Crimp the edges with a fork to seal. Transfer the filled pies to an ungreased baking sheet and refrigerate while forming 6 more pies with the remaining filling and dough.

Pierce the top of each pie once with the tines of a fork. Bake about 20 minutes, or until lightly colored. Cool the pies to room temperature on a rack.

To serve, place a scoop of vanilla ice cream on each of 6 dessert plates. Dust the pies lightly with confectioners' sugar and set 2 on each plate. Serve immediately.

*Makes 12 pies*

# M E N U

◆ ◆ ◆ ◆ ◆ ◆ ◆ ◆ ◆ ◆ ◆ ◆ ◆ ◆

FENNEL AND WATERCRESS SALAD
WITH OLIVES

◆

MOLASSES-GLAZED DUCK WITH
ZUCCHINI AND TURNIPS

◆

PUMPKIN SPOON BREAD

◆

BOURBON-BUTTERSCOTCH
BAKED APPLES

*page 36*

A MEAL OF RICH, dark, and intense flavors, a favorite
menu. Pour a powerful, complex zinfandel.

## FENNEL AND WATERCRESS SALAD WITH OLIVES

2 pounds fennel bulbs,
tough outer layers
discarded, trimmed and
cored, plus fronds, as
garnish
1 large, sweet red pepper
3 tablespoons champagne
vinegar
1 teaspoon prepared
Dijon-style mustard
Pinch of salt
Freshly ground black
pepper
½ cup olive oil
1 bunch of watercress,
tough stems removed
24 Calamata olives (see
Cook's Sources), pitted
and chopped

TASTE THE FENNEL before you buy it to be certain it has a pronounced anise flavor, or the point of this crunchy and tangy first course will be lost.

Cut the fennel into coarse matchstick julienne. Cover with plastic wrap and refrigerate until well chilled. Roast the pepper in the open flame of a gas burner, or under a preheated broiler, turning it, until the skin is charred. In a paper bag, or in a bowl covered by a plate, let the pepper steam until cool. Peel and seed the pepper and wipe it with paper towels. Cut the pepper into matchstick julienne.

In a small bowl whisk together the vinegar, mustard, salt, and a grind of pepper. Slowly whisk in the oil and the dressing will thicken. Adjust the seasoning.

Divide the watercress among 6 plates. In a bowl toss the fennel and the olives with ½ cup of the dressing. Place the fennel in a mound atop the watercress. Garnish with the red pepper and the fennel fronds. Drizzle the remaining dressing over the salads and serve immediately.

Serves 6

## MOLASSES-GLAZED DUCK WITH ZUCCHINI AND TURNIPS

SOMETIMES I LOVE the French style of duck cookery—seared outside, bloodred inside, primal and direct—and sometimes I want an old-fashioned "American" bird, cooked through, tender, the skin glazed and crisp enough to eat. This recipe is of the latter kind, and it comes garnished with its own vegetable side dish, simplifying preparation.

Remove the first and second wing joints from the ducks. Chop the necks, hearts, and gizzards and pat dry. In a small, heavy saucepan over medium-high heat melt together 2 tablespoons of the butter and the oil. Add the wings, necks, hearts, and gizzards and cook, stirring, until well browned, 10 to 15 minutes. Add the chicken broth and thyme and bring to a boil. Lower the heat, partially cover, and simmer, skimming occasionally, for 1 hour.

Strain the stock, return it to the pan, and set it over medium heat. Simmer about 20 minutes, or until reduced to ½ cup.

Bring a pot of lightly salted water to a boil. Add the zucchini and cook until just tender, about 5 minutes. With a slotted spoon, transfer the zucchini to a bowl of ice water. Bring the water back to a boil. Add the turnips and cook until just tender, about 8 minutes. With a slotted spoon, transfer the turnips to the bowl of ice water. When the vegetables are cool, drain them thoroughly. *The dish can be prepared to this point up to 1 day ahead. Cover the stock and vegetables in separate containers and refrigerate.*

Preheat the oven to 325 degrees F. Prick the ducks all over with a fork and pat dry. Set the ducks on a rack in a shallow baking pan and roast them 2 hours, pricking the ducks frequently and discarding the rendered fat from the pan.

In a small bowl stir together the soy sauce and molasses and reserve 3 tablespoons. Brush the ducks with some of the remaining soy mixture. Roast the ducks another 30 minutes and baste every 10 minutes with more of the soy mixture, using it all.

Meanwhile, melt the remaining butter in a large, heavy skillet over medium heat. Add the garlic and ginger and cook, stirring, 1 minute. Add the reduced

*2 ducklings (4½ to 5 pounds each), necks, hearts, and gizzards reserved*

*5 tablespoons unsalted butter*

*1 tablespoon vegetable oil*

*2 cups canned chicken broth or homemade stock*

*½ teaspoon dried thyme, crumbled*

*Salt*

*2 medium zucchini, trimmed and quartered crosswise*

*8 small (about 1½ pounds) turnips, peeled*

*⅓ cup reduced-sodium soy sauce*

*¼ cup molasses*

*3 medium garlic cloves, peeled and minced*

*1 tablespoon minced fresh ginger*

stock and the reserved soy mixture. Cook 1 minute. Add the zucchini and turnips and cook until well coated with the glaze and heated through, 3 to 5 minutes.

Using poultry shears, quarter each duck. Set the duck quarters in the center of a serving platter. Spoon the glazed vegetables around the edge of the platter and serve at once.

▬● *Serves 4 to 6*

## PUMPKIN SPOON BREAD

3 tablespoons unsalted
butter
1 can (16 ounces)
unsweetened and
solid-pack pumpkin
puree
7 tablespoons sugar
1 tablespoon Hungarian
sweet paprika (see
Cook's Sources)
1 teaspoon salt
4 eggs, at room
temperature
⅓ cup buttermilk
1 cup yellow cornmeal,
preferably stone-ground
1 teaspoon baking powder
½ teaspoon baking soda

**M**OIST, TENDER SPOON BREADS—sometimes called cornmeal soufflés—appeared on early American tables and, depending on how sweet they were, made admirable starchy side dishes, desserts, or even frugal suppers. This version, meant to accompany the molasses-glazed duck and vegetables, is sweetened just enough to bring out the flavor of the corn and pumpkin and spiked with a touch of paprika. Serve it with butter and pass the pepper mill.

Preheat the oven to 375 degrees F. In the oven melt the butter in a 6-cup soufflé dish.

In a medium-size bowl whisk together the pumpkin, sugar, paprika, and salt. One at a time, whisk in the eggs. Stir in the buttermilk. Add the cornmeal, baking powder, and baking soda and whisk until well combined. Tilt the hot soufflé dish to coat the bottom and sides with butter. Pour in the pumpkin mixture and bake until puffed and light brown, about 40 minutes. Serve immediately.

▬● *Serves 4 to 6*

# GATHERINGS

THERE ARE OCCASIONS which call for entertaining a crowd, which in and of themselves are all about surrounding one-self with as many congenial friends and relatives as possible. Such events of bountiful camaraderie are inevitably also about the ordinary sort of bounty—lots of food, the best there is, and all of it turned out by a pair of loving hands—*yours*. If thoughts of such marathon cookery have you longing for the hermit's life, I'm with you. I used to wonder frequently how Mom managed holiday gatherings with such aplomb.

When I gave some thought to those rosily remembered holidays, though, I realized something. There weren't all that many of them. We did not, after all, have twenty guests on a regular basis. We also traded hosting holidays with other family members and just as often as we fed the whole clan at an overwhelming bash, we tucked a casserole and two dozen homemade rolls into the Chevy and drove to someone else's house. And, when we did do the hosting honors, I don't remember anyone ever saying it was easy. In fact, I remember my mother working darned hard for days in advance, and there were always plenty of volunteers to put the finishing touches on the feast. Even the Pilgrims got a little help from the Indians.

In short, where is it written that cooking for a crowd should be easy? It isn't (except in certain blithely optimistic cookbooks), and though there are strategies in the menus that follow (most of them designed to help you spread the work out over several days or even weeks), these are precisely the meals in which your sweat, tears, labor, and love are the unique seasoning that will make the event special. Expect to spend some time in the kitchen, but also expect to be lavishly rewarded for your efforts.

# M E N U

PEPPERED PECANS
*page 332*

*or*

TABASCO ALMONDS AND CASHEWS
*page 21*

♦

RADISHES WITH ANCHOVY BUTTER
ON CRUSTY BAGUETTES

♦

GREEN OLIVES WITH MUSTARD SEED
AND SHERRY VINEGAR

♦

BLACK OLIVES WITH CILANTRO,
GARLIC, AND LEMON RIND

♦

SANDWICHES OF MEATLOAF
WITH SUN-DRIED TOMATOES
*page 370*
ON HARD ROLLS WITH
GARLIC MAYONNAISE

♦

HERBED LEMON SHRIMP WITH
SWEET AND HOT PEPPERS

♦

SESAME-MAPLE CHICKEN WINGS

♦

SAUSAGES SMOTHERED WITH
SWEET-AND-SOUR DILLED ONIONS

♦

FRESH FRUIT

♦

CANDY-COUNTER COOKIES
*page 204*

♦

BITCHIN' BROWNIES
*page 43*

I USUALLY RESIST entertaining mobs, but when I do succumb to the lure it's always on my terms. This menu is a good example. The food is lusty and the presentation very casual—a groaning board of mostly room-temperature munchables. Many of the dishes can be done ahead, and some consist of purchased staples—such as good olives—personalized by a little kitchen flair. All are hearty and uncomplicated, meaning I don't have to explain, cheerlead, or even enjoy myself—though I usually do. This menu of culinary extremes goes best with beer: Buy an assortment of your favorites, chill them well, present them in a tub of ice, and let the guests pour as they please.

## RADISHES WITH ANCHOVY BUTTER

♦ ♦ ♦ ♦ ♦ ♦ ♦ ♦ ♦

**T**O EAT THIS LUSTY French classic, spread the butter on a chunk of baguette, bury a radish in the center, and munch away. For the most colorful effect, select pretty radishes and serve them with the tops on. For 20 guests you'll need 40 radishes—about 5 bunches, allowing for those not perfect enough to serve at this party. Leftover anchovy butter can be frozen; it makes a quick and delicious sauce for pasta or grilled fish.

In a medium-size bowl cream together the butter, parsley, anchovies, lemon zest, and pepper. Adjust the seasoning and transfer to a small bowl. Cover and refrigerate. *The recipe can be made 3 days ahead and refrigerated, or it can be frozen for up to 1 month. Soften to room temperature before using.*

Pack the butter into a crock and serve surrounded by the radishes.

*Makes about 1³⁄₄ cups butter*

*1½ cups (3 sticks) unsalted butter, softened*

*½ cup minced Italian parsley*

*16 oil-packed anchovy fillets, drained and minced*

*2 teaspoons minced lemon zest*

*½ teaspoon freshly ground black pepper*

*5 bunches radishes, with tops on*

## GREEN OLIVES WITH MUSTARD SEED AND SHERRY VINEGAR

◆◆◆◆◆◆◆◆◆

5 tablespoons sherry
vinegar
¼ cup yellow mustard
seeds
1 teaspoon dried hot
pepper flakes
1½ pounds brine-cured,
imported green olives
(see Cook's Sources),
drained
¼ cup olive oil

**A**LTHOUGH THIS IS BEST WHEN MADE with imported, gourmet shop olives, it also works with pimiento-stuffed olives from the supermarket.

◆◆◆  ◆◆◆

In a small bowl combine the vinegar, mustard seeds, and pepper flakes and let stand 2 hours, or until the mustard seeds have absorbed most of the vinegar and softened.

In a medium-size bowl toss the vinegar mixture with the olives and the oil. *The recipe can be prepared up to 3 days ahead. Refrigerate, covered. Return to room temperature before proceeding.* Transfer the olives, with their marinade, to a serving bowl.

●—● *Makes about 4 cups*

## BLACK OLIVES WITH CILANTRO, GARLIC, AND LEMON RIND

◆◆◆◆◆◆◆◆◆

¾ cup minced cilantro
¼ cup olive oil
2 tablespoons lemon juice
3 garlic cloves, peeled and
pureed
1½ pounds brine-cured,
imported black olives,
such as Calamata (see
Cook's Sources), drained
Zest of 1 lemon, finely
julienned

In a blender or food processor combine ½ cup of the cilantro, olive oil, lemon juice, and garlic and process until smooth. In a medium-size bowl pour the mixture over the olives. *The recipe can be prepared up to 1 day ahead. Refrigerate, covered. Bring to room temperature before proceeding.*

Toss the olives, their marinade, and the remaining

cilantro. Transfer to a serving bowl and garnish with the lemon zest.

*Makes about 4 cups*

**SERVING STRATEGY** Letting people make their own sandwiches at a casual party like this is a nice touch, but you do need to take simple logistics and portion control into account. I suggest you split the hard rolls and offer them in a napkin-lined basket. Cut the meatloaf into slices that will fit easily onto the rolls you've chosen and present it on a platter or cutting board, close to a generous crock of garlic mayonnaise (recipe follows). Though you've planned sandwiches, don't be surprised if people do what they please with the various components—that's what this kind of casual event is all about.

## GARLIC MAYONNAISE

In a food processor combine the egg yolks, 2 tablespoons of the lemon juice, garlic, mustard, and salt. Process to blend. With the machine running, slowly dribble in the oils. Season generously with black pepper, add additional lemon juice to taste, and process briefly to blend. Transfer to a bowl, stir in the tomatoes, cover, and refrigerate. *The recipe can be made up to 2 days ahead.* Spoon into a 2-cup crock and serve.

*Makes about 2 cups*

3 egg yolks, at room
    temperature
1/4 cup (about) lemon juice
3 garlic cloves, peeled
1 tablespoon prepared
    Dijon-style mustard
3/4 teaspoon salt
2/3 cup olive oil
1 cup corn oil
Freshly ground black
    pepper
6 oil-packed sun-dried
    tomatoes (see Cook's
    Sources), minced

## HERBED LEMON SHRIMP WITH SWEET AND HOT PEPPERS

◆◆◆◆◆◆◆◆◆

S ERVE THE SHRIMP on slices of toasted baguette to preserve every drop of the delicious marinade.

◆◆◆  ◆◆◆

1 cup olive oil

12 whole garlic cloves, peeled

1½ cups finely diced yellow onion

3 fresh jalapeños, stemmed and sliced into thin rounds

3 sweet peppers (1 red, 1 yellow, and 1 orange), stemmed and cut into matchstick julienne

Salt

3 pounds (about 80) medium shrimp, shelled and deveined

½ cup fresh lemon juice, strained

1 teaspoon salt

⅓ cup finely chopped Italian parsley

2 tablespoons minced fresh oregano

1 tablespoon minced fresh thyme

In a large skillet combine the olive oil and garlic cloves. Set over medium-low heat and cook, uncovered, stirring occasionally, 10 minutes. Add the onion and jalapeño and cook, covered, 10 minutes, stirring once or twice. Add the sweet peppers, raise the heat to high, and cook, tossing and stirring often, 5 minutes. Remove from the heat.

Meanwhile, bring a large pot of lightly salted water to a boil. Stir in the shrimp and cook 2 minutes, or until the shrimp are just pink and curled. Drain immediately.

Transfer the hot shrimp to a large bowl. Pour the lemon juice over the shrimp and stir. Pour the contents of the skillet over the shrimp and cool to room temperature. *The shrimp can be prepared to this point up to 1 day ahead. Cover and refrigerate. Return to room temperature before proceeding.*

Stir in the parsley, oregano, and thyme. Adjust the seasoning and serve.

●━◆ *Serves 20*

## SESAME-MAPLE CHICKEN WINGS

◆◆◆◆◆◆◆◆◆

F INGER-LICKING sticky and crunchy, but only slightly sweet, these are at their meaty best when made with the wings from roasting chickens or "oven stuffers."

In a blender or food processor combine the maple syrup, soy sauce, sesame oil, hot oil, garlic, and ginger and process until smooth.

In a large bowl pour the maple mixture over the wings and marinate at room temperature 2 hours. *The wings can be marinated, covered, overnight in the refrigerator.*

Position a rack in the upper third of the oven and preheat to 375 degrees F. Remove the wings from the marinade, reserving it, and arrange them in a single layer on an 11 × 17-inch jelly-roll pan. Bake 25 minutes. Turn the wings and bake them 15 minutes. Brush the wings with half of the marinade and bake 7 minutes. Brush with the remaining marinade, sprinkle with the sesame seeds, and bake another 5 to 7 minutes, or until the wings are very crisp and the sesame seeds are lightly colored.

Cool briefly in the pan, then transfer to a plate. Serve the wings hot or at room temperature.

*Makes 40 wings*

1/3 cup maple syrup (see Cook's Sources)

1/4 cup reduced-sodium soy sauce

3 tablespoons dark sesame oil, from roasted seeds

1 tablespoon Szechuan hot oil

3 garlic cloves, peeled

1 tablespoon coarsely chopped fresh ginger

4 pounds (about 20) large chicken wings, segments separated and tip segments reserved for another use or discarded

2 tablespoons sesame seeds

## SAUSAGES SMOTHERED WITH SWEET-AND-SOUR DILLED ONIONS

FOR THE BEST RESULTS, combine at least two kinds of sausage. If you use an indoor grill or want to light a fire outside, the sausages will be even better than when finished under the broiler. Offer pumpernickel rolls and a jar or two of good mustard for those who would like to make sandwiches.

In a large, nonreactive skillet over medium heat melt the butter. Add the onions, separating the layers, and

4 tablespoons unsalted butter

3 pounds large yellow onions, peeled and sliced thin

5 tablespoons red wine vinegar

2 tablespoons light brown sugar, packed

2 teaspoons salt

*(ingredients continued)*

*½ cup finely minced fresh dill*
*Freshly ground black pepper*
*3 pounds assorted sausages, such as bockwurst, andouille, kielbasa, or knockwurst (see Cook's Sources)*

stir well. Cover and cook 15 minutes. Uncover, stir in the vinegar, brown sugar, and salt, and bring to a boil. Cook hard, uncovered, stirring often, until the liquid has evaporated and the onions are lightly browned, 12 to 15 minutes. Remove the skillet from the heat, stir in the dill, and season the onions generously with pepper. *The dilled onions can be prepared up to 3 hours ahead. Reheat before serving.* Preheat the broiler. Cut the sausages into 2-inch chunks and arrange them on a slotted broiler pan. Broil until crisply brown and heated through, turning them often, about 5 minutes. Transfer the sausages to a platter, top them with the onions, and serve immediately.

*Serves 20*

**SERVING STRATEGY** After a buffet gathering like this, dessert is not only a sweet conclusion to the meal, but also an important group event, bringing back together content, well-fed, but separated clusters of guests for one last shared moment. Dessert also signals gracefully that it's time for things to begin to draw to a close. To achieve this, the host or hostess, or both, should pass plates of cookies and brownies among the crowd. Then, the remaining desserts should be left in place on the buffet table, encouraging those who want more to help themselves and beginning the general movement, however regretful, toward the door.

# MENU

◆ ◆ ◆ ◆ ◆ ◆ ◆ ◆ ◆ ◆ ◆ ◆ ◆ ◆ ◆

CREAMED WILD MUSHROOMS
WITH BACON
*page 222*
ON CONFETTI CORN CAKES
*page 253*

◆

ROAST FRESH HAM WITH
CAMPARI-ORANGE GLAZE

◆

BROCCOLI-LEEK PUREE

◆

PUREE OF BAKED BEETS
AND BAKED GARLIC
*page 136*

◆

WILD RICE DRESSING WITH PEARS
AND CHESTNUTS
*page 349*

◆

LEMON CURD MOUSSE

◆

JACK DANIEL'S
CHOCOLATE WHISKEY CAKE
*page 200*

THIS IS A GRAND MENU for the rare celebratory sit-down holiday feast in my otherwise mostly intimate and unstructured entertaining schedule. I'm driven to such impetuous extremes by the deep, rich flavors and the oddly reassuring Italian–Woodland–Americana mixture of dishes. It doesn't hurt, either, that the main course is a spectacularly glazed, boneless fresh ham, confounding expectations of what to find on a holiday board, and reminding guests how really *good* a pork roast can be.

For the final test of the menu (before it could join the ranks), I actually served it for Christmas dinner. If you have traditions you don't want to tamper with, though, try this spread on New Year's, or at any other special fall or winter event that calls for serious eating.

Although the mushroom recipe is written to serve eight, it is rich enough to provide a light starter for twelve in this menu. (Double the recipe if you've invited big eaters.) Serve the mushrooms over the corn cakes, offering just one cake per guest. Make a triple recipe of the beet puree. If you want a salad after the main course, make a triple recipe of Mixed Greens with Red Wine Vinaigrette and Cheese Toasts (page 50), using Gorgonzola on the toasts. Or, you may omit the toasts and garnish the salad instead with Roquefort-Walnut Shortbreads (page 344).

▀▄▀▄▀▄▀▄▀▄▀▄▀▄▀▄▀▄▀▄▀▄▀▄▀▄▀▄▀▄▀▄▀▄▀▄

## ROAST FRESH HAM WITH CAMPARI-ORANGE GLAZE

♦ ♦ ♦ ♦ ♦ ♦ ♦ ♦ ♦ ♦

1 boneless, oven-ready
   fresh ham (about 10
   pounds), rolled and tied
Salt
Freshly ground black
   pepper
½ cup finely minced
   Italian parsley
3 tablespoons minced
   orange zest
3 garlic cloves, peeled and
   crushed through a press
¾ cup Campari
1 cup fresh orange juice,
   strained
1½ cups (about) canned
   chicken broth or
   homemade stock

**C**AMPARI, THE BRIGHT RED, slightly bitter Italian aperitif, creates not only a handsome lacquer for the roast, but also an assertive edge of flavor that is an excellent foil to the sweet, succulent meat. Order the leg in advance from your butcher (most fresh hams go straight to the smokehouse) and have him bone and tie it. At home, untie it, tuck in the citrus-garlic stuffing, and re-tie the roast, following the butcher's original plan. There will be ham left over for sandwiches, salads, and midnight snacking.

♦ ♦ ♦  ♦ ♦ ♦

Position a rack in the lower third of the oven and preheat to 350 degrees F.

Untie the roast. Season the inside surfaces of the ham lightly with salt and generously with pepper. In a small bowl stir together the parsley, orange zest, and garlic. Spread the parsley mixture evenly over the inside surfaces of the leg. Re-tie the leg, following the arrangement originally used by the butcher.

Set the pork in a shallow, flameproof baking dish just large enough to hold it and bake 3½ hours, occasionally removing the juices from the pan and reserving them.

Add the Campari and orange juice to the pan and bake the ham another 40 minutes, basting often. The ham is done when an instant-reading thermometer inserted into the thickest part registers 165 to 170 degrees F.

Transfer the roast to a cutting board and make a foil tent to keep warm. Degrease the reserved roasting juices and add enough chicken broth to total 2 cups. Add the mixture to the liquid in the baking dish, set it over high heat, and bring to a boil, stirring to deglaze the dish. Taste and adjust the seasoning and strain the sauce into a sauceboat. Carve the roast and serve it, passing the sauce at the table.

—● *Serves 12 to 16*

♦ ♦ ♦ ♦ ♦ ♦ ♦ ♦ ♦ ♦ ♦ ♦ ♦ ♦ ♦ ♦ ♦ ♦ ♦ ♦ ♦ ♦ ♦ ♦ ♦ ♦ ♦ ♦ ♦ ♦ ♦ ♦ ♦ ♦ ♦ ♦ ♦

## BROCCOLI-LEEK PUREE

♦ ♦ ♦ ♦ ♦ ♦ ♦ ♦ ♦

**R**ICH AND DELICIOUS, this bright green puree loses nothing by being prepared a day in advance.

♦ ♦ ♦  ♦ ♦ ♦

3 medium bunches (about
   4½ pounds) broccoli
Salt
1½ sticks (6 ounces)
   unsalted butter
6 large leeks, white part
   only, cleaned, trimmed,
   and chopped
1 teaspoon freshly grated
   nutmeg
1 teaspoon freshly ground
   black pepper

Trim the broccoli and separate the tops into florets. Peel the stalks.

Bring a large pan of water to a boil. Stir in 1 tablespoon of salt. Add the broccoli stalks and cook 5 minutes. Add the florets and cook another 5 to 7 minutes, or until very tender. Drain and transfer immediately to a large bowl of ice water. Cool completely, then drain thoroughly.

In a large skillet over medium heat melt the butter. Add the leeks, lower the heat, and cook, covered, stirring once or twice, until very tender, about 20 minutes.

In batches, in a food processor, puree the broccoli, and then the leeks with their butter, until very smooth. Transfer the puree to a large bowl and stir in the nutmeg, pepper, and 3 teaspoons of salt. *The puree can be prepared to this point up to 1 day ahead. Cool completely, cover, and refrigerate.*

In a heavy saucepan over low heat warm the puree, stirring often, until steaming. Adjust the seasoning and serve.

*Serves 12*

## LEMON CURD MOUSSE

♦ ♦ ♦ ♦ ♦ ♦ ♦ ♦ ♦

6 large eggs
6 large egg yolks
1½ cups sugar
¾ cup fresh lemon juice, strained
2 tablespoons minced lemon zest
2 sticks unsalted butter, well chilled and cut into small pieces
1 cup whipping cream, chilled

**F**OR THIS DESSERT, lemon curd, the oddly named but luscious custard of lemon, eggs, and butter, gets slightly lightened with a bit of whipped cream. The mousse is soft and heavy, and in this menu should be served accompanied by a slice of moist, dark Jack Daniel's Chocolate Whiskey Cake (page 200). At other times of the year, crush fresh raspberries, sweeten them to taste, and use them as a rustic sauce for the tart, yellow mousse.

In a heavy, nonreactive saucepan whisk the eggs and egg yolks. Whisk in the sugar and then the lemon juice. Stir in the lemon zest.

Set the pan over medium-low heat and cook, stirring often with a wooden spoon, until the mixture
thickens. (This will happen rather suddenly, in 7 to 10
minutes.) Do not let the mixture boil. Immediately remove the pan from the heat and add the chilled butter
all at once. Stir until the butter is incorporated and
transfer the custard to a large bowl. Let the custard
stand at room temperature, stirring it occasionally, until it is thick and cool, about 1 hour.

Whip the cream to stiff peaks. Fold the cream into
the cooled custard. Spoon the mousse into individual
serving dishes or ramekins. Cover and chill for *at least*
24 hours. *The mousse can be prepared up to 3 days
ahead.*

━━● *Serves 10 to 12*

◆ ◆ ◆ ◆ ◆ ◆ ◆ ◆ ◆ ◆ ◆ ◆ ◆ ◆ ◆ ◆ ◆ ◆ ◆ ◆ ◆ ◆ ◆ ◆ ◆ ◆ ◆ ◆ ◆ ◆ ◆ ◆ ◆ ◆ ◆ ◆ ◆ ◆

# M E N U

◆◆◆◆◆◆◆◆◆◆◆◆◆◆

"CATFISH-FRIED" CHICKEN

◆

MAPLE-BOURBON GLAZED HAM

◆

PICKLED PEACH SAUCE

◆

NEW POTATO SALAD WITH
PEAS AND MINT

◆

GARDEN SALAD WITH
FRENCH DRESSING

◆

FARMHOUSE POTATO BREAD

◆

PLUM AND APPLE BUTTER

◆

32-LEMONADE

◆

ANGEL FOOD CAKE WITH STRAWBERRIES
AND BROWN SUGAR SAUCE

◆

LATTICE-TOPPED RASPBERRY
AND PEAR PIE

◆

RASPBERRY-BUTTERMILK ICE CREAM
*page 193*

THIS IS A FARM MENU, inspired by tales my father told me
of his life growing up on a Colorado dairy and of sum-
mers spent working on a farm in Iowa in the late thirties, just before the war.

The times were innocent, and hard work, good
food, and old-fashioned virtues were commonplace. The
war changed many things, but one aspect of those days

lives on. My family still celebrates, particularly at late-summer gatherings of the clan, in a manner worthy of our Iowa roots. Every summer ends, and to properly celebrate the passing of another, I offer the following farm-inspired feast.

## "CATFISH-FRIED" CHICKEN

♦♦♦♦♦♦♦♦♦♦

THE SAME CRUNCHY CORNMEAL coating that covers fried Mississippi catfish (an Iowa specialty) does wonders for fried chicken. This recipe will be enough for ten if you are also serving the glazed ham; if not, double it.

Rinse the chicken and pat the pieces dry. In a large bowl combine the chicken and buttermilk and let stand at room temperature, stirring once or twice, for at least 2 hours.

In a wide, shallow bowl mix together the flour, cornmeal, thyme, paprika, salt, and pepper. One piece at a time, shake the buttermilk off and roll the chicken in the prepared cornmeal. Arrange the chicken pieces in a single layer on baking sheets. Let them stand 30 minutes at room temperature to firm up the coating.

Over low heat melt enough shortening in 2 large, heavy skillets to come ½ inch up the sides. Raise the heat to high. When the shortening is almost smoking, add the chicken, skin side down. Lower the heat to medium and cook 12 minutes. Uncover the skillets, turn the chicken, and cook, uncovered, another 12 to 15 minutes, or until a rich, dark brown. The chicken will be just springy to the touch. Transfer to paper towels to drain.

*Serves 10*

2 chickens (3 pounds each), cut into serving pieces
2 cups buttermilk
1½ cups unbleached all-purpose flour
1½ cups stone-ground yellow cornmeal
2½ teaspoons dried thyme, crumbled
2½ teaspoons Hungarian sweet paprika (see Cook's Sources)
2 teaspoons salt
1 teaspoon freshly ground black pepper
2 pounds (about) solid vegetable shortening

## MAPLE-BOURBON GLAZED HAM

1 ready-to-eat smoked ham
(15 to 18 pounds), with
bone in (see Cook's
Sources)
½ cup maple syrup (see
Cook's Sources)
⅓ cup bourbon
1 cup apple or orange juice

THE IOWA FARM was teetotal, so this glaze, it must be admitted, comes from my personal inclination toward good bourbon. Hams, on the other hand, came from hogs raised right on the farm and smoked locally, and were a staple at breakfast, lunch, and dinner.

Let the ham stand at room temperature for 3 hours. If the upper surface is covered with a rind, pull it away with your fingers. With a thin, sharp knife, slice away the thick layer of fat beneath the rind until only about ¼ inch remains. Score a diamond pattern about ⅛ inch deep into the upper surface of the ham. (Stud the diamonds with the traditional whole cloves if you wish, but they make for awkward carving and perilous eating.)

Position a rack in the lower third of the oven and preheat to 325 degrees F. Lay the ham in a large, shallow baking dish or jelly-roll pan. Set it on the rack, add 1 cup water to the pan, and bake 1½ hours.

In a small bowl stir together the syrup and bourbon. Replace the water in the baking dish with the fruit juice. Pour the syrup mixture over the ham. Baste often with the accumulated pan juices until the ham is richly glazed, about 40 minutes.

Let the ham rest at room temperature for at least 20 minutes before carving, or serve the ham cold.

*Serves 12 with leftovers*

## PICKLED PEACH SAUCE

♦ ♦ ♦ ♦ ♦ ♦ ♦ ♦ ♦

**M**Y PATERNAL GRANDMOTHER, Hazel, was a farm wife without peer, running a dairy, raising a large family, and cooking and canning up a veritable storm, more or less single-handedly. I have assorted happy memories of the wonders of her kitchen, where candies, pies, and jams shared the table with rich jellied chicken, mounds of mashed potatoes, and tender, hot-from-the-oven bread and rolls. The bounty was astonishing; and the practiced ease with which that bounty appeared was nothing short of miraculous.

Canning "season" was a year-round business; Hazel was a champ at many a home-preserved delicacy, but none was better than her pickled peaches, particularly when made with the locally grown white ones, which always seemed so spectacularly flavored.

White or yellow, pickled peaches are the perfect accompaniment to a baked ham. For those who would like to experience the flavor without the steamy business of canning, I recommend this sauce. Every bit as flavorful as the inspiration, it keeps, refrigerated, for many weeks.

♦ ♦ ♦  ♦ ♦ ♦

*2 cups cider vinegar*
*2 cups sugar*
*1½ cups dark raisins*
*12 whole cloves*
*1 piece (2 inches)*
  *cinnamon stick*
*3½ pounds slightly*
  *underripe peaches,*
  *peeled, pitted, and sliced*
  *(see note)*

In a heavy, 4-quart, nonreactive saucepan, combine the vinegar, sugar, and raisins. Tie the cloves and cinnamon stick into a piece of cheesecloth and add it to the pan. Set over medium heat and bring to a boil, stirring often to dissolve the sugar. Lower the heat, cover, and simmer, stirring once or twice, 20 minutes.

Uncover, stir in the peaches, and bring to a boil. Lower the heat and simmer, uncovered, stirring occasionally, 15 to 20 minutes. (The peaches should be just tender while still holding their shape.)

Transfer immediately to a heatproof bowl and cool to room temperature. Refrigerate, covered, at least 2 days to develop full flavor. Discard the spice bag.

Transfer the sauce to a bowl and serve, spooning the sauce beside or over slices of the ham.

NOTE Frozen peaches can be substituted. Use 2 bags (20 ounces each) of individually quick-frozen, unsweetened, sliced peaches, and add them to the vinegar mixture without defrosting.

●━● *Makes about 6 cups*

◆ ◆ ◆ ◆ ◆ ◆ ◆ ◆ ◆ ◆ ◆ ◆ ◆ ◆ ◆ ◆ ◆ ◆ ◆ ◆ ◆ ◆ ◆ ◆ ◆ ◆ ◆ ◆ ◆ ◆ ◆ ◆ ◆ ◆ ◆ ◆ ◆ ◆ ◆ ◆ ◆ ◆

## NEW POTATO SALAD
## WITH PEAS AND MINT

◆ ◆ ◆ ◆ ◆ ◆ ◆ ◆ ◆

**T**HE FARM'S GARDEN in Iowa was large, providing virtually all the family's vegetables. New potatoes were combined with baby peas in a rich cream sauce, perfect alongside an Iowa pork roast, and mint grew wild and unbidden, next to the windmill. This salad takes its inspiration from these sources, but it is a lighter and cooler version. When asparagus is in season, use it in place of the peas.

◆◆◆ ⬤⟋ ◆◆◆

*4 pounds small, red-skinned, new potatoes, scrubbed and halved*

*4 cups tender, young, shelled (about 3 pounds unshelled) fresh peas, see note*

*Fresh Mint Dressing (recipe follows)*

*Salt and freshly ground black pepper*

*Sprigs of fresh mint, as garnish*

In a large pan cover the potatoes with cold, lightly salted water. Set over medium-high heat and bring to a boil. Cook the potatoes until they are just tender, about 7 minutes after the water reaches a boil. With a slotted spoon, transfer the potatoes to a large bowl. Return the water to a boil. If using fresh peas, stir them into the boiling water and cook 1 to 2 minutes, or until just tender. Drain the peas and transfer them at once to a bowl of ice water. Cool completely and drain.

Add the peas to the bowl with the potatoes. Add about two-thirds of the Fresh Mint Dressing and gently toss. Season with salt and pepper to taste. Arrange the salad in a serving bowl and drizzle the remaining dressing over the top. Garnish with the mint.

NOTE Frozen peas can be substituted. Use 2 packages (10 ounces each), thawed and drained. They do not require further cooking.

**●— ● *Serves 10***

◆◆◆◆◆◆◆◆◆◆◆◆◆◆◆◆◆◆◆◆◆◆◆◆◆◆◆◆◆◆◆◆◆◆◆◆◆◆◆◆◆◆◆

▀▄▀▄▀▄▀▄▀▄▀▄▀▄▀▄▀▄▀▄▀▄▀▄▀▄▀▄▀▄▀▄▀▄▀▄▀▄▀▄▀

## FRESH MINT DRESSING

◆◆◆◆◆◆◆◆◆

In a food processor combine the eggs, vinegar, mustard, salt, pepper, and mint and process 1 minute, stopping once to scrape down the sides of the workbowl.

With the motor running add the oil in a quick, steady stream. Adjust the seasoning and process again to blend. Cover and refrigerate until use. *The dressing can be prepared up to 1 day ahead.*

**●— ● *Makes about 2½ cups***

◆◆◆◆◆◆◆◆◆◆◆◆◆◆◆◆◆◆◆◆◆◆◆◆◆◆◆◆◆◆◆◆◆◆◆◆◆◆◆◆◆◆◆

*3 eggs*
*5 tablespoons white wine vinegar*
*2 tablespoons prepared Dijon-style mustard*
*1½ teaspoons salt*
*¾ teaspoon freshly ground black pepper*
*3 cups fresh clean, loosely packed mint leaves*
*2 cups vegetable oil*

▀▄▀▄▀▄▀▄▀▄▀▄▀▄▀▄▀▄▀▄▀▄▀▄▀▄▀▄▀▄▀▄▀▄▀▄▀▄▀▄▀

## GARDEN SALAD
## WITH FRENCH DRESSING

◆◆◆◆◆◆◆◆◆

**T**HIS SALAD'S MIDWESTERN sweet-and-sour vinaigrette evolved into the "French" dressing now found in supermarkets. There is nothing particularly French about it, but it is good on crisp, fresh summer vegetables.

This dressing is best if never refrigerated and served at room temperature, so make it the day you use it. Pass a pepper mill when you serve the salad.

◆◆◆  ◆◆◆

Bring a pan of water to a boil. Add the salt and the beans and cook until just crisp but tender, about 5 min-

*2 teaspoons salt*
*2 pounds green beans, trimmed*
*6 beefsteak tomatoes, washed and cut into thick rounds*
*2 pounds cucumbers, peeled, if waxed, and cut on the diagonal into thick slices*
*French dressing (recipe follows)*

utes. Drain and transfer to a bowl of ice water. Cool completely and drain well. *The beans can be prepared up to 1 day ahead. Refrigerate, well wrapped. Bring them to room temperature before proceeding.*

Just before serving, place the beans in a mound in the center of a platter. Arrange the tomatoes at one end and the cucumbers at the other. Pass the dressing separately.

━━● *Serves 10*

◆◆◆◆◆◆◆◆◆◆◆◆◆◆◆◆◆◆◆◆◆◆◆◆◆◆◆◆◆◆◆◆◆◆◆◆◆◆◆◆◆

▀▄▀▄▀▄▀▄▀▄▀▄▀▄▀▄▀▄▀▄▀▄▀▄▀▄▀▄▀▄▀▄▀▄▀▄▀▄▀

## FRENCH DRESSING

◆◆◆◆◆◆◆◆◆◆

3 tablespoons sugar
1 tablespoon Hungarian
  sweet paprika (see
  Cook's Sources)
1½ teaspoons salt
⅓ cup red wine vinegar
2 tablespoons prepared
  Dijon-style mustard
1 egg yolk
Freshly ground black
  pepper
2 cups vegetable oil

In a medium-size bowl combine the sugar, paprika, and salt. Whisk in the vinegar, mustard, and egg yolk. Season generously with pepper. In a slow steady stream whisk in the oil. Adjust the seasoning, cover, and let stand at room temperature until ready to use.

━━● *Makes about 2⅓ cups*

◆◆◆◆◆◆◆◆◆◆◆◆◆◆◆◆◆◆◆◆◆◆◆◆◆◆◆◆◆◆◆◆◆◆◆◆◆◆◆◆◆

▀▄▀▄▀▄▀▄▀▄▀▄▀▄▀▄▀▄▀▄▀▄▀▄▀▄▀▄▀▄▀▄▀▄▀▄▀▄▀

## FARMHOUSE POTATO BREAD

◆◆◆◆◆◆◆◆◆◆

**F**ARMHOUSE THRIFT meant putting everything, including a lowly leftover potato, to good use. One result was these moist, light, and tender loaves, perfect with Plum and Apple Butter (page 376). Resist trying to cut them until they are completely cool; in fact, the bread seems to be even better the day after it's baked—and, if it lasts until morning, it makes spectacular toast.

In a small saucepan cover the potato with cold, lightly salted water. Set over medium heat, bring to a boil, and cook until very tender, about 10 minutes. Drain and force the potato through a sieve or ricer into a large bowl.

In a small saucepan combine the milk, 4 tablespoons of the butter, the sugar, and 1 tablespoon of salt. Set over medium heat and bring just to a boil, stirring to dissolve the sugar. Whisk the milk mixture into the potato and cool to between 105 and 115 degrees F. Sprinkle the yeast over the potato mixture and stir. Stir in 4 cups of the flour. Generously flour a work surface with ½ cup of flour. Knead the dough until smooth and elastic, adding more of the remaining flour if sticky, about 10 minutes. Grease a large bowl with 2 tablespoons of the butter. Add the dough, turning to coat its entire surface. Cover the bowl with a towel and let the dough rise in a warm, draft-free area until it is doubled in volume, about 1½ hours.

Punch the dough down. Knead it until smooth, about 1 minute. Return it to the bowl, cover it, and let it rise until doubled in volume, about 1½ hours.

Grease 2 6-cup loaf pans. Punch the dough down and cut it in half. Shape each piece into a loaf and transfer to the prepared pans. Cover the pans with a towel and let the dough rise until it is level with the tops of the pans, about 45 minutes.

Position a rack in the lower third of the oven and preheat to 400 degrees F. Set the bread in the oven and lower the temperature to 375 degrees F. Bake the loaves until they are a rich, golden brown and sound hollow when the bottoms are tapped, about 30 minutes. Cool the loaves in the pans for 5 minutes, transfer them to a rack, and cool completely, preferably overnight, before serving.

*Makes 2 loaves*

*Salt*

*1 large (about 8 ounces) Idaho baking potato, peeled and cut into 1-inch chunks*

*2 cups milk*

*6 tablespoons (¾ stick) unsalted butter, softened*

*3 tablespoons sugar*

*1 envelope dry yeast*

*5 cups (about) unbleached all-purpose flour*

## 3 2 - L E M O N A D E

32 large lemons, halved
4 cups cold water
3½ cups (about) sugar
Fresh mint, as garnish

**W**HILE IT'S TRUE the orchard in Iowa contained no lemon trees, the WPA did distribute prime California produce around the country, and lemons were frequently abundant and inexpensive. Good Presbyterians abstained from liquor, and this genuine, old-fashioned lemonade made it easy to forget about drinking anything else.

Squeeze the lemons. Strain the juice into a large pitcher. Add the water and sugar and stir until the sugar dissolves. Refrigerate until well chilled. Taste and adjust the sweetening.

Just before serving pour the lemonade over ice in tall glasses and garnish with mint.

Serves 10

## ANGEL FOOD CAKE WITH STRAWBERRIES AND BROWN SUGAR SAUCE

**T**HIS BIG, OLD CAKE is precisely the kind of dessert that ended virtually every farm meal. Be thankful you don't have to regulate the temperature of a wood-burning stove; progress has taken care of that complication and the recipe is surprisingly foolproof. Leftover cake is good lightly toasted and served with a cup of coffee.

*For the cake* Position a rack in the center of the oven and preheat to 350 degrees F. Sift the flour again with ½ cup of the sugar. Repeat this step a second *and* third time. Using an electric mixer, beat the whites in a large bowl until foamy. Add the lemon juice, cream of tartar, vanilla, salt, and lemon extract and beat until soft peaks form. Two tablespoons at a time, add the remaining sugar, beating until the egg whites are stiff and glossy. Sift one-third of the flour mixture over the whites. With a rubber spatula gently but quickly fold the flour into the whites. Repeat, sifting half of the remaining flour at a time and folding until just combined. Spoon the batter into an ungreased 10-inch tube pan. Run a knife through the batter several times to break up any bubbles. Bake until the cake springs back when pressed in the center, 40 to 45 minutes. Invert the pan on a rack and let the cake cool completely in the pan.

*For the berries* Combine the strawberries with sugar to taste. Let them stand until juicy, stirring occasionally, about 30 minutes.

*For the sauce* Whisk the sour cream in a medium-size bowl until smooth and shiny. Whisk in the brown sugar, lemon juice, and vanilla. Cover and refrigerate until ready to serve.

*To assemble* Using a fork, gently pull the cake from the sides of the pan and unmold. Set the cake on a platter. Cut the cake, using a cutter made specifically for angel food cake or a serrated knife, into 1-inch slices, pulling it apart with two forks or with the cake cutter. Set each slice on a plate and top with the strawberries, their juices, and the Brown Sugar Sauce. Serve immediately.

*Serves 10*

ANGEL FOOD CAKE

*1 cup sifted cake flour*
*1¼ cups superfine sugar*
*1½ cups (10 to 12) egg whites, at room temperature*
*2 tablespoons fresh lemon juice*
*1½ teaspoons cream of tartar*
*1 teaspoon vanilla*
*½ teaspoon salt*
*¼ teaspoon lemon extract*

STRAWBERRIES AND BROWN SUGAR SAUCE

*4 pints strawberries, hulled and sliced thick*
*½ cup (about) sugar*

*2 cups sour cream*
*½ cup light brown sugar, firmly packed*
*1 tablespoon lemon juice*
*1 teaspoon vanilla extract*

## LATTICE-TOPPED
## RASPBERRY AND PEAR PIE

♦ ♦ ♦ ♦ ♦ ♦ ♦ ♦ ♦ ♦

**LATTICE CRUST**

*2½ cups unbleached
    all-purpose flour*
*½ teaspoon salt*
*6 tablespoons (¾ stick)
    unsalted butter, well
    chilled and cut into
    small pieces*
*½ cup solid vegetable
    shortening, well chilled
    and cut into small pieces*
*½ cup cold water*
*6 tablespoons whole wheat
    flour*

**RASPBERRY-PEAR FILLING**

*2 cups fresh raspberries,
    picked over, rinsed, and
    dried thoroughly*
*2½ pounds Bartlett pears,
    peeled, cored, and cut
    into ½-inch dice*
*1 cup sugar*
*⅓ cup unbleached
    all-purpose flour*

*1 egg, beaten*
*1 tablespoon sugar*

**E**ARLY IN THE SUMMER, make the pie with peaches or nectarines instead of pears. Either way, a scoop of Raspberry-Buttermilk Ice Cream (page 193) will top it off with old-fashioned summertime goodness.

♦ ♦ ♦  ♦ ♦ ♦

*For the crust* In a large bowl or food processor combine the unbleached flour and salt. Cut in the butter and shortening until a coarse meal forms. One tablespoon at a time, add the water, until a soft dough forms. Sprinkle the work surface with 2 tablespoons of the whole wheat flour, reserving the remaining flour. Turn the dough out onto the floured surface and divide it in half. Form each piece into a disc and wrap each disc well in plastic. Refrigerate at least 45 minutes. *The dough can be prepared to this point up to 1 day ahead.*

*For the filling* Combine the raspberries, pears, sugar, and flour in a medium-size bowl. Let stand 30 minutes, stirring occasionally.

*To assemble* Position a rack in the center of the oven. Set a baking sheet on the rack and preheat to 400 degrees F. Sprinkle the work surface with 2 tablespoons of the reserved whole wheat flour. Roll 1 pastry disc out to a round 14 inches in diameter. Transfer the round to a 10-inch pie pan. Spoon the filling with its juices into the crust. Sprinkle the work surface with the remaining whole wheat flour. Roll the second piece of pastry out to a thickness of ⅛ inch. Cut it into strips ½ inch wide. Arrange the strips atop the pie in a lattice pattern, leaving a fairly generous overhang. Trim the crust and strips, leaving an overhang of ½ inch. Fold the lower crust up over the strips and pinch to seal. Crimp the edges decoratively. Bake the pie 35 minutes. Brush the lattice with the beaten egg and sprinkle with the sugar. Continue baking until the filling bubbles and the crust is golden brown, 10 to 15 minutes. Cool the pie completely on a rack before cutting.

 *Serves 8*

♦ ♦ ♦ ♦ ♦ ♦ ♦ ♦ ♦ ♦ ♦ ♦ ♦ ♦ ♦ ♦ ♦ ♦ ♦ ♦ ♦ ♦ ♦ ♦ ♦ ♦ ♦ ♦ ♦ ♦ ♦ ♦ ♦ ♦ ♦ ♦ ♦ ♦ ♦ ♦ ♦ ♦ ♦ ♦

# MENU

✦✦✦✦✦✦✦✦✦✦✦✦✦✦✦✦

MIXED GAME PÂTÉ WITH
CRANBERRY-BOURBON RELISH

✦

JERUSALEM ARTICHOKE SOUP

✦

ROAST FRESH TURKEY WITH
COUNTRY HAM AND WILD MUSHROOM
DRESSING AND MADEIRA GRAVY

✦

SWEET POTATOES WITH
CIDER AND BROWN SUGAR

✦

BRAISED CELERY WITH ALMONDS

✦

SAUCE APPLE PIE

✦

MAPLE SYRUP ICE CREAM

LIKE AN EARLY-AMERICAN Thanksgiving, this dinner is one with rich flavors and traditional ingredients. I like to think that it is the sort of feast Thomas Jefferson might have served at his great plantation, Monticello. The tradition of Jefferson's day was for lavish feasts of many dishes, and while we may not dine like that now, on Thanksgiving we certainly do, and this particular harvest festival menu is based on my research of those days of elaborate meals. Despite the generous array of courses, much of this Thanksgiving can be prepared in advance, in stages, easing pressure on the busy cook.

## MIXED GAME PÂTÉ

♦ ♦ ♦ ♦ ♦ ♦ ♦ ♦ ♦

**A**MERICA'S ONCE-ABUNDANT wild game might well have been turned into a pâté like this one by Jefferson's French-trained chefs. Today, of course, the meats will probably be farm-raised rather than wild and come fresh or frozen from the butcher. Once the main ingredients are assembled, the dish goes together much like the familiar meatloaf, and since the completed pâté needs at least three days of refrigerated aging to develop full flavor, it can be prepared well in advance of serving.

You might prefer to buy commercial pâté but that would be unfortunate. These are hasty times, however, and there are, in fact, some good pâtés on the market, made by human hands, that will preserve the intent of the menu. There are also some resembling nothing more than bologna with truffles, so shop discriminately, tasting before you buy.

♦ ♦ ♦  ♦ ♦ ♦

Skin the duckling. Remove the breast meat in two pieces and transfer to a small bowl. Add the bourbon, ½ teaspoon of the salt, and ¼ teaspoon of the pepper and marinate at room temperature, turning occasionally, for 1 hour. Cut the remaining meat off the duck and trim away and discard any fat or tendons. Reserve, along with the duck liver.

Bone the rabbit loin (it may be in 2 pieces) and add it to the marinating duck breast. Freeze the remainder of the rabbit, well wrapped, for another use.

In a skillet over medium heat melt the butter. When it foams add the onions, cover, turn the heat to low, and cook, stirring occasionally, until tender, about 15 minutes. Remove from the heat and cool slightly.

In a meat grinder, grind together the cubed venison, pork, pork fat, the reserved duck liver and meat (not the marinating breast meat), the garlic, and the ònions, including the butter in which they cooked. (If

*1 duckling (4½ to 5 pounds), liver reserved*
*⅓ cup bourbon*
*2 teaspoons salt*
*1½ teaspoons freshly ground black pepper*
*½ domestic rabbit (see notes)*
*4 tablespoons unsalted butter*
*1½ cups finely chopped yellow onion*
*1 pound venison (see Cook's Sources or notes), trimmed of fat and sinews and cut into large cubes*
*⅓ pound fresh pork, cut into large cubes*
*¾ pound fresh pork fat*
*3 garlic cloves, peeled*
*1 teaspoon dried thyme, crumbled*
*1 teaspoon dried marjoram, crumbled*
*½ teaspoon freshly grated nutmeg*
*¼ teaspoon cinnamon*
*1 egg, beaten*
*1 pound sliced bacon*
*2 bay leaves*
*3 whole allspice*

you use a food processor, use quick pulses of power, leaving plenty of texture. Do not overprocess.)

Transfer the meat mixture to a large mixing bowl. Add the thyme, marjoram, nutmeg, cinnamon, and egg. Drain the bourbon marinade into the ground meats. Cut the marinated duck breast and rabbit loin into ½-inch cubes. Add the cubes to the ground meats. Add the remaining salt and pepper and mix well.

In a small skillet fry a small patty of the pâté mixture over moderate heat, turning once or twice, until lightly browned and fully cooked. When the meat is cooled, taste and correct the seasoning of the pâté if necessary.

Preheat the oven to 350 degrees F. Line a 9 × 5 × 3-inch (8-cup) loaf pan with the bacon strips, leaving enough of an overhang to enclose the pâté completely. Spoon the pâté into the lined pan, forming a slight mound. Fold the strips of bacon over to enclose the pâté and press the bay leaves and allspice into the bacon in a decorative pattern.

Wrap the filled pan completely in foil and set it in a large baking dish at least 4 inches deep. Place in the oven and add boiling water to reach about three-quarters of the way up the sides of the loaf pan. Bake for 2½ to 3 hours, or until an instant-reading thermometer inserted into the center of the pâté registers 170 degrees F.

Cut a square of cardboard that will just fit inside the top of the loaf pan. Wrap the cardboard in foil. Remove the pâté from the hot water bath. Remove the foil wrapping and set the loaf pan on a plate to catch any juices. Place the foil-covered cardboard on top of the pâté and weigh down with 1 or 2 cans or other heavy objects. Cool to room temperature. Remove the weights and cardboard, wrap the pâté well, and refrigerate for at least 3 days before serving.

Run a knife around the edges of the baking dish, dip the dish briefly in warm water to melt the fat, and unmold the pâté. Wipe away the jellied cooking juices. Slice the pâté thin and serve it garnished with Cranberry-Bourbon Relish (recipe follows).

NOTES The most commonly available domestic rabbit comes from supermarkets, halved, boxed, and frozen. If unavailable, buy a second duck, marinate the breast meat of both, and grind the leg meat of both. Include both livers.

If venison is unavailable, buy an additional pound of lean pork; the effect will be much less gamy, but you will still have a delicious pâté.

*Serves 10 to 12*

♦ ♦ ♦ ♦ ♦ ♦ ♦ ♦ ♦ ♦ ♦ ♦ ♦ ♦ ♦ ♦ ♦ ♦ ♦ ♦ ♦ ♦ ♦ ♦ ♦ ♦ ♦ ♦ ♦ ♦ ♦ ♦ ♦ ♦ ♦ ♦ ♦ ♦ ♦ ♦ ♦ ♦ ♦

## CRANBERRY-BOURBON RELISH

♦ ♦ ♦ ♦ ♦ ♦ ♦ ♦ ♦

**N**O FOOD WRITER or chef can ever tell which of his recipes will capture people and become inexplicably popular. Jeremiah Tower, referring to one of the hits, says he expects to have "invented the black bean cake" carved on his tombstone. This simple little relish—not even a cranberry "sauce," really—may well be my "tombstone" recipe. People who serve it regularly tell me they have to double the recipe just to serve ten or so, and guests often request a copy of it to take home. Go figure.

1 cup bourbon
¼ cup minced shallot
Zest of 1 large orange, grated
1 bag (12 ounces) fresh cranberries, rinsed and picked over
1 cup sugar
1½ teaspoons freshly ground black pepper

In a small, nonreactive saucepan combine the bourbon, shallots, and orange zest. Set over medium-high heat and bring to a boil. Lower the heat and simmer, stirring occasionally, until the bourbon is reduced to a syrupy glaze on the bottom of the pan, about 10 minutes.

Add the cranberries and sugar, raise the heat to medium, and bring to a boil, stirring to dissolve the sugar. Lower the heat slightly and cook, uncovered, stirring occasionally, until most of the cranberries have burst, about 10 minutes.

Remove from the heat and stir in the pepper. Transfer to a bowl, cool to room temperature, cover, and refrigerate. *The relish can be prepared up to 3 days in advance.*

*Serves 8 to 10 as a garnish for pâté*

## JERUSALEM ARTICHOKE SOUP

2 lemons, juiced
3 pounds Jerusalem artichokes
6 tablespoons unsalted butter
2 medium onions, peeled and finely chopped
2 large carrots, peeled and finely chopped
2 large leeks, white part only, cleaned and finely chopped
6 sprigs Italian parsley
1 teaspoon dried thyme, crumbled
5 cups canned chicken broth or homemade stock
Salt and freshly ground white pepper
½ cup (about) whipping cream
Sprigs of watercress, as garnish

**T**HESE TUBERS are, curiously, neither artichokes nor from Jerusalem. In fact, they are members of the sunflower family. Jefferson raised and enjoyed them, but although they're turning up more and more frequently in specialty produce shops, supermarkets, and health food stores (usually bagged and labeled as "sunchokes"), most people are still unfamiliar with their mild, nutty flavor. This rich soup is a good place to make their acquaintance.

Fill a large bowl halfway with cold water and add the lemon juice. Peel the Jerusalem artichokes and drop them into the acidulated water to prevent discoloration.

In a large saucepan over medium heat melt the butter. Add the onions, carrots, leeks, parsley, and thyme, cover, and lower the heat. Cook, stirring occasionally, until the vegetables are tender and lightly colored, about 15 minutes.

Add the chicken broth, increase the heat, and bring to a boil. Partially cover, lower the heat, and simmer 25 minutes. Cool slightly, then strain, discarding the solids. Return the liquid to the pan.

Drain the artichokes and cut them into 1-inch chunks. Add them to the liquid, season lightly with salt and pepper, and bring to a boil. Partially cover, lower the heat, and simmer, stirring occasionally, until the artichokes are very tender, about 45 minutes.

Force the soup through the fine blade of a food mill or puree in batches in a food processor. *The soup can be prepared to this point up to 2 days in advance. Cool to room temperature, cover, and refrigerate.*

Warm the soup over low heat, stirring often, until steaming, thinning as desired with the cream. Adjust the seasoning and serve hot, garnishing each bowl with a sprig of the watercress.

—● *Serves 8*

◆ ◆ ◆ ◆ ◆ ◆ ◆ ◆ ◆ ◆ ◆ ◆ ◆ ◆ ◆ ◆ ◆ ◆ ◆ ◆ ◆ ◆ ◆ ◆ ◆ ◆ ◆ ◆ ◆ ◆ ◆ ◆ ◆ ◆ ◆ ◆ ◆ ◆ ◆

## ROAST FRESH TURKEY

◆ ◆ ◆ ◆ ◆ ◆ ◆ ◆ ◆

I HAVE STRONG FEELINGS about turkey—I love it and prepare it often, not just on the third Thursday in November. It is safe to say our forefathers wouldn't recognize this creature that rises round, white, and icy from thousands of supermarket freezers every holiday season. Indeed, years of genetic manipulation have resulted in a very busty bird, heavy on the white meat Americans prefer. This physical imbalance means substantial portions of nearly any given turkey are either overcooked or undercooked. Despite this, we dutifully roast it up, ingest it with ritual inattention, and then forget about it for the rest of the year.

It needn't be so, and each time I prepare a turkey, using the method outlined below, I gain more converts. Their enthusiasm leads me to hope the turkey will one day regain the respect that led Benjamin Franklin to propose it as the national bird.

By following a few simple rules, and dispensing with a misconception or two, anyone can make a per-

*1 fresh turkey (10 pounds), at room temperature*
*8 tablespoons (1 stick) unsalted butter, softened*
*Salt and freshly ground black pepper*
*¼ cup vegetable oil*
*½ cup canned chicken broth or homemade stock.*

fect turkey—plump, golden brown, and blessed with juicy, perfectly cooked white meat *and* rich, juicy, perfectly cooked dark meat.

*Buy a small turkey.* The ideal bird weighs at least ten pounds but never more than sixteen. This minimizes the imbalance between light and dark meat and allows for faster roasting and a more accurate estimate of doneness. If feeding a crowd, consider roasting two.

*Buy a fresh turkey.* The difference is apparent in the taste. While a fresh turkey once required special ordering, these days they are commonplace. Avoid the self-basting turkey, injected with ersatz yellow stuff that resembles the so-called butter on movie popcorn.

*Roast the turkey unstuffed.* I know it's less festive this way (and I do occasionally break this rule), but when the "stuffing" is baked separately and basted with juices from the turkey roaster, it suffers not at all for never having been near the turkey until they meet on the plate. Again, the turkey roasts more evenly and timings are more accurate.

*Baste the turkey.* The method using cheesecloth, outlined in the recipe below, works well for me. However you choose to baste the bird, use real butter and broth and you'll end up with moister meat.

*Use an instant-read thermometer.* The turkey is done when the thermometer, inserted in the thickest part of the white meat (avoid the bone), registers 160 degrees F. The thigh, when pricked at its thickest point, will yield barely pinkish yellow juices, and a thermometer inserted in the thickest part of the thigh will register 170 to 175 degrees F.

*Take the turkey out of the oven when it's done.* A ten-pound turkey will stay hot enough to eat for *at least* an hour after it comes out of the oven. Make a foil tent and carve the turkey *just* before serving. During that hour you'll have plenty of free time (and oven space) to bake the stuffing, reheat the accompaniments, *and* greet the guests at the door. In case of a major timing snafu (guests caught in a snowdrift, for example), serving the turkey lukewarm with very hot gravy is preferable to keeping it waiting in the oven.

Position a rack in the middle of the oven and preheat to 325 degrees F.

Cut off the first joint of each turkey wing and reserve, along with the neck, heart, and gizzard, for use in the Madeira Gravy (page 325). Reserve the liver for another use or discard.

Rub the breast with 2 tablespoons of the butter. Season the breast and the main cavity lightly with salt and pepper. (Truss the turkey if you wish, although this step is unnecessary if the bird is unstuffed.)

Set the turkey breast side up in a shallow roasting pan just large enough to hold it. Dampen a 10 × 20-inch piece of cheesecloth, double it, and drape it over the turkey breast. About 3½ hours before you wish to eat, set the turkey in to roast.

In a small saucepan melt the remaining butter in the oil and chicken broth over low heat. When the turkey has baked for 30 minutes, baste it through the cheesecloth with half of the butter mixture. Baste again with the remaining butter mixture after another 30 minutes. After another 15 minutes, baste the turkey with the accumulated juices from the roasting pan and repeat every 15 minutes until the turkey is done. Begin checking the turkey for doneness after 2¼ hours.

With a bulb baster remove the cooking juices from the roaster and reserve for basting the Country Ham and Wild Mushroom Dressing (recipe follows). (Be sure to include any juices that have accumulated in the turkey cavity.) Cover the turkey with a foil tent and set aside until ready to carve.

*Serves 8 to 10*

## COUNTRY HAM AND
## WILD MUSHROOM DRESSING

••••••••••

1½ ounces (about 1½
   cups) dried porcini or
   cepes (see Cook's
   Sources)
3 cups (about) canned
   chicken broth or
   homemade stock
10 cups coarsely crumbled,
   day-old, good-quality,
   firm, white bread
6 tablespoons unsalted
   butter
½ pound country ham (see
   Cook's Sources), cut into
   ½-inch cubes
2 medium yellow onions,
   peeled and chopped
1 teaspoon dry thyme,
   crumbled
1 cup finely chopped
   Italian parsley
½ teaspoon salt
1 teaspoon freshly ground
   black pepper
Reserved turkey roasting
   juices

**M**Y FAVORITE NEW YORK gourmet superdeli offers
Smithfield ham ready-to-eat, saving me from the laborious soaking, scrubbing, and simmering otherwise
necessary. Those not so fortunate can order the genuine article by mail (some of these companies now also
offer the hams ready-to-eat; see Cook's Sources) or substitute any good-quality, firm, smoky ham. Dried morels can be substituted for the porcini, to delicious
effect.

•••  •••

Rinse the dried mushrooms thoroughly under cold running water and place in a small bowl. In a small saucepan bring 2 cups of the chicken broth to a boil. Pour it
over the mushrooms and let stand, stirring occasionally, 1 hour.

Put the crumbled bread into a large mixing bowl.
In a medium-size skillet melt 2 tablespoons of the butter over moderate heat until foaming. Add the ham and
cook, stirring, until browned, about 10 minutes. With a
slotted spoon, transfer the ham to the bowl with the
bread. Return the skillet to moderate heat, add the
remaining butter and heat until foaming. Add the onions and thyme, cover, and lower the heat. Cook, stirring occasionally, until the onions are tender and
lightly colored, 10 to 15 minutes. Pour the onions and
butter over the bread and ham in the bowl.

With a slotted spoon, lift the mushrooms from their
soaking liquid and transfer to the mixing bowl. Strain
the soaking liquid through a funnel lined with a coffee
filter or a strainer lined with several thicknesses of
dampened cheesecloth. Reserve the strained liquid for
use in the Madeira Gravy (recipe follows).

Add the parsley to the dressing, season with the
salt and pepper, and stir well to mix. Transfer to a

medium-size baking dish, preferably with a tight-fitting lid. *The dressing can be prepared to this point several hours ahead. Store at room temperature.*

Preheat the oven to 325 degrees F. (Or use the oven in which you baked the turkey.) Degrease the reserved turkey roasting juices and measure them. Add enough of the remaining chicken broth, if necessary, to equal 1½ cups. Spoon the juices evenly over the dressing, cover tightly, and bake for 35 to 45 minutes, or until the dressing is steaming and the sides and bottom are crunchy and brown.

**—• Serves 8**

♦ ♦ ♦ ♦ ♦ ♦ ♦ ♦ ♦ ♦ ♦ ♦ ♦ ♦ ♦ ♦ ♦ ♦ ♦ ♦ ♦ ♦ ♦ ♦ ♦ ♦ ♦ ♦ ♦ ♦ ♦ ♦ ♦ ♦ ♦ ♦ ♦ ♦ ♦ ♦ ♦

## MADEIRA GRAVY

♦ ♦ ♦ ♦ ♦ ♦ ♦ ♦ ♦

**A**LONG WITH TEA, madeira wine was a popular colonial drink, and an effort by the crown to tax the madeira trade out of existence was just one more aggravation leading to the Revolutionary War.

Of course, madeira is a splendid cooking wine, as well, and its special, nutty flavor combines particularly well with ham, wild mushrooms, and turkey. This light gravy ties the whole menu together sumptuously.

♦ ♦ ♦  ♦ ♦ ♦

In a medium-size saucepan over moderate heat melt together 2 tablespoons of the butter and the oil. When it foams add the turkey giblets, neck, and wing tips and cook, stirring often, until browned, 20 to 25 minutes. Add the onions, leeks, carrots, thyme, bay leaf, and parsley stems. Cover, lower the heat, and cook, stirring occasionally, until the vegetables are tender and lightly colored, about 15 minutes.

Combine the madeira and mushroom soaking liquid with enough chicken broth to total 6 cups of liquid.

*6 tablespoons unsalted butter, at room temperature*
*1 tablespoon vegetable oil*
*Reserved turkey giblets, necks, and wing tips*
*2 medium onions, peeled and chopped*
*2 leeks, white part only, cleaned well and chopped*
*3 carrots, peeled and chopped*
*1 teaspoon dried thyme, crumbled*
*1 bay leaf*
*Stems from 1 bunch of parsley*
*1 cup medium-dry (Sercial) madeira*

*(ingredients continued)*

*Reserved mushroom
    soaking liquid*
*4 cups (about) canned
    chicken broth or
    homemade stock*
*¼ cup unbleached
    all-purpose flour*
*Salt and freshly ground
    black pepper*

Add the liquid to the pan, bring to a boil, partially cover, lower the heat, and simmer 30 minutes, skimming as necessary.

Cool slightly and strain, discarding the solids. There should be about 5 cups of stock. Wipe out the pan and return the liquid to it. Set over medium heat, bring to a boil, and cook, uncovered, until reduced to 3 cups, about 20 minutes. *The gravy can be prepared to this point up to 24 hours in advance. Cool to room temperature, cover, and refrigerate. Reheat to simmering before proceeding.*

In a small bowl mash the remaining butter with the flour to form a smooth, thick paste (*beurre manie*). Lower the heat under the gravy to very low. One tablespoon at a time, whisk the butter mixture into it. Raise the heat to medium and simmer, stirring, 5 minutes. Season with salt and pepper to taste before serving.

*Makes about 3 cups*

## SWEET POTATOES WITH CIDER AND BROWN SUGAR

♦ ♦ ♦ ♦ ♦ ♦ ♦ ♦ ♦ ♦

*4 pounds of sweet potatoes,
    peeled and cut into
    1-inch chunks*
*2½ cups unsweetened
    apple cider*
*½ cup dark brown sugar,
    firmly packed*
*8 tablespoons (1 stick)
    unsalted butter*
*1 piece (2 inches) stick
    cinnamon*

HERE IS AN EASY treatment for a trusty Thanksgiving standby, inspired by a surviving Jeffersonian menu. Since this recipe doesn't call for a lot of sugar, the tartness of the cider survives. (Natural, unsweetened cider, by the way, fresh and unfiltered, is preferable to bottled cider or apple juice.)

♦ ♦ ♦ ♦ ♦ ♦

In a large, nonreactive saucepan combine the potatoes, cider, brown sugar, 6 tablespoons of the butter, and the cinnamon stick. Bring to a boil over moderate heat. Lower the heat and simmer, partially covered, stirring occasionally, until the potatoes are very tender, about 45 minutes.

Cool slightly, remove the cinnamon stick, and force the potatoes and their liquid through the medium blade of a food mill or puree in batches in a food processor. Transfer to an ovenproof serving dish. *The potatoes can be prepared to this point up to 3 days ahead. Cover tightly and refrigerate. Return to room temperature before proceeding.*

Preheat the oven to 325 degrees F. (Or use the hot oven in which the turkey was baked.) Dot the surface of the potatoes with the remaining butter, cover tightly with foil, and bake, stirring once or twice, until steaming, about 20 minutes. Remove the foil and bake another 5 minutes before serving.

*Serves 8*

## BRAISED CELERY WITH ALMONDS

H ERE IS ANOTHER RECIPE inspired by a surviving menu from Monticello. Those who never think of celery standing on its own as a vegetable will be pleasantly surprised at the appropriateness of the clean, herbal flavor and the crunch of this dish, in an otherwise rich and tender meal.

In a medium-size, nonreactive saucepan combine the diluted chicken broth, wine, onion, carrot, parsley, cloves, peppercorns, and bay leaf. Set over high heat and bring to a boil. Lower the heat and simmer briskly, uncovered, until reduced to 1 cup, 30 to 40 minutes.

Strain and reserve the stock. *The recipe can be prepared to this point up to 2 days ahead. Refrigerate, covered.*

2½ cups canned chicken broth, diluted with ½ cup of water or 3 cups homemade stock
1 cup dry white wine
1 medium onion, peeled and chopped
1 large carrot, peeled and chopped
6 sprigs of Italian parsley
3 whole cloves
10 peppercorns
1 bay leaf
3 bunches (16 or 18 ribs) celery, large outer ribs only

*(ingredients continued)*

1 large, sweet red pepper,
   trimmed and finely
   diced
2 tablespoons unsalted
   butter
½ cup (about 2 ounces)
   slivered blanched
   almonds

Peel away the celery strings and cut the ribs cross-wise on the diagonal into 2-inch pieces. In a large skillet bring the reserved stock, celery, and sweet pepper to a boil. Lower the heat, cover, and simmer, stirring often, until the celery is tender but retains a slight crunch, about 30 minutes.

Meanwhile, in a small skillet melt the butter over moderate heat. Add the almonds and cook, stirring often, until golden brown, about 5 minutes. Set aside.

When the celery is tender, transfer it, using a slotted spoon, to a heated vegetable dish and cover to keep warm. Return the stock to high heat and boil rapidly until reduced to a few syrupy spoonfuls, about 5 minutes. Stir the almonds and any butter remaining in the small skillet into the reduced juices. Pour over the celery and serve hot.

*Serves 8*

## SAUCE APPLE PIE

I HAVE NEVER BEEN in agreement with those charts claiming to give the best uses for each apple variety. Pie-wise, the results always seem too *al dente* and at odds with my quest for a truly tender crust. In Jefferson's day there were many more apples to choose from—over a thousand varieties—among them many that must have cooked into the meltingly tender, almost custardlike filling my old-fashioned palate prefers.

My first choice for pie, actually recommended on many charts as the ideal apple for sauce, is the Cortland apple, but other sauce apple varieties will produce similar results. For a spectacular early American

Thanksgiving finale, serve the pie à la mode, with a scoop of Maple Syrup Ice Cream (recipe follows).

*For the filling* In a bowl combine the apples, flour, sugar, cinnamon, nutmeg, vanilla, and raisins and let stand at room temperature, stirring occasionally, about 30 minutes.

*For the crust* Position a rack in the middle of the oven. Set a baking sheet on the rack and preheat to 400 degrees F. On a work surface lightly sprinkled with half of the whole wheat flour, roll out one of the prepared pastry discs to form an even round about 14 inches in diameter. Transfer the dough to a 10-inch pie pan.

*To assemble* Spoon the apple filling and any accumulated juices into the pie shell, forming a slight mound in the center. On a work surface lightly dusted with the remaining whole wheat flour, roll out the second pastry disc into a round about 12 inches in diameter. Lay the top crust over the apples. Trim the crusts, leaving an overhang of ½ inch. Fold the lower crust over the upper, pinching it gently but firmly to seal. Crimp decoratively and cut 3 or 4 vent slits into the upper crust.

Set the pie on the heated baking sheet and bake 40 minutes. Brush the crust with the beaten egg, sprinkle evenly with the sugar, and bake for another 10 to 15 minutes, or until the juices are bubbling up through the slits in the crust and the pie is a rich golden brown. Cool the pie on a rack to room temperature before cutting.

NOTE The whole wheat flour used to roll out the pastry adds extra texture and color to the crust. Unbleached all-purpose flour can be substituted.

*Serves 8*

APPLE FILLING

*3 pounds Cortland or other "sauce" apples, peeled, cored, and cut into ⅛-inch slices*
*¼ cup unbleached all-purpose flour*
*½ cup sugar*
*1½ teaspoons cinnamon*
*½ teaspoon freshly grated nutmeg*
*2 teaspoons vanilla extract*
*¾ cup raisins*

*2 tablespoons whole wheat flour (see note)*
*1 recipe chilled pie crust (page 314)*

GLAZE

*1 egg, beaten*
*1 tablespoon sugar*

## MAPLE SYRUP ICE CREAM

2 cups maple syrup (see
Cook's Sources)
2 cups milk
2 cups whipping cream
4 egg yolks
1 teaspoon vanilla

**B**UY ONLY REAL MAPLE SYRUP for this recipe, since the cooking process used will intensify the flavor.

In a medium-size saucepan over moderate heat bring the maple syrup to a boil. Turn the heat to very low and simmer until reduced by half, about 45 minutes. (Counteract the syrup's tendency to boil over by stirring often with a metal spoon.) At the end of the reduction process you will have what appears to be a combination of maple syrup and maple sugar.

Let the reduction cool slightly. Slowly whisk in the milk and cream, return to moderate heat, and bring to a boil, stirring to dissolve the solids.

In a medium-size bowl whisk the egg yolks thoroughly. In a thin stream slowly whisk the hot maple mixture into the egg yolks. Return this mixture to the pan, set over low heat, and cook, stirring constantly, until the mixture is steaming and has thickened enough to coat the back of a spoon heavily, 3 to 5 minutes.

Transfer immediately to a bowl and stir in the vanilla. Cool completely, cover, and refrigerate until very cold, preferably overnight.

Strain the chilled mixture into the canister of an ice-cream maker and churn according to manufacturer's instructions. Transfer to a storage container, cover, and freeze. *The ice cream can be prepared up to 3 days ahead.*

Soften the ice cream in the refrigerator briefly before serving.

*Makes about 1½ quarts*

# MENU

◆ ◆ ◆ ◆ ◆ ◆ ◆ ◆ ◆ ◆ ◆ ◆ ◆ ◆ ◆ ◆

PEPPERED PECANS
◆
NEW ORLEANS OYSTER TARTLETS
◆
BAYOU DUCK CONSOMMÉ
◆
CREOLE ROAST TURKEY
◆
JAMBALAYA STUFFING
◆
CARROTS AND BRUSSELS SPROUTS
GLAZED WITH PEPPER
AND BROWN SUGAR
◆
SWEET POTATO CORN STICKS
*page 267*
◆
MOLDED CRANBERRY SALAD
WITH HONEY MAYONNAISE
◆
PUMPKIN–PEANUT BUTTER PIE
◆
SOUTHERN COMFORT–PEANUT
PRALINE ICE CREAM

THE SOUTH'S INSTINCT for hospitality makes this Creole-themed holiday feast seem beautifully appropriate, even if the Pilgrims never got anywhere near New Orleans. Despite the Louisiana touches, the menu is based on solidly traditional Thanksgiving ingredients, and if you'd like to add a little zip to your holiday, this is the menu for you.

Thanksgiving menus often give the sommelier a headache, but I don't hesitate to make two beverage recommendations for this spicy, peppery menu of culinary extremes. If you are opting for full Creole elegance, drink champagne throughout, selecting one that is well balanced between acid and fruit and not too dry. On the other hand, if you'd like your Thanksgiving to be down-home hearty (same menu, change of attitude)—I confess that's how I'd do it—pour a crisp lager beer.

## PEPPERED PECANS

◆ ◆ ◆ ◆ ◆ ◆ ◆ ◆ ◆ ◆

I'M ALWAYS A SUCKER for alliteration in recipe titles, but that doesn't mean you can't use almonds or cashews (not to mention peanuts), in this peppery Cajun recipe if you'd prefer.

1 tablespoon olive oil
1 teaspoon freshly ground
    black pepper
1 teaspoon freshly ground
    white pepper
1 teaspoon cayenne pepper
1/2 teaspoon dried thyme,
    crumbled
2 egg whites
1 tablespoon
    Worcestershire sauce
1 teaspoon hot pepper
    sauce
1 teaspoon salt
1 pound (about 4 1/2 cups)
    jumbo pecan halves

Position a rack in the upper third of the oven and preheat to 375 degrees F. Brush a large, heavy baking pan with the olive oil.

In a small bowl combine the black pepper, white pepper, cayenne, and thyme. In a medium-size bowl whisk the egg whites until foamy. Whisk in the Worcestershire, hot pepper sauce, and salt. Add the nuts and stir to coat. Sift the pepper mixture over the nuts, tossing quickly to coat the nuts with the spices before the egg whites dry.

Spread the pecans evenly in the baking pan. Bake 5 minutes. Stir the nuts, breaking up any clumps, and bake until they are crisp and brown, stirring once or twice, about 7 minutes. Transfer to a bowl, cool completely, and store airtight until serving. *The recipe can be prepared up to 4 days ahead.*

*8 servings*

◆ ◆ ◆ ◆ ◆ ◆ ◆ ◆ ◆ ◆ ◆ ◆ ◆ ◆ ◆ ◆ ◆ ◆ ◆ ◆ ◆ ◆ ◆ ◆ ◆ ◆ ◆ ◆ ◆ ◆ ◆ ◆ ◆ ◆ ◆ ◆ ◆ ◆ ◆

# NEW ORLEANS
# OYSTER TARTLETS

♦ ♦ ♦ ♦ ♦ ♦ ♦ ♦ ♦

THESE TARTLETS CELEBRATE New Orleans's passion for its local shellfish and feature the briny mollusks, napped with a Pernod-laced *beurre blanc,* in a crisply tender Creole mustard pastry.

♦ ♦ ♦  ♦ ♦ ♦

*For the dough* In a food processor or large bowl combine 3 cups of the flour and the salt. Cut the butter and shortening into the flour until a coarse meal forms. In a small bowl stir together ¼ cup of the ice water and the mustard. Stir the mustard mixture into the dough. One tablespoon at a time add the remaining ice water, until a soft dough forms. Turn the dough out onto a lightly floured surface, divide it in half, and gather each half into a ball. Flatten each ball into a disc, wrap separately in plastic, and refrigerate at least 1 hour. *The dough can be prepared up to 3 days ahead.*

On a lightly floured surface roll out 1 disc of dough to a thickness of ⅛ inch. With a cookie cutter cut the dough into 4-inch rounds. Fit the rounds into 3-inch tartlet molds and trim the edges. Repeat with the second disc. Gather the scraps, roll the dough again, and cut out additional tartlet shells, if necessary. Cover and refrigerate at least 30 minutes. *The shells can be prepared up to 1 day before baking.*

Position a rack in the center of the oven and preheat to 375 degrees F. Pierce the pastry with a fork. Set the tartlet shells on a large baking sheet and bake until golden brown, 12 to 14 minutes. Cool the shells slightly on a rack, unmold them, and cool completely. *The shells can be baked up to 1 day before serving. Store at room temperature in an airtight container.*

*For the filling* In a heavy, medium-size, nonreactive saucepan over moderate heat bring the wine to a sim-

CREOLE MUSTARD DOUGH

*3¼ cups (about) unbleached all-purpose flour*
*¼ teaspoon salt*
*¾ cup (1½ sticks) unsalted butter, well chilled and cut into small pieces*
*¼ cup solid vegetable shortening, well chilled and cut into small pieces*
*½ cup (about) ice water*
*⅓ cup Creole or other mild, prepared whole-grain mustard*

OYSTER FILLING

*2 cups dry white wine*
*24 large shucked oysters, liquor reserved*
*3 tablespoons minced shallot*
*1 cup (2 sticks) unsalted butter, well chilled and cut into 16 pieces*
*2 tablespoons Pernod*
*½ teaspoon freshly ground white pepper*
*Generous pinch of salt*
*Fresh chives, as garnish*

mer. Add the oysters and their liquor and cook until the oyster's gill edges just begin to ruffle, about 1 minute. With a slotted spoon, transfer the oysters to a bowl and reserve. Add the shallots to the wine and bring to a boil. Lower the heat and simmer until the wine is reduced to a syrupy ⅓ cup, about 25 minutes.

Strain the reduction into a small, heavy, nonreactive saucepan. Preheat the oven to 200 degrees F. Reheat the reduction over low heat. Remove from the heat and whisk in 2 tablespoons of the butter. Return the pan to low heat. One tablespoon at a time, whisk in the remaining butter. Whisk in the Pernod and pepper. Adjust the seasoning, adding the salt if necessary. Add the oysters to the sauce, cover, and remove from the heat. Let stand 5 minutes, or until the oysters are heated through.

Meanwhile, warm the tartlet shells in the oven 5 minutes. Arrange 3 tartlets on each of 8 plates. Spoon 1 oyster into each shell. Spoon the sauce over the oysters, garnish with the chives, and serve immediately.

*Makes 24*

## BAYOU DUCK CONSOMMÉ

**T**HIS IS A RICH, dark consommé, filled with tender bits of duck and celery. Duck abounds in the bayou, by the way, which explains the multitude of ways it gets cooked up in the Delta. While a tough, wild duck is the logical candidate for the long-simmered consommé, a supermarket cousin will do as well.

Position a rack in the upper third of the oven and preheat to 400 degrees F. Set the duck breast side up on the work surface. Cut off the wings and reserve. Re-

*1 duck (5 pounds), skinned and fat removed*
*¼ cup vegetable oil*
*2 medium onions, peeled and coarsely chopped*
*2 leeks, white part only, well cleaned and chopped*
*2 medium carrots, peeled and chopped*
*1 medium parsnip, peeled and chopped*

move the breast meat in 2 pieces, wrap, and refrigerate. Cut off the legs with the thighs attached. Cut the legs and thighs apart at the joints. Chop the carcass into 4 pieces. Spread the wings, leg, thigh, and carcass pieces in a single layer on a baking sheet. Bake 30 minutes. Turn the pieces and bake until very brown, pouring off any fat as necessary, about 30 minutes more.

In a large, heavy pot over medium heat warm the oil. Add the onions, leeks, carrots, parsnip, garlic, celery tops, parsley stems, thyme, bay leaves, and peppercorns. Lower the heat and cook uncovered, stirring occasionally, until the vegetables are tender and lightly colored, about 15 minutes. Add the browned duck pieces and the diluted chicken broth. Bring the mixture to a boil, skimming the surface as necessary. Lower the heat until the consommé simmers.

Add the duck breasts to the simmering consommé and cook them until they are almost springy to the touch but pink inside, about 5 minutes. Remove the breasts and cool them completely. Cover the breasts and refrigerate. Partially cover the pan and simmer the stock 4 hours, stirring occasionally. Strain the stock. If necessary, simmer the stock until reduced to 8 cups (or add water to bring the amount up to 8 cups). Cool completely, cover, and refrigerate overnight. *The stock can be prepared up to 3 days ahead.*

Remove the hardened fat from the surface of the stock. Bring the stock to room temperature. In a large bowl whisk together the egg whites and 1 cup of the stock. In a saucepan bring the remaining stock to a boil. Slowly whisk the hot stock into the egg white mixture. Return the stock mixture to the pan, set it over medium heat, and bring just to a simmer, stirring constantly. When the stock simmers, turn the heat to the lowest possible setting and leave the stock undisturbed for 20 minutes. Do not stir. Remove the pan from the heat. Gently ladle the consommé through a strainer lined with several thicknesses of dampened cheesecloth. Cool completely, cover, and refrigerate. *The consommé can be prepared up to 2 days ahead.*

*3 garlic cloves, peeled*

*Tops from 1 large bunch celery*

*Stems from 1 large bunch parsley*

*1 tablespoon dried thyme, crumbled*

*2 bay leaves*

*12 black peppercorns*

*10 cups canned chicken broth, with 10 cups cold water*

*2 egg whites*

*1½ cups (about 4 ribs) thinly sliced celery*

*¾ cup medium-dry (Sercial) madeira*

*Salt*

*Freshly ground black pepper*

Cut the duck breasts into julienne. Combine the consommé, sliced celery, and madeira in a large saucepan. Simmer until the celery is almost tender, about 5 minutes. Add the duck to the consommé and cook until just heated through, about 3 minutes. Adjust the seasoning, ladle into heated bowls, and serve.

●── *Serves 8*

◆ ◆ ◆ ◆ ◆ ◆ ◆ ◆ ◆ ◆ ◆ ◆ ◆ ◆ ◆ ◆ ◆ ◆ ◆ ◆ ◆ ◆ ◆ ◆ ◆ ◆ ◆ ◆ ◆ ◆ ◆ ◆ ◆ ◆ ◆ ◆ ◆ ◆ ◆

## C R E O L E   R O A S T   T U R K E Y

◆ ◆ ◆ ◆ ◆ ◆ ◆ ◆ ◆

T HE SENSATIONAL creole-spiced butter keeps the turkey breast moist and flavorful. See page 321 for advice on achieving the perfect turkey.

••• ◗ •••

½ cup (1 stick) unsalted
  butter, softened
3 garlic cloves, peeled and
  forced through a press
2 teaspoons Worcestershire
  sauce
1 teaspoon Tabasco sauce
1 teaspoon dried thyme,
  crumbled
½ teaspoon rubbed sage
½ teaspoon freshly ground
  black pepper
½ teaspoon freshly ground
  white pepper
½ teaspoon cayenne pepper
¼ teaspoon allspice
1 fresh turkey (16 pounds),
  at room temperature
Jambalaya Stuffing (recipe
  follows)
3 cups canned chicken
  broth or homemade stock
½ cup whipping cream

In a medium-size bowl or food processor combine the butter, garlic, Worcestershire sauce, Tabasco sauce, thyme, sage, black pepper, white pepper, cayenne, and allspice. Process or stir until smooth. Transfer to a small bowl, cover, and refrigerate. *The butter can be refrigerated for up to 4 days, or it can be frozen for up to 3 weeks. Soften to room temperature before using.*

Position a rack in the lower third of the oven and preheat to 325 degrees F. Working from the vent end of the turkey, gently slide your fingers between the skin of the breast and the meat. Rub the spiced butter under the skin and over the meat, using it all. Spoon about half of the stuffing into the cavity, packing it firmly. Truss the turkey or skewer the vent closed. Set the turkey breast side up in a shallow roasting pan just large enough to hold it. Roast the turkey, basting with the accumulated pan juices, until the juices run barely pinkish yellow when the thigh is pierced, about 3¾ hours, or until an instant-reading thermometer inserted in the thickest part of the thigh registers 170 to 175 degrees F.

Transfer the turkey to a heated platter and remove the stuffing. Cover the turkey with a foil tent. The turkey should rest 20 minutes but can stand up to one hour before carving, if necessary.

Degrease the pan juices. Set the roasting pan over medium-high heat. Add the chicken broth and cream and bring to a boil, scraping up any browned bits from the roaster. Boil hard about 7 minutes, or until reduced and thickened slightly, and adjust the seasoning. Strain the gravy into a sauceboat and pass separately.

*Serves 8 to 10*

♦♦♦♦♦♦♦♦♦♦♦♦♦♦♦♦♦♦♦♦♦♦♦♦♦♦♦♦♦♦♦♦♦♦♦♦♦♦♦

## JAMBALAYA STUFFING

♦♦♦♦♦♦♦♦♦

**T**HIS SPICY MÉLANGE of rice, sweet peppers, crabmeat, and *andouille* sausage was inspired by a jambalaya I tasted on my last trip to New Orleans. While I didn't think of it as a turkey stuffing at the time (I was too busy eating, sweating, and smiling), it later occurred to me that the pair might go well together. I was right.

In a heavy, 5-quart saucepan over medium heat warm the oil. Add the sausage and stir until crisp and brown, about 10 minutes. With a slotted spoon, transfer the sausage to a bowl. Add, to the oil in the pan, the sweet peppers, onions, celery, garlic, thyme, bay leaves, cumin, sage, black pepper, white pepper, filé powder, and cayenne. Cover, lower the heat, and cook, stirring occasionally, until the vegetables are tender, about 15 minutes.

*¼ cup olive oil*

*1 pound* andouille *or other spicy smoked sausage, diced ( see Cook's Sources)*

*2 large, sweet red peppers, cored and diced*

*2 medium onions, peeled and chopped*

*3 celery ribs, diced*

*3 garlic cloves, peeled and minced*

*2 teaspoons dried thyme, crumbled*

*2 bay leaves*

*1 teaspoon ground cumin*

*1 teaspoon rubbed sage*

*(ingredients continued)*

*1 teaspoon freshly ground
black pepper*

*1 teaspoon freshly ground
white pepper*

*1 teaspoon filé powder (see
Cook's Sources)*

*¼ teaspoon cayenne pepper*

*5 cups canned chicken
broth or homemade stock*

*1 can (28 ounces)
Italian-style plum
tomatoes, crushed and
drained*

*2 teaspoons salt*

*2¼ cups long-grain rice
(see note)*

*1 cup sliced green onions*

*1 pound lump crabmeat,
picked over*

Stir in the chicken broth, tomatoes, and salt. Raise the heat and bring to a boil. Stir in the rice. Lower the heat, cover, and cook, undisturbed, until the rice has absorbed all the liquid, about 22 minutes. Transfer to a bowl and stir in the sausage and the green onions. Cool completely. *The stuffing can be prepared to this point up to 1 day ahead. Cover tightly and refrigerate. Bring to room temperature before proceeding.*

Preheat the oven to 375 degrees F. Stir the crabmeat into the stuffing. Use half of the stuffing in the Creole Roast Turkey (page 336). In a 2-quart dish bake the remainder, covered, about 40 minutes, or until steaming.

NOTE To enjoy this dish as jambalaya for its own sake, reduce the amount of rice in the recipe to 1¾ cups and proceed exactly as for the stuffing, baking the jambalaya in the oven. Cooked chicken or shrimp can be added in place of (or along with) the crabmeat.

—● *Serves 8*

◆◆◆◆◆◆◆◆◆◆◆◆◆◆◆◆◆◆◆◆◆◆◆◆◆◆◆◆◆◆◆◆◆◆◆◆◆◆◆◆◆◆◆◆◆

▀▄▀▄▀▄▀▄▀▄▀▄▀▄▀▄▀▄▀▄▀▄▀▄▀▄▀▄▀▄▀▄▀▄▀▄▀▄▀▄

# CARROTS AND BRUSSELS SPROUTS GLAZED WITH PEPPER AND BROWN SUGAR

◆◆◆◆◆◆◆◆◆

*2 teaspoons salt*

*2 pounds baby carrots,
peeled*

*2 pounds brussels sprouts,
trimmed, with an X cut
in the root end*

*1½ cups canned chicken
broth or homemade stock*

*6 tablespoons (¾ stick)
unsalted butter*

*⅓ cup dark brown sugar,
firmly packed*

*1 tablespoon freshly
ground black pepper*

THIS PEPPERY, SWEET side dish is also good with a pork roast, a ham, or a roast duck or goose.

◆◆◆  ◆◆◆

Bring a large pan of water to a boil. Add the salt and the carrots and cook until crisp but tender, about 4 minutes. With a slotted spoon, transfer the carrots to a large bowl of ice water. Return the water to a boil, add the brussels sprouts, and cook until crisp but tender, about 5 minutes. With a slotted spoon, transfer the brussels sprouts to a bowl of ice water. When the vegetables are cool, drain thoroughly. *The vegetables can be cooked up to 1 day ahead. Cover and refrigerate separately.*

In a large, heavy skillet over medium heat combine the chicken broth, butter, and brown sugar. Bring to a boil, stirring to dissolve the sugar. Lower the heat slightly and cook hard until reduced by half, about 7 minutes. Add the carrots and cook, shaking the pan occasionally, until they are almost tender and the sauce begins to coat them, about 6 minutes. Add the brussels sprouts and the pepper and cook until just heated through, stirring occasionally, about 4 minutes. Serve immediately.

*Serves 8*

## MOLDED CRANBERRY SALAD WITH HONEY MAYONNAISE

♦ ♦ ♦ ♦ ♦ ♦ ♦ ♦ ♦

USUALLY SHY AWAY from gelatin-stabilized anything, but cranberry salads are imprinted in the American DNA, and it's hard to imagine the holiday without one of these molded creations. The tang of pink grapefruit juice and the piquant honey mayonnaise give the salad a bright kick that is just what a rich and unctuous Thanksgiving menu needs.

*For the mayonnaise* In a medium-size bowl whisk together the egg yolks, vinegar, honey, mustard, salt, and pepper. Slowly whisk in the oil. Adjust the seasoning, cover, and refrigerate. *The mayonnaise can be prepared up to 3 days ahead.*

HONEY MAYONNAISE

*2 egg yolks*
*3 tablespoons cider vinegar*
*3 tablespoons honey*
*3 tablespoons prepared*
  *Dijon-style mustard*
*¼ teaspoon salt*
*¼ teaspoon freshly ground*
  *black pepper*
*1½ cups vegetable oil*

*(ingredients continued)*

CRANBERRY SALAD

3 packages unflavored
    gelatin
1/2 cup cold water
6 cups fresh cranberries,
    rinsed and picked over
1 1/2 cups sugar
2 cups pink grapefruit
    juice, preferably fresh
Lettuce leaves, as garnish

*For the salad* In a small bowl sprinkle the gelatin over the water. In a food processor, in batches, if necessary, coarsely chop together the cranberries and sugar. Transfer to a medium-size, heavy, nonreactive saucepan. Stir in the grapefruit juice. Set over low heat, cover, and cook, stirring occasionally, until the sugar dissolves, about 12 minutes. Uncover, increase the heat, and bring to a boil, stirring occasionally. Remove the pan from the heat, add the softened gelatin, and stir until dissolved. Cool slightly.

Rinse a 5-cup mold with cold water. Pour the cranberry mixture into the wet mold, cover, and chill until set, at least 8 hours and preferably overnight. *The dish can be prepared up to 2 days ahead.*

Line a platter with the lettuce leaves. Invert the mold onto the platter. Wrap it in a hot, damp towel, and shake gently. Let stand until the cranberry salad loosens from the mold. *The salad can be unmolded several hours before serving. Cover loosely and refrigerate.*

Serve the salad and pass the Honey Mayonnaise separately.

*Serves 8*

♦♦♦♦♦♦♦♦♦♦♦♦♦♦♦♦♦♦♦♦♦♦♦♦♦♦♦♦♦♦♦♦♦♦♦♦♦♦♦♦♦♦♦

CRUST

2 1/4 cups (about)
    unbleached all-purpose
    flour
1/4 teaspoon salt
8 tablespoons (1 stick)
    unsalted butter, well
    chilled and cut into
    small pieces
1/4 cup solid vegetable
    shortening, well chilled
    and cut into small pieces
5 to 6 tablespoons ice
    water

## PUMPKIN–PEANUT BUTTER PIE

♦♦♦♦♦♦♦♦♦

**S**ERVE THIS BIG, bright orange and utterly old-fashioned tasting pie with a scoop of the Southern Comfort–Peanut Praline Ice Cream that follows.

♦♦♦  ♦♦♦

*For the crust* In a bowl or in a food processor combine 2 cups of the flour and the salt. Cut in the butter and shortening until a coarse meal forms. One tablespoon at a time, add the ice water, until a soft dough forms.

Turn the dough out onto a work surface lightly floured with half of the flour, reserving the remainder. Gather it into a ball, flatten it into a disc, and wrap it well in plastic. Refrigerate at least 1 hour. *The dough can be prepared up to 3 days ahead.*

Lightly flour a work surface with the remaining flour and roll the dough out to a round about ⅛ inch thick. Transfer the dough to a 10-inch pie pan. Trim the edges, leaving an overhang of ½ inch. Form a high crust and crimp it decoratively. Cover and refrigerate at least 30 minutes. *The formed crust can be prepared up to 1 day ahead.*

*For the filling* In a large bowl mix together the pumpkin, brown sugar, and peanut butter. One at a time, whisk in the eggs. Stir in the half-and-half, Southern Comfort, vanilla, nutmeg, and salt.

Position a rack in the center of the oven and set a baking sheet on it. Preheat to 425 degrees F. Pour the filling into the chilled shell (it will be very full) and set it on the heated baking sheet. Bake 15 minutes. Lower the heat to 350 degrees F and bake another 40 to 50 minutes, or until the filling is uniformly puffed and set. Cover the pie loosely with aluminum foil if the crust becomes too brown. Cool on a rack. The pie will sink and may crack slightly as it cools.

●—● *Serves 8*

PUMPKIN–PEANUT BUTTER FILLING

*1 can (16 ounces) unsweetened solid-pack pumpkin*
*¾ cup light brown sugar, firmly packed*
*½ cup creamy peanut butter*
*3 eggs*
*1¼ cups half-and-half*
*⅓ cup Southern Comfort*
*2 teaspoons vanilla*
*½ teaspoon freshly grated nutmeg*
*¼ teaspoon salt*

## SOUTHERN COMFORT–PEANUT PRALINE ICE CREAM

◆◆◆◆◆◆◆◆◆

THE UNIQUELY MELLOW TASTE of Southern Comfort makes the pie and this ice cream especially delicious. There's no real substitute for it, but these two desserts are so good you'll make them often, and a bottle won't last long.

PRALINE

1 tablespoon (about)
　butter, softened
¾ cup sugar
1 cup roasted, unsalted
　peanuts, husked

ICE CREAM

½ cup sugar
4 egg yolks
3 cups half-and-half
½ cup Southern Comfort
1 teaspoon vanilla

*For the praline* Lightly butter a heatproof plate. In a small, heavy saucepan over low heat, melt the sugar, stirring occasionally, about 15 minutes. Add the peanuts and cook until the mixture is a golden brown and the peanuts are lightly toasted, about 3 minutes. Pour the praline onto the prepared plate to cool, about 1 hour. Remove the praline from the plate and break it into chunks. Store the praline at room temperature in an airtight jar. *The praline can be prepared up to 1 week ahead.*

*For the ice cream* In a medium-size bowl whisk together the sugar and egg yolks. In a heavy, medium-size saucepan over medium-high heat bring the half-and-half to a boil. Slowly whisk the hot cream into the yolk mixture. Return the mixture to the saucepan and cook over low heat, stirring constantly, until the custard thickens and leaves a path on the back of a spoon when a fingertip is drawn across it, about 4 minutes. Transfer the custard to a bowl. Stir in the Southern Comfort and vanilla and cool to room temperature. Cover and refrigerate until very cold, preferably overnight.

*To assemble* With a knife, chop the praline. Transfer the chilled custard to an ice-cream maker and churn according to the manufacturer's instructions, adding the praline when the ice cream is almost firm. Transfer to a covered container and freeze. *The ice cream can be prepared up to 1 day ahead.*

If the ice cream is frozen solid, soften it slightly in the refrigerator before scooping.

*Makes about 2 quarts*

# MENU

◆◆◆◆◆◆◆◆◆◆◆◆◆◆◆

ROQUEFORT-WALNUT SHORTBREADS
◆
SAUSAGE-MUSTARD PHYLLO TRIANGLES
◆
CONSOMMÉ WITH
SWEET POTATO DUMPLINGS
◆
ROAST TURKEY WITH HERBED
WHITE WINE PAN SAUCE
◆
WHOLE WHEAT, LEEK,
AND PARSLEY STUFFING
◆
WILD RICE DRESSING
WITH PEARS AND CHESTNUTS
◆
SOPHISTICATED SUCCOTASH
◆
ANADAMA ROLLS WITH ORANGE BUTTER
*page 61*
◆
HAZELNUT-PUMPKIN CHEESECAKE
◆
CRANBERRY-APPLE TART

ONE OF MY FIRST Thanksgiving menus cooked away from home was this one, composed of all the nostalgic and necessary flavors I remembered from Thanksgivings past but with fresh twists and personalized updatings that made it my own. Try it. You might establish a few new traditions, too.

## ROQUEFORT-WALNUT SHORTBREADS

1½ cups unbleached
all-purpose flour
1 cup walnut pieces
½ pound Roquefort cheese,
well chilled and
crumbled
½ cup (1 stick) unsalted
butter, well chilled and
cut into small pieces
2 egg yolks
1 tablespoon freshly
ground black pepper

THESE SAVORY "COOKIES" are best eaten the same day they're baked, but the dough can be made ahead and frozen.

In a food processor combine all the ingredients and blend until the dough is formed. Divide the dough in half. On a lightly floured surface, form each half into a cylinder 1½ inches in diameter. Wrap and chill until firm, at least 4 hours. *The dough can be prepared ahead and refrigerated up to 3 days, or it can be frozen up to 1 month.*

Preheat the oven to 425 degrees F. Slice the dough into rounds ⅓ inch thick. Arrange the rounds on ungreased baking sheets, spacing them ½ inch apart. (If you are using frozen dough, soften the cut rounds at room temperature 20 minutes.) Bake the cookies until the edges are golden brown, 10 to 12 minutes, reversing the position of the baking sheets once. Transfer to paper towels. Serve the shortbreads warm or at room temperature.

*Makes about 3 dozen*

## SAUSAGE-MUSTARD PHYLLO TRIANGLES

In a medium-size saucepan over moderate heat cook the sausage, stirring often, until it is no longer pink and the fat is rendered, about 15 minutes. Transfer it to a strainer and press hard with the back of a spoon to extract as much fat and moisture as possible. Drain the meat on paper towels.

Wipe the pan. Return the meat to the pan, stir in the cream, mustard, and nutmeg, and set over moderate heat. Bring it to a boil, lower the heat slightly, and cook, uncovered, stirring occasionally, until the mixture is thick enough to mound in a spoon, about 15 minutes. Cool to room temperature.

Brush 2 baking sheets lightly with melted butter. Place a phyllo sheet on the work surface, keeping the remaining phyllo covered with a damp towel to prevent drying. Brush the top of the phyllo sheet lightly with the melted butter. Place another sheet of phyllo atop the first and brush with butter. Cut the phyllo the short way into 5 strips. Place a heaping teaspoon of the sausage mixture at the bottom of 1 strip. Fold the corner of phyllo over the sausage and brush lightly with butter. Continue folding down the entire length of the strip, creating a triangle, brushing lightly with butter after each fold. Repeat with the remaining strips. Arrange the triangles on the prepared baking sheets, spacing them 1 inch apart. Brush the tops with butter. Repeat with the remaining phyllo and filling. *The recipe can be prepared to this point up to 1 day ahead, covered well, and refrigerated.*

Preheat the oven to 350 degrees F. Bake the pastries until golden brown and crisp, reversing the position of the baking sheets once, 20 to 25 minutes. Drain on paper towels. Serve the triangles hot or warm.

NOTE Filled, unbaked phyllo triangles freeze well. Arrange the triangles on unbuttered baking sheets, eliminating the final brushing with butter. When frozen, remove the triangles from the sheets and wrap well. To bake, do not defrost. Arrange the triangles on lightly buttered baking sheets. Brush the tops with the melted butter and bake the triangles in a preheated 325-degree F oven until crisp and golden, 40 to 50 minutes.

*Makes about 25*

*1 pound Italian-style sweet sausage, casings removed, crumbled*
*1 cup whipping cream*
*¼ cup low-salt Dijon mustard*
*½ teaspoon freshly ground nutmeg*
*10 phyllo pastry sheets (see note)*
*1 cup (2 sticks) unsalted butter, melted*

CONSOMMÉ

*¼ cup vegetable oil*

*3 pounds chicken wings,
  backs, and necks*

*3 medium onions, peeled
  and chopped*

*2 large leeks, white part
  only, well cleaned and
  chopped*

*4 carrots, peeled and
  chopped*

*12 cups canned chicken
  broth*

*Stems from 1 large bunch
  of parsley*

*2 bay leaves*

*1 tablespoon dried thyme,
  crumbled*

*2 egg whites*

SWEET POTATO DUMPLINGS

*1½ pounds (2 large) sweet
  potatoes*

*½ cup unbleached
  all-purpose flour*

*2 eggs*

*¼ teaspoon freshly ground
  nutmeg*

*1¼ teaspoon salt*

*⅛ teaspoon cayenne pepper*

TO FINISH

*½ cup medium-dry sherry
  (amontillado)*

*Freshly ground black
  pepper*

*4 cups fresh spinach
  leaves, thoroughly
  washed and julienned*

▼▲▼▲▼▲▼▲▼▲▼▲▼▲▼▲▼▲▼▲▼▲▼▲▼▲▼▲▼▲▼▲

# CONSOMMÉ WITH
# SWEET POTATO DUMPLINGS

♦♦♦♦♦♦♦♦♦♦

**A** CLEAR SOUP, floating with plump orange dumplings and strands of barely cooked spinach, makes an elegant holiday starter. Clarifying a stock is one of the true kitchen wonders, but the process somewhat reduces its flavor. I compensate by beginning with chicken broth, instead of water, and reinforcing the consommé with a final jot of medium-dry sherry.

♦♦♦  ♦♦♦

*For the consommé* In a large, heavy pot over medium-high heat warm the oil. Pat the chicken dry. Add the chicken to the pot and cook, stirring often, until brown, about 15 minutes. Lower the heat to medium. Stir in the onions, leeks, and carrots and cook, stirring frequently, until the vegetables begin to brown, about 15 minutes. Stir in the chicken broth, parsley stems, bay leaves, and thyme. Add enough water to cover. Bring to a boil, skimming to remove the surface scum. Lower the heat, partially cover, and simmer briskly for 2 hours. Cool slightly, then strain, pressing hard on the solids to extract as much liquid as possible. If necessary, return the stock to the pan and simmer until reduced to 2 quarts. *The consommé can be prepared up to 4 days ahead. Cover tightly and refrigerate.*

*To clarify the consommé* Skim the fat from the surface of the stock. Bring the stock to room temperature. Whisk the egg whites together with 1 cup of the stock in a large bowl. In a saucepan bring the remaining stock to a boil. Slowly whisk the hot stock into the egg white mixture. Return the stock mixture to the pan, set it over medium heat, and bring just to a simmer, stirring constantly. When the stock simmers, turn the heat to the lowest possible setting and leave the stock undisturbed for 20 minutes. Do not stir. Remove the pan from the heat. Gently ladle the consommé through a strainer lined with several layers of dampened cheese-cloth. *The consommé can be prepared up to 2 days ahead. Cover and refrigerate.*

*For the dumplings* Preheat the oven to 400 degrees F. Prick the sweet potatoes several times with a fork and bake for about 1 hour, or until very tender. Cool, peel, and force through a strainer, a ricer, or the fine blade of a food mill.

Transfer 1½ cups of the puree to a bowl. Mix in the flour, eggs, nutmeg, ¼ teaspoon of the salt, and the cayenne pepper. *The batter can be prepared up to 1 day ahead. Cover and refrigerate. Bring to room temperature before proceeding.*

Bring a quart and a half of water and the remaining salt to a boil in a large saucepan. Roll rounded teaspoons of the batter between floured palms to form dumplings. Drop the dumplings into the water in batches. After the dumplings rise to the surface, cook another 5 minutes. Remove them with a slotted spoon and set aside.

*To assemble* Bring the consommé to a simmer. Stir in the sherry and dumplings and simmer 5 minutes. Adjust the seasoning and add pepper to taste. Divide the spinach among soup bowls. Ladle the consommé and dumplings over the spinach and serve immediately.

●—● *Serves 10*

◆ ◆ ◆ ◆ ◆ ◆ ◆ ◆ ◆ ◆ ◆ ◆ ◆ ◆ ◆ ◆ ◆ ◆ ◆ ◆ ◆ ◆ ◆ ◆ ◆ ◆ ◆ ◆ ◆ ◆ ◆ ◆ ◆ ◆ ◆ ◆ ◆ ◆ ◆ ◆ ◆ ◆ ◆ ◆ ◆

## ROAST TURKEY WITH HERBED WHITE WINE PAN SAUCE

◆ ◆ ◆ ◆ ◆ ◆ ◆ ◆ ◆

**A** 16-POUND TURKEY will feed 10 easily, even if most go back for seconds, and, if you're lucky (no thirds), there will even be enough left over for the next day's obligatory white bread and mayonnaise sandwich.

*Whole Wheat, Leek, and
  Parsley Stuffing (recipe
  follows)*
*1 fresh turkey (16
  pounds), at room
  temperature, giblets
  reserved*
*1 medium onion, peeled
  and coarsely chopped*
*2 medium carrots, peeled
  and coarsely chopped*
*½ cup (1 stick) unsalted
  butter, softened*
*Salt and freshly ground
  pepper*
*3½ cups canned chicken
  broth or homemade stock*
*¼ cup vegetable oil*
*3 cups dry white wine*
*¼ cup minced mixed fresh
  herbs, such as 2
  tablespoons thyme, 1½
  tablespoons oregano, and
  ½ tablespoon rosemary*

See page 321 for advice on achieving the perfect turkey.

Preheat the oven to 325 degrees F. Spoon the stuffing into the turkey. Truss the turkey or skewer the cavity closed. Arrange the turkey, breast side up, in a shallow, flameproof roasting pan just large enough to hold it. Place the giblets, onions, and carrots around the turkey. Rub the breast with ¼ cup of the butter. Sprinkle it with salt and freshly ground pepper. Dampen a 10 × 20-inch piece of cheesecloth. Fold the cheesecloth in half and drape it over the turkey breast.

In a small pan warm together ½ cup of the chicken broth, the remaining butter, and the vegetable oil.

Roast the turkey 30 minutes. Baste it through the cheesecloth with half of the broth mixture. Roast it 30 minutes longer and baste again, using the remaining broth mixture. Continue to baste the turkey through the cheesecloth every 15 minutes using the accumulated pan juices. The turkey is done when the thigh is pierced with a fork and the juices run barely pinkish yellow, or when an instant-reading thermometer inserted in the thickest part of the thigh registers 170 to 175 degrees F, about 3¾ hours total roasting time.

Transfer the turkey to a heated platter and remove the stuffing. Cover the turkey with a foil tent. Degrease the pan juices. Set the roaster with the juices over medium heat. Stir until the vegetables are browned, about 10 minutes. Add the remaining chicken broth and the wine. Boil until reduced by half, scraping up any browned bits, about 25 minutes. Strain into a small saucepan, pressing hard with the back of a spoon to extract as much liquid as possible. Degrease the sauce and bring it to a simmer. Add the herbs and simmer 5 minutes. Adjust the seasoning. Carve and serve the turkey, passing the sauce separately.

*Serves 10*

## WHOLE WHEAT, LEEK, AND PARSLEY STUFFING

♦♦♦♦♦♦♦♦♦

**A**FIRM, HEALTH FOOD STORE SORT OF whole wheat bread, not one of those squishy impostors from the supermarket, is required for the right texture.

In a large skillet over low heat melt the butter. Stir in the leeks. Cover and cook until very tender, stirring occasionally, about 15 minutes. Transfer to a large bowl and cool.

Stir in the bread. Stir in the broth, eggs, parsley, and salt. Season generously with pepper.

*Makes about 2 quarts*

*¾ cup (1½ sticks) unsalted butter*

*6 large leeks, white part only, well cleaned and chopped*

*1½ pounds day-old, firm whole wheat bread, crusts trimmed, broken into ½-inch pieces*

*1½ cups canned chicken broth or homemade stock*

*3 eggs, beaten*

*2¼ cups minced fresh Italian parsley*

*2¼ teaspoons salt*

*Freshly ground black pepper*

## WILD RICE DRESSING WITH PEARS AND CHESTNUTS

♦♦♦♦♦♦♦♦♦

**T**HIS EASY SIDE DISH is one to keep in mind at times other than Thanksgiving. I like it with pork, duck, or goose and make it often. Substitute fresh apples or dried apricots (soaked for an hour in a little stock) for the pears, if you'd like.

Preheat the oven to 350 degrees F. In a 4½- or 5-quart, flameproof casserole over medium heat melt ½ cup of the butter. Add the onions, bay leaves, and thyme, cover, and cook, stirring occasionally, until the onions are tender, about 15 minutes. Add the chicken broth,

*1 cup (2 sticks) unsalted butter*

*2 medium onions, peeled and chopped*

*2 bay leaves*

*1½ teaspoons dried thyme, crumbled*

*4½ cups canned chicken broth or homemade stock*

*3 cups (about 1 pound) wild rice (see Cook's Sources), rinsed*

*(ingredients continued)*

1½ teaspoons salt

3 large, ripe, firm pears,
  peeled, cored, and cut
  into chunks

24 chestnuts, roasted and
  peeled (see note, page
  227)

Freshly ground black
  pepper

wild rice, and salt and bring to a boil. Cover and bake 30 minutes. Uncover and bake until most of the liquid is absorbed, another 20 to 25 minutes.

Meanwhile, in a large skillet over medium-high heat melt the remaining butter. When it foams add the pears and chestnuts and cook, stirring gently, 5 minutes. Stir the pears, chestnuts, and their butter into the rice and bake until all the liquid is absorbed, another 5 to 10 minutes. Remove the bay leaves. Season to taste with pepper. *The dressing can be prepared up to 1 day ahead and refrigerated. Bring to room temperature. Reheat, covered, in a 350-degree F oven until steaming, about 35 minutes.*

**Serves 10 to 12**

1 large head of broccoli

Salt

10 tablespoons unsalted
  butter

1 pound carrots, peeled
  and cut on the diagonal
  into slices ¼ inch thick

2 medium, sweet red
  peppers, trimmed and
  cut into strips ¼ inch
  thick

2 medium yellow squash,
  scrubbed, trimmed and
  cut into slices ¼ inch
  thick

1 package (10 ounces)
  frozen baby lima beans,
  thawed and drained

1 cup corn, optional (see
  note)

Freshly ground black
  pepper

## SOPHISTICATED SUCCOTASH

WHEN A MENU needs color and crunch, this dish fills the bill. The ingredients are available year-round (so don't wait until Thanksgiving to make it), and since the vegetables can be cut the day before, only a quick sauté is needed before serving.

Cut the broccoli into florets, reserving the stalks for another use. Bring a large pan of salted water to a boil. Add the broccoli and cook until just crisp and tender, 3 to 4 minutes. Drain and immediately transfer to a bowl of ice water. When cool, drain and pat dry. *The broccoli can be blanched up to 1 day ahead. Wrap and refrigerate.*

In a large skillet over medium-low heat melt the butter. Add the carrots and cook until crisp but tender, about 15 minutes. Increase the heat to medium-high, add the peppers, and cook, stirring and tossing, 5 minutes. Add the squash and cook 1 minute. Add the lima beans, corn, and broccoli and season with salt to taste. Cover and cook until just heated through, stirring once or twice, about 4 minutes. Season generously with pepper and serve immediately.

NOTE By definition, succotash should include corn, and if you have some growing fresh in your garden in November (or want to resort to canned or frozen), by all means do so. Your succotash will then be even more colorful, as well as authentic.

*Serves 10*

## HAZELNUT-PUMPKIN CHEESECAKE

I F IT'S HARD FOR YOU to imagine Thanksgiving without a pumpkin dessert but you want to give your usual pie the year off, then consider this worthy substitute.

*For the crust* In a food processor grind the gingersnaps together with the sugar to fine crumbs. With the machine running, slowly add the butter. Press the mixture firmly into the bottom of a 9-inch springform pan and refrigerate until firm.

*For the filling* Position a rack in the center of the oven and preheat to 350 degrees F. In a food processor or mixer combine all of the filling ingredients and process until smooth, stopping once to scrape down the sides of the workbowl. Pour the filling into the crust-lined pan and bake until the edges of the cake just begin to pull away from the sides of the pan, 40 to 45 minutes. The center of the cake will not be firm.

CRUST

*24 gingersnaps*

*2 tablespoons sugar*

*¼ cup (½ stick) unsalted butter, melted*

FILLING

*1 pound cream cheese, at room temperature*

*1 can (16 ounces) unsweetened solid-pack pumpkin* (not *pie filling*)

*5 eggs*

*¾ cup brown sugar, firmly packed*

*½ cup hazelnut liqueur, such as Frangelico*

*1 teaspoon cinnamon*

*1 teaspoon vanilla*

*(ingredients continued)*

½ teaspoon ground ginger

¼ teaspoon freshly grated
   nutmeg

¼ teaspoon ground cloves


TOPPING

1 container (16 ounces)
   sour cream

¼ cup sugar

¼ cup hazelnut liqueur,
   such as Frangelico

12 whole hazelnuts

*For the topping* Meanwhile, in a medium-size bowl whisk together the sour cream, sugar, and hazelnut liqueur. Transfer to a measuring cup with a pouring lip.

Without removing the cake from the oven pour the topping evenly over it, starting with the edges. Spread the topping evenly. Bake the cake another 8 to 10 minutes, or until the edges of the topping just begin to bubble. Cool the cheesecake on a rack. Refrigerate for maximum chilling, at least 12 hours. *The cake can be prepared up to 2 days ahead. Cover carefully to avoid marring the topping.*

*To assemble* Press the hazelnuts lightly around the top edge of the cake. Cut the cake while it is firm and chilled and let the slices stand at room temperature 20 minutes before serving.

**—● *Serves 12***

♦ ♦ ♦ ♦ ♦ ♦ ♦ ♦ ♦ ♦ ♦ ♦ ♦ ♦ ♦ ♦ ♦ ♦ ♦ ♦ ♦ ♦ ♦ ♦ ♦ ♦ ♦ ♦ ♦ ♦ ♦ ♦ ♦ ♦ ♦ ♦ ♦ ♦ ♦ ♦

▼▼▼▼▼▼▼▼▼▼▼▼▼▼▼▼▼▼▼▼▼▼▼▼▼▼▼▼▼▼▼▼

## CRANBERRY-APPLE TART

♦ ♦ ♦ ♦ ♦ ♦ ♦ ♦ ♦

CRANBERRY-APPLE FILLING

1¼ cups fresh, unfiltered,
   unsweetened apple cider

1⅓ cups sugar

1 bag (12 ounces) fresh
   cranberries, rinsed and
   picked over

4 medium, tart apples,
   such as Granny Smith,
   peeled, cored, and cut
   into ½-inch chunks

1 recipe chilled pie crust

**T**HE FILLING for this colorful tart is actually a chunky apple-cranberry sauce, which would make for perfectly good eating alongside the turkey. Prepare it one day before baking the tart, to give it time to thicken. Unsweetened whipped cream is a good accompaniment, if you don't succumb to the notion of a scoop of vanilla ice cream.

♦ ♦ ♦  ♦ ♦ ♦

*For the filling* In a large, heavy, nonreactive saucepan over low heat combine the cider and sugar. Stir to dissolve the sugar, raise the heat, and bring to a boil. Lower the heat and simmer 2 minutes. Stir in the cranberries and apples and bring to a simmer. Cook, stirring once or twice, until the cranberries have burst and the apples are just tender, about 10 minutes. Transfer the filling to a bowl and cool. Cover and refrigerate at least 24 hours. *The filling can be prepared up to 3 days ahead. Bring it to room temperature before proceeding.*

*For the crust* Roll the dough out on a lightly floured surface to a round ⅛ inch thick. Transfer it to a 10-inch tart pan, 1¼ inches deep, with removable fluted sides. Trim and finish the edges. Refrigerate the shell for at least 30 minutes. *The formed shell can be refrigerated, well wrapped, up to 1 day.*

*For the topping* In a food processor, in the order listed, combine the ingredients. Process just until a clumpy, cookielike dough forms, about 20 seconds. Transfer the topping to a bowl and refrigerate 1 hour.

*To assemble* Position a rack in the center of the oven, set a baking sheet on the rack, and preheat the oven to 400 degrees F. Pierce the crust lightly with a fork. Line the shell with parchment paper and fill it with pie weights. Set the tart shell on the hot baking sheet and bake 10 minutes. Remove the beans and foil and bake until the crust is just lightly colored and loses its raw quality, about 5 minutes more. Cool the shell to room temperature on a rack. Lower the oven temperature to 375 degrees F, leaving the baking sheet in place.

Spoon the filling into the partially baked shell. Crumble the topping with a fork and sprinkle it evenly over the filling. Set the tart on the hot baking sheet and bake until the top is browned and the filling bubbles, 30 to 35 minutes. Cool on a rack to room temperature before cutting.

— *Serves 10*

TOPPING

*½ cup pecans*

*½ cup unbleached all-purpose flour*

*⅓ cup light brown sugar, packed*

*6 tablespoons unsalted butter, well chilled and cut into small pieces*

# AUTHOR'S FAVORITES

◆◆◆◆◆◆◆◆◆◆◆◆◆◆◆◆◆◆◆◆◆◆◆◆◆◆◆◆◆◆◆◆◆◆◆◆◆◆◆◆◆◆◆◆◆◆

EVERY HOUSE NEEDS AN ATTIC, and every menu cookbook needs a section like this one, into which the author can tuck those recipes that somehow failed to be included in the previous menus. My files and my head are filled with such much-loved orphans, and the following batch (culled with anguish as the deadline ticked away), while never making it into menus of their own, still deserved to be a part of my new American kitchen.

▓▓▓▓▓▓▓▓▓▓▓▓▓▓▓▓▓▓▓▓▓▓▓▓▓▓▓▓▓▓▓▓▓▓▓▓▓▓▓▓▓▓▓▓▓▓

## SMOKY SWEET POTATO SOUP WITH *CHIPOTLES*

4 tablespoons unsalted
   butter
2 cups finely chopped
   yellow onion
1 leek, white part only,
   trimmed, cleaned, and
   chopped
2 garlic cloves, peeled and
   chopped
¼ teaspoon thyme
⅛ teaspoon freshly grated
   nutmeg
2 large (about 1 pound)
   sweet potatoes, peeled
   and cut into ½-inch
   chunks
2½ cups canned chicken
   broth or homemade stock
½ cup half-and-half
Salt
½ cup sour cream,
   whisked until smooth
   and shiny
3 to 4 tablespoons adobo
   from canned chipotle
   chiles (see Cook's
   Sources)
2 green onions, trimmed
   and sliced thin

**A** RATHER SIMPLE sweet potato soup becomes unexpectedly delicious and dramatic when drizzled with the smoky, brick red *adobo* sauce in which *chipotle* chiles are canned. The piquant jolt of flavor, heat, and color elevates the soup into an important starter. Serve it before a pork roast or the grilled, butterflied leg of lamb that follows.

In a medium-size saucepan over low heat melt the butter. Add the onion, leek, garlic, thyme, and nutmeg, cover, and cook, stirring once or twice, until the vegetables are tender, about 15 minutes.

Add the potatoes and chicken broth and bring to a boil. Lower the heat, partially cover, and simmer, stirring occasionally, until the potatoes are very tender, about 35 minutes. Cool slightly and then force the soup through the medium blade of a food mill or puree it in a food processor. Stir in the half-and-half and adjust the seasoning. *The soup can be prepared to this point up to 2 days ahead. Cool completely, cover, and refrigerate.*

Warm the soup over low heat, stirring often, until steaming. Ladle into bowls. Place a dollop of sour cream in the center of each bowl of soup. Drizzle the *adobo* over each serving to taste, sprinkle with the green onions, and serve immediately.

**—●** *Serves 4*

# SOUTHWESTERN SPICE-COATED GRILLED LEG OF LAMB

✦✦✦✦✦✦✦✦✦

**T**HIS DISH WAS INSPIRED by a recipe from Madhur Jaffrey's *An Introduction to Indian Cooking*. In it, a boneless, butterflied leg of lamb is marinated in a thick puree of onions, chiles, and spices and then slowly grilled. The finished product provides lamb that ranges from medium-rare to well done, pleasing all hands, and the crusty Tex-Mex spiced exterior is a wonderful foil to the juicy meat. Serve it fajitas-style, if you like, sliced thin across the grain and folded, along with salsa and Chunky Guacamole (page 30) into warmed flour tortillas.

2 medium yellow onions, peeled and chopped

6 garlic cloves, peeled and chopped

3 fresh jalapeños, stemmed and chopped

½ cup olive oil

⅓ cup fresh lime juice

3½ tablespoons mild, plain chile powder (see Cook's Sources)

1½ tablespoons ground, toasted cumin (see note, on page 66)

1½ tablespoons dried oregano, crumbled

2½ teaspoons salt

1 boneless (about 7 pounds), butterflied leg of lamb

3 cups mesquite or hickory wood chips

•••  •••

In a food processor, combine the onions, garlic, and jalapeños and process until partially pureed. Add the oil, lime juice, chili powder, cumin, oregano, and salt and process until smooth. In a large, nonreactive bowl pour the puree over the lamb. Cover and refrigerate 24 hours, turning the meat occasionally. Soak the wood chips in water to cover for 30 minutes. Bring the lamb to room temperature. Light a charcoal fire, or preheat a gas grill, and let it burn until the coals are evenly white. Drain the chips and scatter them over the coals or grillstones. Lay the lamb on the grill, 6 inches above the fire, and cook, turning occasionally and basting with the remaining puree, until the thickest portions of the meat are medium-rare, about 50 minutes (see note).

Let the lamb rest on a cutting board 10 minutes before carving in thin slices across the grain.

NOTE You may also bake the lamb on a jelly-roll pan on a rack placed in the upper third of a preheated 400-degree F oven for the same amount of time. The leg will not be quite as crusty and will lack the smoky edge the grill provides, but it will still be delicious.

**━━●** *Serves 8 to 10*

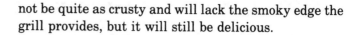

1 small, fresh coconut

4 tablespoons unsalted butter

1 pound (about 24) medium shrimp, shelled and deveined

½ teaspoon salt

3 fresh jalapeños, seeded and minced

3 garlic cloves, peeled and minced

½ cup thinly sliced green onion

1 large, sweet red or orange pepper, stemmed, cored, and cut into ¼-inch dice

1 cup crème fraîche or whipping cream

¼ cup canned chicken broth or homemade stock

1 tablespoon fresh lime juice

½ cup minced fresh cilantro

## COCONUT SHRIMP

**♦ ♦ ♦ ♦ ♦ ♦ ♦ ♦ ♦**

**P**ASSIONATELY HOT and slightly tropical, this sauté evokes Mexico's coastal seafood abundance. I have yet to make it for my friends who hang out on the beach at Puerto Peñasco, but I know when I do it will be as deliciously zesty as it is when stirred up in my own kitchen. The creamy, tart sauce is the perfect foil for the crunchy, sweet shrimp; the appropriate accompaniments are lots of steamed white rice and lots of ice-cold Corona beer.

Preheat the oven to 375 degrees F. With a skewer or screwdriver punch out the eyes of the coconut and drain and discard the liquid. Set the coconut in a baking dish and cook until the shell cracks, about 20 minutes. With a hammer, crack the coconut open. Remove the coconut meat and, with a vegetable peeler, remove the tough brown skin. Coarsely grate enough coconut to yield ⅓ cup and set aside.

In a large skillet over high heat melt 3 tablespoons of the butter. Add the shrimp, season with the salt, and sauté until pink, curled, and just tender, about 2 minutes. With a slotted spoon transfer the shrimp to a bowl and cover them.

Add the remaining butter to the skillet, set it over medium heat, and add the jalapeños, garlic, green onions, and red pepper. Cook, stirring occasionally, until softened slightly, about 2 minutes. Add the crème fraîche and chicken broth and bring to a boil. Lower the heat and simmer the sauce until it is slightly thickened, about 3 minutes. Stir in the lime juice and cilantro.

Spoon the sauce onto 4 plates, dividing it equally. Arrange the shrimp on the sauce. Sprinkle the grated coconut over the shrimp and serve.

*Serves 4*

◆◆◆◆◆◆◆◆◆◆◆◆◆◆◆◆◆◆◆◆◆◆◆◆◆◆◆◆◆◆◆◆◆◆◆◆◆◆◆◆◆

## FRESH TUNA
## SALAD NIÇOISE

◆◆◆◆◆◆◆◆◆

ONCE SPENT an unpleasant summer as the chef in a Southhampton vacation home. The low point of my only foray into "private service" was the tongue-lashing I took for offering a salad Niçoise made with canned tuna. If I had been more culinarily adventurous, I could have used fresh tuna—boats brought magnificent specimens into the Hamptons daily. But I stuck to the basic line I found in all my books on Provençal cooking, and though they did all say that there are as many versions of salad Niçoise as there are Niçoise cooks, when my authorities called for tuna (not all did), they called for canned.

Here, to correct that youthful kitchen indiscretion, is a fresh tuna version of the classic salad. The ingredients are typical, but the creamy Fresh Oregano Dressing is my own touch, and an agreeable one, I think. By all means grill the tuna if you wish—the result is superb. The salad is a meal in itself, needing nothing more than good bread and a cool glass of the pinkish Provençal wine, Bandol, by way of accompaniment.

Salt

1 pound green beans, trimmed

8 red-skinned new potatoes, scrubbed

2 tablespoons olive oil

4 small tuna steaks (about 1½ pounds), cut 1 inch thick, at room temperature

Freshly ground black pepper

4 eggs, hard cooked, peeled, and quartered

Fresh Oregano Dressing (page 80)

2 large, ripe tomatoes, seeded and diced

⅓ cup Niçoise olives, drained

Sprigs of fresh oregano, as garnish

Bring a pan of water to a boil. Stir in 1 tablespoon of salt, add the beans, and cook, stirring once or twice, until the beans are just tender, about 6 minutes. Drain and transfer immediately to a bowl of ice water. Cool completely and drain thoroughly.

In a saucepan cover the potatoes with cold water and stir in 1 tablespoon of salt. Set the pan over medium heat and bring to a boil. Cook the potatoes until they are just tender, about 9 minutes after the water reaches a boil. Drain. *The recipe can be prepared to this point up to 1 day ahead. Wrap the beans and potatoes separately and refrigerate. Bring them to room temperature before proceeding.*

In a heavy, nonstick skillet over high heat warm the olive oil. Pat the tuna steaks dry. Add them to the skillet and cook 1 minute. With a spatula turn the steaks and cook 1 minute. Transfer the steaks to a plate, season with salt and pepper, and cool just to room temperature. (The steaks should remain slightly pink in the center.)

Using a sharp knife, cut the tuna steaks with the grain into thin slices. Divide the tuna among 4 plates, fanning the slices slightly. Divide the beans and eggs among the plates. Slice the potatoes and divide them among the plates. Drizzle the dressing over each salad. Place a mound of the diced tomatoes in the center of each salad and scatter the olives over all. Garnish with the sprigs of fresh oregano and serve.

*Serves 4*

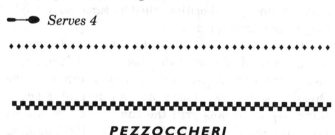

## *PEZZOCCHERI*

THIS TRADITIONAL PASTA from the Lombardy region of Italy just may be one of the world's great dishes. Although I'd heard it described, I'd never seen a recipe until I ran across a box of imported, packaged *pezzoccheri,* the short, thick buckwheat fettuccine which is the basis of the dish of the same name.

The pasta was irrevocably shattered on the several occasions I bought it, so I gave up and devised my own buckwheat noodles. The recipe on the box, however, did give me the authentic sauce ingredients, which I have used in the recipe below. The proportions have been altered to suit my taste, and the method has been adapted to allow much of the work to be gotten out of the way in advance. If you think a man has to be mad these days to make his own pasta, this rustic, colorful, and tremendously flavorful dish of chocolate brown noodles, tossed with pink and white potatoes, bright green Swiss chard, and crisp red onion, in an unctuous sauce of fontina, Parmesan, and garlicky butter, may convince you otherwise.

Serve it as a main course, preceded by excellent, imported prosciutto or another cold, meaty appetizer, and follow the entrée with a green salad and fresh fruit. For authenticity, one of the Lombardy's accommodating red wines (Grumello, Sassella, Inferno) would be an apt choice, but I prefer a white and suggest a Lugana, made from the *trebbiano di soave* grape—light, fruity and well balanced. In a California wine look for a light zinfandel, if you're pouring red, or sauvignon blanc, if drinking white.

1 pound (8 or 9) red-skinned new potatoes, scrubbed and cut into ½-inch chunks
Salt
1 large bunch of Swiss chard, trimmed, cleaned, and stalks and leaves separated
1½ sticks (6 ounces) unsalted butter
4 garlic cloves, peeled and minced
2 tablespoons minced fresh sage leaves (see note)
1 medium red onion, peeled and diced (about 1 cup)
Fresh Buckwheat Noodles (Pezzoccheri) (recipe follows)
Freshly ground black pepper
6 ounces rindless, grated (about 1½ cups) Fontina Val D'Aosta cheese
½ cup grated Parmesan cheese

In a medium-size saucepan cover the potatoes with lightly salted water. Set over medium heat and bring to a boil. Lower the heat slightly and cook until the potatoes are just tender but still hold their shape, about 6 minutes after the water boils. Drain immediately, rinse under cold water, and drain again.

Cut the stalks of the Swiss chard crosswise into ½-inch pieces and set aside. Slice the leaves crosswise into thin strips. Place the leaves in a colander and rinse under cold water. Set aside in the colander in the sink.

Bring a medium-size saucepan of lightly salted water to a boil. Cook the chard stalks until tender but still crunchy, about 4 minutes. Pour the stalks and boiling water over the chard leaves in the colander. Transfer immediately to a bowl of ice water and cool. Drain well and squeeze out as much water as possible. *The recipe can be made to this point up to 3 hours ahead. Cover the potatoes and the chard separately with plastic wrap and store at room temperature.*

Position a rack in the upper third of the oven and preheat to 375 degrees F. Butter a 9 × 13-inch oval gratin dish.

In a large skillet over low heat melt the butter. Add the garlic and cook, stirring occasionally, until fragrant, about 2 minutes. Add the sage and red onion and cook, stirring, until the onion is softened but not browned, about 5 minutes. Add the potatoes and chard and toss to coat with the contents of the skillet. Cook, covered, until heated through, about 5 minutes.

Bring a large pot of lightly salted water to a boil. Add the buckwheat pasta and cook until tender but still firm, 10 to 20 seconds. (If the noodles have been fully dried before cooking, cook about 1½ minutes.) Drain immediately and transfer to a large bowl. Add the potato mixture and stir gently to mix. Season lightly with salt and generously with pepper. Add the fontina and Parmesan cheeses and toss again. Turn the pasta into the prepared gratin dish. Cover tightly with foil. *The recipe can be prepared to this point up to 1 hour ahead. Hold at room temperature.*

Bake the pasta 10 minutes. Uncover and bake until the cheeses are melted and the dish is heated through, about 7 minutes.

NOTE The taste of fresh sage does much to make the dish successful; if you can't locate it, don't resort to the dried version. Substitute, instead, another full-flavored, fresh herb (oregano, marjoram, or rosemary) or do without.

*Serves 6*

## FRESH BUCKWHEAT NOODLES *(PEZZOCCHERI)*

**F**OR THOSE WHO DO make their own fresh pasta (you know who you are), this is a sound addition to the repertoire. The deep brown color and nutty, whole-grain flavor of this pasta make it a unique and delicious partner to pork, wild mushrooms, or leeks. Look for buckwheat flour at a health food store or see Cook's Sources.

*3 large eggs, at room temperature*
*¼ teaspoon salt*
*1 cup buckwheat flour (see Cook's Sources)*
*1¼ cups (about) unbleached all-purpose flour*

In a small bowl whisk together the eggs and salt. In the bowl of a food processor fitted with the metal blade, combine the buckwheat flour and 1 cup of the unbleached flour. Process briefly to blend. With the machine running, slowly pour in the eggs. Continue to process until a lumpy dough forms, about 10 seconds. Turn the dough (it will be damp and crumbly) out onto the work surface and knead, flouring it lightly with additional unbleached flour to prevent sticking, until the dough is smooth, 3 to 5 minutes. Wrap the dough airtight in plastic wrap and let it stand at room temperature for 45 minutes.

Cut the dough into quarters and flatten each with your palm. Adjust the rollers of a pasta machine to their widest setting and roll each piece of dough through the machine. Fold each strip of pasta dough in half crosswise and roll it through the machine again. Reset the rollers to the next narrower setting, fold the dough in half crosswise, and run each piece through the machine twice. Adjust the machine to the next to the last setting and repeat the above procedure. The resulting pasta should be slightly thicker than typical fettuccine. Let the pasta dough rest at room temperature, uncovered, for 20 minutes.

Using the pasta machine's fettuccine cutter, cut the pasta into long strips and trim the strips 5 or 6 inches long. Toss the noodles with additional white flour to prevent sticking and spread out on a baking *sheet. The pasta can be used at once or prepared up to 3 days ahead. When completely dry, wrap the noodles in plastic wrap and store at room temperature.*

━● *Serves 6*

✦✦✦✦✦✦✦✦✦✦✦✦✦✦✦✦✦✦✦✦✦✦✦✦✦✦✦✦✦✦✦✦✦✦✦✦✦✦✦✦

▀▄▀▄▀▄▀▄▀▄▀▄▀▄▀▄▀▄▀▄▀▄▀▄▀▄▀▄▀▄▀▄▀▄▀▄▀▄▀

## CHINATOWN CARRY-OUT DUCK AND PASTA SALAD WITH JALAPEÑO-SESAME DRESSING

✦✦✦✦✦✦✦✦✦✦

**DRESSING**

1 medium fresh jalapeño
2 garlic cloves, peeled
1 tablespoon minced fresh
   ginger
1 egg
¼ cup red wine vinegar
3 tablespoons soy sauce
1 tablespoon sugar
1 tablespoon dark sesame
   oil, from roasted seeds
¾ cup peanut or corn oil

**SALAD**

1 package (about 8 ounces)
   soba, Japanese
   buckwheat noodles (see
   Cook's Sources)
Salt
2 tablespoons dark sesame
   oil, from roasted seeds
1 tablespoon peanut or
   corn oil
2 scallions, trimmed and
   sliced thin
1 large ripe mango
1 Peking duck, cut into
   bite-size pieces

**B**Y ALL THE LAWS of cookbook writing, including two buckwheat pasta recipes back-to-back is bad planning—but this recipe and the preceding one are so different, and so good, they both deserve to find their way into print.

I think crisp-skinned Peking duck is the finest of all possible duck preparations, and since the process is awkward to duplicate at home and the restaurant version often costs the same as starting from scratch, I never hesitate to star carry-out Peking duck in low-labor meals.

Prepare the thick, spicy dressing the day before, stop on the way home to pick up the duck, and spend only 30 minutes putting together the salad. (Be certain to ask that the restaurant cut the duck into bite-size pieces—those Chinatown cleavers will do the job far better than you can.)

No Chinatown? See my alternate roasting method below. Not Peking duck by any means, but it will result in crisp, relatively fat-free duck and make a good salad.

•••  •••

*For the dressing* Over the open flame of a gas burner, or under a preheated broiler, char the jalapeño (impale it with a fork for easier handling over an open flame) until the skin blackens and blisters. Cool to room temperature and remove the stem.

In a food processor fitted with the metal blade combine the unpeeled jalapeño, garlic, ginger, egg, vinegar, soy sauce, and sugar and process until smooth, about 1 minute. With the machine on, dribble in the oils in a slow, steady stream. Adjust the seasoning. *The dressing can be prepared up to 1 day ahead. Refrigerate, covered, allowing the dressing to return to room temperature before proceeding.*

*For the salad* Add the *soba* to a pot of lightly salted, boiling water and cook according to package directions until just tender, about 5 minutes. Drain immediately, rinse well under cold water, and drain again. In a bowl toss the *soba* with the oils and half of the scallions.

Divide the *soba* among 4 serving plates. Cutting down to the pit, through the skin and flesh, quarter the mango. Remove the skin segments, slice each quarter into thirds, and release the slices from the pit with a small knife. Arrange the duck pieces and mango slices over the noodles. Drizzle the dressing over the salads and sprinkle them with the remaining scallion before serving.

**●** *Serves 4*

● ● ● ● ● ● ● ● ● ● ● ● ● ● ● ● ● ● ● ● ● ● ● ● ● ● ● ● ● ● ● ● ● ● ● ● ● ● ● ● ● ●

## SORT OF
## CHINESE ROAST DUCK

♦ ♦ ♦ ♦ ♦ ♦ ♦ ♦ ♦ ♦

Preheat the oven to 325 degrees F. Pull all the loose fat from the duck cavity. Prick the skin all over with a fork. In a small bowl stir together the soy sauce, molasses, and sesame oil.

On a rack in a shallow baking dish roast the duck for 2 hours, occasionally removing fat from the pan and pricking the duck skin.

*1 duckling (4½ to 5 pounds)*
*3 tablespoons soy sauce*
*2 tablespoons unsulfured molasses*
*1 tablespoon dark sesame oil, from roasted seeds*

Brush the duck with one-third of the soy mixture and continue roasting, brushing with the remaining soy mixture every 10 minutes, until the duck is cooked through and is crisp and shiny, 30 to 40 more minutes. Remove the duck from the oven and cool to room temperature. *The duck can be roasted up to 3 hours in advance and reserved at room temperature, or it can be roasted 1 day ahead and refrigerated, covered. Bring the duck to room temperature before using.*

—● *Serves 4*

## LAMB AND GOAT CHEESE ENCHILADAS WITH CHILE-PEANUT SAUCE

**B**OWLS OF RED CHILE-SPRINKLED peanuts are common Mexican bar snacks and directly inspired the rich and spicy sauce on these enchiladas. The combination goes well with lamb (although pork would be a delicious substitute), and the salty tang of mild chèvre completes what turns out to be a deeply complex tasting entrée.

To the right food-loving friends this is as show-stopping a main course as a leg of lamb would be to a more conservative crowd—which is my way of justifying what might otherwise seem to be a lot of work for "mere" enchiladas. Start with Chunky Guacamole (page 30) or half-portions of Coconut Shrimp (page 358), and follow the enchiladas with crisp greens with Fresh Oregano Dressing (page 80). A smooth amber beer, like Dos Equis, will cool the subtle fires.

*2½ pounds lamb stewing meat (from the shoulder, for example), trimmed of external fat and tissue*

*4 cups canned chicken broth or homemade stock, diluted with 1½ cups water*

*¼ cup olive oil*

*½ cup finely chopped yellow onion*

*3 garlic cloves, peeled and minced*

*⅓ cup unbleached all-purpose flour*

*4 teaspoons mild, plain chile powder (see Cook's Sources)*

*2 teaspoons ground cumin, from toasted seeds (see notes, page 66)*

Preheat the oven to 400 degrees F. In a 4½- or 5-quart Dutch oven combine the lamb and diluted chicken broth. Cover and bake 45 minutes. Uncover, stir, and bake another 50 to 60 minutes, or until the lamb is very tender. Cool to room temperature. With a slotted spoon, remove the lamb from the broth. Shred it. Strain the broth (there should be about 4 cups). Refrigerate the broth, covered, and the lamb, well wrapped, for 24 hours.

Remove the hardened fats from the surface of the broth. In a 2½- or 3-quart saucepan over medium heat warm the oil. Add the onions and garlic, cover, and cook, stirring once or twice, until tender, about 15 minutes. Uncover, stir in the flour, chile powder, cumin, and oregano and cook, stirring constantly, 3 minutes. Slowly whisk in the broth. Bring to a boil, lower the heat, and cook, uncovered, skimming, 40 minutes, or until the sauce is thickened and reduced by about one-quarter. Remove from the heat and whisk in the peanut butter. Adjust the seasoning. Cool to room temperature. *The sauce can be prepared to this point up to 3 hours ahead.*

Preheat the oven to 400 degrees F.

In a medium-size bowl combine the shredded lamb, the pickled jalapeños, and 1½ cups of the lamb sauce. One at a time, dip each of 4 tortillas in the remaining lamb sauce and set each tortilla in a round, single-serving gratin dish. Spread half of the lamb mixture over the 4 tortillas, dividing it evenly. Dip 4 more tortillas in the lamb sauce and lay them over the meat mixture in each dish. Top the second layer of tortillas with the remaining lamb filling. Dip the remaining 4 tortillas in the lamb sauce and lay them over the meat-layered tortillas. Pour any remaining sauce over the top tortillas.

Crumble the goat cheese over the enchiladas and cover each dish tightly with foil. *The enchiladas can be assembled to this point up to 1 hour before baking.* Bake 15 minutes. Uncover and bake another 5 to 7 minutes, or until the cheese is lightly colored and the enchiladas are steaming hot and tender. Sprinkle each enchilada with the diced onion and serve immediately.

*Serves 4*

*1 teaspoon dried oregano, crumbled*

*⅓ cup chunky peanut butter*

*6 pickled jalapeños, finely diced*

*12 corn tortillas, 6 inches each*

*4 ounces soft, mild chèvre, such as Montrachet*

*½ cup diced sweet red onion*

## SPARERIBS WITH
## MOLASSES-MUSTARD GLAZE

♦ ♦ ♦ ♦ ♦ ♦ ♦ ♦ ♦

2 sides pork spareribs
    (about 6 pounds),
    cracked by the butcher
Salt
Freshly ground black
    pepper
¾ cup Molasses-Mustard
    Glaze (recipe follows)

Possibly the perfect glaze for ribs—and certainly a change from the typical tomato-based sauces. If you find you like it a lot, make a double or triple batch: It keeps well in the refrigerator and is good on chicken or lamb, or as a glaze for a big country ham.

Serve the ribs with Simple Orange Slaw (page 43) and Buttermilk Biscuits (page 27).

♦ ♦ ♦  ♦ ♦ ♦

Preheat the oven to 350 degrees F. Cut each side of ribs in half. Season each half generously with salt and pepper and wrap tightly in foil. Lay the foil packages on 1 or 2 baking sheets and bake about 70 minutes, or until the ribs are very tender. Open the packages and cool the ribs to room temperature. *Prepare to this point up to 2 days ahead. Discard the juices and refrigerate the ribs, tightly wrapped in plastic.*

Preheat the oven to 400 degrees F. Cut the ribs into 2-rib sections. Line two jelly-roll pans with foil. Brush the ribs generously with Molasses-Mustard Glaze and arrange the sections meaty side up on the foil-lined sheets. Bake 5 minutes. Repeat the glazing process twice more, allowing the ribs to bake 10 minutes after the final coating of glaze. Serve the ribs hot or warm.

━━● *Serves 4*

♦ ♦ ♦ ♦ ♦ ♦ ♦ ♦ ♦ ♦ ♦ ♦ ♦ ♦ ♦ ♦ ♦ ♦ ♦ ♦ ♦ ♦ ♦ ♦ ♦ ♦ ♦ ♦ ♦ ♦ ♦ ♦ ♦ ♦ ♦ ♦ ♦ ♦ ♦ ♦

½ cup unsulfured
    molasses
⅓ cup dark brown sugar,
    packed
⅓ cup cider vinegar
¼ cup prepared Dijon-style
    mustard

## MOLASSES-MUSTARD GLAZE

♦ ♦ ♦ ♦ ♦ ♦ ♦ ♦ ♦ ♦

In a medium-size, heavy saucepan whisk together all the ingredients. Set the pan over medium heat and bring to a boil, stirring. Lower the heat and simmer, uncovered, for 5 minutes. Transfer to a heatproof container and cool to room temperature. Cover and refrigerate. The sauce will keep several weeks.

━━● *Makes about 1½ cups*

◆◆◆◆◆◆◆◆◆◆◆◆◆◆◆◆◆◆◆◆◆◆◆◆◆◆◆◆◆◆◆◆◆◆◆◆◆◆◆◆◆◆◆

*¼ cup prepared coarse-grained mustard*
*1 tablespoon dry mustard*
*1½ teaspoons Tabasco sauce*
*1 teaspoon dried thyme, crumbled*
*½ teaspoon salt*

## PORK SCALLOPS WITH RAISINS AND VINEGAR

◆◆◆◆◆◆◆◆◆

**T**HIS IS A QUICK little sauté, belying the myth that pork dishes are always sturdy, long-simmered affairs. It is made with pork tenderloin, as tender and flavorful as veal, but much more affordable, and the sauce is quickly concocted of such pantry staples as chicken broth, raisins, and vinegar. Tenderloins frequently come sealed in ryovac and will keep well, letting you turn out a fairly spontaneous but elegant meal. Team the scallops with Pilaf of Wild Rice with Leeks and Mushrooms (page 76).

◆◆◆  ◆◆◆

In a small saucepan bring the chicken broth to a boil. Pour it over the raisins in a small bowl and let stand until they are plump and soft, about 30 minutes.

Starting with the larger end of the tenderloin, slice off 6 to 8 pieces ½ inch thick. (Reserve the remaining tapered end of the tenderloin for another use.) One at a time, place the pork pieces between 2 sheets of wax paper. With a meat hammer or the bottom of a skillet or saucepan gently flatten the pork into 3-inch rounds.

In a medium-size skillet melt 2 tablespoons of the butter over moderate heat until foaming. Dredge the scallops in the flour and shake off the excess. Sauté half of the pork scallops, turning them once, until slightly browned, about 4 minutes per side. Transfer to a plate. Repeat with the remaining scallops.

*⅔ cup canned chicken broth or homemade stock*
*¼ cup mixed dark and golden raisins*
*1 pork tenderloin (about ¾ pound)*
*6 tablespoons unsalted butter*
*½ cup unbleached all-purpose flour*
*¼ cup sherry wine vinegar*
*⅛ teaspoon salt*
*¼ teaspoon freshly ground white pepper*

Add the vinegar to the skillet and raise the heat to high. Bring the vinegar to a boil and cook hard, stirring and scraping up browned bits from the bottom of the pan, until the vinegar is reduced to a thick, syrupy glaze, about 5 minutes.

Stir in the raisins and chicken broth and bring to a boil. Return the pork scallops (and any juices from the plate) to the skillet. Season with the salt and pepper. Lower the heat, cover the skillet, and simmer 5 minutes.

Divide the pork scallops among heated plates. Set the skillet over very low heat and whisk in the remaining butter, 1 tablespoon at a time. Adjust the seasoning, adding an additional splash of vinegar, if desired, and pour the sauce over scallops. Serve immediately.

*Serves 2*

## MEATLOAF WITH SUN-DRIED TOMATOES

¼ cup olive oil, preferably from sun-dried tomatoes

3 cups finely diced yellow onion

1 cup finely diced celery

6 garlic cloves, peeled and minced

2 teaspoons dried basil, crumbled

2 teaspoons dried oregano, crumbled

2 teaspoons dried thyme, crumbled

3 pounds lean ground beef

IF THE SUN-DRIED TOMATOES are the catsup of the eighties, it seems perfectly natural to stir them into a meatloaf, especially when the results are this tasty. Nothing is so reassuring as a cache of leftover meatloaf waiting in the refrigerator for comforting suppers or demon-chasing midnight snacks, and the recipe makes plenty. Serve some of it hot with Parmesan Mashed Potatoes (page 284) and Vegetables with Herbed Butter Sauce (recipe follows), and enjoy the rest cold on crusty hard rolls with Garlic Mayonnaise (page 295).

In a medium-size skillet over moderate heat warm the oil. Add the onions, celery, garlic, basil, oregano, and thyme and cook, covered, stirring once or twice, until the vegetables are tender, about 15 minutes. Cool slightly.

Position a rack in the middle of the oven and preheat to 350 degrees F. In a large bowl combine the ground beef, the sausage, and the sautéed vegetables and their juices. Stir in the tomatoes, parsley, eggs, bread crumbs, salt, and pepper and mix thoroughly with your hands. Form the meat into two oval loaves and transfer them to a large, shallow baking dish.

Bake, occasionally pouring off the accumulated juices from the pan, 1½ hours, or until an instant-reading thermometer inserted in the meat registers 160 degrees F.

Serve hot or warm. Allow the chilled meatloaf to return to room temperature before serving.

● *Serves 12*

◆◆◆◆◆◆◆◆◆◆◆◆◆◆◆◆◆◆◆◆◆◆◆◆◆◆◆◆◆◆◆◆◆◆◆◆◆◆◆◆◆◆◆◆◆◆

*2 pounds sweet Italian-style sausage, casings removed*

*1 cup coarsely chopped oil-packed sun-dried tomatoes (see Cook's Sources)*

*1 cup minced Italian parsley*

*4 eggs, beaten*

*½ cup fine, dry bread crumbs*

*1 tablespoon salt*

*1 tablespoon freshly ground black pepper*

# VEGETABLES WITH HERBED BUTTER SAUCE

◆◆◆◆◆◆◆◆◆◆

W E HAVE FORGOTTEN the simplicity of fresh vegetables napped with butter. My father grew up on a dairy, surrounded by all the good things that abundant, sweet, fresh milk provides, so margarine was forbidden in our house. Even when the vegetables were less than astonishing, butter always made them taste good. Fresh herbs may not be as easy to come by as good vegetables or sweet butter, but when they can be found, their judicious addition to this mostly do-ahead sauté adds dimension. The vegetables, of course, can vary with market availability from the obvious (sweet peppers and broccoli) to the less familiar (wild mushrooms and sugar snap peas). Here is a rough blueprint.

*Salt*

*4 medium carrots,
    trimmed, peeled, and cut
    on the bias into ½-inch
    pieces*

*½ head of cauliflower,
    trimmed and cut into
    small florets*

*½ pound green beans,
    trimmed and cut on the
    bias into 1-inch pieces*

*6 tablespoons unsalted
    butter*

*1 medium onion, peeled
    and finely diced*

*1 garlic clove peeled and
    minced*

*1½ tablespoons minced
    fresh herbs, such as
    oregano, thyme,
    marjoram, or rosemary,
    or ¼ cup minced fresh
    basil*

*Freshly ground black
    pepper*

*1 tablespoon fresh lemon
    juice, strained*

Bring a pot of water to a boil. Add 1 tablespoon of salt and when the water returns to a boil stir in the carrots and cauliflower. Cook, stirring once or twice, until the vegetables are just tender, 7 to 8 minutes. Drain and transfer to a bowl of ice water. Cool thoroughly and drain completely.

Bring a pot of water to a boil. Add 1 tablespoon of salt and when the water returns to a boil stir in the green beans. Cook, stirring once or twice, until the beans are just tender, about 5 minutes. Drain and transfer to a bowl of ice water. Cool completely and drain thoroughly. *The vegetables can be prepared up to 1 day ahead. Wrap well and refrigerate.*

In a large skillet over low heat melt the butter. Add the onion and garlic and cook, covered, stirring once or twice, 7 minutes. Add the carrots, cauliflower, and the green beans, raise the heat, and cook, tossing and stirring, until the vegetables are heated through and well coated with butter, about 3 minutes. Stir in the herbs. Season the vegetables with salt and pepper to taste. Remove the skillet from the heat, stir in the lemon juice, and serve immediately.

■—● *Serves 6 to 8*

# PARSNIPS BRAISED WITH HAM AND ORANGE JUICE

W HAT'S YOUR FIRST food memory? Most of us don't have strong recollections of bottled formula or baby food from a jar, giving credence to my theory that all infants are born with innate good taste and only lose it later in life. James Beard recalls, in *Delights and Prejudices,* that on all fours he crawled into the pantry and devoured an onion, "Skin and all." You don't have to be Proust to know these early culinary experiments can inform a lifetime of eating and remembering.

There's a wonderful simplicity in that onion of Beard's. My own earliest recollection is a little more prosaic, but no less intense. Across the street from my house lived an elderly lady named Emma Brandon, called "Brandy." At her invitation, and with my mother's permission, and with the two of them watching from their respective sides, I was allowed to cross the street. Brandy's home (small house, big porch), sat in beds of lily of the valley. Inside it was full of dark old furniture and the secret smells of someone else's life. I was five and she was probably eighty-five, and I suppose we dined on various things, but the purpose of the journey and the object of my interest was always the same: Parsnips. She cooked them up as simply as an eighty-five-year-old would, and I can't explain the appeal of their odd, silky texture and ripe, bittersweet taste to a five-year-old, but appeal they did. I ate my fill of them then, and still do, and though this is a gussied-up approach to braising these savory roots, I'd like to think Brandy would approve.

*4 tablespoons unsalted butter*

*¼ pound smoky, baked ham, trimmed and cut into ¼-inch dice*

*1 pound small parsnips (see note), trimmed and peeled*

*1 cup canned chicken broth or homemade stock*

*½ cup fresh orange juice, strained*

*1 tablespoon light brown sugar, packed*

*Salt and freshly ground black pepper*

*2 tablespoons finely minced Italian parsley*

Preheat the oven to 350 degrees F.

In a flameproof baking dish over low heat melt the butter. Add the ham, raise the heat slightly, and cook, stirring once or twice, until the ham is lightly browned, about 10 minutes.

Add the parsnips, chicken broth, and juice to the baking dish. Sprinkle with the brown sugar. Cover the dish and bake until the parsnips are just tender, 25 to 30 minutes.

With a slotted spoon, transfer the parsnips to a warmed serving dish. Set the baking dish over high heat, bring to a boil, and cook hard, stirring often, 5 minutes, or until the liquid is slightly reduced. Season to taste with salt, sprinkle generously with pepper, and pour the liquid over the parsnips. Sprinkle with the parsley and serve immediately.

NOTE Only later in life did I learn parsnips were once as widely eaten as the potato is now. Their fall from grace was primarily due to their aggressive flavor, one I crave when the wind turns cold. Oversized, they become tough and stringy; the best-testing are small to medium and have been left in the ground past an early frost, to turn their starches into sugar.

*Serves 4*

◆◆◆◆◆◆◆◆◆◆◆◆◆◆◆◆◆◆◆◆◆◆◆◆◆◆◆◆◆◆◆◆◆◆◆◆◆◆◆◆◆◆◆◆◆◆◆◆

## RASPBERRY-THYME VINEGAR

◆◆◆◆◆◆◆◆◆

4 cups imported
   champagne or white
   wine vinegar
⅓ cup sugar
1 cup fresh raspberries,
   picked over, rinsed, and
   patted dry plus
   additional berries, as
   garnish
4 sprigs fresh thyme,
   rinsed and patted dry
   plus additional sprigs,
   as garnish

I CAN'T SAY WHERE the idea of combining raspberries and thyme came from, but it's a pairing I like, and one that seems to make a kind of rustic sense, especially in a sauce for chicken or other birds.

The shelves of all kinds of food stores are awash these days with flavored vinegars, some of them actually made of high-quality vinegar, flavored with fresh and genuine ingredients. Still, for an atypical combination of flavors, and to be certain that you are using the highest-quality flavored vinegar possible, make your own.

The infusion process, whereby best-quality purchased vinegar is warmed, then steeped for a few days with flavorings, is quick and easy. The results will cost less than a store-bought product, and strained and garnished with fresh whole berries, strips of citrus peel, sprigs of herbs, and so on, the vinegars make unique gifts—and, if you experiment wisely, delicious ones.

◆◆◆  ◆◆◆

In a nonreactive saucepan combine the vinegar and sugar and bring almost to a boil, stirring to dissolve the sugar. Place the berries and thyme in a 5-cup heatproof, nonreactive container and pour the vinegar over them. Cool to room temperature, cover, and let stand at room temperature for at least 48 hours and up to 2 weeks.

Strain the vinegar, discarding the softened berries and discolored thyme. Transfer the vinegar to a storage bottle (or to a decorative decanter), add a few fresh raspberries and a sprig of thyme as garnish, and store in a cool place, out of direct sunlight. The vinegar will keep for a year or longer.

*Makes about 1 quart*

◆ ◆ ◆ ◆ ◆ ◆ ◆ ◆ ◆ ◆ ◆ ◆ ◆ ◆ ◆ ◆ ◆ ◆ ◆ ◆ ◆ ◆ ◆ ◆ ◆ ◆ ◆ ◆ ◆ ◆ ◆ ◆ ◆ ◆ ◆ ◆ ◆ ◆ ◆ ◆ ◆ ◆ ◆

## CRANBERRY–RED PEPPER CHUTNEY

◆ ◆ ◆ ◆ ◆ ◆ ◆ ◆ ◆

**O**NE REASON THE SHELVES of gourmet shops are so clogged with chutneys of every color and flavor combination is that they are relatively easy to make. Just combine and simmer, what could be easier? Many commercial chutneys, though, are overspiced and cooked far too long, yielding thick and unappetizingly brown purees. Here's a colorful, chunky exception, both a condiment and a garnish, and delicious when paired with smoked meat or poultry and sharp cheese. Keep some on hand for yourself and pack the rest into attractive jars for holiday gift-giving.

*2 cups cider vinegar*
*2½ cups sugar*
*2 tablespoons yellow mustard seeds*
*2 teaspoons dried red pepper flakes*
*1 tablespoon salt*
*1½ pounds large, thick-fleshed, sweet red peppers, stemmed, cored, and cut into ¼-inch dice*
*2 bags (12 ounces each) cranberries, rinsed and picked over*

◆ ◆ ◆  ◆ ◆ ◆

In a heavy, nonreactive pan stir together the vinegar, sugar, mustard seeds, pepper flakes, and salt. Set over medium heat and bring to a boil, stirring often to dissolve the sugar.

Add the sweet peppers and cranberries, bring to a boil, then lower the heat and simmer, uncovered, stirring occasionally, about 40 minutes, or until bright red, thick, and shiny.

Pack the chutney into hot, sterilized jars and seal. (Sterilize and seal the jars according to the manufacturer's directions.) Process 15 minutes in a hot water bath. *For short-term storage the chutney can simply be spooned into a large, clean jar and kept, covered, in the refrigerator. It will last for months.*

*Makes about 5 cups*

♦♦♦♦♦♦♦♦♦♦♦♦♦♦♦♦♦♦♦♦♦♦♦♦♦♦♦♦♦♦♦♦♦♦♦♦♦♦♦♦♦♦♦

## PLUM AND APPLE BUTTER

♦♦♦♦♦♦♦♦♦

THIS IS A WONDERFUL use of late summer fruit. For maximum color, flavor, and pectin, the fruits are not peeled and the apples are not cored. If you don't have a food mill, preferably a stainless steel one with three interchangeable blades, you really should, and this recipe is the perfect excuse to invest in one (see Cook's Sources).

♦♦♦  ♦♦♦

*2 pounds slightly underripe, unpeeled red plums, such as Santa Rosa, quartered and pitted*

*2 pounds unpeeled, uncored Jonathan or McIntosh apples, stemmed and quartered*

*2 cups fresh, unfiltered, unsweetened apple juice*

*2 cups sugar*

*2 teaspoons cinnamon*

*2 teaspoons vanilla*

In a heavy, nonreactive saucepan combine the plums, apples, and apple juice. Set over medium heat and bring to a boil. Lower the heat, partially cover, and simmer, stirring occasionally, 25 minutes. Uncover and cook, stirring occasionally, until the apples are very tender, 20 to 30 minutes. Cool slightly.

Force the mixture through a food mill fitted with the medium blade, discarding the peels and seeds. Return the puree to the pan. Stir in the sugar and cinnamon. Set the pan over medium heat and bring to a boil, stirring constantly. Lower the heat and simmer briskly until the plum and apple butter is thick and glossy, stirring often, about 40 minutes. Remove from the heat and stir in the vanilla. Spoon the hot butter into hot, sterilized jars. (Sterilize the jars according to manufacturer's instructions.) Cool, cover, and refrigerate. *The butter can be stored in the refrigerator up to 3 weeks, or it can be sealed (according to manufacturer's instructions), processed in a water bath for 15 minutes, and kept 1 year.*

**━●** *Makes 3 pints*

✦✦✦✦✦✦✦✦✦✦✦✦✦✦✦✦✦✦✦✦✦✦✦✦✦✦✦✦✦✦✦✦✦✦✦✦✦✦✦✦✦

## DARK CHOCOLATE–RASPBERRY MOUSSE

✦✦✦✦✦✦✦✦✦

**T**HE TART RED bits of raw raspberry and the crunch of seeds against the rich chocolate background make this a sensational dessert, at once earthy and elegant. Chocolate mousse, like many of the better things in life, is sometimes dismissed as *déclassé*, but when I make this—and I serve it often—sophisticated folks just clean their plates and ask for more.

✦✦✦  ✦✦✦

In a small bowl crush the raspberries roughly with a fork. Stir in the sugar and the *framboise* and let the mixture stand at room temperature.

Make a modified double boiler by setting a large, heavy ceramic bowl over a saucepan of water. The bottom of the bowl should just touch the water.

Place the chocolate and butter in the bowl and set the double boiler over low heat, about 10 minutes, stirring occasionally as the chocolate melts. Do not let the water boil.

Meanwhile, whip the cream to the point *just before* it will hold soft peaks and refrigerate.

Separate the eggs, stirring the yolks into the raspberry mixture and placing the whites in a medium-size bowl. Whisk the whites to the point *just before* they will hold soft peaks.

*1½ cups fresh raspberries, picked over, plus additional berries, as garnish*

*¼ cup sugar*

*2 tablespoons framboise (raspberry eau-de-vie), see note*

*10 ounces bittersweet chocolate (see Cook's Sources), chopped*

*4 tablespoons unsalted butter*

*2 cups whipping cream, chilled*

*3 large eggs, at room temperature*

Transfer the bowl with the melted chocolate to the work surface. Stir in the raspberry mixture all at once. Stir in 1 cup of the whipped cream. Fold in the egg whites until just incorporated. Spoon the mousse into a large bowl or into individual serving cups and chill, covered with plastic wrap, until firm, 2 hours for individual cups and 6 hours for the large bowl. *The mousse can be prepared up to 2 days ahead.*

Whip the remaining whipped cream to soft peaks. Garnish the mousse with the whipped cream and perfect, beautiful raspberries.

NOTE A bottle of *framboise,* the "water of life" distilled from raspberries, can seem like a pricey purchase for only 2 tablespoons—unless you've tasted it. It is colorless, but Francine the caterer exclaimed, on experiencing it for the first time, that she had "Never tasted anything so red." A bottle will keep a long while, unless you make a lot of mousse or develop the pleasant habit of offering guests a pony of chilled *framboise* to sip with after-dinner coffee.

*Makes about 1 quart, serving 8 to 10*

# COOK'S SOURCES

+ + + + + + + + +

MANY MORE CHOICE INGREDIENTS are offered for the cook's pleasure than ever before, but readers still lament that some essential ingredients are hard to locate. My experience is that many cooks just haven't fully explored their local markets, and, assuming the worst, are frequently mistaken about what is and is not available. Give your town's specialty merchants the benefit of the doubt, lobby them to stock harder-to-find items, and when they do so, support them by buying. When all else fails, resort to mail order. Even in New York, where pretty much everything anyone would want to eat is for sale, sending away for special ingredients is still a Christmas morning kind of thrill, and I order often. Here are the sources I recommend.

## SOURCES

1. Dean and Deluca
   560 Broadway
   New York, NY 10012
   800-221-7714
   In New York State,
   212-431-1691

2. Balducci's
   11-02 Queens Plaza South
   Long Island City, NY 11101
   800-822-1444
   In New York State,
   800-247-2450

3. Walnut Acres Organic Farms
   Penns Creek, PA 17862
   717-837-0601

4. Maid of Scandinavia
   3244 Raleigh Avenue
   Minneapolis, MN 55416
   800-328-6722
   In Minnesota,
   800-851-1121

5. Williams-Sonoma
   P.O. Box 7456
   San Francisco, CA
   94120-7456
   415-421-4242

6. Sunnyland Farms, Inc.
   P.O. Box 8200
   Albany, GA 31706-8200
   912-883-3085

7. Everett and Kathryn Palmer
   Box 246
   Waitsfield, VT 05673
   802-496-3696

8. Texas Wild Game
   Cooperative
   P.O. Box 530
   Ingram, TX 78025
   512-367-5875

9. Vella Cheese Company
   P.O. Box 191-315
   Sonoma, CA 95476
   800-848-0505

10. Delftree Corporation
    234 Union Street
    North Adams, MA 01247
    413-664-4907

11. Earthy Delights
    618 N. Seymour Street
    Lansing, MI 48933
    800-367-4709
    In Michigan, 517-371-9089

12. The Mozzarella Company
    2944 Elm Street
    Dallas, TX 75226
    214-741-4072

13. The Game Exchange
    107 Quint Street
    San Francisco, CA 94124
    415-282-7878

14. American Spoon Foods
    411 East Lake Street
    Petoskey, MI 48770
    800-222-5886
    In Michigan,
    800-327-7984

15. Santa Cruz Chile and Spice Co.
    P.O. Box 177
    Tumacacori, AZ 85640
    602-398-2591

16. Embassa Foods
    1048 Burgrove Road
    Carson, CA 90746
    213-537-1200

17. The Blue Corn Connection
    8812 Fourth Street NW
    Albuquerque, NM 87114
    505-897-2412

18. Manchester Farms
    P.O. Box 97
    Dalzell, SC 29040
    803-469-2588

19. D'Artagnan, Inc.
    399-419 St. Paul Avenue
    Jersey City, NJ 07306
    800-327-8246
    In New Jersey,
    201-792-0748

20. Wolferman's
    P.O. Box 15913
    Lenexa, KS 66215-5913
    800-255-0169

21. Durham–Night Bird Game
    and Poultry Company
    650 San Mateo Avenue
    San Bruno, CA 94006
    415-873-5035

22. Burger's Smokehouse
    RFD 3 Box 126
    Highway 87 South
    California, MO 65018-9903
    314-796-4111

23. Early's Honey Stand
    P.O. Box K
    Spring Hill, TN 37174-0911
    800-523-2015

24. Ducktrap River Fish Farm
    Box 378
    Lincolnville, ME
    207-763-3960

25. Aidell's Sausage Company
    1575 Minnesota Street
    San Francisco, CA 94107
    415-285-6660

26. Virgil L. Morse & Son
    Waldoboro, ME 04572
    207-832-5569

27. Maytag Dairy Farms
    P.O. Box 806
    Newton, IA
    800-247-2458
    In Iowa, 800-258-2437

28. Neuske-Hillcrest Farm
    Meats
    Highways 29 and 45
    Wittenberg, WI 54499
    800-382-2266

29. Craigston Cheese Company

45 Dodge's Road
Wenham, MA 01984
508-468-7497

30. Hollow Road Farms
    Stuyvesant, NY 12173
    518-758-7214

◆ ◆ ◆ ◆ ◆ ◆ ◆ ◆ ◆ ◆ ◆

## INGREDIENTS AND EQUIPMENT

(Numbers following items indicate the mail order sources, above, that carry that product.)

*Ancho* chiles
   1, 2

Arborio rice
   1, 2

Black walnuts
   6

Blue cornmeal
   1, 2, 17

Brine-cured hams,
   ready to eat
   1, 2, 22, 23, 28

Buckwheat flour
   1, 2, 3

Buckwheat groats
   3

Bulgur
   1, 2, 3

Cheeses, general and specific
   1, 2, 9, 12, 27, 29, 30

Craigston Camembert
   1, 2, 29

Dried Cherries
   1, 2, 14

Dry-cured country hams,
   ready to eat
   1, 2, 22, 23

Dutch process cocoa
   1, 2, 5

Embassa *chipotles*
   1, 16

Exotic and wild mushrooms
   1, 2, 10, 11, 14

Fish grilling basket
   1

Fresh mozzarella
   1, 2, 12

Fresh sauerkraut
   26

Hungarian sweet paprika
   1, 2

Imported chocolate
   1, 2, 4, 5

Irish oats
   1, 2, 5

Maple syrup
   1, 2, 3, 7

Maytag blue cheese
1, 2, 27

Olives
1, 2, 5

Pancetta
1, 2

Plain chile powder
15

Quail and/or squab
1, 2, 18, 19, 21

Saffron
1, 2

San Remo sun-dried tomatoes
1

Sausages
1, 2, 8, 19, 22, 23, 25

Smoked fish
1, 2, 5, 24

Soba noodles
1

Stainless steel food mill
1

Vacuum-packed roasted chestnuts
1, 2, 5

Vella Sonoma Jack cheese
1, 2, 9

Venison
1, 2, 8, 13, 19, 21

Wolferman's muffins
1, 2, 20

# METRIC CONVERSION CHART

♦ ♦ ♦ ♦ ♦ ♦ ♦ ♦ ♦ ♦ ♦

## LIQUID AND DRY MEASURE EQUIVALENCIES

| Customary | Metric | |
|---|---|---|
| ¼ teaspoon | 1.25 | milliliters |
| ½ teaspoon | 2.5 | milliliters |
| 1 teaspoon | 5 | milliliters |
| 1 tablespoon | 15 | milliliters |
| 1 fluid ounce | 30 | milliliters |
| ¼ cup | 60 | milliliters |
| ⅓ cup | 80 | milliliters |
| ½ cup | 120 | milliliters |
| 1 cup | 240 | milliliters |
| 1 pint (2 cups) | 480 | milliliters |
| 1 quart (4 cups, 32 ounces) | 960 | milliliters (.96 liter) |
| 1 gallon (4 quarts) | 3.84 | liters |
| 1 ounce (by weight) | 28 | grams |
| ¼ pound (4 ounces) | 114 | grams |
| 1 pound (16 ounces) | 454 | grams |
| 2.2 pounds | 1 | kilogram (1000 grams) |

♦ ♦ ♦ ♦ ♦ ♦ ♦ ♦ ♦ ♦ ♦

## OVEN TEMPERATURE EQUIVALENCIES

| Description | °Fahrenheit | °Celsius |
|---|---|---|
| Cool | 200 | 90 |
| Very slow | 250 | 120 |
| Slow | 300–325 | 150–160 |
| Moderately slow | 325–350 | 160–180 |
| Moderate | 350–375 | 180–190 |
| Moderately hot | 375–400 | 190–200 |
| Hot | 400–450 | 200–230 |
| Very hot | 450–500 | 230–260 |

♦♦♦♦♦♦♦♦♦♦♦♦♦♦♦♦♦♦♦♦♦♦♦♦♦♦♦♦♦♦♦♦♦♦♦♦♦♦♦♦♦

MICHAEL MCLAUGHLIN, a Colorado native, moved to New York City ten years ago; his goal to become a food writer. A year later he worked at an Upper West Side gourmet shop called The Silver Palate. One year after that *The Silver Palate Cookbook*, on which he collaborated with the shop's owners, was published to wide acclaim.

In 1984, he opened a restaurant dedicated to one of his favorite foods, chili. The restaurant, called the Manhattan Chili Co., and located in Greenwich Village, soon became Manhattan's premier purveyor of top-notch chili as well as other imaginative Southwest-accented fare. The restaurant inspired Michael's next book, *The Manhattan Chili Co. Southwest American Cookbook*.

Following these outstanding successes, Michael turned his attention to writing about food and cooking full time. He recently completed *The Back of the Box Gourmet*, which will be published in 1991, and he is a regular contributor to *Food & Wine*, *Bon Appétit*, *COOK'S*, and *House Beautiful*, as well as other national publications. Michael is now hard at work on another cookbook.

♦♦♦♦♦♦♦♦♦♦♦♦♦♦♦♦♦♦♦♦♦♦♦♦♦♦♦♦♦♦♦♦♦♦♦♦♦♦♦♦♦

# INDEX

*(continued)*

(continued)